MW01620423

MANUAL OF FREEDIVING

Underwater on a single breath

Umberto Pelizzari - Stefano Tovaglieri

MANUAL OF FREEDIVING

Underwater on a single breath

GG
IDELSON-GNOCCHI

MANUAL OF FREEDIVING

Underwater on a single breath

by Umberto Pelizzari and Stefano Tovaglieri

Published by Idelson-Gnocchi Ltd., Subsidiary Publisher Division of
IDELSON-GNOCCHI Srl – Editori dal 1908 - www.idelson-gnocchi.com
Sorbona · Grasso Morelli · Liviana Medicina · Grafite · Idelson Gnocchi Ltd.
Via M. Pietravalle, 85 - 80131 Naples, Italy - Tel +39-081-5453443 - Fax +39-081-5464991
12255 NW Hwy 225-A Reddick, FL 32686 USA - Tel. +1-352-5911136 - Fax +1-352-5911189

Idelson-Gnocchi Ltd. Publishers is Member of:

- DEMA, Diving Equipment & Marketing Association
  www.dema.org
- FPA, Florida Publisher Association
  www.flbookpub.org
- HDSUSA, The Historical Diving Society USA
  www.hds.org

Library of Congress Cataloging-in-Publication Data
[Manual of Freediving - Underwater on a single breath]
ISBN 1928649270
Translated from the Italian by William Trubridge

Cover photograph by © Alberto Muro Pelliconi. All rights Reserved.
Drawings and Tables by Nicola Refolo

CONTENTS

Part two
THE ART OF NOT BREATHING

Part three
BECOMING AN APNEIST

FOREWORD

To the reader, freediver or instructor

One evening several years ago, in the swimming pool of a village in the Milanese hinterland where an apnea course was being held, it befell us to see the following scene. An instructor was repeatedly telling his student to "Relax!" The aspiring apneist, standing in the shallow end of the pool, stretched his arms downwards and lowered his shoulders (...as if this is the way to relax!) with a perplexed expression that became truly dejected when the instructor gave him the command: "Don't hyperventilate!"

The student looked at him with an air of demoralization that seemed to say "Well what can I do then?"

This small episode demonstrates the educational gaps of modern apnea. On one side an instructor attempting to transfer a new approach to apnea that favours relaxation over physical force, but who doesn't know how to teach this technique; on the other side a student, impregnated with old ideas, who thinks it is sufficient to 'fill up with air' before diving. The two weren't able to understand each other because, in spite of their good intentions, they both lacked educational tools: for teaching and for learning.

This manual was created to cover such a gap and to become a tool of communication between student and teacher.

In these pages we have tried to gather together all the knowledge that in recent years has contributed to the changing methodology of apnea. Much of the wisdom is fruit of our experiences; we have learnt both from our mistakes and from our successes, and our intention is to put this learning at the disposal of future apneists.

Manual of Freediving is also the fruit of the labour of instructors at the Apnea Academy, the international school of apnea founded in 1996, which in recent years has become a theoretical and practical laboratory of the highest level. For years we have accumulated contributions from those that teach apnea, until at the end we found ourselves with something approaching a manual that formed the original nucleus of this book.

Maybe from these pages will be born a future champion, someone who will succeed in writing his name in the history of apnea, however our goal will be realised if with this book we succeed in transferring the 'pleasure of water', the awareness that apnea is within reach of everyone and that it is a way of regaining contact with our aquatic roots, a way of living well with oneself and with others. Above all, for our part we will feel fulfilled if with this work we manage to infect the reader with at least a small part of our passion for the sea and for apnea.

Anyone expecting a manual that deals solely with physical technique may be disappointed (although clearly this is included). We make the assumption that apnea is first of all a mental sport. The mind must be trained to a greater extent than the body, and for some this will represent a radical change from the normal way of practicing and thinking about this sport. You can rest assured that in some way this will also change your way of life out of the water.

Manual of Freediving does not take the place of an instructor. Don't make the error of thinking it is enough to read these pages before confronting the sea. Consider instead that you have at your disposal a new learning instrument that you can adapt to your use, according to your technical level and to your ability in the water. We have built a sort of teaching path, beginning with the theory (first and second parts) and finishing with the practical (third part). However each reader may use and read this manual according to their own curiosity and needs.

Our work on paper ends here. We'll see you again in the water!

Umberto Pelizzari
Stefano Tovaglieri

ACKNOWLEDGEMENTS

The realisation of this manual was possible thanks to the original project of creating a school for the instruction and research of subaquatic apnea, called the Apnea Academy (www.apnea-academy.com), to which the following people have contributed:

Renzo Mazzari
Marco Mardollo
Prof. Luigi Magno (Hyperbaric Medicine)
Prof. Luigi Odone (Psychology)
Dr. Nicola Sponsiello (Dietology)
Dr. Angelo Azzinari

Other than the above mentioned persons, founders of the Apnea Academy, this manual owes credit to the contribution of:

Dr. Carlo Besnati
Dr. Stefano Correale (Otorhinolaryngology)
Dr. P. De Ferrari
Prof. Mauro Ficini (Hyperbaric Medicine)
Dr. Lorenzo Manfredini (Psychotherapy)
Dr. Pierpaolo Martini
Sandro Sola
Francesca Strologo (Logopaedist)
Dr. A. Tedeschi
Paola Traldi
Engineer Davide Zanatta

A very warm thankyou to all the instructors of the Apnea Academy who haven't been named, but whose hard work during apnea courses has assisted in the gathering and synthesis of much of the information exposed in this manual.
A special thankyou to Doctor Umberto Berrettini for consultation of medical science.

FOR THE ENGLISH EDITION

Dr. Matt Brown for help with medical vocabulary
David Trubridge for help with nautical vocabulary
Mauro Porco for Italian phraseology
The Library of Santa Teresa di Gallura for their patience
Maurizio Candotti Russo for his enthusiasm and expertise
Dr. Chiara Gnocchi and Dr. Guido Gnocchi (owners of Idelson-Gnocchi Publishers Ltd)
for making this publication possible

CONVERSION TABLE

To convert a depth from meters into feet you can use the table below, or the formulas:

$$\text{meters} = \text{feet} \times 3.28$$
$$\text{feet} = \text{meters} \times 0.305$$

Meters	Feet	Meters	Feet	Meters	Feet	Meters	Feet	Meters	Feet
1	3.3	33	108.3	65	213.3	97	318.2	129	423.2
2	6.6	34	111.5	66	216.5	98	321.5	130	426.5
3	9.8	35	114.8	67	219.8	99	324.8	131	429.8
4	13.1	36	118.1	68	223.1	100	328.1	132	433.1
5	16.4	37	121.4	69	226.4	101	331.4	133	436.4
6	19.7	38	124.7	70	229.7	102	334.6	134	439.6
7	23.0	39	128.0	71	232.9	103	337.9	135	442.9
8	26.2	40	131.2	72	236.2	104	341.2	136	446.2
9	29.5	41	134.5	73	239.5	105	344.5	137	449.5
10	32.8	42	137.8	74	242.8	106	347.8	138	452.8
11	36.1	43	141.1	75	246.1	107	351.0	139	456.0
12	39.4	44	144.4	76	249.3	108	354.3	140	459.3
13	42.7	45	147.6	77	252.6	109	357.6	141	462.6
14	45.9	46	150.9	78	255.9	110	360.9	142	465.9
15	49.2	47	154.2	79	259.2	111	364.2	143	469.2
16	52.5	48	157.5	80	262.5	112	367.5	144	472.4
17	55.8	49	160.8	81	265.7	113	370.7	145	475.7
18	59.1	50	164.0	82	269.0	114	374.0	146	479.0
19	62.3	51	167.3	83	272.3	115	377.3	147	482.3
20	65.6	52	170.6	84	275.6	116	380.6	148	485.6
21	68.9	53	173.9	85	278.9	117	383.9	149	488.8
22	72.2	54	177.2	86	282.2	118	387.1	150	492.1
23	75.5	55	180.4	87	285.4	119	390.4	151	495.4
24	78.7	56	183.7	88	288.7	120	393.7	152	498.7
25	82.0	57	187.0	89	292.0	121	397.0	153	502.0
26	85.3	58	190.3	90	295.3	122	400.3	154	505.2
27	88.6	59	193.6	91	298.6	123	403.5	155	508.5
28	91.9	60	196.9	92	301.8	124	406.8	156	511.8
29	95.1	61	200.1	93	305.1	125	410.1	157	515.1
30	98.4	62	203.4	94	308.4	126	413.4	158	518.4
31	101.7	63	206.7	95	311.7	127	416.7	159	521.7
32	105.0	64	210.0	96	315.0	128	419.9	160	524.9

THE HISTORY OF APNEA

Introduction

The word apnea is derived from the Greek *a-pnoia* or 'without breathing.' Taken literally, apnea doesn't include any reference to the aquatic, however in current terminology it is used to refer to the sport of freediving: immersion underwater without the aid of respiration.

Freediving is a codified sport, with defined categories, registered records, athletes of the highest level, and naturally, thousands of enthusiasts who practice it for enjoyment.

The origins of this discipline have been lost in the depths of time, and are a weave of legends, chronicles and stories passed down by word of mouth. Its history is not incidental.

More than any other sport, freediving draws on atavistic reflexes of the human being. It is enough to consider that amniotic fluid, which develops the foetus, is very similar to seawater; furthermore if upon birth a baby is immersed in a pool of water it will instinctively swim breaststroke, and will be able to hold its breath for 40 seconds. The baby will retain this ability until learning to walk.

This impulse may be obscured in the individual by the dominance of the upright position, but in the collective memory of humanity – and therefore in history – the practice of apnea has left indelible traces: legends, myth and historical stories right up to the most recent chronicles of athletes of our time, who haven't just written incredible pages in the history of the sport, but have also rewritten the textbooks of human physiology.

Every apneist has heard the famous quote of the French doctor Cabarrou who, when asked if it was possible for a man to descend deeper than 50 meters, declared "*il s'ecrase, donc, si rompe*" (he will be crushed, therefore he will burst). However that was before **Enzo Maiorca**, who broke the barrier in Ustica in 1962, diving to 51 meters and returning unharmed to the surface.

The history of the world records is also the history of apnea: any athlete who has exceeded the limits of those who came before has opened the door on a new evolution of diving techniques, putting in place a teaching progression that has formed new champions.

In this introduction we have gathered together the major events in the history of apnea, so as to allow the apneist to understand the heritage of those who came before him and thus to understand better the techniques and exercises of the following chapters. Without mentioning that over the course of centuries the history of apnea maintains its fascination.

ORIGIN OF APNEA: FROM MYTH TO HISTORY

In populations settled on the shores of seas and lakes, freediving was born out of the necessity to draw food from the bottom of the water's glass.

'The shellfish eaters'

The most ancient evidence of freediving was found by palaeontologists on the coast of the Baltic Sea, where a civilization that has been given the Danish name of *Kojkkenmodinger* or 'the shellfish eaters' was settled between 7,000 and 10,000 years ago. The name was suggested after fossilized remains of shells were discovered close to the settlement's dwellings; evidence that this civilization had acquired the knowledge and adequate practical technique of immersion to gather shellfish from the bottom of the sea.

In the excavations that bought to light the rest of the Mesopotamic civilizations between the Euphrates and the river Tigre (4,500 BC), and in the sixth Egyptian dynasty that reigned on the Tiber (3,200 BC), there were found the remains of numerous ornamental objects fashioned from mother-of-pearl – a material that can only be obtained by diving to the bottom of the sea.

Apnea was certainly practiced in all of the cultures bordering on the Mediterranean basin, and this has been confirmed by traces visible in both archaeological findings and chronicles handed down through Greek and Latin literature. Many ancient writings describe the trade of *porpora* ('purple'), a precious substance used as red dye for the garments of kings and emperors (and later the cardinals; high priests of the church). This royal colouring was extracted from the hypobranchial glands of either *Murex brandaris* or *Bolinus brandaris*, gastropod molluscs very common to the Mediterranean, that could obviously only be gathered by apneists.

That the practice of apnea was part of the daily life of the population of the Mediterranean is evidenced by the numerous myths and legends of those that came before us.

Glaucus, the 'green mariner'

The mythological figure closest to being a pre-alphabet apneist is certainly **Glaucus**, the 'green mariner.' The myth belongs to the Minoan civilization that, from the island of Crete, reached its maximum splendour between 2000 and 1570 BC, expressing commercial and military power over a wide area of the Mediterranean.

In the Minoan myths Glaucus was son of Minos, king of Crete, and Pasiphae, "she that lights everything." The baby Glaucus fell into a pot of honey and drowned. He was then brought back to life by the prophet Polido, thanks to a magic plant.

The legend came to Greece, but during its 'transfer' the history changed radically. Glaucus was transformed from fisherman to a god of the coasts by virtue of a magic herb that had the power to resuscitate fish. From his home offshore of Delo he visited the Greek ports every year to give much sought-after answers to the people of the sea. Diverse and unlucky were the events of his love life: enamoured of the nymph Scylla he turned to Circe for help. This was a grave error: Circe was in love in her turn with Glaucus, and transformed Scylla into a sea-monster, kept to guard Ariadne, who was abandoned by Theseus on the island of Naxos, but who was stolen by Dionysus...

A picture of a fisherman reproduced in a Minoan mural discovered on the island of Thera, which dates back to the 16th century B.C.

The character of the coastal god is traceable through many famous works of literature: in *Metamorphosis* by Ovidio, in Dante's paradise (song I, 68), and in more recent times he was honoured by Luigi Ercole Morselli in the tragedy *Glaucus*, and mentioned by Gabriele D'Annunzio in *Alcyone.* Every artist has represented Glaucus according to the style of their time, but they have all shared the same fascination for the man that lived underwater.

The visual representation that most certainly depicts this god is a mosaic, conserved near the 'Cabinet of Medals,' in Paris, where he appears as a centaur of the sea, a creature especially associated with the name of Glaucus. In iconography he is often mistaken for Proteus and the tritons. The colossal herm of the Vatican, representative of a sea god with a thick beard, is therefore of uncertain attribution to Glaucus.

However the character of Glaucus is curious also because in another myth he died in the sea. It is told that the sea god Poseidon was so impressed by one of his exceptional dives that instead of sending him back to the surface he welcomed him in to his court, between the Naiads and Sirens. When the body of Glaucus finally resurfaced he was covered in seaweed and shellfish, and his beard had assumed the colour of the sea.

From myth to history

The artistic representation of Glaucus is a child of myth, but the image presented in a Babylonian bass relief dating back to 1885 BC is definitely true to the every day life of the fishermen of the age: the picture shows a man breathing underwater from a bottle that is attached to his chest by means of a tube held tight between his lips. This example is only one of many descriptions of 'proto-subs' handed down to us through the Classics.

In the story of the Greco-Persian war, the Greek historian **Erodoto** tells of the fisherman Scylla and his daughter Cyana, who swam underwater in a dark night of 480 BC to cut the mooring and anchorage lines of the Persian fleet that had Athens under siege. The ships of the Persian king Xerxes thus unanchored were driven onto the rocks by the northerly wind.

Another Athenian historian, **Tucidide**, told that in 415 BC, during the siege of Syracuse, Athenian divers sawed through the sharpened underwater stakes that were preventing Athenian boats from entering the harbour.

The philosopher **Aristotle** recounts a similar story of the sub-aquatic Grecians who destroyed the barricades of the port of Tyre, and explains that in order to stay longer underwater these ancestors of modern scuba divers used a *lebeta*; probably a type of mouthpiece connected to a sealed bottle.

Always a careful observer of natural phenomena, Aristotle tells of the most common problems that even now befall scuba divers (pain in the ears, nosebleeds etc), and mentions "an upside down pot full of air, that remains sealed, and in which the man keeps his head".

Another of the legends has for its hero the most famous pupil of Aristotle, the Macedonian king **Alexander the Great**. It tells that Alexander decided to brave the bottom of the sea and (first man in history to do so) he lowered himself underwater closed into a kind of made-to-measure glass barrel. The fable, since it is probably only a matter of myth, continues to report that upon returning to the surface on one occasion, Alexander the Great claimed to have seen a monster parading menacingly in front of him for three days and three nights.

The *urinatores*

In the Roman epoch of the fourth century BC, a force of genuine sub aquatic commandos was created and given the name '*urinatores*' (from the Latin verb that means 'to go underwater'). They had numerous tasks including retrieving snagged anchors, dismantling underwater barricades and defences, and other acts of war conducted under the water.

Concerning the *urinatores* there is a story handed down orally, but never written, regarding the island of Mozia (now called San Pantaleo), the last Punic bastion of the conquest of Sicily. Mozia was enclosed by a stretch of relatively shallow water called '*lo stagnone*' (the big pond), and was defended by 13 Carthaginian triremes that the Romans tried to assail from land, using catapults. With every attack the triremes raised their anchors and sailed into open water through a stretch of water at the eastern end of the *stagnone*, thwarting any hostile attempt by the Roman army. This carried on for a long time, the people of Mozia resisting every siege, until a corps of *urinatores*, working underwater and only at night, succeeded in planting huge stakes across the channel to open water. The Carthaginian triremes collided with these stakes, and it is told that they all sunk and were hidden in the mud that was many meters deep in this stretch of the seafloor.

Recently a scuba diver came across one of these triremes after a violent storm. It has now been fully recovered and is installed in the courtyard of a school in Marsala.

Cleopatra, the last queen of Egypt (69-30 BC), used divers to arrange a dreadful joke on her guest, none other than her lover Marco Antonio, who was addicted to fishing. Swimming underwater, and under precise orders from the empress, the divers affixed a petrified fish to Marco Antonio's hook.

The Latin historian **Tito Livio** (59 BC-17 AD) testified that during the reign of the Macedonian king Perseus (212 BC-166 BC), underwater divers recovered incredible treasures from shipwrecks. The laws of Rhodes awarded divers with a share not just proportional to the value of the object, but also to the risk: someone who dove to 16 cubits (just past 7 metres) would take half of the booty.

If in the Mediterranean civilization there are still very visible traces of the practice of apnea from remote times (one need only visit a village of Greek sponge divers to witness ancient practices and customs of work), we must not forget that these techniques of immersion were (and still are) practiced at all latitudes.

The world is large, and the sea is greater still; infinite are the isles and populations that through contact with the sea have found a way of life, sustenance and recreation. First among these are the Polynesian fisherman, but there are also the pearl divers of India, Yemen and the Persian Gulf, while the Spanish chronicles of the conquest of America tell of the amazing underwater capacities of the native Antilleans and their successful recoveries of sunken galleons.

The Ama

Exceptional, even today, are the practices of the Japanese and Korean Ama, who have earned their living with the same technique of fishing for over two thousand years. They are all woman, divided into three ranks defined by age and underwater capacity. Between 17 and 50 years old, these women swim on average 8–10 hours per day in water that barely exceeds 10° Celsius, naked save for a small loincloth, and with a net that straps from the shoulders to the waist, passing between the breasts, and serving to hold the catch. Previously they collected pearl-yielding oysters; nowadays they also gather crustaceans and molluscs like the *awabi* (similar to our abalone – *Halliotis lamellose* – even if theirs are measurably bigger).

German engraving from 1555, labelled with "Subaquatic attacker", the swimming soldier is supplied with a buoy similar to that designed by Leonardo Da Vinci.

Returning from the East, and with the passing of centuries the history of apnea becomes entangled indissolubly with the history of Scuba: man has always sought to exceed the limits of our respiration with the use of technical instruments. Technology has always improved the efficiency of these instruments, allowing man to stay on the sea bottom for consistently longer periods.

Naturally of course **Leonardo Da Vinci** (1452 – 1519) made illustrations and designs for rudimental underwater equipment: a mouthpiece almost identical to those actually in use, webbed gloves and a strange diving suit that looks very similar to a modern oxygen aqualung. In successive centuries the development of Scuba technology has overshadowed apnea. It is not until the twentieth century that the apneists return to the scene.

Before arriving at our present time, where a great number of people dive in conditions of great security, it is necessary to retread the history of deep freediving, and therefore the modern records.

HISTORY OF THE RECORDS: THE FIRST BY A GREEK FISHERMAN

To relive the dawn of freediving we must turn the clock back almost a hundred years. The scene is the Aegean Sea, and more precisely the Greek island of Simi. The protagonist is a sponge fisherman, **Haggi Statti**. At this time he could not have imagined that his name would become legendary in the history of apnea. The year is 1913. Haggi Statti is 35 years old when he is presented onboard *Regina Margherita* of the Royal Italian Navy, anchored in the bay of Picadia on the island of Karpatos. His task is to recover the ship's anchor, which has sunk to a bottom of about seventy-five meters. As payment he asks for a small sum of money, and the permission to be able to fish with explosives; a terrible practice that makes sushi on the seafloor.

Haggi Statti, Greek sponge fisherman, who in 1913 'fished up' the anchor of the Regina Margherita of the Royal Italian navy from –76 meters with a dive time of about 3 minutes.

The ship's doctors, and in particular Giuseppe Musengo, the official doctor responsible, were more than a little incredulous as to Haggis Statti's actual capacity. He didn't exactly have the physique of a superman: 175 cm tall with a thin bony body of around 60 kg, delicate musculature, an elevated heart rate (between 80 and 90 bpm), an emphysema in the lower lung, reduced hearing ability due to a hole in one eardrum, and the total lack of an eardrum in the other ear.

However his most astonishing feature was an inability to hold his breath out of the water for more than one minute.

Nevertheless the locals all asserted that Haggi Statti could remain underwater for seven minutes without breathing, and that he had already many times touched a depth of one hundred meters, being dragged to the bottom by a stone tied to the end of a rope. He would then ascend back to the surface using his arms to pull his way back up this rope.

In the end Haggi Statti surprised everyone. After several days searching the seafloor between depths of 60 and 80 meters he recovered the Regina Margherita's anchor, **returning from a depth of 76 meters after an immersion of around three minutes**.

All the testimonies, the scrupulous medical reports and the accounts of the veracity of the event can be found in the archives of the Italian Navy's Historical Office in Rome.

In awe and admiration, doctor Musengo wrote "Statti returned from every dive energetically and entirely under his own steam; this is demonstrated by the way in which he jumps into the boat unassisted and shakes his head to clear his nose

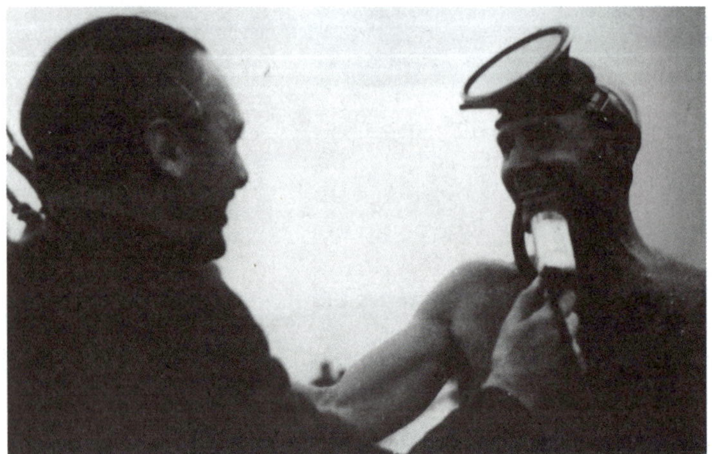

and ears of water that has penetrated them. He is able to reach a depth of 110 meters, with the capacity to stay at 30 meters for about 7 minutes."

In 1912, one year before Haggi performed this feat, a Hungarian was born who would later be naturalised as an Italian and establish the first official freediving record: **Raimondo Bucher**.

In 1949 Raimondo Bucher took with him to the bottom of the sea at –30 m a parchment sealed in a canister and became the 'world's deepest man'.

When in 1949 he announced that he would take with him to the bottom of the lake of Naples, at 30 meters depth, a parchment enclosed in a metal cylinder that he would pass, as if it was the baton in a relay race, to a diver who would be standing on the muddy bottom, scientists declared that this mad captain of the air force would certainly die from the crushing pressure. According to official medicine of the time, the physiological variations entailed by depth of immersion during apnea were brutally regulated by Boyle's Law (pv = k, the volume of a gas is inversely proportional to the pressure exerted on it).

They had not yet discovered the phenomenon of blood-shift, or haemo-compensation or pulmonary filling: the air in the lungs, which is compressible, is substituted for liquid, in this case blood, which is incompressible (the phenomenon of blood-shift is described in more detail in *Chapter 3*).

Bucher's bet

Nevertheless Bucher pulled it off, and became the 'deepest man' in the world. He later admitted that he had descended to this depth for a wager made with the same diver that was waiting on the bottom: he won 50,000 lira, which in 1949 was a considerable sum.

The winning bet of Bucher opened the way for a long succession of records in 'absolute variable weight,' where maximum depth is reached with the aid of ballast of unlimited weight. The ascent could be made with the help of a balloon.

Bucher remained the 'deepest man' in the world for two years, until 1951 when, also in Naples, **Ennio Falco** and **Alberto Novelli** both descended to –35. Bucher waited only one year before in Capri, 1952, he reclaimed the record with a –39 meter dive. At this time waterproof cases for cine cameras had just been invented, and Bucher's –39 meters constituted the first record documented on film.

The equipment that Raimondo Bucher used is very interesting. His **snorkel** was a piece of **gas piping**. The **mask** was rudimental, with a capacious internal volume, and the first problems of compensation were already encountered at about ten meters. Not to mention the **flippers**, which, being made of very soft rubber, supplied a pitiful amount of force. Moreover the dimensions of the blade were greatly reduced – at the time you could see apneists diving with fins only slightly longer than their feet.

The record of Santarelli

In 1956 Falco and Novelli returned to the stage, setting a new world record of –41 meters at Rapallo. After another interval of four years news arrived from Brazil that **Americo Santarelli** had reached –43 meters in Rio de Janeiro. 1960 was a year for records: Santarelli came to Italy and in the waters off Cape Circeo touched the depth of –44 meters.

Soon after at Syracuse, **Enzo Maiorca**, the man who would dominate the history of apnea for the next thirty years, descended to –45 meters. Americo Santarelli moved to Santa Margherita Ligure and superseded this with –46. The unphased Maiorca promptly put three meters between himself and the Brazilian with a dive of –49 meters, still in his home waters. Then in 1961 for the first time Enzo reached the milestone of –50 meters.

The next year, at Ustica, he easily moved the mark to –51 meters. Science was resoundingly contradicted. Who can guess the state of mind of Maiorca as he set out from the surface to descend beyond –50 meters, with all the world's medical theory against him. In such circumstances do you see the greatness of the man.

Americo Santarelli retired, and Maiorca, now bereft of adversaries, registered 53 meters at Syracuse in August of 1964 and 54 meters at Acireale the following July. The peace for Maiorca lasted only a year; in 1965 three new adversaries appeared on the horizon: **Teteke Williams**, **Robert Croft** and **Jacques Mayol**.

A journalist of the time said of these three athletes that they were like thunderbolts in a clear sky for Maiorca: the first a thunderclap, the second a raging storm, and the third an infinite tempest.

Until this time CMAS (the World Confederation of Sub-Aquatic Activities) had validated all the records. However the arrival of the new claimants coincided with more severe policies: The –59 of Williams achieved in Polynesia in September of 1965, Mayol's –60, made in the Bahamas in June of 1966, and the –64 meters of Croft (Florida, February 1967) weren't accepted as valid, even if they were entered directly into the annals of freediving.

However Enzo Maiorca wasn't to be caught resting on his laurels, and in November of 1966 he descended to –62 meters in the waters of Syracuse, with all the proper officials. However the fact that Croft had arrived at –64 meters wasn't to his liking: in Cuba, in September of 1967, he descended to the same depth.

Maiorca and Mayol: the challenge

The techniques were diverse. Croft, gifted with an impressive lung volume (nine and a half litres!) would dive naked of equipment – without fins or mask – and made the ascent by pulling himself up the guide rope. Mayol introduced the technique of yoga and mental concentration in an attempt to make up for a physique that wasn't exactly comparable to Tarzan.

As for Maiorca, commitment and determination constituted the basic elements of his style of diving "headlong into the blue." Croft, who evidently didn't attach much importance to CMAS, persisted with his records: in December 1967 he reached –67 cleanly in Florida, but scarcely a month later and also in Florida, the Shanghai-born Frenchman Jacques Mayol touched –70 meters.

The American responded in August of 1968 with a handsome –73. As far as CMAS was concerned it was all wasted effort: they didn't validate any of these performances. Croft was forced to leave the scene due to a pulmonary emphysema.

A recent photo of Jacques Mayol, father of the new technique of apnea.

However there was enough incentive to take Enzo Maiorca to –72 meters, and just a year later, and still in the waters of Ognina, to –74 meters. A single month passed before Mayol reached –75 and straight after –76 in Japan.

On the 5th of December 1970, following a very serious decision from their medical commission, CMAS announced that they would no longer be validating any freediving records. One of the reasons they gave was the danger to the supporting scuba divers.

For CMAS these performances had a scientific interest only, and the confederation gave them an academic, but worthless, acknowledgement as experiments. Mayol took sides with the research. Maiorca initially didn't want anything to do with it, but in the end ceded to the spirit of competition.

The controversies of the Seventies

Inflamed by the –76 of Mayol, Maiorca swam past him into the abyss to –77 meters. He would repeat the feat with punctuality at Ognina and Genoa in the Augusts of the next two years taking the baton to –78 and –80 meters. Mayol decided to move the challenge to the home of his rival, and in 1973 he presented himself on the island of Elba, where he surpassed the Sicilian by a good six meters.

The reaction of Maiorca was almost immediate, and the next year he chose Sarrento as a venue to give a definite lesson to his rival: in September of 1974 he descended to –87 meters. But in the following year Mayol, still at Elba, flew down to –92 meters, and thirteen months later on the 23rd of November he reached the mythical depth of –101 meters.

The records of the two great rivals in these years had a backwash of controversy that gave little honour to the discipline of apnea. Mayol maintained that he didn't brave the abyss to set records, but for means of medical research only. His Sicilian rival rebutted that if Mayol really only wanted to carry out experiments then he wouldn't need to bring his squad of scuba divers and medics, his television crew, photographers, press, judges, officials and sponsors.

In 1983 Jacques Mayol touched –105 meters and in 1988, at Syracuse, Enzo Maiorca also exceeded the momentous threshold, taking his mark to –101 meters – a fitting finish for a huge sporting career.

The Eighties: equipment evolves

In these thirty years of history freediving equipment also underwent a remarkable evolution. The masks, packed with silicon to reduce their internal volume and thereby facilitate equalisation, were subsequently replaced with contact lenses.

With the current depths there were two possibilities: you could descend with bare eyes (like most of the South American apneists) or you could use contact lenses. The little rubber fins were also abandoned to make way for longer and more rigid designs. The fins used by the last generation for competitions reached almost a meter in length, and in the most sophisticated cases were fashioned from carbon fibre. It is thanks to this new equipment that man has made such incredible progress, especially in constant weight.

Constant Weight: the record of Makula

This discipline has a history equally rich and fascinating. Constant weight requires that the athlete descends and ascends under their own force, without being able to touch the line and without releasing the weight belt that was used for the descent.

With these rules, the first to set a record of –50 meters was **Stefano Makula**, a Roman of Hungarian origin like Bucher, who in 1978 opened a personal challenge with Enzo Maiorca and his two pupils **Nuccio** and **Mario Imbesi**. The brothers both touched –52 in September of 1978, but in the same month Maiorca descended to –55 meters. In 1979 Makula equalled Maiorca, even if in the same year they were both superseded by **Enzo Liistro**, who reached –56 meters. In June of 1980 Nuccio Imbesi moved the mark to –57 meters.

Sixteen months passed before Makula descended to 58 meters in October of 1981. But all was not over: in November of the same year, Mayol (who else!) was the first to break the 60 meter barrier, with a dive to –61.

Another year passed in relative peace amongst the worlds deepest, with the exception of some sporadic appearances from Makula, first with constant Weight dives and then with variable weight. However his attempts were never validated, until in 1988 at Gianuttri his dive of –102 meters in variable weight was officially confirmed. The next year, on the 23rd of October at Ponza, he was the victim of a serious accident in an attempt to reach –110 meters.

Pipin

Meanwhile there began to circulate in Europe the name of a very strong Cuban apneist, **Francisco 'Pipin' Ferreras**, who all the divers of the Caribbean were talking about with an almost reverent awe. They told of his descent in constant weight to –67 meters in the autumn of 1987 and of a successive –69 meters in 1988, in the waters of Key Largo. These performances were never validated, as he would ascend by pulling on the line, which was strictly forbidden by the regulations.

Then came a very important year for freediving. The Frenchman **Frank Messegué**, on Reunion island, reached –62 meters in constant weight, reopening the competition in this discipline eight years after Mayol's –61 meters.

Pipin began practicing the discipline of variable weight according to the rules, and at Cuba on the 3rd of November 1989 he plummeted down to –112 meters, and was given the title of 'world's deepest man.'

Variable weight is modified

At this point an adjustment was made. The Italian Federation of 1989 (one of the few world federations that continued to recognise freedives after the veto of CMAS) created a new set of directives. Constant weight wasn't affected, but several rules of variable weight were changed. Following the new ruling an athlete could use a ballast of no more than a third of their bodyweight to achieve maximum depth, which could then be left on the bottom while the athlete ascended under their own power. The use of balloons or inflatable wetsuits was not allowed.

These two disciplines of constant and variable weight were officially recognised by the Federation, whilst the category of No Limits, or absolute variable weight (the old variable weight practised by Mayol and Maiorca in which the athlete descends with unlimited ballast and returns to the surface by means of an inflated balloon), was no longer recognised, although it was still 'officialised' by the presence of CMAS judges.

Thus we resume the story, with Messegué's –62 meters for constant Weight, the –87 meters of Maiorca for variable weight and Pipin's –112 meters in No Limits.

In September of 1990, several months after having achieved 112 meters, and after transferring to Maiorca's Sicily, Pipin took the record in constant weight from –62 to –63 meters, and that of variable weight from –87 to –92 meters.

Pelizzari's first record

This was the moment in which **Umberto Pelizzari** entered the scene. On the 11th of November 1990, in the waters of Porto Azzurro, he set his first world record in the discipline of constant weight, passing Pipin on his way down to –65 meters.

From this day forth there began a great rivalry between the two, which has been compared to that of Mayol and Maiorca of the preceding years. In 1991 Pipin failed in an attempt at constant weight before he improved his No Limits depth to –115 meters, on the 6th of July.

In October of the same year, and still at Porto Azzurro, Pelizzari responded, establishing world records in all three disciplines in the course of one month: on the 2nd, 22nd and 26th of October he reached –67 meters in constant weight, –95 meters in variable weight and –118 meters in No Limits.

A new rivalry

In May of 1992, on his own island of Varadero, Pipin took Pelizzari's most cherished record, constant weight, with a dive of –68 meters. It was only to be for a few months: on the 17th of September 'Pelo' descended two metres further: –70 during the Blue Olympiad at Ustica.

In the course of the same event Pipin, first attempting –101 meters in variable weight but exiting with a blackout, went on to revenge himself with –120 meters in No Limits, on the 20th September 1992. Pipin persisted in variable weight, and after abandoning the idea of –101 meters he surpassed Pelizzari by a single meter to take the record to –96.

Pelizzari replied on the 11th of October in the waters of Montecristo, after much delay for bad weather, reclaiming the title of 'deepest man' with a depth of –123 meters in No Limits. However one month later on the 12th of November at Freeport in the Bahamas Pipin descended to –125 meters.

He improved on this depth three more times: in Sicily in July of 1994 with –126, in November of the same year in Florida with –127 and on the 30th July of 1995, back in Syracuse for –128 meters.

The birth of AIDA

At the end of 1993 a group of French scuba divers, medics, technicians and apneists created **AIDA** (International Association for the Development of Apnea) whose purpose was to regulate and standardise freediving world record attempts. AIDA now forms the greatest world refereeing body in the sport. They commenced activities in 1994, and were present at all the official attempts of an international level.

On the 26th of July at Cala Gonone in Sardinia, Pelizzari succeeded in variable weight where Pipin had failed two years before at Ustica: overtaking the Cuban by five meters as he set the mark at –101. He then bettered himself in the same discipline on the 22nd of July the following year, with a depth of –105 meters.

Six days before on the 16th of July, in the course of the same event at Villasimius, a village fifty kilometres from Cagliari, Pelizzari had set a new constant weight record of –72 meters.

At the end of September 1995 **Eric Charrier**, a Corsican of thirty-three years, attempted –73 meters. However he had a problem in the ascent that required the intervention of surface support, which is categorically prohibited by the rules that validate attempts. The press release stated, "At the moment in which he arrived in contact with the air Eric Charrier was unconscious. Within a few seconds he was taken onboard the support boat where he was administered with oxygen. He regained consciousness after about a minute."

CMAS recognises constant weight records

On the 15th of December 1995, under the presidency of **Achille Ferrero**, CMAS made a decision that surprised everyone: to review their stance of the 5th of December 1970 and resume the recognition and validation of freediving records, although limited solely to constant weight.

It was a technically important decision that rewarded the most demanding and authentic of the three sporting categories. The rules for constant weight remained unchanged, and from 1996 this discipline was once again officially recognised in the hundred other countries that support CMAS.

In this season of 1996 two new protagonists stepped into the limelight: the Italian **Gianluca Genoni**, close friend of Pelizzari and for years his surface safety diver, who achieved his first world record on the 17th of August with a variable weight dive to –106 m, and the Frenchman **Michel Oliva** (the strongest of the constant weight freedivers to have come out of France), who equalled the constant weight record in October, touching the depth of –72 m.

New recruits for competitive apnea

Pelizzari concentrated himself exclusively on the two disciplines with ballast, and in the space of a week between the 9th and the 16th of September he re-conquered the records of variable weight, with –110 m, and No Limits, with –131 m. Then in 1997 Genoni took the variable weight record all the way to –120 meters.

In October of the same year at Porto Venere Pelizzari claimed the constant weight title, descending to –75 m, before being defeated the following year by the Cuban **Alejandro Ravelo**, who surfaced successfully from –76 m. 1998 was the year of Genoni as he broke his own variable weight record with –121 m and claimed the No Limits record with –135 m.

On the 6th of June 1999 a new French name, **Loïc Leferme**, took the No Limits title from Genoni, moving the mark to –137 meters. However Genoni wouldn't surrender and at the end of the summer of 1999 he reclaimed supremacy with –138, and improved his variable to –122 m.

After almost two years absence from the world's deepest, Pelizzari returned to the scene. Despite adverse weather conditions, on the 18th of October he attained supremacy in constant weight, diving to –80 m, and in the same week he was the first man to break the wall of –150 meters in No Limits. Pelizzari was the new 'deepest man' in the world, even if due to the bad conditions he was forced to call off an attempt on the variable weight record. Two years later he claimed the title in this discipline also, with – 131 m in the waters of Capri on the 2nd of November 2001. With this record Umberto Pelizzari decided to finally withdraw from the competition for world records.

In recent years freediving has moved away from the mythical rivalry between Pipin and Pelizzari. Young apneists are asserting themselves internationally with performances at the highest level. The nationalities of these athletes demonstrates the fact that apnea has now diffused throughout the world. Other than the apneists we have already mentioned there is the Czechoslovakian Martin Stepanek, the Austrian Herbert Nitsch, the Venezuelan Carlos Coste, the Frenchman Guillaume Nery, the Italians Davide Carrera and Alessandro Rignani Lolli, the Grecian Manolis Yankos, Pierre Frolla from Monaco and many more.

The sequence of depths and dates above summarizes fifty years of history: they were exhausting meters, conquered centimetre after centimetre with majestic flights into the abyss. During this half century a score of athletes attempted to improve the human aquatic potential, driven by their cultures, ambitions and diverse techniques. And by their women, naturally...

THE APNEA OF THE WOMEN

The history of women's apnea began in the early sixties. On the 26th of June 1965, twenty-one year old **Giuliana 'Jolly' Treleani** dove to –31 meters, taking the title that was established with –30 m the previous year by **Hedy Roessler**, who in her turn had overtaken the –25 m of **Francesca Trombi**.

A few months later the English **Evelyn Petterson** descended to –33 meters in the Bahamas, but Giuliana reclaimed the record with –35 m at Eolie on the 24th of July 1966. Petterson responded with –38 meters, again at the Bahamas. Giuliana travelled to Cuba together with Enzo Maiorca, and reached –45 meters. These are all records in variable weight, but at this time in Cuba the sister of Treleani, **Maria**, descended to –31 m in constant weight.

The daughters of Maiorca

The Maiorca sisters, daughters of Enzo, appeared on the scene in 1978 when **Patrizia** straight away set a record in constant weight. The next year her sister **Rossana** caught her up, and together they went down to –40 m.

In 1980 Patrizia suspended her diving due to pregnancy, but her sister Rossana continued alone to –45 meters. There followed six long years of quiet, until in 1986 Rossana joined her father in the waters of Crotone for *Operation Pythagoras*, a series of experimental dives that concluded with a new record in variable weight of –69 meters.

In 1987 the Maiorca sisters returned to the waters of Syracuse: Patrizia surpassed by a meter her sister's variable weight record, with –70; Rossana exceeded Patrizia by five meters in constant weight. In 1988, and again at Syracuse for *Operation Aretusa*, Patrizia confirmed her –70 meters, while Rossana reached –80.

One year later **Angelo Bandini**, a twenty eight year old student of Mayol from Rimini trounced everyone, men included: –107 meters in No Limits.

From 1990 to 1993 there was only Rossana Maiorca, who dedicated herself exclusively to the discipline of constant weight, taking the record to –59 metres, a depth that surpassed the personal best of her father Enzo. The next year she decided to retire in order to dedicate herself to her family.

At this point there were no Italian heroines on the world record scene. The queen was undoubtedly the Cuban **Deborah Andollo**, ex-championess of synchronized swimming, who was in her national squad for twelve years. In a short time she also took herself to the top of freediving with performances of –67 in constant weight, –95 in variable weight and –115 meters in No Limits.

In Sardinia, September 1998, **Tanya Streeter** made her debut in the blue circus of the world's deepest women with –67 meters in constant weight. This woman, with an English and American passport, lives on the Cayman Islands in the Caribbean, where she trains all year. She specialises in the hardest and purest discipline, constant weight, in which she has reached –70 meters.

Europe is well represented by the youthful Turk Yasmin Dalkilic, who has the potential to outstrip both Andollo in variable weight and No Limits and Streeter in constant weight. Yasmin, the Canadian Mandy Rae Cruickshank, and the American Annabel Briseno are considered the athletes that will dominate the women's freediving scene in the future.

THE DISCIPLINES

Constant Weight: the athlete reaches maximum depth using the force of their legs only before returning in the same fashion, without ever touching the guide rope. The use of ballast or other variations in weight is prohibited. This is the most pure and demanding discipline, but at the same time the most significant and important for apneists, who today descend past 100 meters.

Variable weight: the athlete can utilise a ballast of up to 30 kg for the descent, but cannot use any balloon or inflatable wetsuit for the ascent. The athlete must use only their own resources: legs and arms. Depths presently achieved are beyond –130 meters.

No Limits: This is the old variable weight of Maiorca and Mayol, in which the athlete reaches the maximum depth with an unlimited weight of ballast and ascends to the surface with the help of a balloon. It is a kind of escalator, where the real difficulty is pressure compensation for the great depths, which today exceed –170 meters.

Free Immersion: Consists of freediving without fins; the athlete pulls on the guide rope in the descent and ascent. We are at about –100 meters.

Static Apnea: The athlete must remain underwater as long as possible. He can assume any position in the water or on the surface as long as all airways are completely immersed for the duration of the performance. Record times are around 9 minutes.

Dynamic Apnea: The athlete swims longitudinally as far as possible in a swimming pool. Maximum distances are over 200 meters.

Part one

BEFORE ENTERING THE WATER

APPROACHING APNEA

CHAPTER

1

The apneist is not a Superman, but a normal person, dedicated to this sport because he or she has discovered and experienced the sensations, the peace and the pleasure that are unique to apnea. Freediving is a sport for everyone!

However the practice of this discipline requires a healthy psychophysical condition. Improvement of performance depends upon an awareness of oneself, and on psychophysical development induced by training. For this reason before taking the first steps, or rather the first fin strokes, it is important to know exactly what aspects of fitness are required for apnea.

As is common sense, a trusted doctor and a good instructor will help the aspiring apneist evaluate the mental and physical condition required to practice this discipline or to participate in a course *ad hoc*.

Without adequate equipment freediving is out of the question, since it is an outdoors activity that requires the use of dedicated gear. Therefore it is critical to know the particular functions of each piece of equipment – how it is put on and used – and how to maintain gear so that it will continue to be efficient over time.

1.1 THE FIRST RULE: VERIFY PSYCHOPHYSICAL CONDITIONS

In the introduction we defined subaquatic apnea as an outdoor sport; it is undoubtedly a recreational activity practiced in a world that has very different characteristics to the *terra firma*. The risks are therefore both environmental and individual, or tied to an awareness of one's own technical, mental and physical capacity. For this reason it is imperative to assess one's personal condition before enrolling in an apnea course.

General Rules

Lack of good training is the most common cause of accidents; apneists who are overweight, who smoke, who drink excessively, or who are in inappropriate mental and physical condition expose themselves to the greatest risk, whilst an apneist who is in good form will improve their safety and that of their companions. In order to be free of nervous tension during apnea there are several precautions and good habits that should be observed.

Sleep well and do not consume alcohol the night before an intended day of diving. Allowing adequate time for the digestion of meals will prevent excessive stress and thereby reduce the possibility of an accident.

On the long term an adequate physical preparation, specifically in the water, the practice of particular techniques of relaxation and respiration, periodic medical check-ups, and a calibrated diet will all add to the enjoyment and intensity of the experiences that are unique to apnea.

In particular if you:

- smoke
- are older than 45
- are overweight
- have recently had a surgical operation
- take medication
- suffer from cardiac or respiratory trouble

and you wish to initiate or resume the practice of apnea, then it is important for your safety that you undergo a thorough medical exam and a physical recovery programme.

Cardiovascular fitness

Water is about 800 times denser than air, producing a consistent resistance against our body that causes a significant loss of energy. To move in a liquid environment requires strength and energy.

All non-competitive sports that increase general physical endurance – cycling, jogging, swimming, aerobics and gymnastics, cross country skiing and many more – will stimulate cardiovascular activity, and are therefore beneficial for physical preparation. Cardiovascular fitness implies a stronger heart and better vascularisation (blood circulation), and therefore better muscular oxygenation. In fact this condition favours the maintenance of a constant body temperature, as well as a good level of awareness and self-control, and most importantly requires less work of the heart, allowing the athlete to recover more quickly between one dive and the next.

Pulmonary Fitness

Clearly an efficient respiratory system is essential in order to achieve good results; on the other hand the preparatory breathing for apnea, whether static or dynamic, will considerably develop the primary airways, the trachea and lungs. Some conditions that impede respiration – or the exchange of gases with the blood – give the apneist all sorts of problems that inevitably reduce performance, but most importantly reduce safety.

For this reason apneists with colds, influenza, sinus infections, or with an excessive production of mucous that obstructs the frontal sinuses or the bronchi, or who show asthmatic symptoms, should visit a specialist in medicine for aquatic sports. Naturally a precaution that everybody can take is that of **not smoking**.

Spirometric exams that can be taken at any sports clinic will give you all the information necessary to evaluate your respiratory ability. You can analyse and discuss this with your instructor, and by comparing it with another exam after several months of training you will be able to evaluate modifications made to training.

At present the effects of pressure on an apneist who is taking pharmacological therapy are still unknown. Therefore it is recommended to dive only when you feel well or after having received the approval of a doctor; being able to relinquish apnea in certain conditions of health is a sign of maturity that distinguishes the good apneist from the foolish.

Psychological fitness

From the point of view of psychology, by fitness we mean the capacity to recognise and control emotions connected with the specifics of apnea (for example fear of the water, of depth or of loss of control) as well as emotive factors ingrained in man.

Apnea does not lend itself well to competitiveness – it is better to talk in terms of improving physical and psychological potential rather than contending with oneself or others.

The psychological factors that should be considered in the practice of this sport are inferiority or superiority complexes, humiliating experiences, obstacles to personal ambition and the possible difficulties of interaction with people that participate with you in a course or even just in a freediving excursion.

An **Inferiority complex** is a factor that will emerge when confronted with new tasks, or during a situation over which we do not have control. In these conditions repressed feelings of withdrawal, suppression or heavy self-criticism may be triggered.

On the other hand a **superiority complex** may cause an exaggeration of the idea of personal capacity or a reduced alertness to danger. This attitude is hazardous because it can translate into absent-mindedness or traumatic accidents.

Humiliating experiences, even if only occasional, can provoke a sense of inferiority, the feeling of inadequacy in what one's doing, or a sense of hostility towards an instructor or companion who is perhaps being more assertive than they should.

The difficulty of achieving set goals even in reasonable circumstances can generate different forms of nervous tension that result in **anxiety**.

Unlike the weather, we can condition the climate in which we carry out lessons or training, and as a consequence minimise the incidence of a complex.

All these possible difficulties can occur at any moment during the day. Therefore we must be able to recognise weakening in our emotional defences and the consequent anxiety, fear, lack of concentration etc, so that we can intervene to control the emotion.

1.2 FROM MASK TO BALLAST: HOW TO CHOOSE EQUIPMENT

Immersing oneself in the hydrosphere, which has physical and chemical characteristics very diverse to the atmosphere that we live in, requires the use of special equipment that supports adaptation to the environment. The most obvious obstacles to the freediver are the incapacities to see, to breathe, to move efficiently and to maintain warmth.

These obstacles have been overcome with the production of four fundamental pieces of freediving gear: **mask**, **snorkel**, **fins** and **wetsuit**, which depending on thickness requires a certain amount of **weight**.

New materials and the experience of apneists has been put at the disposal of manufacturers, allowing them in recent years to make ever more sophisticated equipment that increases the safety and comfort, and therefore the performance of all apneists from the beginner to the champion.

Apneists should have the technical know-how to be able to adequately maintain their equipment. It is essential to have faith in your equipment in order to be totally relaxed in the water and to dive with safety and enjoyment.

The mask

There are two types of mask in production: **large volume** and **reduced volume**. The first is for use with Scuba equipment while the second is best for apneists.

An effective mask for freediving must first of all have a reduced volume: In the descent the apneist is forced to subtract air from the lung's reserve, and to discharge this air through the nose in sufficient quantity to prevent the mask from squashing against the face due to the increasing hydrostatic pressure. This 'mask squeeze' can have a painful suction effect, which may also cause the rupture of capillaries in the eyes. During the descent it is sufficient to blow a little air into the mask to avoid this danger, or if for some reason this is not possible then the descent can be terminated.

Clearly then, the lesser the interior volume of the mask, the smaller the amount of air that needs to be emitted during the descent, and this benefits performance, especially for deeper dives. A reduced volume mask requires about a litre of air for compensation during a very deep dive.

However for someone who operates at five or six metres, perhaps between the waves, it may be more suitable to adopt a larger mask that has a greater volume but a superior field of vision. Visibility is definitely an element to take into con-

A BRIEF HISTORY OF MASKS

In the 1940's, soon after the Second World War, there was a rubber mask called the 'Monogoggle' on the market. Manufactured in France, it exacerbated the basic defects of Asian goggles: the nose was kept outside and therefore the mask could only be used to a few meters depth before the pressure literally sucked the eyeballs out of the sockets of the unfortunate wearer. The first mask that did cover the nose was excessively sized, and didn't allow for much of a descent due to the amount of air wasted on compensating it. Then in 1951 the professor Luigi Ferraro, decorated with gold medals of military valour for having single-handedly sunk four enemy merchant ships using his 'Gamma Man,' a kind of underwater commando unit, went to work as a technical consultant for the company of Cressi in Genoa, and together with the 'Rondine' fins (the first shoed fin) patented the 'Pinocchio' mask – in practice a 'Monogoggle' that didn't have the nose outside, but included it comfortably within. The 'Pinocchio' (which is still in production) is the progenitor of all modern underwater masks of reduced volume. Today studies carried out by all the businesses involved in the sport have allowed for the creation of models designed specifically for apnea: small, but with good visibility, equipped with two lenses placed on the same plane, and with an extremely soft and comfortable skirt.

sideration. Masks with twin lenses are ideal for both reduced internal volume and enhanced visibility.

Until recently the **skirt** (the part in contact with the face) has been made exclusively from rubber of varying softness. Nowadays almost all models on the market have adapted to silicon, even more soft and durable than rubber. The fit on the face is improved. Regardless of material, the contour of the skirt must be adapted to the profile of the face. It is important that the housing for the nose does not create points of constriction, and that the freediver can squeeze it easily with their fingers in order to equalise. Many models have indents on the side of the nosepiece that make it easy to insert the fingers.

Another point to assess carefully is the forehead. If the **frame**, compressed by the pressure of water, squeezes excessively on the skull then it will cause pain that could ruin a dive.

All models of production masks allow for the quick adjustment of the **strap** even whilst in water. Usually you need only to press the plastic buckle that frees the strap and alter it to the desired length. Releasing the buckle to return to its position will once more jam the strap.

Impaired vision is no longer a limitation to underwater activities. There are models of masks that incorporate corrective lenses as a substitute for normal spectacles.

Choosing an appropriate mask for your face entails testing it out of the water to see if it will adapt to your physiognomy. To do this you will need to tilt your head to look upwards, place the mask on your face and breathe in through the nose, creating a slight depressurisation. If the mask sucks into your face and remains attached then you can be sure that it will not let in any water.

When a mask is new, especially if it has a silicon skirt, it is best to wash it inside and out before the first use with a specific detergent that can be found in the shop, or with toothpaste or dishwashing detergent, so as to eliminate any traces of silicone oil, preventing it from misting in the future. However don't forget when the mask is dry to wash the inside of the glass with saliva before diving. This operation serves to degrease the mask, preventing it from fogging during the dive, and can be done any time before entering the water.

Snorkel

The word snorkel is derived from the German *Schnorchel*, a device for aerating submarines, but also used to describe a big nose. By appearances a snorkel seems very simple, and of little importance: a shaped tube with an attached mouthpiece. However the snorkel does have great importance, given that it allows a freediver to breathe on the surface with the face immersed in the most efficient way possible.

It is best to avoid snorkels with corrugated bends: water can rest in these grooves, becoming a nuisance and causing a noise during breathing.

The most important part of a snorkel is the tube, or to be precise its cross-section. If it is too narrow the diver will use more energy breathing and will tire sooner. If instead the cross-section is too wide, the apneist will find it difficult to completely empty the snorkel of water. The ideal tube must have an intermediate diameter.

Fins

Fins are an apneist's means of propulsion, and are perhaps the piece of gear that has recently been known to develop the most radically. Not so long ago the only option was rubber fins of moderate length that could be used either for apnea or for scuba diving. Then long fins were created for the specific use of the apneist, with rubber foot pockets and techno-polymer blades of up to a metre in length. Two guides were fixed to the shoes, as well as one or more screws to attach the blade. Finally, in recent times, blades have been fashioned from carbon fibre: a costly material that assures the highest performance.

Carbon fibre, although it hasn't diffused much into the underwater market due to the higher price, has become a discriminating factor, especially in deep dives. Weight and thickness are impressively reduced. Its principal characteristic is its 'snap,' or rapidity of return, and the consequent reduction of dead time. This return is remarkable, especially for its good weight/rigidity ratio and the elastic quality of the material. Elasticity allows the blade to be responsive, particularly in the turn of a dive. When the apneist inverts the phase of the fin-stroke the blade reacts immediately to all the force applied to it. This is also due to the fact that when subjected to a force carbon fibre will flex uniformly over its whole surface.

The **foot pocket** must satisfy two principle requirements: it must fit the foot perfectly, without creating any constrictions, and at the same time it must transmit the movement created in the leg muscle to the blade. To meet these demands fins of superior quality are created using two types of rubber of different toughness. The softer is used for the part that holds the instep and the ankle, while the tougher rubber is

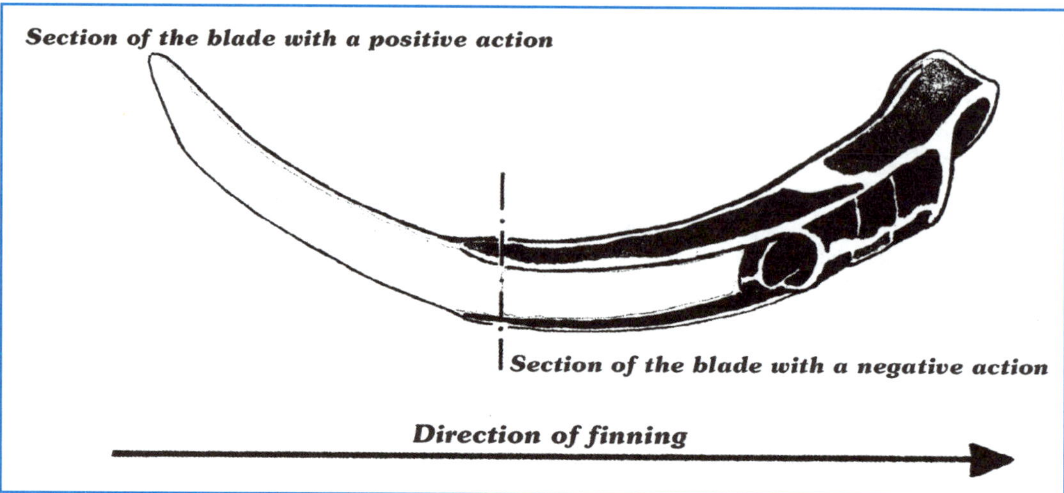

used for the sole, the side spars and for holding the toes whilst leaving them free to move, as in a sandal. In this way the foot pocket will have a comfortable fit whilst binding the foot efficiently so that muscular action can be transmitted without dispersion of energy. The 'shoed' fin that opens at the point in such a way as to leave the toes free is the other patent (with the 'Pinocchio' mask) of Professor Luigi Ferraro: the 'Rondine', product of his experience during the war, was a 'secret' but very primitive fin with a tough rubber foot pocket that massacred the toes of the diver.

The **blades** are the propellers with which the athlete steers himself into the depths and returns with a proportional consumption of energy. The overwhelming majority of fins in production are techno-polymer, an elastic material with a reasonable 'snap' back to its original position. The design of the blade usually includes some parallel longitudinal flutings that channel the water and eliminate the phenomenon of lateral sliding under force.

Presently, in specialist shops, you can choose between blades of different rigidity that satisfy all requirements. The softer models are adapted for people with long-limbed musculatures, whilst the stiffer models are for more robust legs and a heavier, and therefore less hydrodynamic physique. The firmer blade will allow for more efficient propulsion, but at the same time its use requires greater strength; it is therefore necessary to evaluate the physical and technical qualities of each for an educated choice. There is no ideal choice of fin; it depends on the apneist's physique and degree of training.

Fins do not require much care. It is sufficient to rinse them in freshwater after each dive in the sea, and to avoid leaving them exposed to the sun, which can vulcanise (bake) the rubber of the shoe, making it porous and therefore less durable. At the end of the season remember to check the screws that attach the shoe to the blade: remove them, and clean and lubricate them with a spray or liquid antioxidant.

Wetsuits

There are numerous models of freediving wetsuits that satisfy any requirement. Between these you can choose from made to measure full body suits either with high waist or shoulder strapped trousers, single lining or double lining, in black, green, grey, camouflage etc, with or without a zip.

Above all a wetsuit should keep you warm, especially if it is to be worn in the winter or pre-season; it must be of sufficient thickness to isolate the body from cold water. It is therefore imperative that the suit is the right size, with a cut that fits the body like a glove. There cannot be any gaps that water will flow through, dispersing body heat, and it must be made out of the highest quality **neoprene**; soft and elastic so as not to restrict movement of the thorax and thereby limit breathing.

Another characteristic of good neoprene is incompressibility. During the descent the pressure squeezes the neoprene, reducing its thickness and hence its ability to trap heat, as well as causing a significant variation in buoyancy.

Single lining is definitely better suited for competitive apneists, or those who are diving frequently during all seasons; the *Double lining* is instead suited for less frequent divers, who are active for perhaps a fortnight in the summer and don't need a very technical suit. However we will try and explain in more detail the differences between these two types of neoprene.

The **single lining** has only one layer of material lining that can be on the inside or the outside – the other surface is smooth. If the rubber is in contact with the skin then the suit will be softer, warmer and have a better grip. On the other hand there are two advantages with having the lined surface next to the skin: donning or doffing of the suit is easier due to slide of the material on the skin, and there will be greater insulation out of the water: the wetsuit will dry quicker due to the neoprene being in direct contact with the air, and this is an advantage during boat trips in the cold months. With the lining on the outside the suit will be more resistant to abrasion, but it will also be more difficult to remove since the neoprene won't slide easily on the skin.

A wetsuit has a **double lining** when the layer of neoprene is the filling of a sandwich, between two layers of material. This is the most durable wetsuit on the market: its tougher structure means it won't tear easily when scraped against rocks and neither will it rip when removed hurriedly or with little care. The disadvantages are a relatively high rigidity, especially after several dives, and a lesser insulation compared to a single lined suit of the same thickness. In spite of this it is the most popular suit for scuba divers, owing to its greater durability.

Finally there is the **open cell**, a suit in which the pores of the neoprene are in contact with the skin. Both sides of the neoprene are vulcanised, with a central spongy zone containing cells full of air. The advantages of this scheme are its softness and greater insulation, whereby the porous material adheres to the skin, reducing water infiltration to a minimum. On the other hand the open cell has two inconveniences: it is exhausting to put on or take off and it is very delicate. There are two possible ways of putting on an open cell suit. When the water is warm you can soak the suit, lubricate it with shampoo and then slip it on, always taking the greatest care with how you handle the material, as even the pressure of a finger can rip it. If instead the water is cold and you don't want to put on a wet wetsuit, dust the interior with talcum powder, which will reduce friction against the skin, making it easy to slide on.

There are **two types of open cell**: unlined and single lining. The **unlined** is smooth outside and extremely soft, as it conserves the elastic quality of the neoprene. It is good for the winter because of how quickly it dries, however it is delicate and tears easily. It only takes one clumsy scratch to put a finger right through, and if you come against the rocks or coral it rips like pastry. The **single lining** is just as warm, but has the advantage of being tougher, given that the external lining protects it from abrasion due to contact with the sea floor, and renders it more resistant to tears. However it takes longer to dry, thus in the winter you may be colder during the boat trip, since it will disperse more heat.

The most common forms of wetsuit are the **two-piece** and **single-piece**. The two-piece consists of jacket and trousers, while the single-piece is a full body cut (jacket and trousers) and is generally used in warmer waters. The two-piece has an incorporated hood, while the single-piece seldom has an attached hood, although it may be supplied as an accessory. The trousers of the two-piece should preferably be high waist, as

GETTING DRESSED

Start by putting on the trousers: insert the legs, first one then the other. Then take the neoprene by the fingertips, and unroll the trousers as far as they will go. When putting on the jacket, which in the apneist's case is usually zipless, insert the arms until the hands clear through the cuffs, then push your head through the neck, helping yourself by bringing the arms down to your sides. Seize the ends of the jacket and pull it with short tugs onto the stomach. Do the same with the back, pulling on the 'beaver's tail' that dangles behind. To finish attach the clip or press the Velcro together. With a smooth outer surface the procedure is the same, although proceed with delicacy to avoid leaving scratch-marks or inadvertently ripping the material. If the trousers are high waist then when putting on the jacket hold the top of the trousers with one hand, keeping the waist in place so it doesn't make annoying folds that allow water to infiltrate. Naturally if putting on a jacket with a zip the operation is simple and less exhausting. On the whole these wetsuits are not the best for apneists since they aren't as flexible or as warm – a small amount of water will always pass through the zip. However they are not to be excluded for those enthusiasts who only freedive in the summer, as the ease with which they are put on can outweigh their other inconveniences.

this will create less restriction on the thorax during respiration. High waist trousers may be easily removed if nature happens to call in the middle of the sea.

Smooth neoprene suits can also come with a **metallic trimming**, also called *aqua stop*, used for the wrists, ankles and face opening: it limits the infiltration of water, but on the other hand makes the donning and doffing of the suit a little more difficult as it won't slide on the skin. Pay attention to roll this surface over when manoeuvring in the suit and the problem will be resolved.

Regarding care and maintenance, a wetsuit should be treated as a garment of clothing. Creases will make the suit less comfortable and liable to deteriorate more rapidly, especially if they are in the jacket. For this reason avoid leaving the suit in a bag for a long time, and never with the weight belt resting on top. Like every other piece of equipment that we have discussed, the wetsuit needs to be washed in fresh water after use in sea or chlorinated pool water. After having dried it well, re-hang the suit on a clothes hanger in a dark and dry place – a wardrobe is ideal.

If the seams of the lining become frayed then they can be resealed by burning the nylon with the flame of a lighter. Small tears in the neoprene can be repaired with a neoprene glue available in dive shops. When the rip is more extended consult the shop owner for repair.

Weight Belt

The weight belt is made of two parts: the belt itself (in rubber or nylon) and the weights. Its function is to balance the positive buoyancy of the wetsuit. The belt should preferably be made from stretchable rubber that will keep the weights fixed in place around the waist at depth. Don't forget that during the descent the body is squeezed by the hydrostatic pressure, which diminishes lung volume, and a nylon belt will tend to rotate or slide up towards the chest. The elastic will instead accommodate for the increasing pressure. Buckles are produced in stainless steel or plastic. Steel will be the stronger of the two, and also locks better.

The lead weights can be a half-kilo, a kilo or two kilos. Other than the standard weights there are other quick release weights, which can be attached or removed without having to unclasp the belt to unthread them. It can be helpful to keep a weight of this kind on the belt so that if it is necessary to vary weighting at the last minute it can be done instantaneously, without having to undo the belt. It is also important to keep a metal ring on the belt that the karabiner of the signal buoy can be clipped onto. Remember that the last weight on the end opposite the buckle should be fixed: if you have to abandon the belt on the bottom it will be possible to recover it without risking the weights sliding off into the blue.

There are a few measures to take when storing the weight belt for a long period of time. If the belt is rubber then it is best to remove the weights and the buckle, wash and rinse it, and dust it with talcum powder before rolling it up into a loose coil. If it is made of woven nylon then rinse and dry it before storing it, obviously without the weights.

One last suggestion: never transport your weight belt in your bag! It is the easiest way to quickly damage the bag or the rest of your gear.

INSTRUMENTS

The level of technical sophistication reached by some manufacturers has made compact and efficient instruments available for freediving. The use of a watch, depth meter or computer improves the practice of apnea in terms of safety and quality of diving.

Watch

These must be suitable for underwater use and therefore resistant to pressure. Other than keeping track of the time, if the watch includes a chronometer (analogue or digital) then it can also be used to measure dive times. There are many such models on the market.

Other important evaluations to make when buying a watch are the readability of its numbers or needles, and the length of the wrist strap, which must be able to accommodate the increased circumference of the wrist with the wetsuit cuff.

There are also analogue watches with small digital displays that register the depth clearly and save it in the memory.

Depth meter

An instrument that serves to measure profundity. Whether it is analogue or digital the data must be easily read from the face. Any quality depth meter should indicate the maximum depth reached.

Computer

Recently apneists have also been able to 'computerize' themselves like their underwater relatives with the regulator. Several manufacturers have created instruments specifically for freedivers. Other than depth and dive time, these devices will memorize all dives and the surface intervals.

It is possible to interface them with a PC, download all the data, and analyse total times, descent and ascent times. This is extremely useful for evaluating performance in deep freediving and for setting targets and personalised training programs.

OTHER ACCESSORIES

Wetsuit vests

These are often used by freedivers, especially in the cold months. Vests are usually worn with high waist trousers as a substitute for the 'Farmer John' trousers (with shoulder straps), as the latter can be more of a nuisance. The insulation supplied by either options is similar, although if anything the vest will be superior as it has a higher neck and therefore covers a greater area. With regards to the material the same arguments apply as with the full suit. There are vests with single or double lining, of varying colours and thickness, although usually the vest is made in two or three millimetre neoprene. In fact too thick is sometimes irritating, especially at the collar and armpits where the jacket can press tightly, causing a rash from the seams rubbing against the skin.

Socks

Their function is to keep the feet warm in cold water and to prevent rashes or blisters occurring at the points of chafing with the foot pocket of the fin. They are made in single lined or double lined neoprene. There are also much heavier socks (booties) with rubber souls that are worn with open heeled fins and have an adjustable strap, but these aren't effective for freediving.

If the water temperature allows you can wear normal cotton socks, the advantage being that they protect the feet but do not add to buoyancy.

Gloves

These protect from the cold and safeguard the hands from cuts and scratches, which are inevitable when you are in contact with the bottom. In the winter, after an hour of being in cold water, neoprene gloves become indispensable to avoid numb hands that will render any operation difficult.

On the other hand neoprene gloves cause a very annoying loss of sensitivity. There are varieties that have a graining on the palms made from lots of small balls set in relief to improve the grip.

In seasons when the water is less cold it is best to opt for softer gloves, made from cloth or a synthetic anti-slip material. They may have no value as insulation, but in compensation they prevent the hands from scratches whilst retaining their sensitivity.

Bermuda shorts

These are neoprene shorts that cover the thighs down to the knees, and are put on over the wetsuit in order to limit the flow of water between jacket and trousers.

They are mainly worn in the coldest winter months or in lakes, where the water is in general colder than the sea. Their thickness varies between 2 and 3 mm. When choosing the size keep in mind the various layers that will be worn underneath. Owing to their function it is imperative that the waist and the thigh collars are close fitting to prevent water entry.

Ankle weights

These are small weights set in belts worn round the ankles. They serve to stop the fins from floating on the surface and are only useful in shallow water; at depth they are worthless and unadvisable as the pressure renders the whole body negatively buoyant, and therefore also the fins.

Ankle weights can be of varying type and weight. The most widely used are made of a lead weight (usually half a kilo) with two slots through which a rubber or Velcro strap passes for attaching it to the ankle. Another type of ankle weight is made of a small bag of durable cloth full of small balls of lead that is opportunely shaped to wrap around the ankle and fasten with a quick release buckle. Ankle weights make finning on the surface more exhausting, and since their weight adds to the weight on your belt they will compromise buoyancy on the surface, and therefore relaxation and respiration prior to a dive. However for the practice of apnea in shallow depths it is best to use plenty of weight. Carefully evaluate the option of using ankle weights, considering that the greatest advantage will be a more balanced body position when floating.

Dive knife

This will serve to free oneself in the unlikely event of entanglement in a net or fishing line abandoned on the bottom. For the apneist, who must reduce gear to the bare essentials, a small knife is sufficient, as long as it is tapered, neatly designed, and has a pointed blade. One edge of the blade should be smooth, the other serrated to cut thick ropes. The handle is a matter of personal taste, as long as it can be held and used safely with gloves, and the hilt must be such that when you pull out the knife you don't run the risk of sliding a finger on the blade and cutting yourself.

A plastic sheath can have a quick release button, or the knife may also be fixed by means of a rubber ringlet, which holds the end of the hilt in place. The knife can be attached to the calf or arm by means of two rubber straps with buckles, or it can be fixed to the weight belt. This last option has one inconvenience: if the weight belt must be abandoned then the knife is lost. The advantage is better hydrodynamics of the limbs.

Regarding the maintenance of the blade, as for the rest of the equipment it should be rinsed in fresh water after every dive session. If you are storing the knife for a length of time rub the blade with a layer of protective silicon oil to avoid rusting. Do not worry if spots of rust still appear: it is almost certainly superficial incrustation that will disappear straight away after brushing it with sandpaper or with a wad of cotton wool soaked in oil.

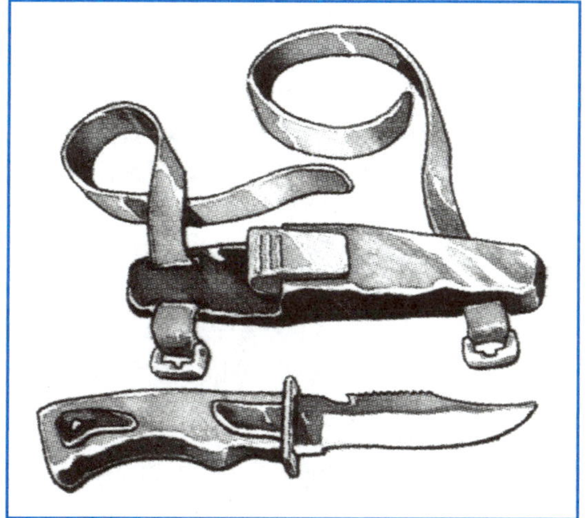

To finish, remember to periodically substitute the sheath's fastening straps, which can crack and break with use. Also from time to time take the knife to a knife-grinder for sharpening. A knife that doesn't cut is a useless tool!

Underwater torch

The purpose of this piece of equipment is to illuminate the seafloor, restoring the true colours that the water has filtered out of the sunlight, and to light up the fissures and caves where darkness reigns. A good beam of light will restore brilliant colour and the ability to see into nooks and crannies that would otherwise be inaccessible to our vision.

The principle requirement of a torch for apnea is merely to illuminate what is hidden to our eyes with a beam of direct, compact and bright light. A good underwater torch should be pressure resistant, with reduced dimensions, easily handled and not cumbersome. The power supply can be either normal batteries or rechargeable batteries, normally nickel-cadmium. In general the second solution is more costly but you may save money on batteries in the long run. When recharging pay attention to the manufacturer's instructions. The switch is generally magnetic, so care must be taken not to expose the torch to other magnetic sources that could damage it.

The reflector and the bulb determine the characteristics of the beam of light. If swapping the bulb verify that the voltage corresponds to the power supply to avoid blowing its filament. Clean the reflector occasionally with a dry cloth; this will enhance the light. To finish, remember that your hands are precious in the water; therefore fix the torch to the wrist with a strap so that your hands are free without the preoccupation of having to hold the torch.

Stroboscope

This is a small flashing light that can be fixed to the arm with a Velcro strap, and is very useful when you are diving in cloudy water of reduced visibility. When training in a lake a stroboscope is essential in order to be well visible to companions who are supplying assistance. Generally powered by a battery, the lamp emits flashes of white light that are extremely penetrative through water containing a lot of suspended particles.

If you are diving in turbid water, in particular lakes, remember that the stroboscope is synonymous with safety. Never economise on safety. Being clearly visible to your companions is of the highest importance.

Signal buoy

There are two types of signal buoy on the market: the traditional spherical and the torpedo. The first has the advantage

of being better visible by boat pilots when the sea is choppy; the second has less resistance and therefore saves the energy of the apneist who is pulling it. Every signal buoy has the function of indicating on the surface the presence of an apneist below. For this reason they are made with bright colours like red, orange or yellow.

They are connected to the apneist by means of a line that is attached on one end to a ring underneath the buoy, and on the other end to a karabiner on the weight belt. The length of the rope must be several metres longer than the operating depth. If it is too long then the buoy will remain far away from the divers, leaving them less identifiable to boats in transit. If instead it is too short then it will be a resistance during the dive, tiring and slowing down the freediver.

Fin straps

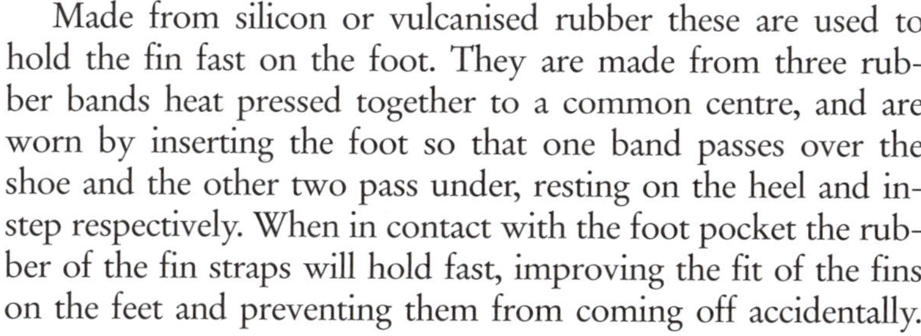

Made from silicon or vulcanised rubber these are used to hold the fin fast on the foot. They are made from three rubber bands heat pressed together to a common centre, and are worn by inserting the foot so that one band passes over the shoe and the other two pass under, resting on the heel and instep respectively. When in contact with the foot pocket the rubber of the fin straps will hold fast, improving the fit of the fins on the feet and preventing them from coming off accidentally.

Box of small pieces of equipment and spare parts

It would be a pity to miss out on a day of freediving just because we have broken a mask strap and we don't have a spare! A small kit with a few pieces of essential spare parts and several tools like pliers, scissors and a screwdriver should always be within close reach. Several articles to include are:

- straps and buckles for the mask
- a spare snorkel
- demister for the mask
- silicon spray
- neoprene glue
- needle and thread
- spare batteries and bulbs for the torch
- a small first aid kit
- nylon fishing line of 3mm diameter
- a lighter

Include other spare parts according to the equipment you are using.

Free Diving Logbook

The 'Diary of a Freediver:' a folder containing paper for taking notes during apnea courses, or recording training progress and competition results for the competitive apneist. Freediving is a sport that depends heavily on the right equipment and experience.

It is important to collect ordered information on practical experiences, the local marine weather and any equipment used.

The diary is an item of proven worth that is of concrete benefit to training, stimulating a personal dialogue necessary for the registration of our experiences and favouring self-awareness of our actions. It also acts as a memory that is indelible over time and easily consulted.

ADAPTING THE BODY TO WATER

CHAPTER

2

Every human being spends about nine months before birth in their mother's belly, well-protected inside a sac called the *amnion*, and immersed in *amniotic fluid*, which at the end of gestation amounts to 500-600 ml of water containing albumin, urea and potassium, sodium and calcium salts in solution. A liquid that is in many ways very similar to seawater.

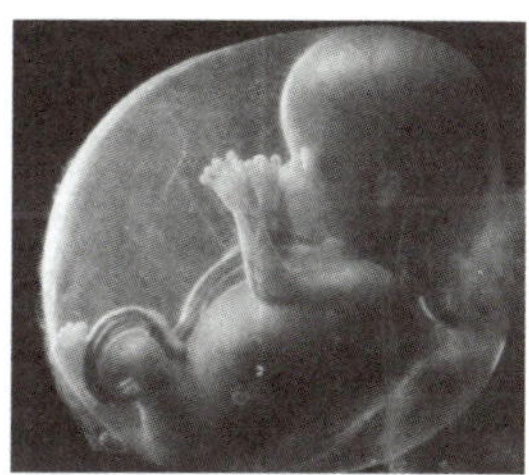

Our bodies are constituted mainly of water: 97% of a human embryo; 80% of a newborn and 60% of an adult individual.

The origin of this system is still disputed, but its function is to protect the foetus from pressure and trauma. Amniotic fluid is usually drained before birth, at the moment when the membrane of the water sac ruptures. Its coloration varies according to the stage of pregnancy (towards the end it is whitish).

Even though we may have aquatic origins our natural adaptation to water often has little consequence, especially if too much time passes after birth before relearning to swim. To submerge in a world with such different physical and chemical qualities to the terra firma on which we live requires a knowledge of how our body adapts to water: that it is 800 times more dense than air, disperses heat 25 times as rapidly, refracts light differently, thereby altering vision underwater, and impedes hearing, since sound travels four times faster underwater.

It is necessary then to study several physical laws that explain the occurrence of certain phenomena in the physics and chemistry of the hydrosphere. The laws of Archimedes, Boyle and Dalton explain all the effects of immersing a body in water, in an environment with significant variations of pressure, salinity, transparency and temperature.

Every good apneist should possess this knowledge. It is the only way to guarantee safe behaviour. This part of the manual is dedicated to the study of the body's adaptation to water, the analysis of breathing on land, the production of muscular energy, and how vision, weight and heat exchange are altered underwater.

2.1 THE PHYSICS OF IMMERSION

It is important for the apneist to know the laws that govern the behaviour of a body immersed in liquid, as it will reduce the factor of the 'unknown,' helping to prevent stress. In this way we can create a good foundation for relaxation.

Archimedes principle of buoyancy

To begin let us state the law:

A body immersed in liquid receives a force upwards that is equal to the weight of the volume of liquid displaced.

Translating this into practice, we can say that if a 400 g (weight force) buoy has a volume of 1 litre (and would therefore displace 1 kg of water) then it will receive a hydrostatic force upwards of 1 kg. The resultant force is equal to 600 g upwards, and the buoy will float on the surface. In this example the hydrostatic force is greater than the weight force and the object is said to be **positively buoyant.**

If we put a weight belt in the water that totals 7 kg and displaces only 1 litre of water = 1 kg, then the resultant force will be 6 kg downwards, and the weight belt will sink. The weight force in this case is greater than the hydrostatic force and the object is said to be **negatively buoyant.**

Finally, if an apneist is underwater, weighing 75kg and displacing 75 litres of water = 75 kg then the positive and negative forces will cancel. We say that the diver is **neutrally buoyant**, or the weight force and hydrostatic force are equal and therefore the diver moves neither up nor down but stays in the same position.

Positive, negative and neutral: these are the three states of buoyancy that every apneist will confront during freediving. It is therefore necessary to adopt precise strategies of 'weighting;' that is to use a certain quantity of ballast to neutralise the positive buoyancy of the body and any equipment worn such as wetsuit, mask, gloves and socks. Even the intended type of activity should be considered for weighting. Snorkelling in shallow water, deep freediving, static apnea, spearfishing by either waiting at depth, shooting from the surface or hunting under rocks; all of these situations require different weighting to ensure safety and enjoyment.

In order to determine correct weighting it is important to understand the fluidic quality of the water in which we dive. What is the weight of the volume of water displaced by our

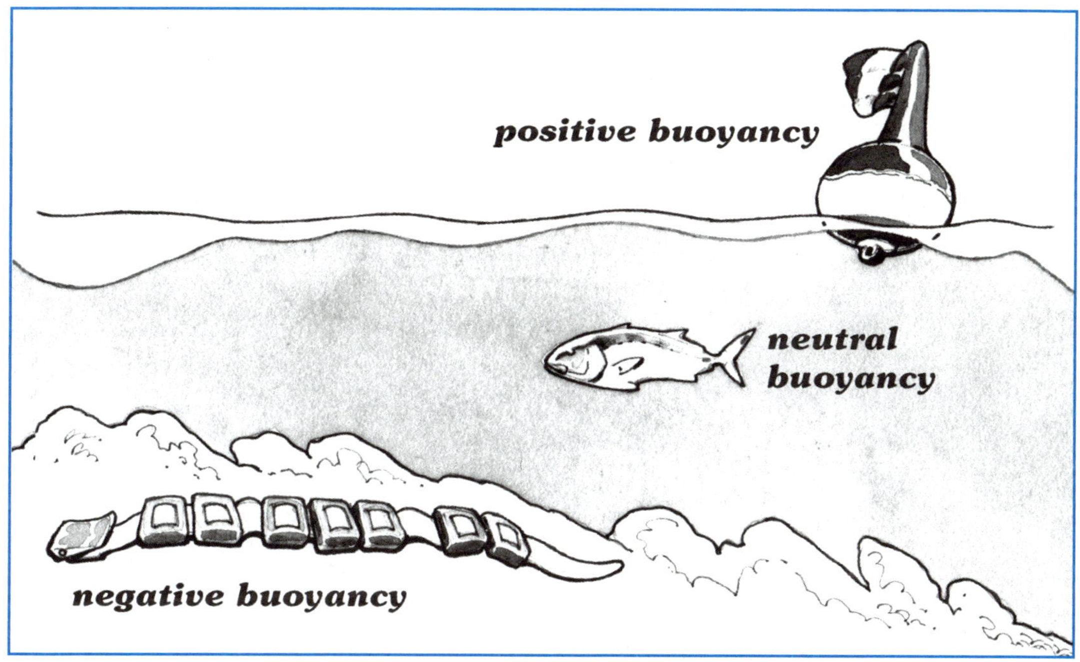

The three different situations: positive buoyancy that causes floating, neutral buoyancy in which the forces are balanced and one remains at the same depth and negative buoyancy that causes sinking.

body? The specific weight of freshwater is always less than saltwater; therefore the buoyancy force is less. This means that the weight worn in a swimming pool will be insufficient for the sea, because the seawater has a greater weight due to the presence of dissolvent. Buoyancy will even be different for equal equipment between the Mediterranean and the Red Sea, where the salinity reaches values above 4%. We would therefore have to use a different amount of weight.

Variations in buoyancy also influence muscular work due to either the greater or lesser resistance to the legs when finning. Hence if an ascent from 30m to the surface in the sea requires a certain quantity of muscular energy then the same ascent in freshwater will require a greater amount.

In short, the four main factors that vary buoyancy in water are: equipment, the amount of air inhaled, density of the water and the hydrostatic pressure determined by depth.

Obviously a 7mm thick wetsuit confers a greater buoyancy than a 4mm suit. Likewise a maximum inhale will afford a slightly more positive buoyancy than an incomplete inhale. However this is all relative to the operating depth, which influences buoyancy in a way that is determinable.

To conclude, we should mention the possibility of using mobile weight, which can be used by an apneist with particular requirements, who needs to economize on energy during the descent. This technique will be discussed later in more depth.

Pressure

The underwater environment has very different physical and chemical characteristics to the world in which we live above the surface. Water is denser than air and acts on the organism to produce modifications that are of great consequence to the apneist. The aspect that requires the most attention is the **pressure**.

Each dive exposes the body to a variation of pressure in proportion to depth: increasing in the descent, diminishing in the ascent. As we will see, this increase and decrease of pressure requires specific behavioural strategies that explain the training and technique of diving.

Physics teaches us that liquids are practically incompressible while gases are compressible. Water constitutes about 70% of our body mass. The remaining 30% is either solid (also incompressible) or spaces containing gas, which are subjected to the same pressure variations as those that affect us during our diving. This explains why when we immerse the 'empty' spaces of our body and equipment they are subjected to a squeeze. Hence the ears, lungs and mask must all be compensated (we will talk of this in detail in *Chapter 7*).

Pressure is perceived by a phenomenon known as 'squeeze.' In open water freediving, and at times in a pool if there is a

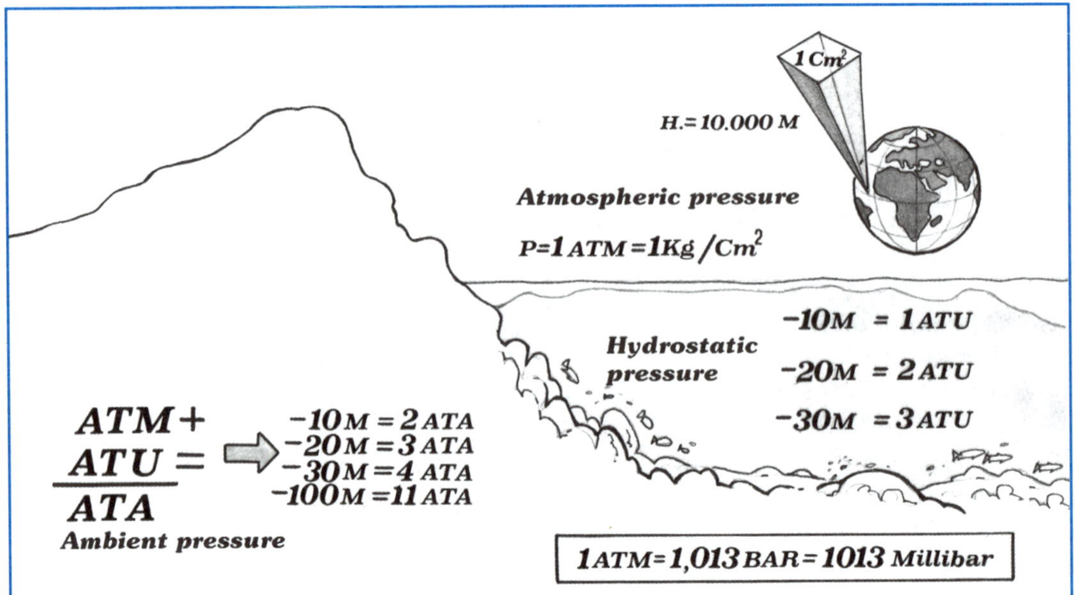

A graphical representation of atmospheric pressure (ATM), *hydrostatic pressure* (ATU) *and ambient pressure* (ATA).

'hole' deeper than three meters, one of the phenomena that warns of a significant variation in pressure is the annoying pain in the ears caused by water pressure on the eardrum, or the squashing of the mask onto the face if air isn't exhaled into it through the nose.

In physics, water pressure is a result of the application of a force downwards from the surface, given by:

$$P = F/S = 1kg/1cm^2 = 1 \text{ ATM} = 1.013 \text{ Bar} = 1013 \text{ MILLIBAR} = 760mmHg$$

With reference to diving it is necessary to define what is meant by

- **Atmospheric pressure**
- **Hydrostatic pressure**
- **Ambient pressure**

Atmospheric pressure (ATM)

The pressure exerted by the weight of a column of air with a height of 10,000m (the height of the atmosphere that circles the earth) on a square centimetre at sea level.

Hydrostatic pressure (ATU)

The pressure exerted by the height of the column of water above each square centimetre of an immersed body. Every 10m of depth is equal to 1 ATM.

Ambient Pressure (ATA)

Also called absolute pressure, this is the sum of the atmospheric pressure at sea level, which is always 1 ATM, and the hydrostatic pressure that varies by 1 ATM every 10m of depth. In other words:

$$ATA = ATM + ATU$$

Therefore:

at sea level	ATA = 1 ATM + 0 ATU =	1 ATA
at –10 meters	ATA = 1 ATM + 1 ATU =	2 ATA
at –20 meters	ATA = 1 ATM + 2 ATU =	3 ATA
at –90 meters	ATA = 1 ATM + 9 ATU =	10 ATA

The laws that follow are necessary to explain what effects this pressure will have during a dive.

Boyle's Law

Boyle's Law states that:

The volume of a gas at constant temperature is inversely proportional to the pressure exerted on it.

$$P \times V = K \quad \text{when temperature is constant}$$

or:

$$P_1 \times V_1 = P_2 \times V_2$$

This means that during a freedive descent our lung volume is reduced in proportion to the pressure acting on it. At a depth of 50 m an apneist will have a lung volume one sixth that of its volume on the surface.

For a better model of the effects of this law, imagine taking a balloon underwater that on the surface has a volume of 6 litres. This is what will happen:

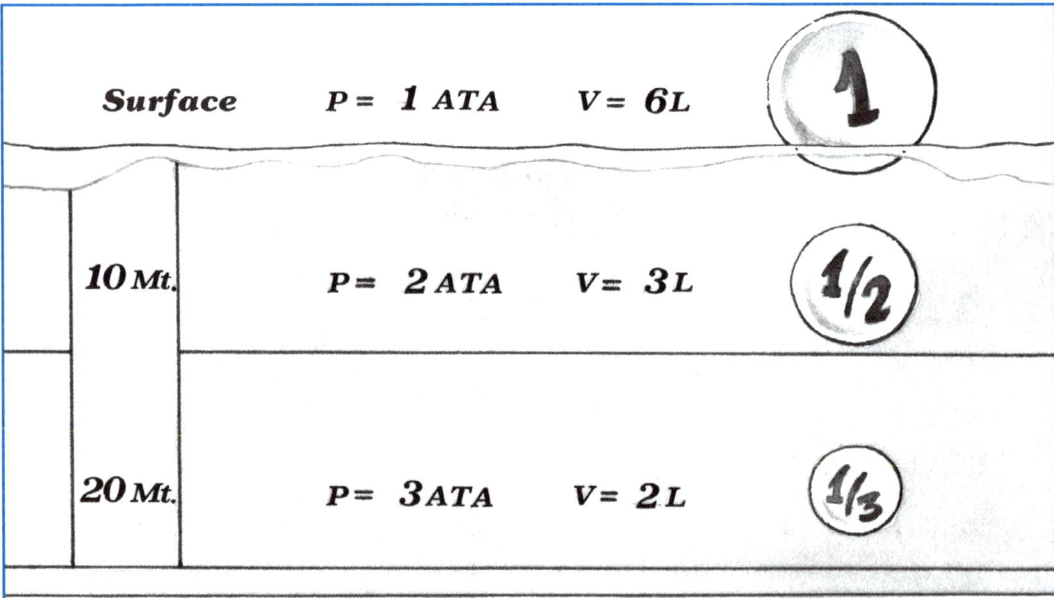

This also means that the further you descend and the greater the ambient pressure, the more the volume of the mask will be reduced, squeezing it against the face. Let us analyse what happens to the mask during descent and ascent. If on the surface the volume of air contained in the mask on the face is for example 100 cc, then after descending to a depth of ten meters the internal volume will have reduced by half, or 50 cc, and the pressure will have doubled to two atmospheres. 50 cc of air must therefore be emitted out of the nose to equalize the ambient pressure. In practice, air can be taken from either a respirator or the lungs and exhaled into the mask.

Dalton's law states that:

Dalton's Law

The pressure exerted by a mixture of gases (in our case air) is equal to the sum of the partial pressures of the gases.

As we know, our atmosphere is made up of a mixture of gases that we call air. These various gases are present in different percentages. In order to easier explain the subject we have simplified the actual data to the following generalization:

AIR = 21% Oxygen (O_2)
78% Nitrogen (N_2)
0.04% Carbon Dioxide (CO_2)

As we have seen, at sea level atmospheric pressure is given by:

$$1 \text{ ATM} = 1\text{kg/cm}^2 = 1 \text{ Bar} = 760 \text{ mmHg}$$

The partial pressures of the individual gases that comprise air will vary in proportion to their percentages.

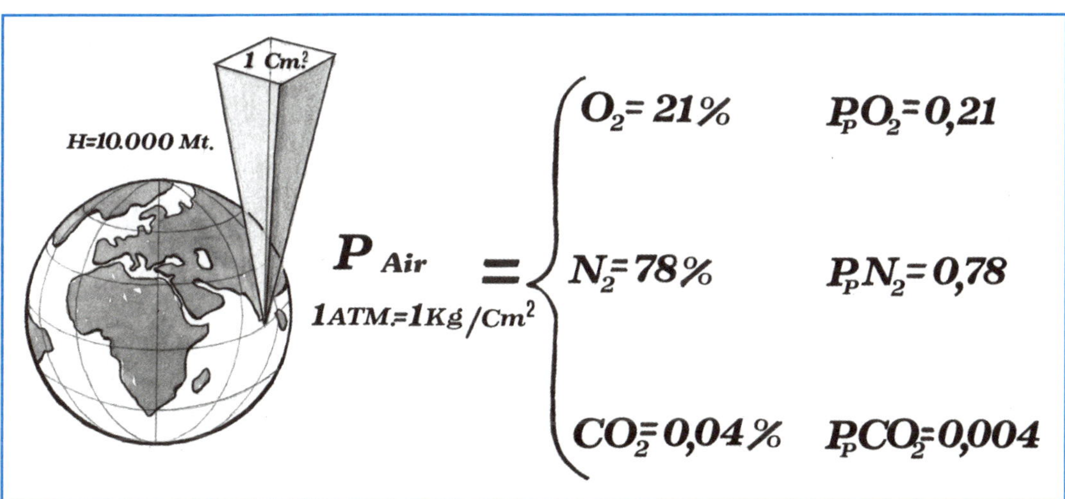

In more practical terms, this means that at sea level the pressure of air will be equal to the sum of $P_P\ O_2 + P_P\ N_2 + P_P\ CO_2$, or:

$$\begin{array}{ccccccc} P \text{ air} & = & P_P\,O_2 & + & P_P\,N_2 & + & P_P\,CO_2 \\ \downarrow & & \downarrow & & \downarrow & & \downarrow \\ 1 \text{ ATM} & = & 0.21 \text{ ATM} & + & 0.786 \text{ ATM} & + & 0.0004 \text{ ATM} \end{array}$$

With the last breath before a deep dive the apneist will inhale as much air as possible into the lungs, but only 21% of this is oxygen. During the descent, any movement on the bottom and the ascent, all cells will respire in order to survive, and muscles will function thanks to energy produced by the presence of oxygen. Oxygen metabolises to become carbon dioxide. Therefore the partial pressure of oxygen (P_P O_2) and the partial pressure of carbon dioxide (P_P CO_2) will vary in relation to the ambient pressure, but also to the activity of the apneist.

Gases in the lungs are exchanged between blood and alveolar air (air which arrives in the alveoli of the lungs) as a direct consequence of the pressure gradients of single gases. Dalton allows us to closely study the oxygen and carbon dioxide cycles in relation to the percentages with which they comprise respired air. We will see later (*Diffusion*, page. 72) the importance of Dalton's law in understanding how and why gases are exchanged in the lungs during respiration.

2.2 THE OXYGEN CYCLE

From the first airway into the lungs, to the alveoli, to the red blood cells and then on to all the cells of our body, oxygen passes, activating the oxidative processes that sustain the life of cells. To be able to talk of respiration and energy production at a muscular level it is necessary to understand the systems concerned. We start then with an analysis of the respiratory and cardiovascular systems so as to discover how the muscles of an apneist convert oxygen into movement.

CARDIOVASCULAR SYSTEM

For the apneist the activity of the cardiovascular system is a bit like the clock of a marathon runner. A clock gives rhythm to the runner and dictates when to start and when to finish. In apnea the rhythm is given by the pulsing of blood passing through the arteries.

Heart

The heart is the central organ of the cardiovascular system. Of the greatest importance for the apneist, it gives the rhythm for preparation before apnea, for the dive itself, and for the recovery between one performance and the next.

The heart is a hollow muscle that has the capacity to function like a pump; expanding and contracting, it sucks blood that is delivered continuously by the veins and pushes it to the peripheries of the body through the arteries. It is situated in the thoracic cavity between the two lungs and rests on the diaphragm that separates it from the abdominal cavity.

Internally the heart is composed of four cavities: two upper **atria** and two **ventricles** beneath. From a longitudinal perspective there is a **right heart** comprised of the right atrium and ventricle, and a **left heart** comprised of the left atrium and ventricle.

The left and right cavities are not connected to each other, but each atrium communicates with the ventricle beneath by a hole equipped with a one way valve: the **atrioventricular valve**. In this way the blood from the atrium passes into and fills the ventricle, forcing the valve closed so that when the ventricle contracts blood does not reflux back into the atrium.

Blood returning from the periphery flows into the atria by way of the veins, while from each ventricle an artery transports blood back towards the periphery. There is another valve at the entrance to the artery that permits blood-flow from the ventricle into the artery but not in the reverse direction.

Blood vessels

Blood vessels that branch off from the heart towards the peripheral parts of the body are called **arteries**; the inverse vessels that converge from the tissues and peripheral organs back to the heart are called **veins**.

The arteries, stretching away from the heart, branch out abundantly and at the same time diminish in width, taking their name to **arterioles**; these then continue to still smaller vessels called **arterial capillaries**, which in time connect to **venal capillaries** that join together to form veins of increasing width. Therefore the capillaries represent the point of union between the arterial and venous systems.

Arteries

The arteries are a system of tubes with muscular, elastic walls that convey the blood expelled by the ventricle and distribute it to the periphery through a network of fine vessels, permeating all of the tissues of body.

Two large principle arteries drain blood from the heart:

1) The **aorta** departs from the left ventricle, initiating the greater circulation: fresh and oxygenated blood disburses from here to be distributed to the periphery.

2) The right ventricle is connected to the **pulmonary artery**, which is responsible for the lesser circulation: blood col-

lected from the periphery is transported through the pulmonary artery to the lungs where it will offload carbon dioxide and be re-oxygenated.

A wave of blood pushed by the contraction of the ventricle into the principal arteries is propagated by their elastic walls at a velocity of 9 meters per second. However in the arterioles of the periphery the velocity drops to one millimetre per second in order to facilitate gas exchange between blood and cellular tissue.

Veins

The veins are vessels that bring blood back to the heart from the peripheral tissues, where they begin as microscopic vessels. Along their course they meet to form vessels of increasing width until they result in two thick trunks: the **vena cava superior** and the **vena cava inferior** that both drain into the right atrium. The vena cava superior collects blood from the head and upper limbs, while the vena cava inferior is responsible for gathering blood from the rest of the body. A third principle vein collects blood from the lungs and drains into the left atrium: this is the **pulmonary vein** that carries blood that has been oxygenated and cleaned of carbon dioxide back to the heart.

Thus it would be inaccurate to say that all veins carry venal blood and all arteries carry arterial (oxygenated) blood. In fact as we have seen the pulmonary artery transports blood deficient of oxygen whereas the pulmonary vein transports freshly oxygenated blood. The definitive difference between artery and vein is that the first has a centrifugal course, transporting blood away from the heart, while the latter transports blood into the heart.

Capillaries

These are the microscopically thin conduits that represent the terminals of the arterioles and the beginning of the venous system. To comprehend the vastness of the network formed by these capillaries one need only consider that the capillaries of a single person could be spread out over a surface of about 6,300 square meters.

CARDIAC CYCLE

The work of the heart consists of two distinct phases that repeat continually: a phase of contraction called **systole**, and a phase of relaxation called **diastole**. During the diastolic phase both the atria and the ventricles are relaxed and blood enters the atria. As they are gradually filled a pressure difference is created between the atria and the still empty ventricles.

The atrioventricular valves yield to the pressure of the mass of blood in the atria, and open, allowing the ventricles to fill in a short space of time. At this point the atria contract, forcing the remaining blood into the ventricles, which then also enter a phase of contraction. The pressure this causes in the ventricles closes the atrioventricular valves. The blood contained in the ventricles is forced by the contraction into the aorta or pulmonary artery. This finishes the phase of contraction, or systolic phase, and the cycle begins again as the atria refill with more blood.

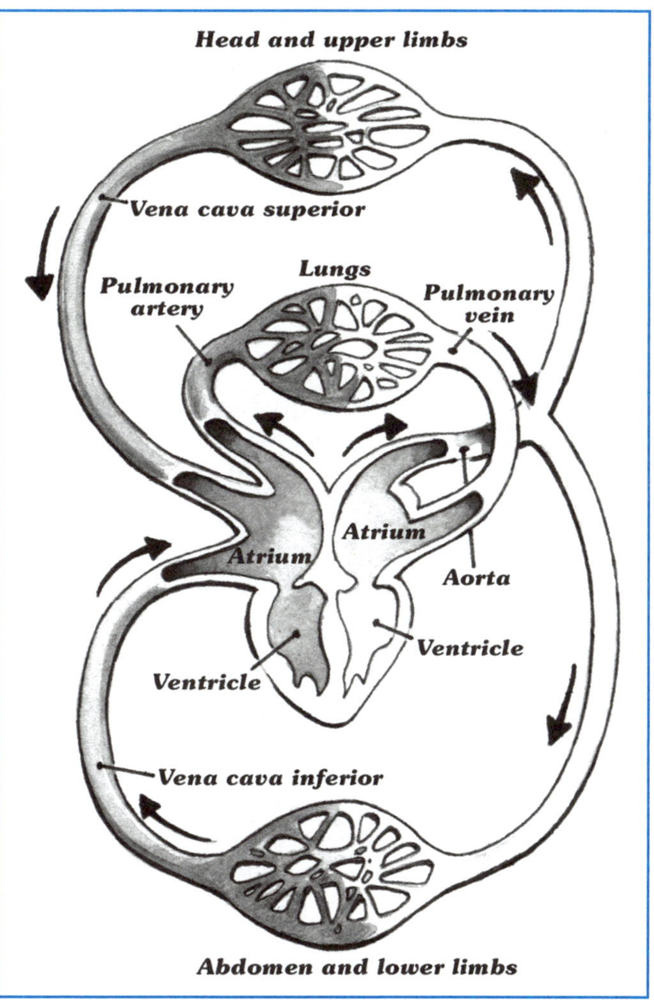

A diagram showing the circulation of blood.

Normally, at **rest conditions** the heart contracts 50-100 times in one minute, and pumps about 5 litres of blood in the same amount of time. These quantities increase during physical activity. During intense muscular exertion cardiac flow increases remarkably, reaching values above twenty litres per minute.

In highly trained apneists the heart rate can drop to values well below average – as low as 30–40 beats per minute – with great advantage to apnea. As we will see in *Chapter 4*, bradycardia (reduction of heart rate) can also be induced by particular techniques of autogenic training, but in particular it is one of the most interesting of the physiological features of the dive reflex (see *Chapter 3*).

Greater and lesser circulation

Distribution of blood is achieved by a circular system that has the same point of departure and arrival: the heart. We need to distinguish between the *pulmonary circulation* or *lesser circulation* and the *systemic circulation* or *greater circulation*.

Pulmonary circulation begins with the pulmonary artery, which originates from the right ventricle and penetrates the lungs, where it divides into numerous branches that form a fine network of microscopic capillaries wrapping around the walls of the lung's alveoli. After having been oxygenated in the capillaries, the blood then passes into venous vessels, which in their turn merge into the pulmonary vein that terminates in the left atrium.

The blood is then forced through the left atrioventricular valve (mitral or bicuspid valve) into the left ventricle from whence initiates the grand circle of **systemic circulation**, starting with the aorta and spreading to all districts of the body through the arteries and arterioles. Upon reaching the tissues, arterial blood relinquishes its nutritional substances and its oxygen, at the same time collecting cellular refuse and carbon dioxide. It is then returned to the right atrium of the heart, passes through the right atrioventricular valve (tricuspid valve) into the right ventricle and is channelled once more into pulmonary circulation through the pulmonary artery.

Blood

Blood is a liquid that circulates throughout the body by means of the cardiovascular system. It has four main ingredients:

- **plasma (50%)**
- **red blood cells (45%)**
- **white blood cells (5%)**
- **platelets**

Plasma is a yellowish solution made up of 93% water that carries red and white blood cells and numerous other substances that need to be distributed to all cells of the body: salts, proteins, fats, sugar as well as special proteins like antibodies and hormones, and a certain amount of dissolved gas.

Red blood cells have the function of transporting oxygen. Oxygen transport is made possible by a substance called haemoglobin that is contained in these specialised cells. Haemoglobin is a complex molecule characterized by a ferrous (iron) terminal that has a particular affinity to oxygen: it oxidises. When blood is rich in oxygen it has a vivid red colour; when the oxygen content is reduced it becomes a dark red. Carbon dioxide is transported by various mechanisms: about half is dissolved in plasma and the remainder combines with haemoglobin after the latter has delivered its oxygen. When it reaches the lungs, haemoglobin instantly releases carbon dioxide and binds to oxygen. A normal adult individual possesses about 5 litres of blood; each cubic centimetre of blood contains around 5 million red blood cells.

RESPIRATORY SYSTEM

Respiration is the process of O_2 metabolism. It is made possible by the cardiovascular and respiratory systems, in which the blood circulating in the body reloads with oxygen and at the same time frees itself of carbon dioxide. As for circulation, a good knowledge of the respiratory system will assist in the comprehension of the diaphragmatic breathing techniques and autogenic training that we will discuss in *Chapter 4*.

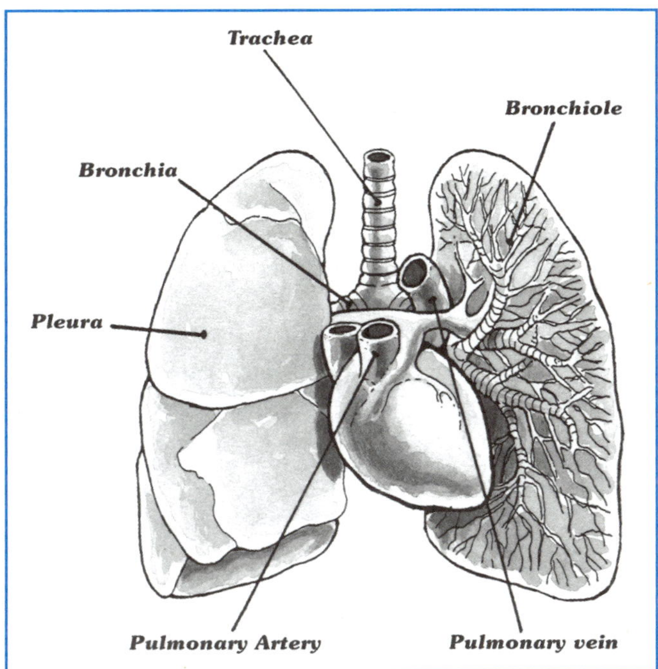

The cardiopulmonary system.

The organs assigned to gas exchange are the lungs. Air arrives in the lungs by means of the primary airways, which begin in the **nasal passage** and **oral cavity**, and continue into the **trachea**, a pipe that penetrates the thorax and divides into two bronchi, which enter a lung each. The two lungs are located in the thoracic cavity, which they fill almost completely; each has the rough shape of a 20 cm high cone. The right is divided by two deep incisures into three lobes, while the left is divided by a single incisure into two lobes.

The bronchi that penetrate the lungs divide into thinner pipes (**lobar bronchi**), which in their turn divide like the branches of a tree into ever thinner pipes (**bronchioles**), finally ending with the **terminal bronchioles**, which form bunches of microscopic vesicles called **alveoli**. Gas exchange between blood and air occurs at the level of alveoli. If you were to spread the alveoli out flat they would cover a surface of 60–80 square meters. The walls of the alveoli are incredibly thin, such that oxygen can simply diffuse across into the blood of the capillaries.

Gas exchange in the alveoli of the lung.

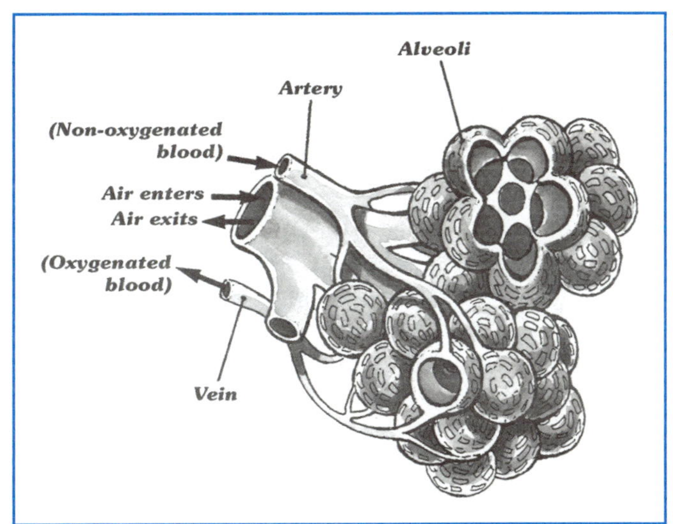

Respiration

Respiration is composed of two distinct actions: **inspiration**, which is the entry of air into the lungs, and **expiration**, the expulsion of air from the lungs.

The mechanics of respiration consist of the combined movement of the musculature of the thoracic cage and diaphragm, which with their rhythmic contraction and relaxation increase and decrease the volume of the thoracic cavity. This movement isn't just responsible for storing oxygen to support apnea, but also determines variations of buoyancy in water.

The inspiration involves:

a) contraction of the intercostal muscles with the consequent raising of the ribs;

b) contraction of the diaphragm (a dome shaped muscle that is the 'floor' of the thoracic cavity).

The lifting of the ribs and lowering of the diaphragm cause an increase in the volume of the thoracic cage. In accordance with Boyle's law, as the volume of the thoracic cavity gradually increases, its pressure diminishes with respect to the external ambient pressure and a certain quantity of air from outside is thus drawn inside.

During **expiration** the thoracic cage is lowered and the diaphragm is raised, reducing the volume of the thoracic cavity and thereby expelling air out of the lungs.

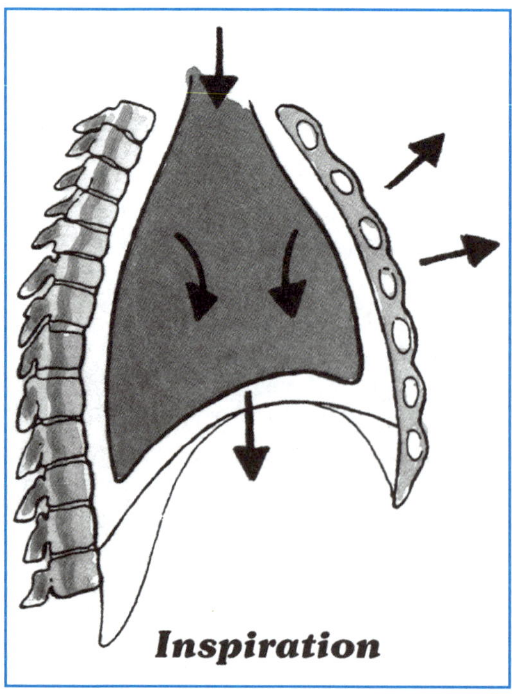

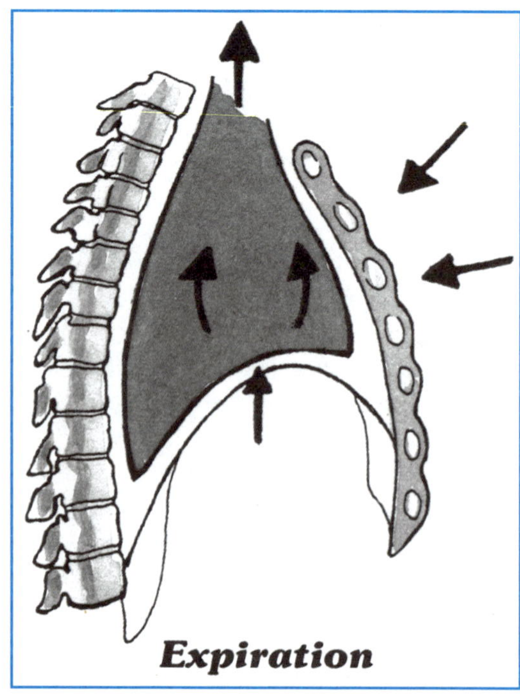

At rest, each act of respiration will introduce about 500 ml of air into the respiratory system (this volume can increase to over 2500 ml during a forced inspiration).

The modifications of thoracic volume that are essential for respiratory mechanics are caused by movement of the ribs, which are controlled by muscular contractions, especially of the diaphragm. Therefore in preparation for apnea it is necessary to adopt techniques of diaphragmatic respiration that will guarantee optimum ventilation and maintenance of the right balance of oxygen and carbon dioxide, whilst avoiding hyperventilation and the consequent excessive decrease of CO_2 in the blood.

A Spirometric exam will help to better understand the mechanisms of respiration, and gives measurements of the following:

1. **Frequency:** the number of acts of respiration (breaths) per minute (13–16/min). Frequency is generally inversely proportional to body size.

2. **Rhythm:** the succession of acts of respiration.

3. **Tidal volume:** the quantity of air that enters and exits the respiratory system (350–500 ml).

4. **Inspiratory reserve volume:** the maximum quantity of air that can be inhaled with a forced inspiration on top of a normal inspiration (2000-3000 ml).

5. **Expiratory reserve volume:** the maximum quantity of air that can still be exhaled with a forced exhalation after a normal exhalation (1000-1500 ml).

6. **Vital capacity:** the sum of tidal volume and inspiratory and expiratory reserve volumes (3500-5000 ml).

7. **Residual Volume:** the air that remains in the respiratory system after a forced exhalation (1500 ml).

8. **Total pulmonary capacity:** the sum of vital capacity and residual capacity (6000 ml).

9. **Bronchial-tracheal Dead space:** of the 500 ml of air in a normal inspiration only 2/3 arrives at the alveoli, while the

rest remains in the larger airways that constitutes the dead space. The **anatomical dead space** corresponds to the cavity of the respiratory system that does not contain alveoli, and the **physiological dead space** represents the actual volume of gas that is not put in contact with the blood. In physiological conditions the two variables should correspond.

Oxygen, nitrogen and water vapour

The constituents of atmospheric air that are important for respiration are **oxygen**, **nitrogen** and **water vapour**. The last serves to keep the mucous lining of the airways moist. Oxygen represents 21% of air and nitrogen the remaining 79%; carbon dioxide is found as a trace: 0.04%.

The composition of inhaled air is very different in terms of oxygen and carbon dioxide percentages to that of exhaled air. In exhaled air oxygen reduces from 21% to 16.3% and carbon dioxide increases from 0.04% to 4.5%. The difference in composition is due to gaseous exchange in the alveoli: some of the oxygen passes from alveolar air into the blood, and an equal quantity of carbon dioxide passes from the blood into the alveolar space.

There is a small increase in the concentration of nitrogen in exhaled air. This difference is not genuine, but linked simply to the varied proportions of exhaled oxygen and carbon dioxide. In fact atmospheric nitrogen does not participate in any chemical reactions in the organism; it is not metabolised,

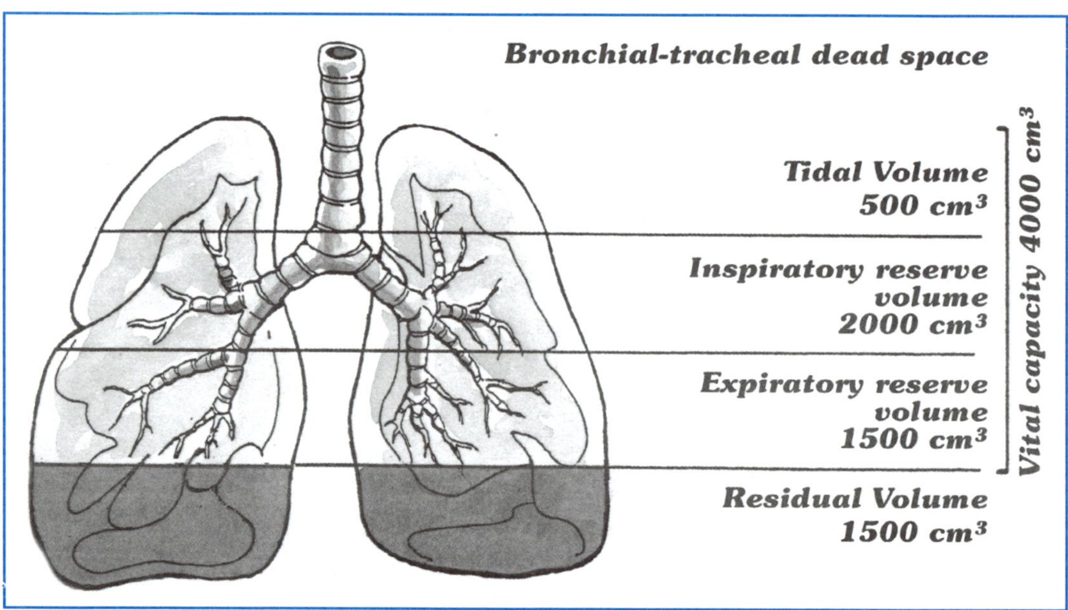

and in respiration it serves only as a diluent of oxygen. Nevertheless this gas is dissolved into the blood and absorbed by all the tissues (especially fat tissue) without ever reacting with any component.

Diffusion

As we have seen, atmospheric pressure at sea level is 760 mmHg. Air pressure is nothing but the sum of the partial pressures of each constituent gas, and the partial pressure of each gas is strictly proportional to the concentration of gas in the mixture (Dalton's Law). Furthermore a gas will tend to pass from a point of high pressure to a point of lower pressure in order to restore an equilibrium.

The blood that circulates in capillaries around the walls of the alveoli is bought into contact with air contained in the alveoli. This blood has come from the pulmonary artery and is therefore poor in oxygen. Its partial pressure of oxygen is 40 mmHg while the partial pressure of carbon dioxide is 46 mmHg. In the alveolar air the partial pressure of oxygen is 100 mmHg while that of carbon dioxide is effectively nil.

In order to balance these pressure differences a certain quantity of oxygen will diffuse from the alveoli into the blood, while a certain quantity of carbon dioxide diffuses from the blood into the alveolar air.

Meanwhile the reverse procedure occurs in body tissues: freshly oxygenated blood from the heart comes into contact with the cells and liquids of the tissues that are rich in carbon dioxide and poor in oxygen, which has been rapidly consumed. Here also there is gaseous diffusion in two directions, but in this case oxygen passes from the blood to the cells, while carbon dioxide passes from the cells into the blood. It is here that blood loses its arterial characteristics, becoming venous blood that returns towards the lungs to be replenished with oxygen.

Stimulation of respiration

The fact that we can deliberately modify the rhythm and intensity of our breathing demonstrates that it is in part under the control of our will. The impulses that ensure autonomous respiration come from a part of the brain called the **respiratory centre**, which continually dispatches these impulses through nerves to the respiratory muscle (intercostal muscles and diaphragm).

The respiratory centre receives very precise information about the pressure of CO_2 from chemical receptors that analyse blood composition. If the carbon dioxide concentration of blood that passes through the respiratory centre is analysed and found to be even slightly increased then the centre begins action to correct the excess of gas and restore the O_2–CO_2 equilibrium by stimulating the respiratory system and modifying the intensity and profundity of respiratory movement.

For this reason it is not possible to arrest respiration for longer than a certain period of time. The diaphragmatic contractions are a clear manifestation of the organism, which, upon reaching high values of CO_2, 'asks' the apneist to resume respiration by contracting the diaphragm: effectively a 'punch in the stomach.' This also explains why the necessity to breathe diminishes after voluntarily deep inspirations and expirations, which lower the concentration of carbon dioxide in the blood.

Muscle

Why does one athlete achieve great results in constant weight whilst another only in variable? After all, they have both trained incessantly for years before the record, following an ascetic regime of life based on exercise, rest, an inflexible diet and little else. The answer is complex and depends on a myriad of small details, such as mental condition or even the shape of the foot pockets or the blades of the fins. However in a constant weight record, which depends predominantly on personal resources of strength and endurance, one of the principle factors that determines victory is physiology: the muscular fibre of the leg, and especially the thighs, must generate a certain power in the space of a couple of minutes or maybe a little more, whilst maintaining a low consumption of oxygen with respect to that of the variable weight diver.

Research has allowed us to analyse how muscles adapt to exercise – or the lack of it – and to what extent muscles can be modified to adapt to the different necessities of the various disciplines, such as the prolonged force of a dynamic apnea or constant weight dive, or the need of relaxation in a static apnea. This information helps us to understand why world record breakers triumph, but also allows us to better comprehend the capacity of the average person.

Muscular structure

Skeletal musculature is the most abundant tissue in the human body and also one of the most adaptable. Intensive weight training can double or triple muscular mass, while the total cessation of use after a trauma can reduce this mass by 20 percent in two weeks.

A muscle is a bundle of cells, or **fibres** held together by connective tissue. A single fibre is formed from an outer membrane, many nuclei spaced along the fibre just beneath the membrane, and thousands of internal filaments – the **myofibrils** that are found in the cytoplasm. The largest human muscle fibres reach a length of 30 centimetres and a diameter of 0.05-0.15 millimetres, and contain thousands of nuclei.

Myofibrils have the same length as the fibre and form the part of the cell that is able to contract in response to a nerve impulse. The motor nerve cells, or motor neurons, extend from the spinal marrow to a group of muscle fibres that form a motor unit. In leg muscle a single motor neuron can innervate more than a thousand muscle fibres. Where greater precision is necessary, such as in the control of a finger or eyeball, a motor neuron will control less fibres, maybe even just one. The contraction of myofibril is effected by its miniscule components, the **sarcomeres**, which are connected at their extremities to form the myofibrils. Each sarcomere is composed of two protein filaments, **actin** and **myosin**, which interact to cause the contraction. Muscular contraction involves a kind of telescopic shortening of the sarcomere: the actin filaments at the ends of the central myosin filament slide towards its centre.

A component of the molecule of myosin, the so-called **heavy chain**, determines the function of the muscular fibre. In the adult this chain exists in three varieties, or isoforms, described as I, IIa and IIb: the fibres that contain them are given the same name. Type I fibres are also called **slow twitch**, while IIa and IIb are called **quick twitch**: the maximum velocity of contraction of a single type I fibre is about a tenth of the velocity of a type IIb, and the velocity of type IIa is between the two.

Other than the three different types of fibre, there are hybrids containing two isoforms of myosin in variable proportions. The functional characteristics of hybrid fibres are similar to that of the dominant types.

Muscle material

The velocity of contraction of muscular fibre depends on the way in which the fibre utilises adrenaline triphosphate (ATP) to extract energy in the heavy chain of myosin. The slow twitch fibres are based on a relatively efficient aerobic mechanism, while the quick twitch depend mostly on anaerobiosis.

Thus slow twitch fibres are important for activities that require endurance such as cross country running, cycling and swimming, while quick twitch fibres are prevalent where strength is required, such as in weightlifting, sprints or at the start of a deep freedive and the take off from the bottom, where pow-

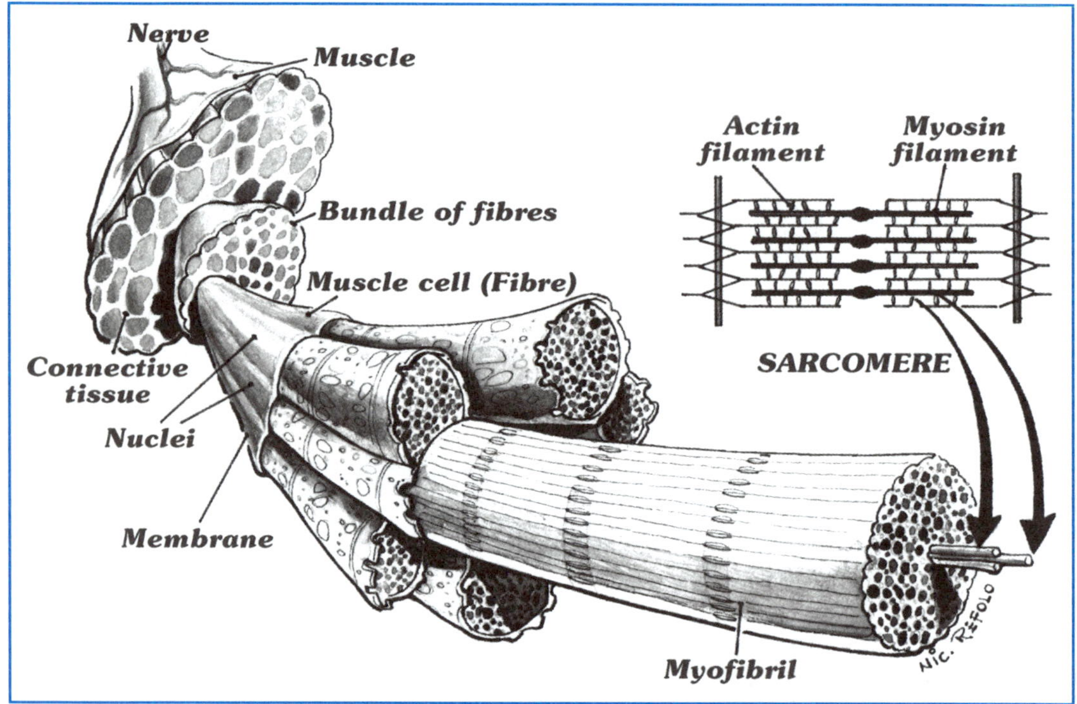

erful muscle is required to overcome the unfavourable hydrostatic forces.

The average adult has about the same amount of quick twitch as slow twitch fibres, but like other species human beings have a great variation. There are people who have quadriceps made up of 19 percent slow twitch fibre, and others with 95 percent. The latter could become a good marathon runner, but would not have success as a sprinter and even less as an apneist; the reverse applies for someone with only 19 percent slow twitch fibre.

'Putting on muscle'

It is important to note that muscular fibre cannot multiply: during aging we will lose muscle fibre, but it is impossible to regenerate. Thus a muscle can grow only by increasing the width of its fibres.

This widening is caused by the creation of further myofibrils. The mechanical action that training exerts on tendons and other connective structures of the muscle triggers the synthesis of protein messengers, which activate genes that induce muscle fibre to produce more contractile protein. These proteins, principally actin and myosin, are necessary for the large quantities of additional myofibril produced by the fibre.

To stimulate the production of new protein while maintaining an adequate relationship between cellular volume and number of nuclei, it is necessary also to synthesize the latter. Muscle fibre has multiple nuclei, but these cannot divide inside the fibre; new nuclei must be donated by so-called satellite cells (staminal cells). Spaced between the many nuclei on the surface of a skeletal muscle cell, these satellite cells are separate from the muscle cells, and have only one nucleus, which can reproduce by division. After fusion with the muscle fibre they serve as a source of nuclei to supply the growing fibre.

Satellite cells proliferate in response to training-induced stimulus. A popular theory supports that intense exercise inflicts micro-tears in muscle fibre. The damaged areas then attract satellite cells, which are incorporated into the muscle tissue and start to produce protein to fill the gaps. As these cells gradually multiply some will remain satellites while others enter to join with the fibre. Their nuclei become indistinguishable from those of the muscle cell, and with these additional nuclei the fibre is equipped to secrete more protein and create more myofibril.

In order to produce a protein a muscle cell (like all other cells of the body) must have a 'blueprint' that specifies the order in which the amino acids are to be assembled, thus indicating which protein will be created. This blueprint is contained in the different genes of the cellular nucleus, and the process by which its information exits the nucleus and enters the cytoplasm where the protein is synthesized starts with **transcription**. Transcription occurs in the nucleus when information in the gene (codified in DNA) is copied into messenger RNA (mRNA).

The mRNA then transports the information from the nucleus to the ribosome, which assembles the amino acids into the protein specified by the mRNA, for example actin or one of the isoforms of myosin. This process is called **translation**.

Muscle transformation

Conversion of muscular fibre is possible. In fact if muscles are repeatedly subjected to selected training stimuli, such as resistance training with heavy weights, then the number of type IIb quick twitch fibres diminishes as they are transformed into type IIa quick twitch. The nuclei stop expressing IIb genes and start to express those of IIa.

If the intense exercise continues (heavier weight, slower execution, lower number of repetitions) for a month or more, then the type IIb fibres will completely transform into type IIa. At the same time the fibres will increase their production of protein, becoming thicker.

Quick or slow twitch?

The conversion between the two types of quick twitch, IIa and IIb, is a natural consequence of training or of its cessation. But what can we say about the conversion between slow and quick twitch fibres, types I and II? Here the results are less clear. Many experiments conducted in the last 20 years have failed to prove that this conversion is possible. However at the start of the nineties evidence was obtained that a rigorous training regime can convert slow twitch fibre into type IIa quick twitch.

If a certain type of exercise can convert type I into IIa, it would be fair to ask if other types of exercise can effect the reverse. It would seem possible, even if so far no studies conducted on humans have demonstrated it with certainty. We do know that top endurance athletes generally have higher proportions of slow twitch fibre (up to 95 percent) in their main muscle groups, such as in the legs.

However it is still unclear whether these athletes are born with a higher percentage of type I and then find their way into sports in which they can take advantage of their inherent potential, or if they have gradually raised their percentage of this type of fibre through prolonged training. We do know that if type IIa fibre can be converted into type I, then the time required is decidedly longer than what is necessary to transform type IIb into IIa.

Maybe the great marathon runners truly were 'born different.' Therefore the same would apply for the quickest sprinters. With respect to freediving, sprinters will obviously have the advantage of a reduced percentage of type I fibre. However an aspiring freediver with too much type I fibre should not give up: it has been demonstrated that hypertrophy produced by resistance training will increase type II fibre twice as fast as type I. In this way weight training can enlarge the cross section of muscle formed of quick twitch without altering the ratio between slow and quick twitch fibres in the muscle.

The muscles of the apneist

We will now examine which fibres concern the apneist, so that we may know how to train them, and also what type of strength (endurance, speed, explosive etc) must be developed.

So far there has been no research to clarify whether a constant weight freediver or a spear fisherman should have a musculature prevalent in type I or II fibres. The hypotheses formulated on the basis of tests on top athletes, conducted by medical specialists in the field, are contradictory. For now we are limited to observe that during a deep constant weight freedive the athlete employs his muscles in a quick and powerful action (the ideal descent velocity is greater than 1 m/sec) to overcome the resistance of buoyancy.

This resistance gradually decreases until it disappears completely at the point of neutral buoyancy; the apneist then proceeds in negative buoyancy, freefalling. We can thus hypothesize that if at the beginning there is the necessity of rapid and powerful finning supported by quick twitch (IIa and IIb) fibres, then the successive phase of the freefall will be characterised by a phase of muscular relaxation, during which the energy source (ATP) is regenerated, in a deficit of oxygen, to supply new power and speed after the turn and during the ascent towards the surface. Setting out from the bottom, the apneist must overcome negative buoyancy; however during the ascent the diminution of hydrostatic pressure is favourable and buoyancy increases towards the surface, reducing the burden on the legs.

In conclusion, a balanced development of muscle mass, characterised by an equal ratio of type IIa and IIb fibres, should be advantageous to the performance of the apneist.

Production of muscular energy

The apneist must be acquainted with the energy giving mechanisms that support muscular activity for two reasons: **to plan their training** and **to economise by distributing their effort in the water.**

The capacity of muscles to continually contract and relax creates movement: the more this activity is protracted over time, the greater the endurance of our physique.

The contraction of a muscle is the consequence of two factors: a neural stimulus and a chemical reaction that requires energy to function. It is important to understand the nature of the reaction that permits muscular contraction and above all how the necessary energy can be acquired to sustain muscular activity for a long period. The main energy source that the muscle can use to contract is the chemical energy liberated by the fission of adenosine triphosphate (ATP).

ATP has the special property that after its division it can be reconstructed through other chemical reactions. This is an important property, since the quantity of ATP present in the muscle cell is very small and sufficient only for a limited number of contractions. After the first 8-10 seconds of an intense activity it must be reproduced by other pathways. Exhausted ATP can be restored by our organism in two ways: the aerobic or anaerobic systems.

The aerobic system

In the aerobic system (*see figure on page 63*) oxygen delivered by the blood is the comburent, while food substances that have been appropriately transformed will have the role of fuel.

This system can be compared to a combustion engine. In the analogy there is a machine (muscle = motor) in which the fuel (glycogen = petrol) and the comburent (oxygen in both cases) are mixed (process of oxidation) to produce chemical energy, which is transformed (combustion) into mechanical energy, or movement. In our case the movement is a contraction of the muscle fibre that moves muscle, which in its turn moves the limb.

The anaerobic system

In the anaerobic system (*see figure on page 63*), the reserve energy sources of the muscle are transformed without the use of oxygen. The employment of this system creates problems in the reconstruction of the energy, in so much as it requires a certain amount of time for oxygen to oxidise food sources and transport them to the cell to produce new energy. The aerobic mechanism is used when the muscular activity requires a limited intensity of exertion. The organism will have enough time to transform food sources with oxygen, and there is enough chemical energy produced to reconstruct ATP. In this condition muscular work can be sustained for a long time, even for several hours. Thus for this system of energy supply the capacity of the organism's respiratory and circulatory systems to obtain oxygen from the air and transport it through the blood to the involved muscles is very important.

This becomes impossible during an freedive. The only air which the apneist has access to is that which is contained in the lungs, and furthermore in a deep dive the phenomena of *blood shift* (see *Chapter 3*) induces a selective vasoconstriction so that less blood, and therefore less oxygen, flows through the peripheral tissues.

Our organism generally uses the aerobic system in activities of greater duration, such as long distance running, swimming or cross-country skiing, where the action must be protracted for hours.

A hypothesis credited to observation and experimentation on top apneists is that the aerobic system intervenes only at a particular moment during a freedive descent, just after passing the point of neutral buoyancy at about 12 meters. At this depth *blood shift* is not yet significant, but exertion needn't be as intense as at the surface, where the hydrostatic force

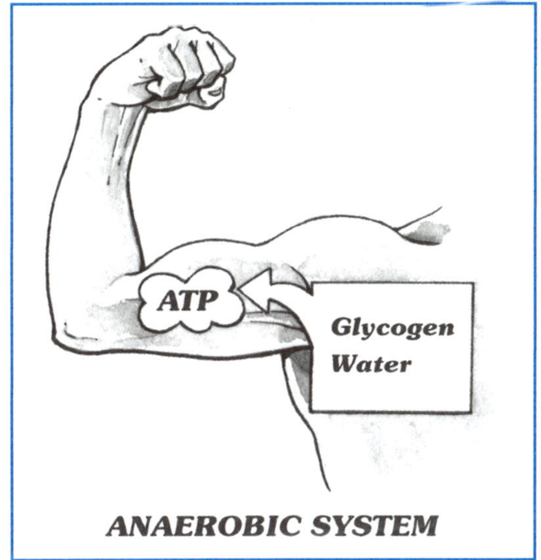

ANAEROBIC SYSTEM

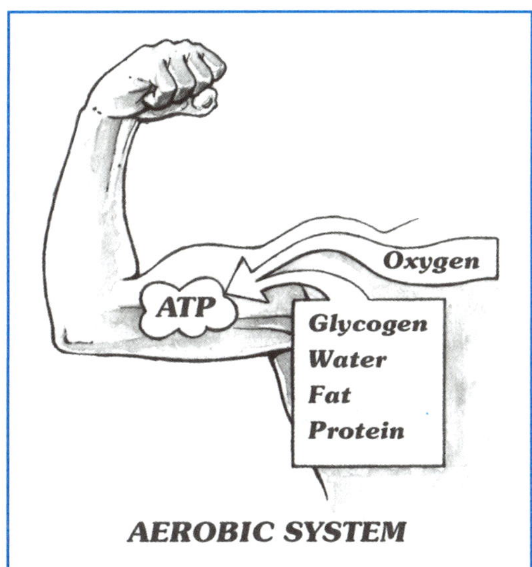

AEROBIC SYSTEM

must be overcome. Muscular work becomes easier and more fluid, there is no need to develop power, oxygen levels are still good and blood flow to the periphery is still important.

The anaerobic mechanism intervenes when the organism must produce maximum force for a short duration. In this case an elevated power is employed, requiring a high energy consumption in a short time period. Anaerobiosis is certainly the most important energy-giving mechanism for the apneist. During performance of this kind muscles will mainly use stored energy sources, predominantly sugar.

This type of activity is where the sprinters, jumpers, throwers and weightlifters reign. Such forms of energy use develop different chemical reactions in the muscles that determine very different bodily sensations/signals. It is important to be able to recognize these sensations/signals in order to put in place intelligent behaviour that can support and facilitate what is happening in the organism. For example, when our body must reconstruct energy reserves it will not only use oxygen but also an elevated quantity of water.

For this reason prolonged activity causes thirst, despite how strange it may seem that we lose liquid whilst being immersed in water! Sweating cannot be blamed for this loss – it is due to other factors dependant on the production of hormones that stimulate diuresis. Therefore the body must be replenished with liquid both for rehydration and for the reconstruction of material energy that is necessary after prolonged activity.

2.3 UNDERWATER VISION

If you have ever put your head underwater with eyes wide open, you will know that seeing under the water is unlike seeing above it. Without a mask we do not have distinct vision; objects are confused and clouded. Eyes are designed to see through air, a gas with very different physical qualities to water. The index of refraction in liquid is different from that of a gas mixture, for which reason light rays undergo modifications in water.

The eye

The eye is the organ dedicated to collecting impressions of light. It is therefore responsible for the sense of sight, one of the channels through which we experience the world. It is comprised of a principal structure – the eyeball – and other different accessories.

The **eyeball** is a sphere situated in the orbital cavity made of three concentric membranes called the sclera, choroid and retina, as well as fluids and semi-fluidic substances.

The **sclerotic membrane** or **sclera** is a thick, resistant, white layer that becomes thinner and transparent at the front of the eyeball, to allow the passage of light, where it takes the name **cornea**.

The **choroid** is very rich in blood vessels; it changes aspect and colour anteriorally in correspondence with the cornea to form a diaphragm of muscle constituting the **iris**. At its centre the iris is breached by a circular hole, the **pupil**. The iris

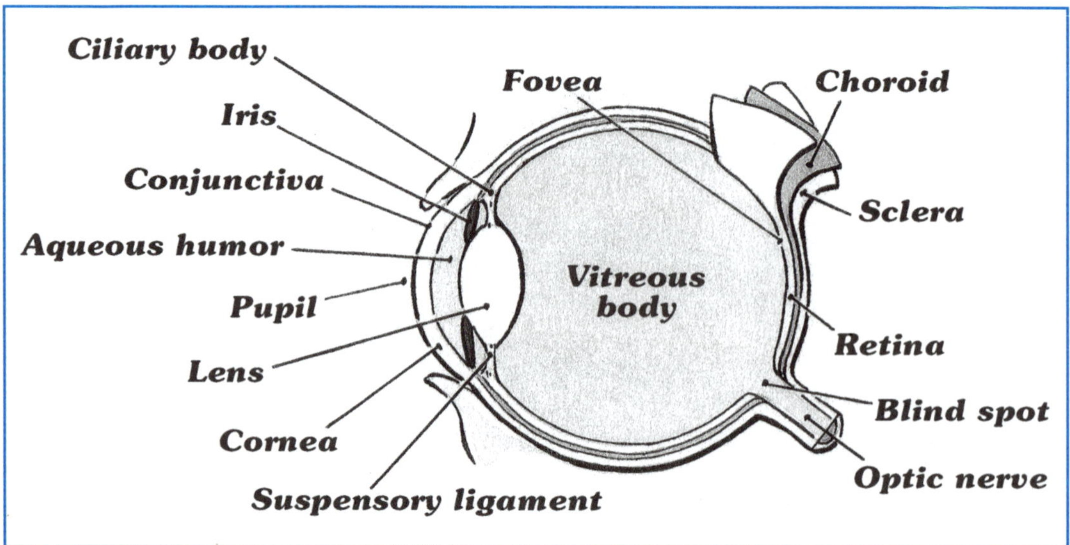

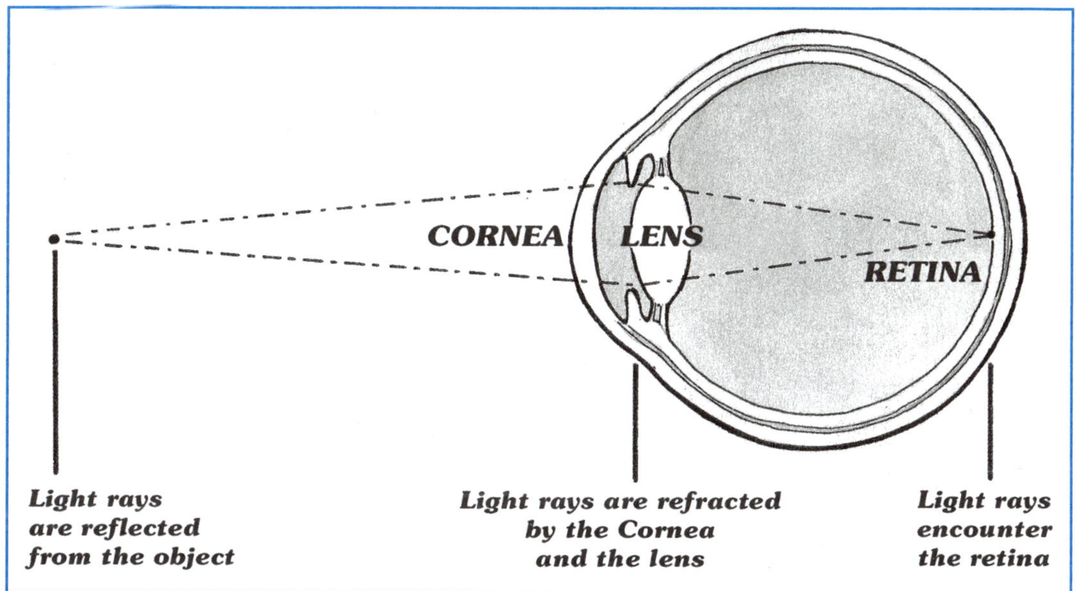

is the coloured part of the eye, and this colour is given by the presence of pigmented cells, whose density determine gradations of colour that differ from person to person.

The hole of the pupil appears black because it is an aperture through which light enters (similar to the aperture of a photographic camera). If we could look at an eye cut transversely we would discover a large space between the cornea and iris, called the **anterior chamber**, full of a clear, colourless and mainly aqueous liquid; light passes through this liquid before reaching the pupil. The duty of the iris around the pupil is to regulate the size of the pupil's hole according to ambient light intensity.

Continuing inwards, following the iris is the **lens** itself, convex on both sides, which refracts light rays entering the eye. The lens is very transparent and elastic, and can therefore continually change its own shape. It is contained in an epithelial capsule, attached to the rest of the eye by miniscule muscle fibres. When these muscles are inactive the tension is reduced, and the lens becomes more convex. By means of minor variations of the tension on the lens its curvature can be varied, producing a near or distant focus of the eye. This regulation is called the **power of accommodation**.

After the lens, light will cross through the **posterior chamber**, full of a semi-fluidic substance called **vitreous humor**. The back of the eye, behind the vitreous humor, is lined with the **retina**, the sensitive film of the 'camera.'

The cells of the retina are organised into nine layers, of which the most interesting and important is the layer containing the **rods** and **cones**; sensitive cells responsible for the phenomenon of vision. Together these form a very thin layer that collect the light.

If the refractive materials of the eye in front of the retina are intact then the image is formed perfectly in focus on the retina. The optic nerve that is connected to the retina will then transfer the subsequent nerve impulses to the visual cortex. This is good reason to keep your eyes closed when possible in apnea, in order to reduce nerve stimulation to a minimum and thereby save oxygen.

Vision through air

The **cones** of the retina are sensitive to optical stimuli and are dedicated exclusively to the perception of colour. In the light of day, light rays cross the cornea, aqueous humor, pupil, lens and vitreous humor to arrive at the retina. The lens focuses the light rays on the centre of the retina (fovea), where the cones are particularly abundant. A sharp image of the observed object is formed at this point, giving distinct vision. The cones situated outside of the fovea register vision indistinctly – this is why when we concentrate our gaze on a given object other objects around it will appear with less detail.

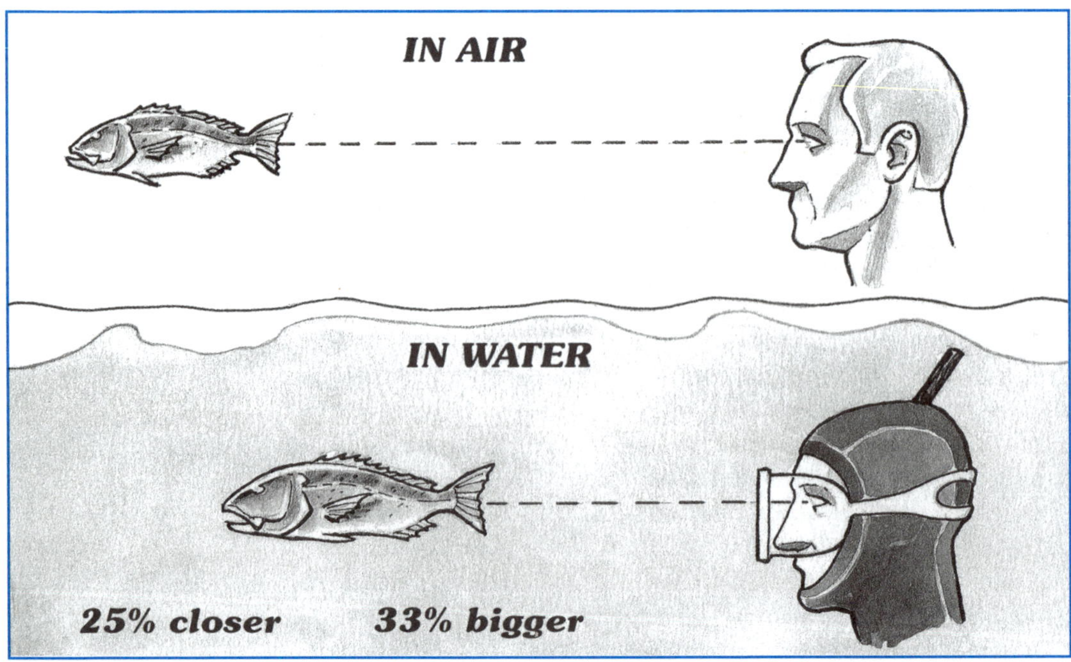

During evening and night light levels are too reduced to be able to stimulate the cones, but are sufficient to stimulate the rods, which, unlike the cones, are not sensitive to the light frequencies that confer colour recognition.

The **rods** contain a red substance called **rhodopsin**, which is decomposed and drained of its colour in the presence of living light, but reconstructed in the darkness. This explains why when we pass from a lit room to a darkened room we feel like we have become blind. Once the rhodopsin is reconstructed the rods recover their function, and it is then possible to see objects even in conditions of scarce light.

Vision through water

Water, as we have discussed, has a different index of refraction to that of air, which means light rays are refracted in a different way. In consequence, the focal point falls behind the retina and the image read on the retina by the nervous system is out of focus. Vision of objects is therefore indistinct. The mask assumes a corrective function. By wearing a mask we are in effect putting in front of our eyes a bubble of air – the element through which our eyes are accustomed to seeing. This permits a distinct vision of objects, even if the system has a small inconvenience. Light rays reaching the eyes of the diver pass first through the water, then through the glass of the mask (which has a different index of refraction to both water and air), and finally through the air contained in the mask. The result is that the final image that is read on the retina is altered from reality: it is 33% larger and 25% closer.

Absorption of colours

Other than refracting light, water also absorbs it. This phenomenon alters the colours of the spectrum, as different wavelengths are absorbed in relation to depth: in the first ten meters red and orange disappear, between ten and twenty meters yellow and green fade, and past twenty meters only blue light remains.

Thus when diving deeper than twenty meters the ambient light is predominantly blue, and an underwater torch is essential to be able to see all the true colours. A torch will light up the seafloor like a charm, displaying it in true and extraordinary polychrome: anyone who, as a kid, took a brown starfish to the surface from even just a meter's depth will remember lifting a brilliant red creature from the water, but would not have known that they had just carried out a genuine science experiment.

2.4 HEAT

It is a common experience when entering the water – whether swimming pool, lake or sea – to have a sensation of cold. The reason is that body heat is dispersed twenty five times faster in water than in air.

In spite of this it only takes a few minutes for the organism to adapt. A restriction of the peripheral blood vessels reduces the flow of blood and slows the dispersion of body heat; this condition favours the maintenance of a constant body temperature of about 36°, which is necessary for vital functions.

However if the body remains in the water long enough then the dispersion of heat will be such that the organism will react by contracting muscle (shivering) in an attempt to produce heat: however this mechanism requires energy that in a brief amount of time will be exhausted. So if the body disperses heat for a long period of time then body temperature will also start to fall and shivers will become more intense and prolonged; in this condition hands and feet become numb, increasing exposure to other accidents.

If body temperature drops below 35° hypothermia will occur, at 32° reasoning capacity fails, and below 32° there is an immediate threat to life.

With cold water the choice of whether to wear gloves, socks and a hood of adequate thickness should be made carefully, considering also the variation in buoyancy that this equipment will entail. If cold should catch up with you, and even if you are expecting it to, don't hesitate to exit from the water and warm up. The responsibility of a good apneist is shown in the recognition of when to concede a dive if ambient conditions are unfavourable. Remember that apnea is for enjoyment and pleasure, not for sufferance!

ADAPTING THE BODY TO APNEA

CHAPTER

3

Although the human body has evolved to live on land, in the tailor-made environment of technological civilization, man, as is his nature, has dared to challenge the 'sixth continent', and he has done so from a position of inferiority with respect to many other mammals. Nevertheless, in spite of everything he has achieved results that are, to say the least, extraordinary. Over the course of millennia the road has been slow but progressive: first the collection of food in shallow water, then diving for sponges and pearls and the retrieval of sunken treasure, all in ever deepening depths. However in recent decades the progression of apnea has recorded a major growth.

Man has attacked the wall of supposedly insurmountable medical barriers; the multitudinous questions of pressure, heat loss and suchlike. The human body is constituted in the main part by water, and the foetus lives in amniotic liquid. The newborn, perhaps delivered underwater like a miniature cetacean, can be immersed in a warm pool and stay there with its eyes open, without swallowing water or becoming distressed, and swimming breaststroke as if it had received lessons inside the womb: in short the baby is delightedly comfortable, for the precise reason that it is habituated to living in the liquid element. However with the passing of months, if this natural predisposition is not cultivated adequately and constantly, it will die out and be lost in clumsy attempts of swimming, flailing arms, crying and the swallowing of water, and everything will have to be learnt from scratch.

Apnea is the temporary and voluntary suspension of breathing. In man it is a transitory condition. We can survive weeks without eating and a few days without drinking, but only several minutes without breathing. 'Aquaticity' is a fundamental attribute for the apneist. It allows us to behave, in a world completely diverse to the terrestrial, as if it was a natural *habitat*, and to use the few available minutes to their full extent.

'Comfort' in the water must be learnt slowly and gradually: in the pool, on the surface, then in immersion. To be able to develop a good foundation the apneist must closely study his or her behaviour, listening to and feeling their contact with the liquid element without the aid of any equipment, which is used only at the conclusion of this base preparation. It is now recognised by all apnea schools that anyone who succeeds through willpower to control their survival instincts, or to contain negative thoughts and impulses (which are the cause of almost all accidents), has reached a high level of aquaticity.

In preparing for apnea we must remember that all the senses, vigilant and developed in the terrestrial environment, will change underwater. If these changes are not well understood they can cause serious problems. For this reason in Chapter 2 we have dealt with the perceptive modifications to which our body is subjected in immersion; we have studied how ways of thinking, seeing and discerning colour are all changed by water. In this chapter we will consider the modifications produced by immersion under apnea. We will start with some important observations of man's aquaticity, in order to understand how the *dive reflex* is shared with many other mammals, and through the study of *blood shift* we will analyse the cardiorespiratory modifications and their correlation with the nervous system.

3.1 AQUATIC NATURE OF MAN

The similarity between man and the sea is incredible, whether from the point of view of chemistry or physical function. Our body is constituted principally of water: in the adult it contributes 60% of total mass, in a baby 80%, and an incredible 97% of a human embryo. As Jacques Mayol said, "there is a veritable ocean in all of us".

The ocean inside us

From a chemical point of view, the sea is similar enough to the internal liquids of its inhabiting creatures that it almost constitutes their external 'blood' and 'lymph'.

Human blood also has a salt composition comparable to that of the sea in preceding eras, when animal life began to manifest itself on our planet. Even today however, blood has a concentration of sodium chloride (normal cooking salt) stronger than that of the sea.

But the analogy doesn't finish there. Blood feeds all the tissues of the body though the transport of oxygen and protein, indispensable for cellular respiration and nutrition. In a certain sense the sea acts in the same way by carrying with itself the plankton that comprise the base of the food chain of the different marine species.

Like blood, the sea also has a respiratory function: the majority of marine animals are able to respire thanks to oxygen dissolved in seawater. As doctor Brooks wrote: "life that was born in the sea could not make its way on land unless at the same time the forces of evolution finally succeeded in creating an organism capable of carrying with it a scrap of the ocean". As it emerges from the sea life is individualised, but maintains with it "a tiny piece of the sea. In the most ancient of our genetic memories man still possesses a recollection of his aquatic past".

If this is true for the adult human, then what can we say about the neonate who has just finished spending nine months in a liquid habitat? The foetus grows in the womb, fed and completely enveloped in amniotic fluid – in this phase the neonate is as good as living in water. Its lungs are 'short circuited:' they exist but do not function and will only initiate respiration after birth, as a reflex to the umbilical chord being cut. The oxygen required by the millions of tiny cells that constitute the foetus is supplied by blood circulation, nourished by the placenta through the umbilical chord. The placenta is a kind of 'second mother', an intermediary between baby and mother. In the final weeks of gestation the foetus begins to practice the respiration reflex, inhaling amniotic fluid. Another impressive amphibious characteristic of the human foetus is inherent in the heart. During the nine months of intrauterine life the cardiac muscle evolves by transforming from a heart with two cavities, like that of a fish, to three cavities, as of a reptile, and finally to the four cavities that defines a mammalian heart.

It is easy to imagine the intimate relationship and the strong bonds between the neonate and the liquid element – the 'primordial broth' from which we exited. This is the reason why newborn babies immersed in water don't find it completely unpleasant. It is as though there is a continuity between the water of the mother and the water in which the baby is immersed: the newborn finds itself in its element, as if it had never left.

There is one more aquatic quality of man connected to the early days of life: in its first three months the neonate's haemoglobin has a greater affinity with oxygen than an adult's, but after three months this feature tends to gradually diminish. This means that even from the physiological point of view the baby is predisposed to apnea for its first hundred days of life.

Water births

Underwater birth has been practiced with remarkable success for years in many countries. It has come to be considered a modern technique, although in many 'primitive' cultures the act of submerging the woman in water in the difficult moments of labour and birth is a practice derived from the most ancient tradition. Examples are the pygmy populations that live in the forest bordering the Ituri River in Congo, any tribe that occupies the Peruvian part of the Amazon forest, and the aborigines of the western coast of Australia. Some cases of birth in water were documented also in the ancient Maori population of New Zealand and the Indians of the Panama.

This technique avoids the trauma of an abrupt passage from the familiar liquid universe of the mother's belly to the dry and completely unknown universe of terrestrial life.

A very complex investigation was carried out, conducted with a psychoanalytical method on a sample population of children from 4 to 10 years of age, all born underwater. It emerged that the percentage of individuals who were markedly extroverted, communicative, optimists was about 70% higher than the percentage amongst contemporaries born with a normal technique of childbirth. According to psychologists and doctors this is attributable to the fact that the first force received by the newborn is not gravitational – violent and towards the ground – but that of water: sweet, homogenous and upward.

Return to the origins

The late professor Luigi Odone, lecturer of clinical psychology at the University of Genoa, was occupied for years with the psychodynamic aspects and the psychological profile of ability of the apneist. He maintained that in apnea underwater man returns to his origins, since during prenatal life he has expected an aquatic existence that subsequently he never completely forgets. Man's unconscious knows a thing or two about his origins and his relationship with nature, the elements and the universe.

We are born marine animals, whether in the ontogenitic sense (birth of an individual) or phylogenetic sense (birth of a species). According to professor Odone, the process of psychological development in man is nothing but a recapitulation on the preceding process of developmental biology. More than a level of memory, it brings a level of intuition: where the memory fails to reach consciously we succeed with the unconscious.

In the moment we dive beneath the surface, we apply that which is defined as a 'deep regression', a capacity to return the psyche to a state of calm. In water we joyously reclaim that dimension (which is a return to Eden, in its original purpose) of relief from tension, of comfortable security, of the peace that we knew in the womb. Birth involves a dynamic biology, a force towards life and the struggle to survive (to cry, to move, to chew the mother's nipples...). From the moment in which the neonate comes into the world there is an end to the homeostasis, or as Freud defines it, the equilibrium without a driving force that has defined the first nine months of life. Only in an aquatic environment do our minds succeed in reaching a harmonisation with the archetypal sensations of peace and happiness.

The two worlds, one above and one below water, are therefore considered 'parallels' without connection. This explains why we can only achieve impressive performance in apnea in the liquid element.

Professor Odone claimed that it would be very difficult to explain this phenomenon in scientific terms; we must simply accept it, grounding it on intuitive understanding and senses.

3.2 THE DIVE REFLEX

To appreciate the true meaning of this reflex, which is shared by all mammals, humans included, it is necessary to observe in detail the behaviour of a neonate who is immerged in its very first month of life: the ease with which the baby remains in the water will surprise us. One could say that this is the neonate's natural environment.

We cannot forget that for the nine months between conception and birth the natural environment is liquid – at any rate more similar to a pool than a cradle. There is good reason why many obstetricians have for years supported childbirth in water as a means of reducing the impact of birth into a strange reality. This type of passage into 'terrestrial life' will be less traumatic. It is also the very first experience in water, which, if continued constantly through the first months of life, will leave indelible traces in the psyche of the individual.

In the deepest of our genetic memories man still possesses the recollection of his aquatic past. Hence from birth we carry with us a small hereditary kit of reflexes enduring from the evolution of species. These reflexes are involuntary actions that have the purpose of supplying the first adaptation to the environment. For example a neonate immersed in water shows an apnea reflex, and swims (swim reflex), adopting efficient movements.

The **dive reflex** is in all of us; it only remains for the apneist to reawaken this reflex in themselves. Physiologically, the reflex is characterized by **bradycardia** (reduction of cardiac frequency), **selective peripheral vasoconstriction** of organs that are resistant to hypoxic conditions, and a **reduction of oxygen metabolism**.

When we submerge, even if only in shallow water, we will experience the physiological modifications that impart a better adaptation to the liquid environment. For example it is the dive reflex that explains why experimental tests conducted on dry apneas or apneas in hyperbaric chambers have always given different results relative to those conducted in water.

The physiological modifications

Other than the already cited reduction of heart rate, there is also a significant reduction in blood pressure and a general muscular decontraction that involves all muscles of the locomotor system. A convincing example is the elongation of the vertebral column, a result of the position and loss of weight force given by flotation.

Another interesting parameter observed in record breakers is the relative production of CO_2. The percentage of CO_2 measured in exhaled air varies with the different types of apnea performed. After a static apnea on dry land CO_2 will have undergone a predictable increase. The same apnea performed in immersion will afford astonishing measurements of gas in the exhalation, decidedly contrary to what would be expected in theory. The percentage of CO_2 is maintained at a constant level after a static apnea in a pool, and even actually diminishes after a deep dive of the same duration. This is simply incredible! Many tests have been made in this field of research, but there is still much to be discovered.

It is primarily the cardiovascular system that renders incredible dives possible. Many human dive responses have also been observed in marine mammals: blood that irrigates the periphery of the body is recalled to the core of the torso, and the heart rate is reduced, insuring greater economy of oxygen use. The seal for example, which can dive to about 300 meters, slows its pulse from 120 beats per minute down to 20.

Studies of apneists

Several studies of Umberto Pelizzari have revealed that in a stationary apnea in water his cardiac frequency gradually slows to 30 beats per minute. The phenomenon is even more evident during apnea at depth. Pelizzari himself recounts, "I often linger a while on the bottom, after a descent to over one hundred metres, and I concentrate exclusively on my heartbeat. It may sound unbelievable, but I feel a pulse only once every 7–8 seconds. The doctors on my team smile when I tell them of this impression and maintain that it is impossible for a man's heart rate to reduce to nine beats per minute. We shall see. I am convinced that as soon as a Holter (the instrument used to record an electrocardiogram) is created that is water resistant to over a hundred meters, then even this phenomenon may be verified".

Bradycardia isn't confined to marine mammals, but is present in all other warm-blooded animals with pulmonary respiration: not only the beavers and hippopotamuses that (given their habitat) one would expect, but even dogs, if they are constrained to keep their head underwater, show an obvious slowing of the heart. The phenomenon has even been verified in the duck (which is of course a bird, not a mammal) where it was defined as a dive reflex or 'washbasin reflex', since one need only immerse the face in a bowl of water to provoke an automatic reduction of heart rate. The dive reflex is an instinctive reaction, fully developed even in neonates and the smallest children who, although they may yet be unable to swim, will automatically show apnea reflexes if immersed in a pool.

This phenomenon can be nullified with the intervention of appropriate drugs: experiments have been made on seals that caused them to interrupt a dive and ascend to the surface with obvious signs of difficulty.

Many unanswered questions

Forwards progress has been made into the scientific understanding of man's responses to apnea, but there are still many uncertainties and physiological phenomena that await explanation. Doctor Luca Torcello, who has followed Umberto Pelizzari since his emergence into the world of depth, has conducted many medical tests on him during training. In an interview several years ago he confessed that at the start of every set of tests they would set off in the direction of research, with the hope of giving an answer to existing questions, but at the end of each test numerous mysteries remained unsolved and, moreover, new problems and questions had emerged. According to him we are only at the beginning of a mysterious and fascinating road: we know neither its direction nor its destination, but we must walk it all the same. However it will take time, much time.

Anyone subjected to extreme pressure during apnea can react, from a physiological point of view, in a unique and unpredictable manner. To halve the atmospheric pressure that we have at sea level we must scale a mountain to 5000 meters, but to double it we need only dive to 10 meters. This gives an idea of how much more conditions vary in water than in air, and of what extreme conditions are to be found past 100 meters depth. If everyone who lives and breathes in 1 atmosphere of pressure was subjected to such extreme variations would they all react in the same way?

One would imagine that the limits of man in freediving are linked to the time of immersion. This is not necessarily true. With modern equipment it is now possible to descend to 150 meters and return in less than 3 minutes. But a freedive in which you are dragged down to maximum depth on a weighted sled and towed back up to the surface by a balloon can be considered a static apnea in so much as it does not require any physical exertion. There are apneists who can hold their breath for over eight minutes: if the result of a freedive was indeed dependent on time than they would be able to descend to 400 meters. Unfortunately this is not the case.

The real problem is in compensating the eardrums. With the increase of depth there is an increase of pressure on the tympanic membrane that forces it inwards. At this point we must compensate, taking air from the lungs and directing it towards the ears to force the eardrum back to its normal position. If we don't compensate then the membrane will rupture. This is what gives us the real limiter that makes deep apnea so difficult. In a constant weight dive to –60 meters lung volume will be a seventh of its initial volume, making it very difficult to 'rob' air from the lungs to push into the ears. The solution to the problem is in the reduction of compensation frequency, and in the use of the diaphragm (*see Chapter 7*). In No Limits Pelizzari and others are studying a completely new and extremely difficult technique of compensation. It consists in removing the internal nose plug at eighty meters and completely flooding the airways. Where there is water there can be no air: it is this saving of air that should permit compensation at a greater depth. This technique is especially complicated and is practiced only at the highest level.

3.3 BLOOD SHIFT

In the fifties the French doctor of physiology Cabarrou came to the conclusion that man wouldn't be able to descend past a depth of 50 meters: "*Après, il s'ècrase*," ("beyond, one will be crushed") he affirmed. Almost a decade passed before the 'facts' were contradicted. It was Enzo Maiorca who, on the 15th of August 1961, was the first man to break the mythical wall of 50 meters.

Doctor Cabarrou deduced his terrible prophecy of the crushing future of apnea past 45 meters by using several hypothetical containers that would resemble the human thoracic cage in composition and resilience. But the thoracic cage is not just a static container that contains heart and lungs; it is also the packaging of a complex physiological mechanism that responds to precise rules.

Ten years later we had the reply to the innumerable questions triggered by Maiorca's dive. Initially it was argued that the feat could be explained by hereditary factors and progressive training, but the true explanation has since been identified as bradycardia and the *blood shift*.

The proof of the existence of *blood shift*

In 1974 at Elba Jacques Mayol underwent a very delicate medical test that consisted in the taking of a blood sample during a dive. A catheter was introduced into his elbow, in the vena cava superior, allowing doctors to measure the venal intrathoracic blood pressure at depths of 40 and 60 meters.

It was noticed that the quantity of blood contained in the thorax during the dive increased from 1 to 2.2 litres. This demonstrated the recall of blood into the thorax; the so-called **blood shift** studied and theorized for the first time in 1968 by Karl Shaefer, a physiologist in the US Navy. It is the blood shift that belies the theory of Cabarrou. This physiological mechanism is manifested in all apnea dives, and is proportional to depth and pressure.

The explanation is simple. At sea level the atmospheric pressure is 1 bar. Descending underwater the hydrostatic pressure increases by 1 bar every 10 meters, so at 20 meters we have 3 bar, at 30 meters 4 bar and at 100 meters 11 bar. This pressure acts on the body, but what interests us is to observe how the lungs behave. With an increasing pressure, air contained in the lungs reduces in volume progressively, in accordance with Boyle's law. Therefore at one hundred meters the air in the lungs will occupy 1/11 of the initial volume: our lungs will thus be 11 times as small as their volume was on the surface. The problem is that the free space created by this pulmonary compression could not be left empty, or there would be an implosion, just as Cabarrou hypothesized – a thoracic squeeze given by the weight of the water and external atmospheric pressure.

Why the thorax is not crushed

This disturbing image is prevented by the *blood shift*. Blood is recalled from the peripheral zones of the body, where there are no vital organs, and is pushed into the lungs, where it occupies the free space left by the reduction of air volume due to increased pressure. Blood is a liquid and therefore incompressible; this explains how we can adapt to pressure without imploding.

But the *blood shift* is not only a passive phenomenon that counteracts hydrostatic pressure: it is also an active phenomenon that gives a more rational exploitation of oxygen, saving it for the critical organs like the brain and heart, at the loss of peripheral organs and tissues.

Doctors maintain however that is the phenomenon of *blood shift*, which today allows us to plumb depths that were considered impossible until several years ago, that could one day constitute the physiological limit of man in apnea. The reason is that at greater depths we may find the heart is engulfed by the elevated quantity of blood arriving from the peripheries, making it impossible to continue beating. The conditional is in this case obligatory, especially after all the contradictions of subaquatic medicine in the last thirty years of the history of apnea.

Dolphins (which of the marine mammals are the closest relative to humans) and other cetaceans habitually reach depths

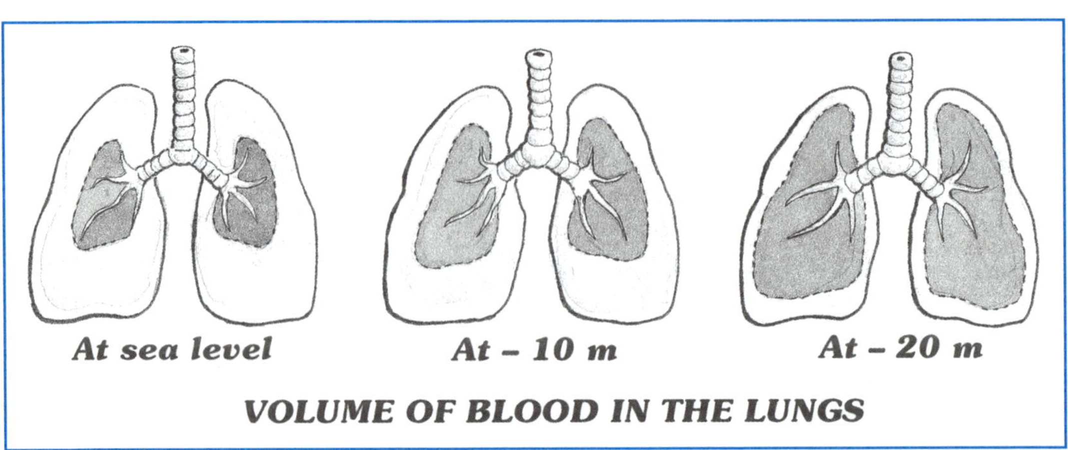

VOLUME OF BLOOD IN THE LUNGS

of great magnitude. The sperm whale and the elephant seal are the undisputed champions of depth, being able to descend to well over a thousand meters. When the sperm whale dives it stores about 3,000 litres of air in its lungs, equivalent to a 20-litre scuba bottle filled to 150 atmospheres. Upon arriving at 1,000 meters, where the pressure is 101 atmospheres, the volume of gas contained in its lungs will have reduced to about 1/100, or 30 litres. At this point the sperm whale should implode – its immense body should burst inwards, falling to pieces. Obviously this doesn't occur, but instead at this depth the animal even has the strength to engage in furious struggles with the giant squid, its food of choice. This is only possible because the marine mammal has made incredible adaptations to the (essentially hostile) environment in which it lives and moves.

As well as collapsible lungs, seals, whales and dolphins also have collapsible tracheas and bronchi, due to the fact that the cartilage they are constructed from is not rigid, as it is in humans. Furthermore they have supple ribs, which are not connected anteriorally to the sternum, and are therefore more flexible under compression.

3.4 EARS, NOSE, MOUTH

The ears, nose and mouth are all delicate organs for the apneist. Problems in the primary airways or in the ears mean suspending freediving; therefore it is important to treat these body parts with great attention. Taking care of them requires an understanding of their function and most importantly knowing how to make them more resilient and train them so that they will always be in good condition.

The ear

Due to its anatomic configuration, the ear is the organ most exposed and sensitive to the effects of pressure variation during immersion. Before describing manoeuvres for compensation of the cavity connected to the organ of hearing (*see Chapter 7*), we will give an overview of the anatomy and physiology of the ear and Eustachian tube, which will help to better comprehend the problems related to it.

If directly exposed to temperature and pressure variations during underwater activity, the ear can sustain lesions that, other than being very painful, may permanently compromise hearing function. Hearing function can be schematically summarized as:

- **Transmissive**: sound is transformed into mechanical stimuli (conducted by the external ear & middle ear, the latter formed by the eardrum and ossicular chain).
- **Nervous**: the mechanical stimuli move the liquid contained in the inner ear (cochlea) to create a nervous impulse.

Anatomy and physiology of the ear

The ear can be divided into three sections: outer, middle and inner. The **outer ear** is formed by the auricle, whose concave shape has the function of collecting sound and conveying it into the ear canal. Sound is carried inwards by the ear canal, which is closed at its internal extremity by the tympanic membrane (eardrum).

The eardrum is a very thin and elastic membrane, rounded in shape, with a diameter of about 1 cm, forming an airtight separation between external and middle ear. Its function is to amplify acoustic vibrations, and together with the structure of the middle ear it transforms these vibrations into precise mechanical stimuli, i.e. from sound waves into movement.

The **middle ear** is situated in a little bone cavity next to the eardrum, and contains a chain of three small bones called ossicles: the **hammer** (connected to the eardrum), the **anvil**, and the **stirrup**. The ossicular chain must have a maximum liberty of movement to be able to supply a high fidelity of sound; therefore it is necessary that the middle ear is always clear and clean. To this end we are supplied with **Eustachian**

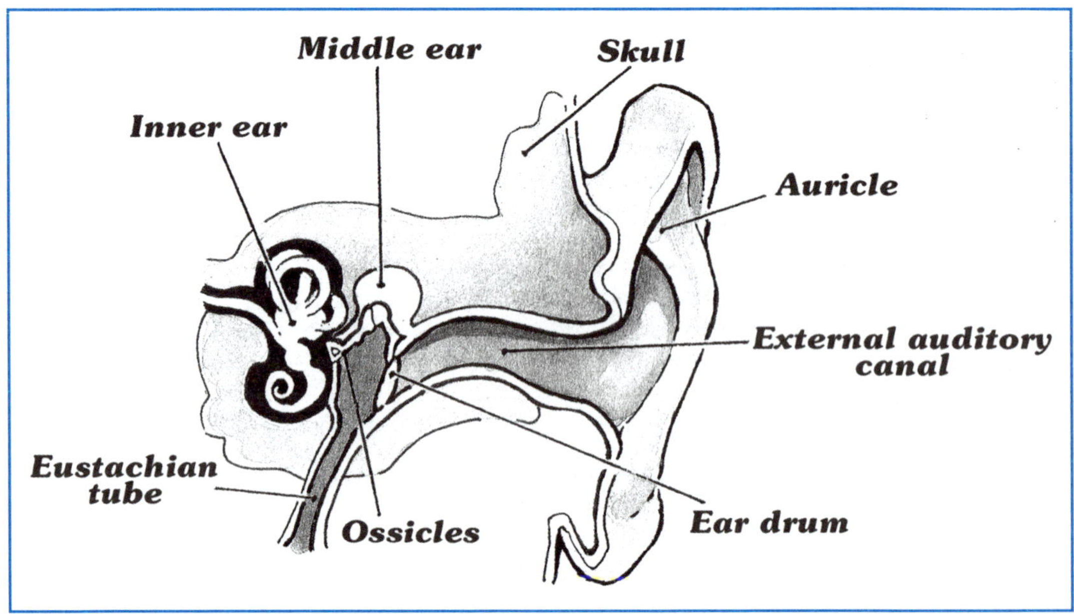

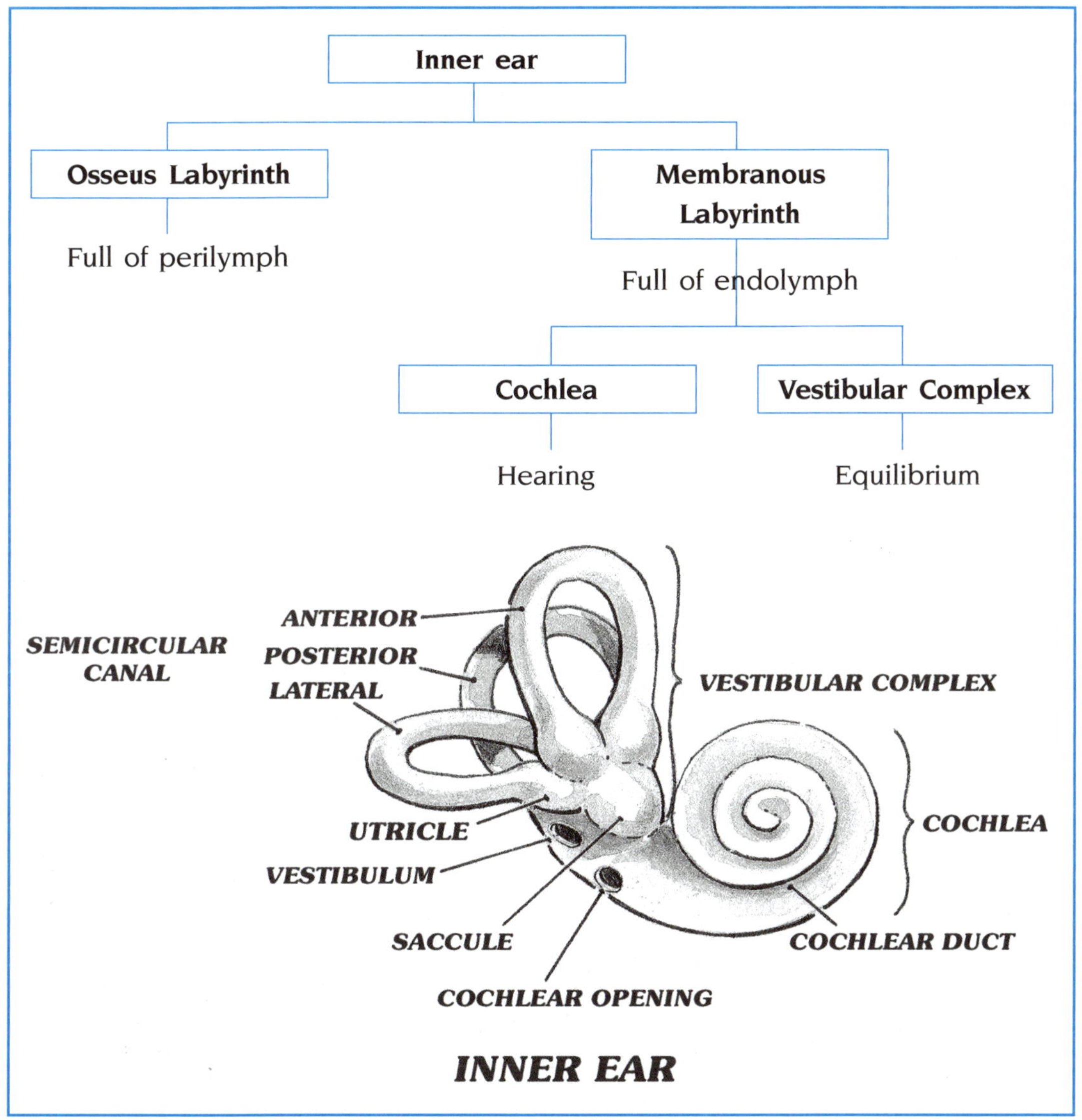

INNER EAR

tubes, the bone and cartilage canals that connect the cavity of the eardrum to the nasopharynx.

Vibrations are propagated inwards from the external ear, transformed into mechanical impulses by the three small bones and transmitted through an orifice, called the vestibulum, to the inner ear – the headquarters of hearing. Sudden changes of pressure or temperature can damage this structure suddenly and permanently, or slowly and gradually, producing very uncomfortable consequences.

The **inner ear** is also a very delicate structure, consisting of a series of cavities and channels called the **membranous**

labyrinth, which contain liquid endolymph, and an **osseous labyrinth** that tightly encloses and protects this structure. The space between the two labyrinths is full of another liquid called perilymph. The anterior part of the inner ear, the cochlea, is responsible for the sense of hearing, while the posterior half is concerned with the sense of equilibrium.

Sense of equilibrium

The sense of equilibrium is supplied by the intricate actions of three structures: the semicircular canals, the utricle and the saccule. The **semicircular canals** are three tubes full of endolymph in which sensitive cilia (fine hairs) are free to move. Each canal describes a semicircle in one of the three dimensions of space, meaning that any movement or rotation of the head will move liquid in at least one of the canals, stimulating the cilia. The **utricle** and the **saccule** are two small bags that are connected together to form the **vestibule**. The semicircular canals extend from the utricle, while the saccule opens into the cochlea. These two cavities also contain sensitive cilia, protected by a gelatinous medium containing minute crystals of calcium carbonate that respond to variations of gravity and linear acceleration.

A constant weight freediver will assume a head-down position. This is the exact opposite of the position we adopt walking on land. The vestibular complex (semicircular canals) receive stimuli that are therefore difficult to interpret. The increase of pressure during the descent and the subsequent necessity of compensation, the downward position of the head, the velocity of descent and the cold water after the thermocline are all factors that limit depth. This explains why in variable weight and No Limits athletes will use a sled that allows them to descend with the head kept in the upward position.

Sense of hearing

The sense of hearing is supplied by the nervous structure of the **cochlea**. Its neural receptors are ciliated (hairy) cells connected to the organ of Corti and stimulated by movement of the cochlear liquid. These cells transform the mechanical stimulus into a bioelectric nerve impulse, which is in turn transmitted to the central nervous system by the vestibular nerve.

The cochlear liquid is agitated as a consequence of movement of the ossicular chain. This is possible since the **osseous labyrinth** of the cochlea is penetrated at two points on the side of the middle ear to form two membranes: the **vestibulum** and the **cochlear opening**. The vestibulum is firmly attached to the stirrup, which strikes against its surface during movement of the eardrum and ossicular chain. This movement creates a force on the cochlear liquid. Being a liquid, and therefore incompressible, this force must be compensated elsewhere, and this is the role of the cochlear opening. An introflexion of the vestibulum will correspond to an extroflexion of the cochlear opening.

The combined anatomical features and actions of all these auditory structures permits the faithful perception of sound. An adequate compensation is based on the integrity and competence of the structures, united with a good knowledge of compensation manoeuvres and one's own capacity. The Eustachian tubes are used to ensure an equal pressure on both faces of the eardrum and to prevent lesions, pain or irritation during immersion. A superficial or inadequate compensation can result in either immediate and permanent auditory damage or gradual and progressive damage.

Anatomy and physiology of the Eustachian tube

The Eustachian tube is an **osseous-cartilaginous canal** that connects the inner wall of the eardrum with the lateral wall of the nasopharynx. It extends in an oblique direction, inwards, downwards and forwards. In an adult, the complete length is between 36 and 40 mm, 10–12 of which constitutes the upper bony tract, while the rest is the lower cartilaginous portion.

The **bony portion** is formed by an expansion of the tympanic bone, and is situated under the base of the cranium, projecting along the thickness of the pyramid of the temporal bone. It has a passive role in tubular function.

The **cartilaginous portion** follows on from the bony portion, and curves and widens progressively towards the na-

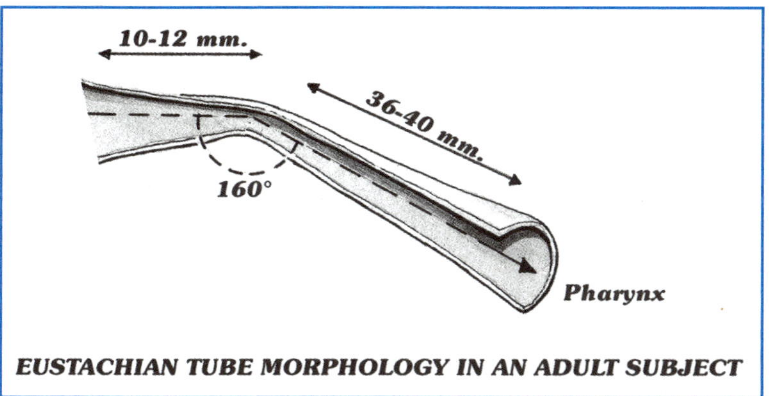

EUSTACHIAN TUBE MORPHOLOGY IN AN ADULT SUBJECT

sopharynx. Its elastic quality is determined by fibro-elastic lamina that form the external walls of the entire Eustachian tube. The cartilaginous tube has two further elastic layers: the **lateral lamina** in the upper section, and the **medial lamina** in the lower section. The latter has longitudinal incisions that isolate the cartilaginous plates, augmenting the tube's elasticity.

The **orifice of the tube** opens into the lateral wall of the nasopharynx and contains the nasopharyngeal tonsils, a member of the lymphatic structures of Waldeyer's ring.

The two portions of the Eustachian tube appear as separate organs, different in both macro and microscopic structure and morphology. They are both shaped like transversely flattened cones that join to form a tubular isthmus with a downwards angle of 160°. The diameter of the tube at this isthmus is 2 mm.

In conditions of repose the tube is closed; its walls are collapsed and are only opened by means of active physiological mechanisms (swallowing, chewing, yawning, belching, humming etc) or passive mechanisms (autoinsufflation manoeuvres, pressure differences between the two extremities) whose function involve the middle ear.

Tubular dynamics are provided by intrinsic and extrinsic musculature, which overcome the elastic force of the cartilaginous trunk (the only mobile portion of the tube) and the surface tension of the tube walls. **Intrinsic muscles** open and close the orifice of the tube, while the extrinsic muscles reinforce this action indirectly, having other specific functions. To facilitate tube opening the mucous producing cells of the respiratory epithelium secrete a substance that reduces surface tension between the mucous on the walls.

The tubular epithelium is not uniform over its entire surface: the epithelium of the osseous section, thin and poor in glands like the middle ear, passes into the thicker epithelium of the cartilaginous section, which is rich in ciliated cells, mucous producers and lymphatic structures like those of the nasopharynx and nasal canal. These different qualities allow a suitable connection between the auditory and respiratory systems. The Eustachian tube has both anatomical and functional connections with adjacent structures.

The 'tubular aerobics' illustrated in Chapter 7 have the purpose of training the correct use of jaw, tongue and soft palate in order to open the Eustachian tube and improve compensation. These are simple exercises that will improve awareness and control of the structures implicated in compensatory manoeuvres.

Eustachian tube function

The Eustachian tube has three important functions that together guarantee maximum functionality and protection of the structures of the middle ear (ossicular chain and eardrum).

- **Function of aeration or ventilation**: by means of periodic active opening the tube ensures the middle ear cavity is adequately aired so that an equal pressure is maintained on the two faces of the eardrum. This condition allows proper functioning and optimum motility of the middle ear complex, and therefore an accurate mechanical transmission of sonic stimuli. The function of aeration affords easy adjustment to changes in posture and pressure. Abrupt variations of external pressure (take-off and touch-down of aeroplanes, underwater diving, cable car trips etc) provoke either an outward or inward flexion of the eardrum, which may cause sensations of muffling or irritation and, in the case of filling with fluid or inflammation of the eardrum, pain. In the absence of pathology such situations are easily resolved by the active opening of the tube (manoeuvre of compensation) or with a passive mechanism induced by a pressure difference greater than 15 mmHg.
- **Function of defence or protection**: the Eustachian tube also has the task of protecting the middle ear from any chemical, physical or biological agents that could alter its function. In the case of pathogens, the tissue of the tubes and adjacent pharynges are equipped to activate an immune defence against pathogens already known to the organism. The secretion of mucous rich in bacteriolytic enzymes forms a protective barrier.
  There are also mechanical factors that constitute a great obstacle to the movement of any agent up the tubes. They are represented by the semi-permanent surface contact of the tubular walls and by a 'valve' mechanism, which gives a greater resistance to airflow towards the middle ear than towards the nasopharynx.
- **Drainage function**: the tubes also have the task of clearing excess secretions from the canal, and of freeing the eardrum from fluid-creating pathogens. Drainage occurs thanks to the synchronous vibration of the cilia hairs, which are abundant in the cartilaginous section towards the nasopharynx.

PREVENTION AND HYGIENE

Optimal functioning of the Eustachian tube is given by perfect integrity and tonality of all structures that directly or indirectly intervene in the mechanics of the tube. These structures need to be constantly trained and looked after (*see Chapter 7*).

Nose

Having clear and clean nasal passages is essential for the integrity of the Eustachian tube orifice. The latter is located in the lateral wall of the nasopharynx, next to the end of the lower turbinate bone. During prevalently oral respiration this zone is not benefited by passage of air from the external environment. This means that viruses and bacteria may colonize it without disturbance, making it a permanently dangerous source of pathogens close to tube and therefore the middle ear.

It is well known that acute and chronic inflammations act on respiratory mucous to make it oedematous and thick, presenting mechanical obstacles to the opening of the tube and making it impossible to compensate for several days. In light of this, it is advisable to breathe nasally in order to drain the mucous, eliminate any threatening pathogens and sustain the function of the tubes.

For the same reason the nose must be kept clean. To this end it is helpful to blow the nose at least ten times a day, even in absence of colds or allergies, in order to remove any residue issuing from the auricular area or the paranasal sinuses. Sniffing is particularly bad for the health of the tube orifice; it creates an abrupt pressure change that in the long term can make the tissues around the orifice loose and hyper-mobile, with consequent changes to tonality, elasticity and therefore the proper functioning of this area.

Hygiene of the nostrils

Other than these simple daily routines, there are additional measures that can be taken to safeguard the nasal area.

Preventative pharmacological therapy supplies nasal drops and sprays that help to clear the airways and drain any inflammations of the nasopharynx. These consist in a solution that literally washes the nasal passages. You can treat both nostrils simultaneously (by tilting the head the liquid enters one nostril and exits from the other) or one at a time (the liquid enters and exits the same nostril).

Those who practice yoga will be familiar with Yal Neti, literally the 'nose wash'. Its use is recommended before respiratory exercises as a way of cleaning and purifying the nose.

Every day the nose transmits thousands of litres of air that is carrying countless particles of dust and pollution. The purpose of Yal Neti is to cleanse the nose, which, according to yoga masters, is a 'pranic antenna' capable of absorbing prana energy present in the air (*see Chapter 4*).

For us westerners it has been proven that nasal washes have valuable preventative and curative purposes. In particular, thermal therapy uses a water vapour with dissolved minerals such as sulphur, sulphide and sodium salts. It is an advisable treatment for the spring and summer periods, with the aim of draining the mucous from the nasopharynx and Eustachian tubes. The most common therapies are: nasal aerosol, insufflation, inhalation, the Politzer technique and the nasal wash.

Hygiene of the ear

The only area directly accessible is the external ear. Just as for the nose, there are simple but important daily routines.

The ear canal must always be clear and clean. Normally the ear cleans itself by moving earwax and detritus to the entrance of the canal, from where it is easily removed. The use of cotton buds is widely discouraged since they can be pushed dangerously far and very frequently damage the eardrum – instead of removing residue the cotton bud pushes and compresses it towards the end of the canal. In this way it is easy to form a plug of wax that must be removed with the help of a doctor, who will use a needle-less syringe full of warm water. The water is squirted into the canal, infiltrates between the plug and the eardrum and expels the wax.

For more banal and frequent incidents like dry waxy residue, pimples or crusts inside the canal it is advisable to carry out localized treatment with warm and sterile water and wait for spontaneous resolution of the problem. The temperature of the water is always important; the further it is from body temperature the easier it will be to provoke the sudden movement of water into the internal ear, where it can damage the nerve cells and cause temporary vertigo.

The special 'Proplug' made in America combats this problem efficiently, isolating the eardrum from the cold, but maintaining its communication with the external environment to allow compensation.

With regards to the middle ear, the only way of insuring cleanliness and health is through constant exercise of the tubes. For this purpose 'tubular aerobics' and the frequent chewing of gum or caramel are recommended, as the associated mastication and swallowing encourages opening of the Eustachian tubes.

THE PROPLUG

This is an anatomical plug designed specifically for underwater use. The two versions for the left and right ears are adapted perfectly to the external opening of the ear canal. For this reason they come in different measurements. A small hole, "Scott's valve", allows for the maintenance of equal pressure between the interior and exterior of the canal.

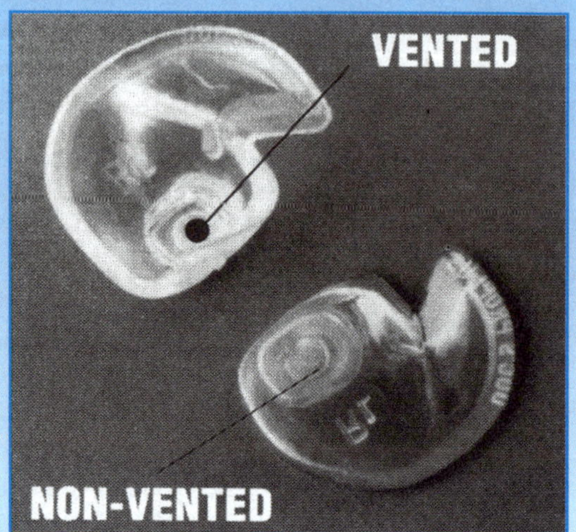

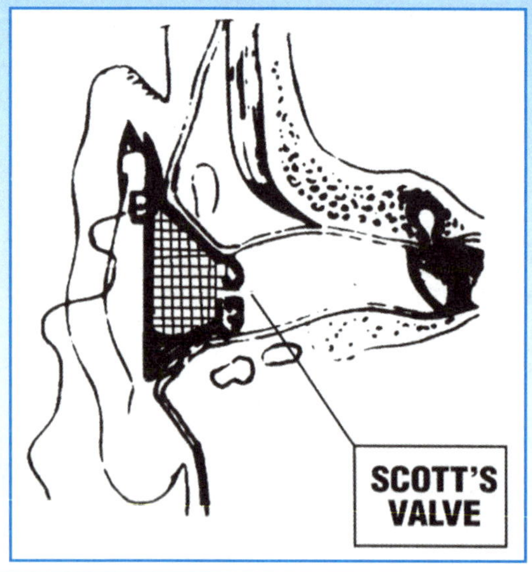

The plug guarantees efficiency of compensation but prevents the circulation of water that would inevitably chill the eardrum and canal, exposing the ear to annoying pathologies such as otitis. In particular the maintenance of body temperature in the area around the eardrum improves the sensitivity of the eardrum to pressure and favours compensation.

Furthermore the middle ear is greatly benefited by heat therapy of insufflation, where warm vapour is directed into the orifice of the Eustachian tube towards the eardrum. In all cases of acute or recurrent inflammation in this region it is best to see a doctor who can help to eliminate the pathogenic source and prevent further aggravation of the pathology.

PERIODIC CHECK-UPS

Anyone who freedives regularly, whether competitively or recreationally, constantly exposes their ears to a condition of stress. Therefore it is advisable to receive regular check-ups with clinical instruments – they are very simple but important. Check-ups are especially necessary in cases where ear

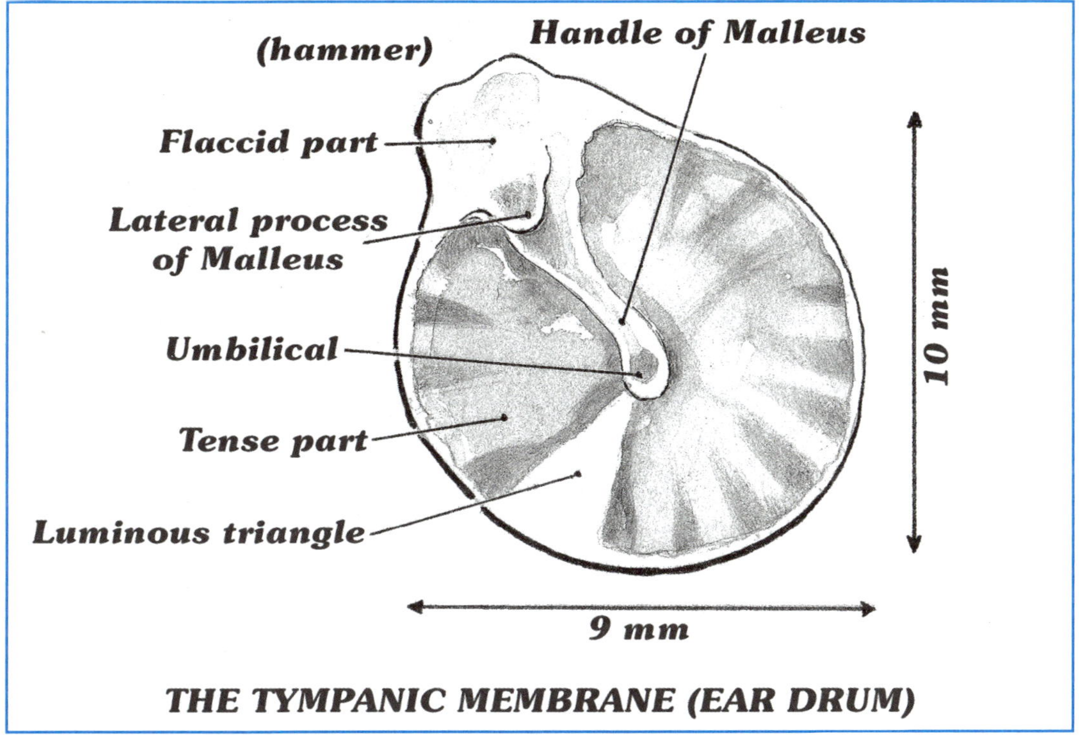

THE TYMPANIC MEMBRANE (EAR DRUM)

problems of any nature have been experienced during or after a dive.

The routine examinations are not intrusive or painful; they examine the ear's functionality and the integrity of its structure.

Direct otoscopy

This consists in the direct examination of the eardrum. In absence of pathology it appears smooth, with a uniform outline and a translucent mother-of-pearl colour. The hammer should be visible in transparency, and the light of the otoscope (the instrument used for examination) should reflect off the eardrum, creating a luminous triangle in the lower part. In all cases of afflicted eardrums these properties are absent, substituted by other appearances that depend on the precise pathogen.

Tonal Audiometry

The tonal Audiometer allows an evaluation in qualitative (Hz) and quantitative (dB) terms of a possible loss of hearing due to transmission and/or neural problems. This exam is carried out in a noise proof chamber and the patient receives sonic stimuli of varying intensity and frequency through headphones.

The responses are represented graphically on an audiogram. Frequency in Hz is plotted on the x-axis and intensity in dB on the y-axis (*Figures A and B on page 90*).

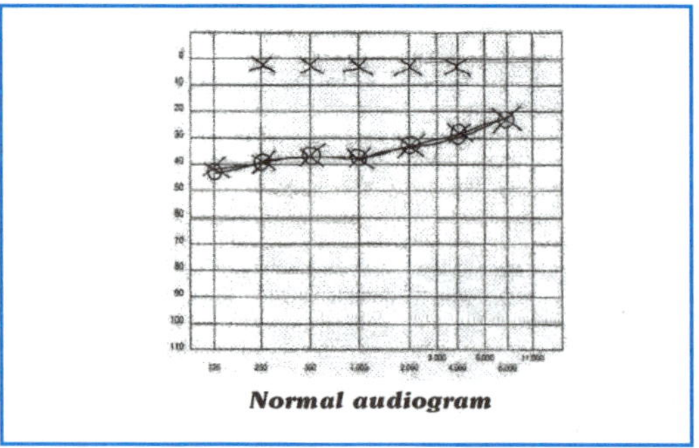
Normal audiogram

Fig. A

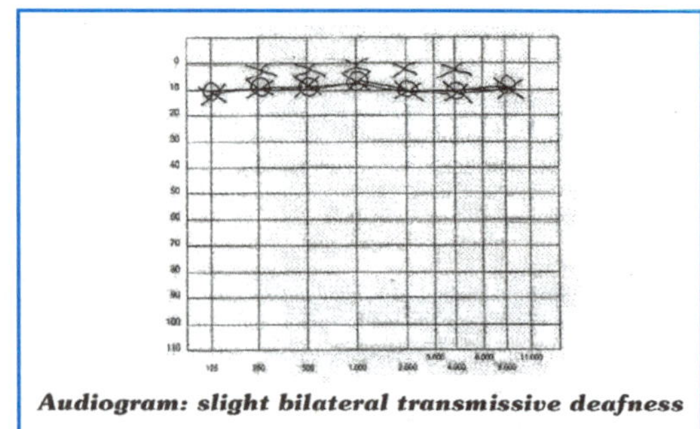
Audiogram: slight bilateral transmissive deafness

Fig. B

o Right ear x Left ear	Transmissive function
> Right ear < Left ear	Neural function

Impedance meter

The impedance meter is an objective evaluation of mobility, and therefore of functionality, of the eardrum and ossicles: the technique is not invasive, and doesn't require any collaboration on the part of the patient as long as he or she is immobile for the duration.

The test consists in tympanometry, which measures the eardrum's compliance, or pliability, and the assessment of stapedius reflex. Both measurements are obtained using an impedance meter probe, which stimulates the external ear canal with pressure and sound, and simultaneously monitors the effects.

Tympanometry

Tympanometry, represented graphically by the tympanogram (*Figure C*) examines the effects of pressure variations on the mobility of the transmission system. The impedance meter probe delivers air compressed to a pressure normally between +/–200 mmH_20 (it can reach values of +/–400 mmH_20). If the transmission system is free and functioning then the pressure flux will meet with maximum pliability, and therefore minimum impedance (resistance). The level of impedance will rise with any increase in the rigidity of the system. Normal values of compliance are around 0.5 cm^3 of air for pressure levels of +/–50 mm H_2O.

TYPE A CURVE: normal tympanogram

TYPE B CURVE: flat tympanogram. Usually the peak is absent and the values of compliance (y-axis) are more or less equal over the whole range of pressure.

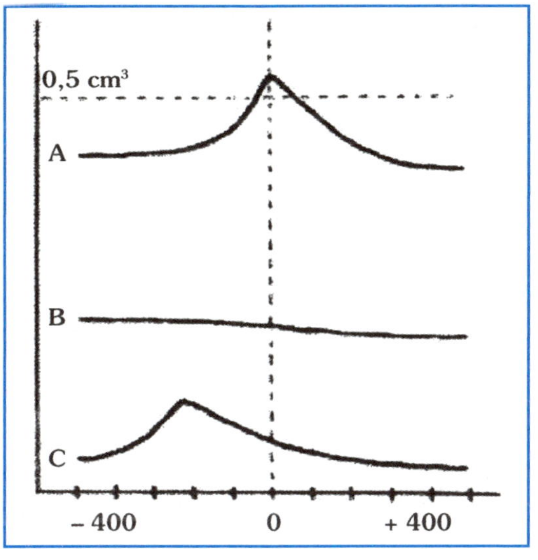

Fig. C

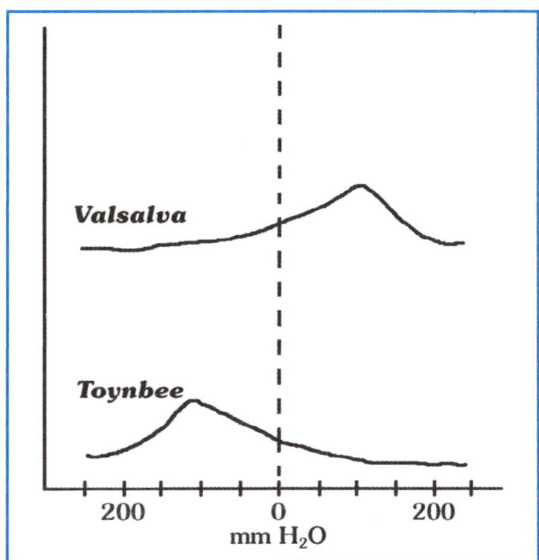

Fig. D

The middle ear is completely occupied by liquid, which reduces and impedes the motility of the eardrum and ossicular system (usually attributable to middle ear otitis and mucous serum).

TYPE C CURVE: the peak has moved to values of negative pressure (< 50 mmH_2O).

This is a sign of tubular dysfunction, derived from a depressurisation of the interior of the eardrum cavity, with a consequent contraction of the eardrum.

With an intact eardrum there are two possible manoeuvres that can be performed using tympanometry to evaluate functionality of the tubes. They are called 'forced ventilation trials' and are usually carried out one after the other:

Valsalva manoeuvre: the patient exhales whilst holding the nose closed and with the mouth shut (*see Chapter 7*). If the tubes are functioning properly the peak of compliance will be positioned towards values of positive pressure; if it is blocked the peak remains in the same position.

Toynbee manoeuvre: the patient must swallow three times consecutively without opening the mouth, and whilst holding the nose closed. This manoeuvre gives the opposite effect of the preceding test; the peak of compliance is positioned towards negative values (*Figure D*). A hypomobile or blocked tube will not permit such flexing of the eardrum and this alters the configuration of the tympanogram.

Sinuses

The sinuses are cavities of bone in the face: they are coated in mucous and are connected to the nasal cavity through numerous ducts. In normal conditions compensation of facial sinuses doesn't present any problems, in so much as the pressure is balanced spontaneously through direct communication with the upper airways. Nevertheless the freediver must be careful in cases of mucous congestion due to inflammatory conditions (sinusitis, colds); an abundant secretion of mucous can obstruct the passages that connect to the nasal cavity and create problems of compensation during the descent. If the increase of external pressure is not balanced spontaneously by air moving through the passages then a depression will be created in the sinuses, which will act as a sucking force on the mucous and draw blood out of the capillaries. This produces a swelling of the mucous, causing an intense pain that can often be associated with rupture of capillaries and epitasis (nosebleed).

Teeth

Even though it is very rare, it can happen that, due to the increase of pressure during a descent, a small amount of air trapped in a dental cavity or under a badly made filling can press against the pulp inside the tooth, causing pain.

Part two

THE ART OF NOT BREATHING

BREATH AND RELAXATION

CHAPTER

4

Dive deep oh mind,
Into the ocean of divine beauty.
You will discover a new gem,
Instant after instant.
- Yogic epigram

Learning to breathe and relax is the best way to prepare oneself, whether for a freedive into the depths or for a more simple immersion where the aim is to stay underwater for as long as possible.

Until a few decades ago there was a dominant way of thinking, which for simplification we will call 'forced apnea', that utilized a series of 'coercive' techniques, and whose main purpose was to force the body past the limit. Hyperventilation, which is dangerous as well as inefficient, is the progeny of this approach to apnea.

The first person to break these habits was Jacques Mayol. The French apneist adopted breathing and relaxation techniques from ancient oriental disciplines (especially Yoga) and their westernised versions (autogenic training and mental training). It was Mayol who gave birth to the idea of 'relaxed apnea' as opposed to 'forced apnea'. Obviously this meant a radical transformation of training and preparation methods for many apneists, but the results and performances weren't long in coming.

In this chapter we have tried to summarise the physiological arguments that favour relaxed apnea, and have proposed a series of techniques and exercises to learn and apply to your own body and mind. We will talk of stress, anxiety and boredom and of the risks (and benefits) that these altered psychological states represent for the apneist. In freediving we must eliminate all sources of stress, or at least those that depend on ourselves; we will thus attempt to use breathing and relaxation techniques to reach the tranquillity necessary for positive experiences, i.e. for enjoyable apnea that gives a feeling of well-being.

One need look no further than the way we fix our minds on the passing of time during a static apnea to appreciate that the limits are first mental and then physical. If we truly believe this then sooner or later we will succeed in exceeding ourselves.

4.1 STRESS, ANXIETY AND BOREDOM

Anxiety is a sensation that arises automatically in situations that are considered problematic or potentially dangerous. Initially it triggers a positive reaction that 'prepares' the person for the situation; in practice a state of alertness takes over that improves the base condition, mobilising it to confront 'the danger'.

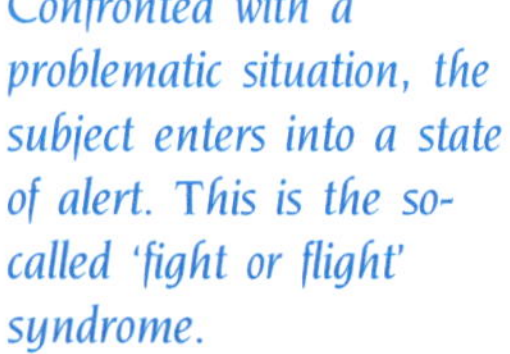

Confronted with a problematic situation, the subject enters into a state of alert. This is the so-called 'fight or flight' syndrome.

Every individual reacts differently to stimuli, and this difference is dependent on many factors: familiarity with the en-

WHAT HAPPENS TO OUR BODY DURING ANXIETY?

Vasoconstriction: lack of tissue oxygenation. Reduced oxygen supply to all tissues. Favours an increase in heart rate.

Muscular contractions and cardiac arrhythmias: signs of cardiac malfunction that are presented in various forms. In general reduces cardiac output and contributes to vasoconstriction.

Hypoxia: general lack of oxygen. Stimulates a reduction of bodily function and increases heart rate.

Muscular anesthesia: if caused by anxiety, produces a reduction of muscular activity along with a certain sensation of physical powerlessness and general discomfort.

Difficulty breathing: negative state of mind brings an increase in rate of respiration without profit. Difficulties in breathing are often accompanied by a shortness of breath.

Vomiting, diarrhea and indigestion: anxiety can have consequences to the digestive system, typically manifested by nausea and indigestion. These malfunctions cause a chain effect by negatively influencing circulatory and neuromuscular systems.

vironment, level of experience, preceding stimuli etc. As a consequence each person has their own threshold, and a situation that is thought by one person to be problematic or dangerous is not necessarily the same for others.

If the stimulus is considered 'dangerous' or 'problematic' then a series of reactions will be triggered that involve the nervous and endocrine systems and prepare the person for confrontation or evasion **('fight or flight' syndrome)**. The subject enters into a state of alertness.

If the stimulus is optimal and the reaction is optimal then performance will be optimal. If the stimulus is excessive then the reaction becomes excessive and performance decreases.

The 'fight or flight' syndrome induces a strong reaction of the autonomous nervous and endocrine systems, which raise the production of numerous hormones, among which adrenalin and noradrenaline, products of the adrenal glands, have a pivotal role. Noradrenaline is produced and applied also at a cerebral level. This molecule increases the frequency and force of the heartbeat, facilitates respiration by provoking a dilation of the bronchi, and raises the level of concentration and alertness. All this brings the individual into a state of maximum readiness. However the effects of these hormones are not completely positive; they can also cause an inhibition of creative and cognitive function in favour of the activity of the most primordial part of our brain (brainstem and limbic system).

If anxiety is protracted for a long period of time it will generate **stress** – a permanent state of tension. The human being will be in a continual state of alarm, consuming masses of energy, and mental and physical performance will deteriorate.

AVOID STRESS BY UNDERSTANDING IT

The causes of stress

It is important to be familiar with the factors that generate stress so that it may be recognised before it progresses to panic. Accidents are never caused by a single stressful factor. They are often the consequence of the sum of many stressful factors, which, if not identified, lower the level of control of the situation, resulting in panic and possible accidents.

Stress is learnt

Nobody is born with stress, but is exposed to it through an educative process aimed at resolving the relationship of dependence on parents. Stress, the imbalance between problems and answers, is an experience tied to each educational moment of upbringing. This upbringing is defined by a learning curve that allows the resolution of increasingly difficult problems and helps to develop fear and anxiety in a positive way. Experience and instinct favour the ability to keep stress at a minimum.

Stress is social

We are all born 'associable', not sociable: only through social experiences do we learn to understand ourselves with respect to others: initially in the family and successively in school and society. Everyone has need of other people to satisfy two primordial requirements: recognition and protection. Therefore we learn to interact with each other through the experience of social pressure and fear, which are both great causes of stress. The safety of apnea is based on a system of pairs, and therefore allows for new acquaintances to be made with other freedivers. This makes it a very social and rewarding activity.

Stress and the individual

Every individual is different from another, not just biologically but also in character and psychology. Stress is a personal feature and cannot be shared – it varies from individual to individual based on the extent of perceived risk. If someone is confronted with a risk greater than they can manage then the negative stress will grow, developing into a traumatising panic, to the point of causing an accident.

Boredom is also a cause of stress to the organism: it is a situation of repetition, of *routine*, of 'been there, seen that, done it all' – uninteresting, monotonous and grey. In this case the reaction is minimal and does not trigger the optimum condition, meaning the subject performs poorly, does not obtain results, and the brain becomes detached, wanders and misbehaves. In the athlete this can be caused by monotonous, repetitive and therefore tedious training. The effect will be a lack of attention with consequent reductions in commitment and results.

To conclude J.E. Mc Grath has defined stress as "**the result of an imbalance between demands made to the individual and the capacity of the individual to respond to these demands**"; we can say therefore that everybody receives a certain level of stress every day, which can be positive, since it alerts of danger or of a problem to solve, and keeps the attention active.

However there are factors that can change *positive stress* into *negative stress*. These factors are: the possibility of choice, the level of control and the ability to anticipate the consequences.

Possibility of choice

It often happens that the obligation to resolve a problem generates tension or **negative stress**. On the other hand to choose to undertake a problem involves the evaluation of one's own ability and the decision to confront the problem; this **stress is positive**. In static apnea for example, a companion might declare: "Today you're going to do 4 minutes", when your best performance is 3:30; the stress induced by the imposed choice in this case is negative. The effect is different if you feel capable of 4 minutes and therefore choose to attempt it voluntarily.

Level of control

If there is command of the situation and everything is under control then stress is positive, since it keeps the subject alert and capable of solving problems efficiently. If stressful factors are added to the situation (for example currents, flooding of the mask, loss of a fin etc), then control of the situation is depleted and the stress becomes negative, bringing the subject to the threshold of panic.

Ability to anticipate the consequences

The level of stress is diminished if the subject understands the situation; stress will be positive since the consequences can be anticipated, providing the opportunity to prevent any possible complications. On the other hand ignorance arouses a strong negative stress, since one can only expect the unexpected. All apneists must understand the details of their environment, the weather and the activity they are performing in order to reduce the level of stress and to enjoy themselves.

CAUSES OF STRESS IN APNEA

A healthy condition, good technical preparation and good equipment will all help the apneist to stay one step ahead of stress.

An understanding of the causes of stress and how to recognise and deactivate them allows us to interrupt the chain of stressful factors that can result in an accident. **An accident is never caused by a single factor** but by the sum of many factors, which, if not recognised and resolved, will expose us to an unpleasant experience. The categories into which we can group the causes of stress are:

1. **Physical causes**
2. **Psychological causes**
3. **Causes due to equipment**
4. **Environmental causes**
5. **Lack of technical capacity and training**

Physical causes

The psychophysical condition changes every day. A good training, the participation in advanced apnea courses, and a trusted companion are all beneficial to the enjoyment of apnea; on the other hand, poor physical form promotes physical stress. Not smoking, receiving regular check-ups and following an adequate diet are habits for greater safety and enjoyment. If fatigue takes over at any moment then that is the best occasion for a break or to conclude underwater activity. Don't carry on with the next descent! It is also important that the physically fittest members of the group adjust to the rhythm of activity set by the weakest.

Deteriorating marine weather conditions increase physical fatigue and therefore stress. In this case it is best to change the program or location in such a way as to adapt to the situation.

Psychological causes

People who suffer from active psychosis, depression, who abuse alcohol or use drugs or psychotic medicines should not freedive. They require personal attention.

The use of alcohol negatively influences the perception of

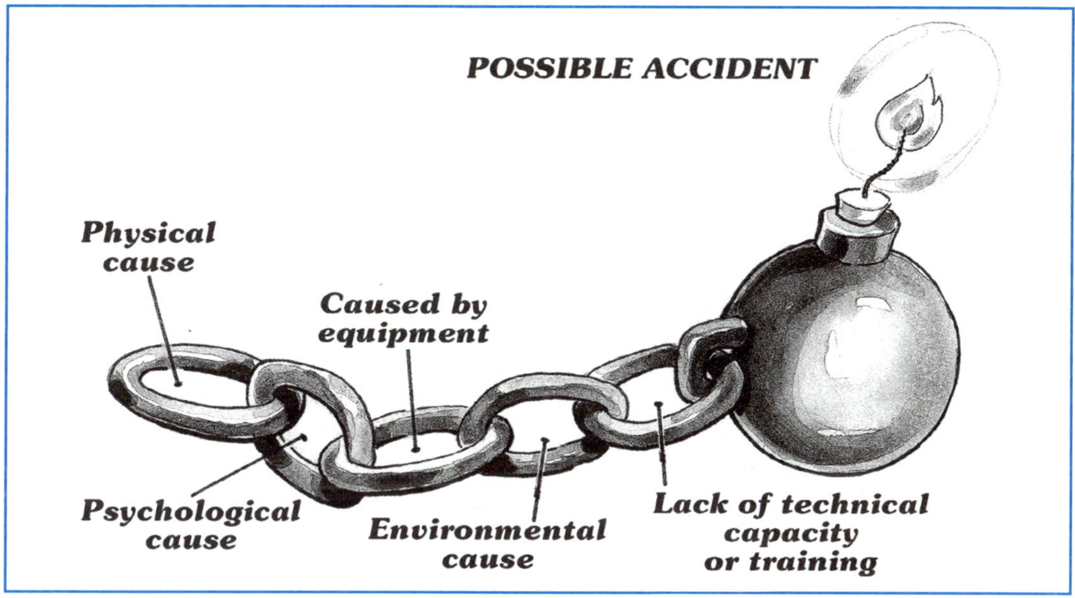

reality and slows reflexes. If someone makes use of medicinal drugs it is important that there is precise confirmation from a doctor that they do not contraindicate activities in apnea underwater.

It is not a single stressful event that causes an accident, but the concatenation of many factors that, if not recognised and resolved, cause exposure to possible accidents.

Every freediving companion must be sensitive to these situations and if necessary resolve them with an intervention that guarantees the well-being and enjoyment of all.

Causes due to equipment

Freediving takes place in a natural environment and therefore requires special equipment. This gear (*see Chapter 1*) should guarantee comfort, safety and enjoyment; it must be good quality, well serviced and used correctly. The loss of a piece of equipment, bad maintenance or a badly fitting wetsuit will create discomfort and therefore stress.

An apneist must know how to identify problems related to unsuitable equipment, and be able to resolve them. If a companion does not have all the essentials for immersion, one must – with responsibility and sensitivity – persuade them to concede the activity.

Environmental causes

Even an expert apneist can find himself in difficulty if the environmental conditions are unsuitable or unknown. Strong winds, extreme temperature, little visibility and swift currents are all factors that can increase the level of stress. If the marine weather conditions are unfavourable then one should forfeit the dive – it is a sign of responsibility.

Lack of technical capacity and training

Technical capacity and training are the basis of safety and enjoyment. Not knowing how to behave in a situation that requires specific technical abilities will increase the level of stress and the possibility of an accident.

4.2 TECHNIQUES OF RESPIRATION

Respiration doesn't just mean 'filling up with air'. Incorrect movements or tight upper body muscles can often lead us to believe we are breathing, when in fact we are doing it incorrectly. In other cases we are incapable of using all the air present in our lungs. These two limitations can negatively influence performance in apnea. We need to remember that the depth or distance reached and the time in apnea all depend on various factors such as training, technique, equipment and so forth, but most of all on how we prepare for the performance, and therefore on how we relax or breath before beginning the apnea.

The control that is afforded by a good level of relaxation and correct technique of respiration during the preparation not only guarantees minimum use of oxygen by reducing its metabolism, but also a greater awareness of oneself, an inner peace and safer diving.

By developing our breathing we will be taking care of our entire system of body and mind. Through a regular daily practice movements will find harmony with the breath and will no longer be forced, but rather an opportunity to listen to and feel the breath. The awareness of breathing gives it regularity and fluidity.

Awareness of the breath

Many meditative techniques make reference to the dynamics of respiration, and diaphragmatic respiration is the type of breathing that allows not only the greatest concentration but also a better contact with the body. The first step towards being able to acquire a greater sensitivity of yourself is to become aware of your own breathing.

Normal automatic respiration does not require any particular participation: the breath follows its own rhythm. Only at times, and for various reasons, do we voluntarily intervene in respiratory action; however even in these cases we do not dedicate genuine attention to our breathing. We must become habituated to listening attentively to our breath and we must visualise it, feeling the passage of air through the lungs.

Whether in the gym or in the water, close your eyes and try to 'feel' the breath pass through your body. It can seem bizarre, especially at the start, and we may feel ridiculous, but if we draw out respiration whilst remaining completely calm, then we will become much more aware and sensitive to the breath. To begin with we will address discomforts of position and the contraction of muscles that could be peacefully inactive; continuing with this discovery, as we succeed in sensing our body in a new way, we will observe with new eyes the movements that were occurring before. Walking, climbing stairs, sitting, running, swimming and also finning are all complex movements that require the coordination of many muscles.

For example when we first learn to ride a bicycle we are quickly fatigued because we are engaging a lot of muscular energy in order to maintain the necessary balance even just to travel a few hundred meters. By repeating the movement it is perfected and becomes automatic, and we can therefore travel great distances with a trifling amount of force.

The learning of underwater propulsion happens in the same way. We pass from conscious control at the start to automatic movement when we have earned greater aquaticity, with the significant difference that we must do it all without breathing. It will therefore be essential to eliminate all unconstructive movements that use unnecessary muscles. To do this we will have to sense the muscles, i.e. make ourselves aware of their existence and status: whether they are in tension or repose.

The first step to becoming conscious of our body and visualising every movement is to control respiration.

IMPROVING THE ELASTICITY OF THE RIBCAGE

To breathe correctly we must have a soft and elastic diaphragm and ribcage. It is essential to possess a good thoracic mobility that allows for ample movement during diaphragmatic inspiration and expiration. An elevated mobility of the ribcage reduces residual lung volume – the air that remains in the lungs after a complete exhalation.

Working on ribcage mobility increases the important ratio of Total Capacity:Residual volume that determines our comfort and ability to compensate to a greater depth. In the following pages we propose several exercises for improving the elasticity of the ribcage.

Remember that all the exercises proposed in the following pages should be performed only after obtaining verification from your doctor that there are no clinical contraindications.

EXERCISES FOR THE IMPROVEMENT OF THE ELASTICITY OF THE RIBCAGE (costovertebral and intercostal joints)

EXERCISE 1

Note: *do not move the chest forwards or backwards during the exercise*

Execution

- Sit on a bench or a seat without a back with arms hanging by the sides: during one long and slow inspiration rotate the arms and shoulders outwards; hold this position for an inspiratory apnea of 3-5 seconds (*Fig. 1*).
- During the expiration rotate the arms and shoulders inwards; hold in this position for a 3-5 second expiratory apnea (*Fig. 2*).
- Repeat for 10-12 complete cycles.

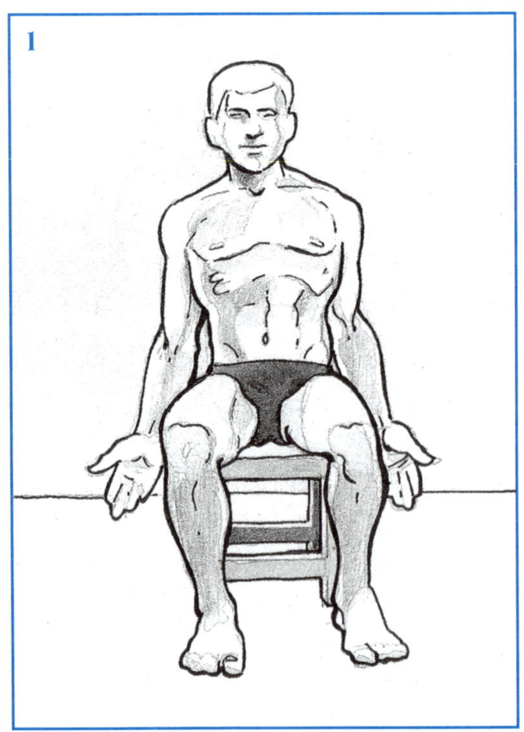

Inspiration + inspiratory apnea of 3-5 seconds.

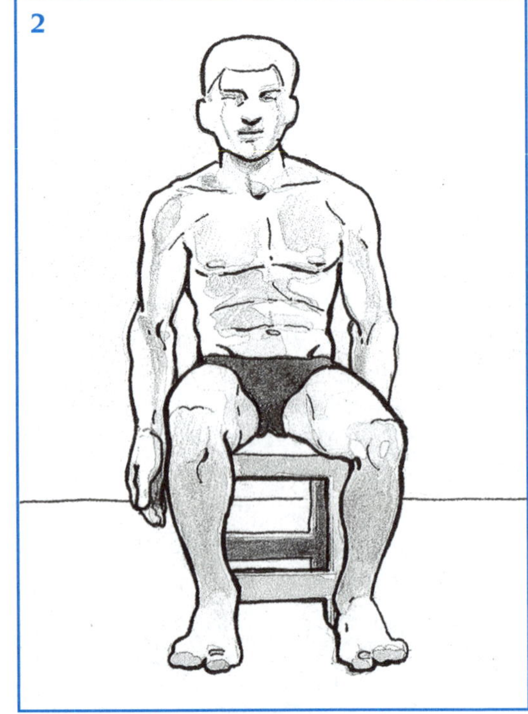

Expiration + expiratory apnea of 3-5 seconds.

EXERCISE 2

Execution

- Sit as in the previous exercise and place hands opposite each other with the fingertips resting at the point where the two clavicles meet (sternocostoclavicular joint).
- During a long and slow inspiration raise the elbows, without moving the fingers off the clavicles; hold in this position for an apnea of 3-5 seconds (*Fig. 1*).
- During the expiration bring the elbows down until the inner arms touch the ribs, and maintain a light pressure during an expiratory apnea of 3-5 seconds (*Fig. 2*).
- Repeat for 8-10 complete cycles.

Inspiration + inspiratory apnea of 3-5 seconds.

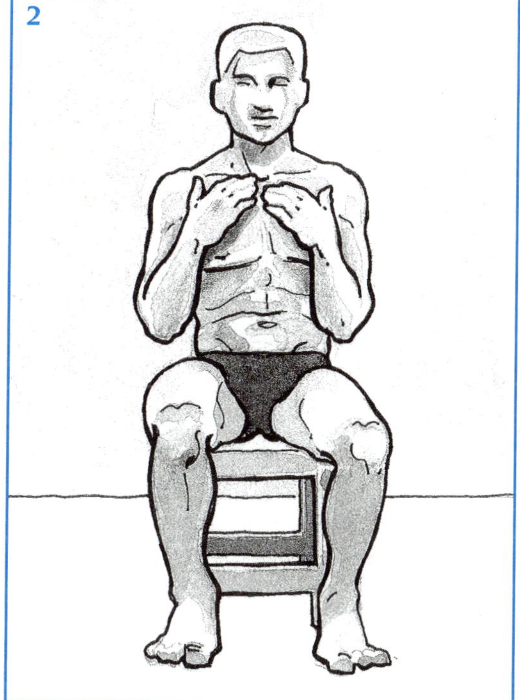

Expiration + expiratory apnea of 3-5 seconds.

EXERCISE 3

Note:
never force the movement, never tense the body.

Execution

- Sit as in the preceding exercises. During a long and slow expiration, lengthen the arms forwards, holding one hand with the other, and bring the head forwards into the space created between the arms.
- Gently stretch the arms forwards; hold for an expiratory apnea of 3-5 seconds (*Fig. 1*).
- From this position, with a long and slow inspiration bring the arms behind the back, grasp the hands together and gently stretch the arms downwards, bringing the head posteriorally (looking up) and the shoulders back and down. Hold for an inspiratory apnea of 3-5 seconds (*Fig. 2*).
- Repeat for 6-8 complete cycles.

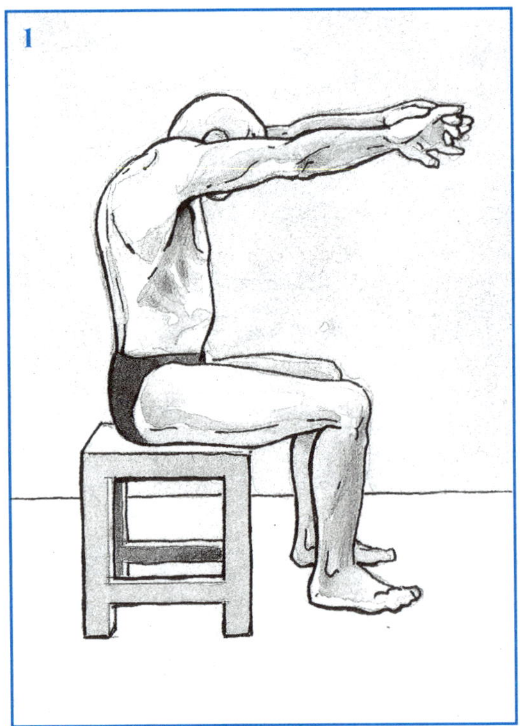

Expiration + Expiratory apnea of 3-5 seconds.

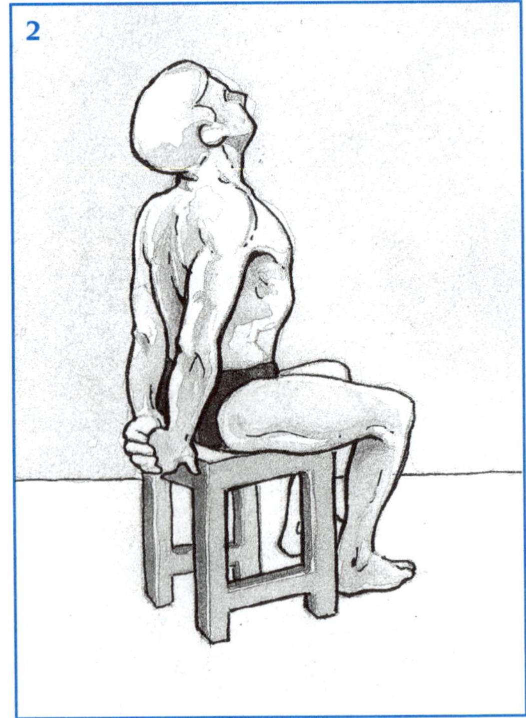

Inspiration + Inspiratory apnea of 3-5 seconds.

EXERCISE 4

Execution

- Lie supine, with legs bent and slightly apart so that the soles of the feet are in contact with the ground, and with fingertips opposite each other in the centre of the ribcage at the bottom of the sternum, and palms in contact with the ribs.
- During a long, slow and deep expiration gently follow the lowering and shrinking of the ribs and thorax with the hands, without pressing at the finish; hold for an expiratory apnea of 3-5 seconds (*Fig. 1*)
- Using the hands, hold the ribs in the position they reached at the end of the expiration, and start a long and slow inspiration through the mouth (*Fig. 2*).
- At the end of the inspiration lift the hands suddenly off the thorax: this produces a quick entry of air through the open mouth and an abrupt expansion of the thorax. After 2-3 normal breaths repeat the sequence. Repeat for 4-5 complete cycles.

Note:
do not press hard on the ribs; the inspiration must always be performed with mouth completely open; the removal of the hands must happen as quickly as possible; always intersperse the cycles with several normal breaths.

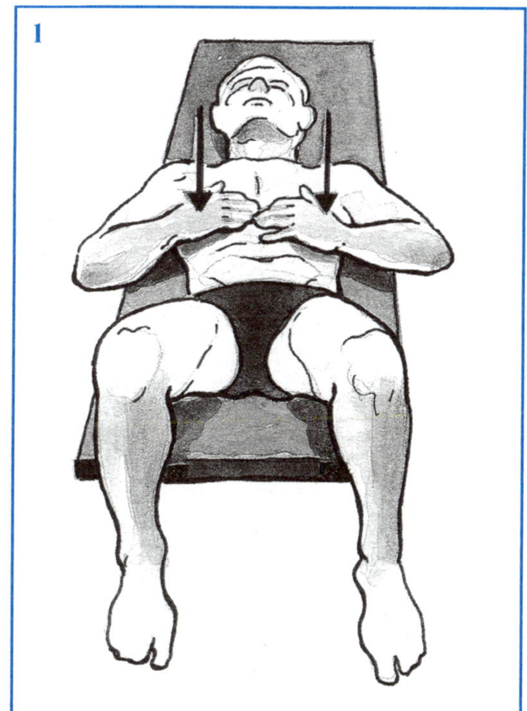

1

Expiration + Expiratory apnea of 3-5 seconds.

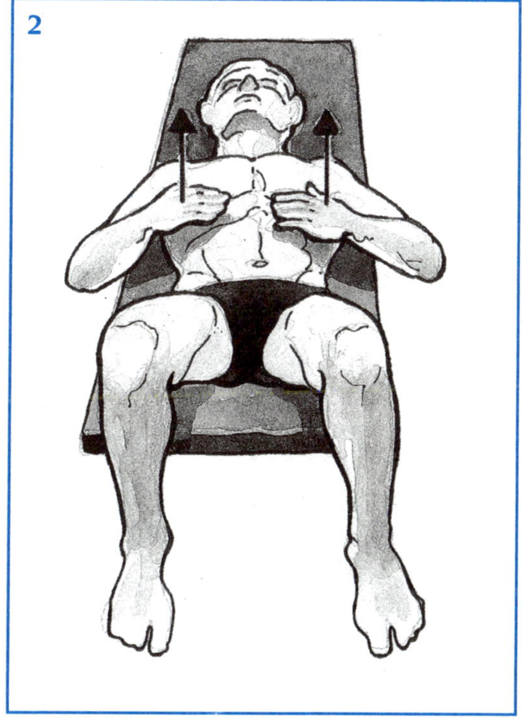

2

Inspiration + Inspiratory apnea of 3-5 seconds.

EXERCISE 5

This exercise is a lateral variation of the preceding exercise, and is performed with the body in lateral repose.

Execution

- Lie on one side, with legs easily bent and head resting on the bottom arm.
- Place the hand of the upper arm on the side of the corresponding ribcage.
- During an expiration, follow the lowering of the side of the ribcage with the hand. Without pressing, gently hold the position reached at the end of the expiration and remain for an expiratory apnea of 3-5 seconds (*Fig. 1*).
- During the successive inspiration through the mouth, hold the ribs in the same position, and only at the end of the inspiration allow them to spring up by quickly removing the hand (*Fig. 2*).
- Repeat 3-4 times on each side.

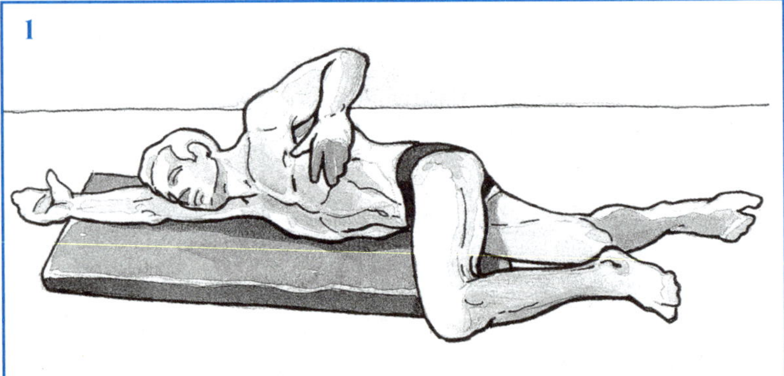

Expiration.

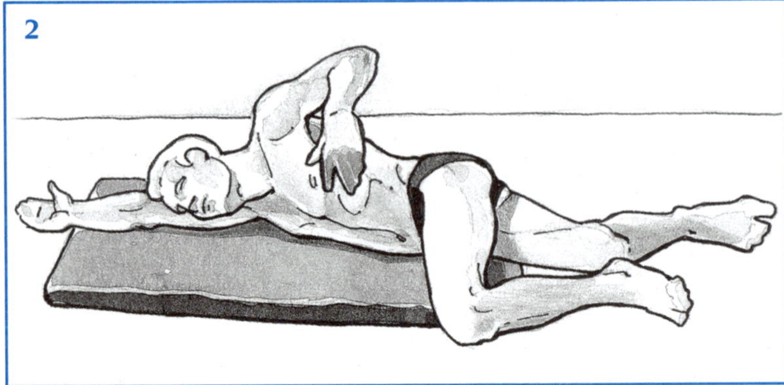

Inspiration.

YOGA BREATHING TECHNIQUES

By developing our breathing through yoga we will be taking care of our entire system of body and mind. Through a regular daily practice movements will find harmony with the breath and actions will no longer be forced, but rather an opportunity to listen to and feel the breath. The awareness of respiration gives it a regularity and fluidity: when this quality becomes stable and is maintained the mind becomes attentive and alert, inactive but awake: prepared.

Yoga is a tool, a system and an approach to life. The awareness that yoga imparts will have a great impact on our behaviour throughout our lives. An intelligent approach to Yoga always takes into account who we are, what we are doing and what we want, and quickly generates the need to apply the concept of 'opposite action'.

Any action that is made in the life of relationships, whether with oneself or with others, is never perfect, no matter how well it is thought out. A close observation of an action during the daily practice of yoga reveals the need to insert movement, gestures and breaths that have the opposite nature to the standard movements, gestures or breaths produced during the day – the counterpoises, the compensations, the re-equilibrating actions.

A freediver who performs prolonged descents underwater requires a breath that has opposite features to an apnea. In this way the principle action is balanced by the opposite action, and can be continued without damage.

EXERCISES TO IMPROVE RESPIRATORY SENSITIVITY

We propose these exercise as the foundation of respiratory technique. The body must remain completely relaxed and conscious of the breath.

What follows is the base exercise in the techniques of breathing. The execution is as follows:

Raise the arms slightly whilst inhaling, then lower them with the exhale, resting for a moment with empty lungs. With every inspiration lift the arms higher, until they are completely raised with the seventh or eighth respiration. Maintain the pause between each respiration. Observe the breath. This condition is most easily achieved by closing the eyes, de-contracting the body and imagining that the air entering and exiting the nose is a fluid that fills our body, thereby changing its colour.

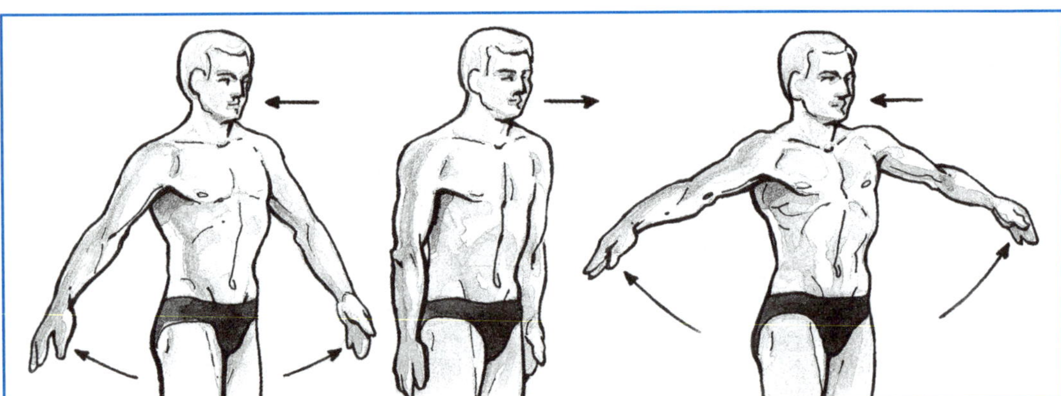

In the following pages we propose two programs of increasing difficulty that are specifically aimed at training respiration. Note that:

- EX indicates expiration
- IN indicates inspiration
- PAUSE is a brief apnea (of about 5 seconds duration) that is inserted between cycles of respiration

We recommend that the inspiration is through the nose and the expiration through the mouth. It is important to put in practice all the considerations we have made regarding the awareness of the breath.

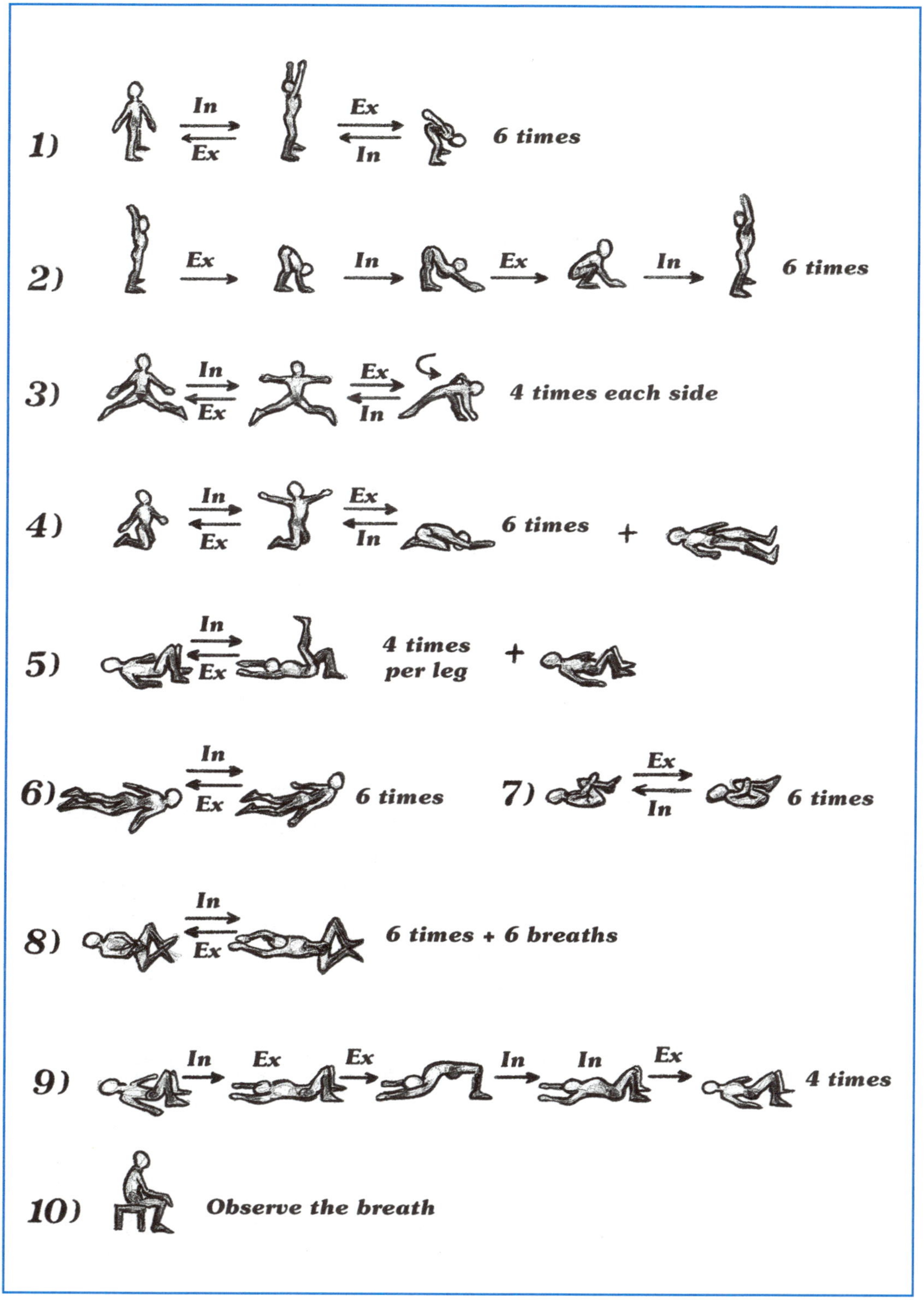

1) In Ex Ex In 6 times
2) Ex In Ex In 6 times
3) In Ex Ex In 4 times each side
4) In Ex Ex In 6 times +
5) In Ex 4 times per leg +
6) In Ex 6 times
7) Ex In 6 times
8) In Ex 6 times + 6 breaths
9) In Ex Ex In In Ex 4 times
10) Observe the breath

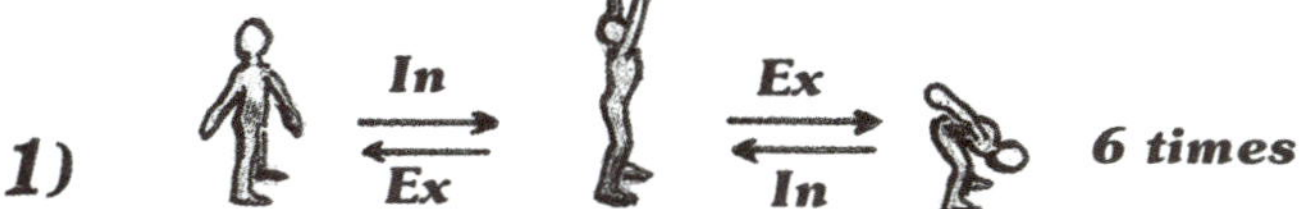

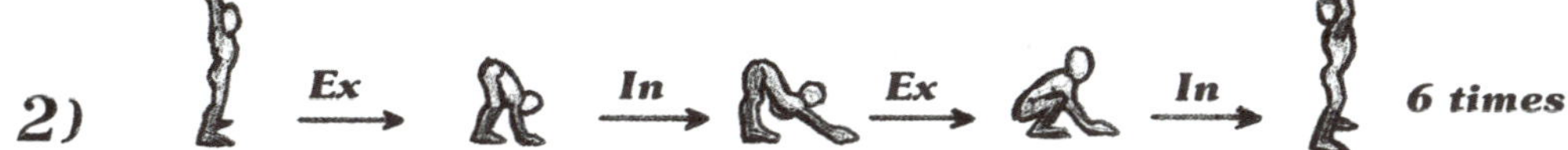

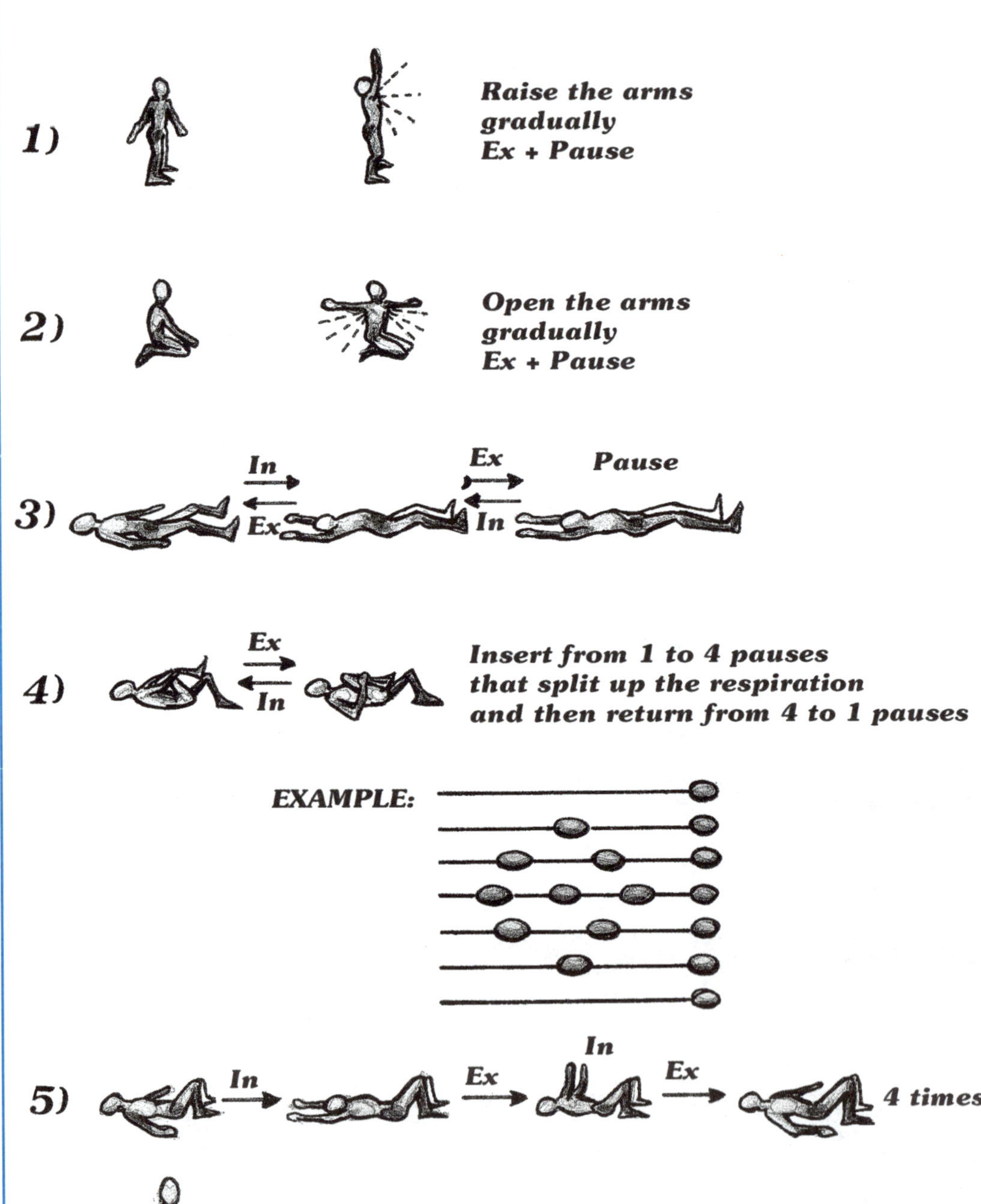
1)
Raise the arms
gradually
Ex + Pause
2)
Open the arms
gradually
Ex + Pause
3)
In
Ex
Ex
In
Pause
4)
Ex
In
Insert from 1 to 4 pauses
that split up the respiration
and then return from 4 to 1 pauses
EXAMPLE:
5)
In
Ex
In
Ex
4 times
6)
Observe the breath,
respiring without retention

PRANAYAMA

Jacques Mayol was responsible for introducing yoga into freediving training; he was convinced that the true path towards good results and a pleasurable experience was the path of internal discovery, of introspection and of the return to the origins. In other words, to a sporting discipline he added the discipline of the mind.

Western culture, which teaches the separation between body and mind, didn't offer Mayol suitable techniques, so inevitably he turned to the East and its ancient cultures, in which spirit and body are treated together, and reunited through particular techniques of meditation, respiration and movement. Yoga is one of these techniques. It is impossible to summarize into a few lines the ideas of a culture as complex as that which forms the origins of yoga. We will therefore limit ourselves to some general information.

Several sacred texts dating back to 2000 BC refer to prana as 'the sum of all energy contained in the universe'. According to yogis life is characterized by its ability to attract prana inside itself, to accumulate prana and transform it to act on both the internal environment and the external world.

For us westerners, the term energy denotes something that is more material and less vast. For the yogis, the same idea is a more subtle form of prana. They insist that prana is present in the air; however it is not oxygen, nor nitrogen nor any other gas. Prana exists in food, in water and in sunlight; but it is neither vitamin, nor heat, nor UV rays. Air, water, nutrition and sunlight transmit the prana on which all animal and vegetable life depends. Prana penetrates through the whole body even to where air does not reach. Prana is our real sustenance, because without it no life is possible. However prana is also a form of electrical energy. It involves tiny negative ions or tiny packets of energy in an almost pure state. Therefore there exists a 'metabolism of electricity'. The organism absorbs atmospheric electricity, utilizes it, and releases it through the skin; the more active this system is in absorbing negative ions and evacuating excess electricity, the more alive and healthy is the organism. The sun, cosmic rays, and the mass of moving and evaporating water are the principle factors of ionisation, and charge the air with prana. Dust, smoke and clouds on the other hand remove prana from the air. By favouring the exchange of prana through our skin and our lungs, which are genuine sponges for this electricity, we will bring vitalising energy to all the cells of the body.

The technique of yoga that is used to absorb and distribute prana through our body takes the name pranayama (prana is energy, ayama means to control or to master). All yoga exercises, not just pranayama exercises, have this precise objective.

To translate 'Pranayama' as 'respiratory exercises' would be limiting, but at the same time it would be presumptuous to think oneself capable of grasping all its implications without having investigated, studied and understood the culture that has generated it.

However we can borrow some techniques and basic concepts and adapt them to our culture, to our habits of life, and naturally to our sportive requirements.
Yogis dedicate much attention to the care of the nose, considered a true pranic antenna. This care must become habit also for the apneist. The widening of the nostrils modifies the shape of the funnel formed by the lower part of the nose, and guides inhaled air towards areas in the nasal cavity where the nerve endings are most numerous, and where the yogis locate our main physiological apparatus for capturing prana.
Therefore it is beneficial for training during respiratory exercises (and the practice of pranayama), to inhale whilst actively widening the nostrils, aiding the perception of the passage of fresh air into the nose. Improvements to this ability will favour concentration on the process of absorption of air and prana.

For those that prefer the 'certainty' of physiological science it may help to understand the localization of the olfactory system in our central nervous system.
Over the course of evolution our brains have enlarged like a city that grows progressively. There is the historical part: the antique city that embraces the oldest quarters, which in our brain is the 'reptile' or 'primitive' part – the paleocortex. Then there is the new districts of the city, or the neocortex. The most sensitive nerve endings that cover the area of the olfactory receptors are in direct contact with the 'old city', or with the part of our brain that is the seat of instinct, inherited from our most distant ancestors. With reflexive mechanisms we touch the 'visceral brain' and therefore organs such as the heart, blood vessels, bladder, intestine and gall bladder.
Through other connections we also influence the pituitary gland and the hypothalamus that both lie in the primitive brain; in this way we stimulate, through the use of hormones, the whole endocrine system – the 'chemical nervous system'.
Given the importance of the vicinity of the olfactory centre to the paleocortex, it is worth knowing the morphology of the nose and in particular the aerodynamic formation of its internal structure.
The current of air entering each nostril is subdivided into three passages. In the olfactory region, situated at the summit of the nasal dome, the flow of air reverses direction and thus comes into contact with the area capable of perceiving odour. In normal respiration only a small part of the inhaled air volume touches this olfactory zone. To increase the efficiency of respiratory exercises it is essential to consciously direct air towards this area.
To help reach this objective we can imagine smelling a rose during slow respiration. There is good reason why many yogis make use of incense, which perfumes the air and thereby stimulates the olfactory centre, favouring the passage of air towards the sensitive part that captures prana.

After this description of the nose – which we have defined as a pranic antenna – we will try to understand the purpose of prana, and especially through what pathways it can be distributed to benefit our organism. According to yogic anatomy our body is traversed by a network of a good 72,000 nadi – in Sanskrit literally 'tubes'. These nadi cross each other several times, descending towards the base of the vertebral column, passing through several strategic 'Chakra' points. In this subtle tubing the yogis distinguish two main conduits: Ida and Pingala. Ida is the left, the lunar nostril, which refreshes. Pingala is the right, the solar nostril, which warms.

To perform pranayama correctly it is important that both nostrils are clear and clean. This is why 'neti', the nasal wash, is practiced before any session of pranayama.

It is easy to see how little attention we give our nostrils, especially if we live in a polluted or dusty environment. An adult subject takes on average 12 breaths per minute, with a volume of ventilation of about 500 cc. This means that our noses filter 6 litres of air in one minute, 360L in an hour, and 8,640L in one day. Copious litres of air, containing immeasurable particles of dust all passing under our very noses!

This is why yogis, who originally lived a long way from our polluted cities, have learnt to clean the nostrils. Jala neti is the nasal wash; its aim is to purify the nostrils before practicing pranayama by cleaning them with simple salted water.

THE NASAL WASH

The instrument that yogis use for the Jala neti is the Lota; a kind of teapot with a conical spout adapted to fit the nostril. The water can be hot, cold or lukewarm. Use one teaspoon of salt per litre of water.

The technique is simple: incline the head backward, insert the spout into the left nostril until it is watertight, and let the water penetrate into the nose. It will then drain by itself out of the other nostril.

Important: during the whole operation the mouth must remain open, whether breathing or not. Remember after the cleansing to dry the nostrils and the nasal chamber.

To do this, hold your hands behind your back and lean forwards. Then exhale powerfully through the nostrils, tilting the head downward. Successively inhale and expel air forcefully through the two nostrils, whilst raising the head. Repeat with the head leaning to the left and then to the right. Continue for several minutes until both nostrils are completely dry.

DIAPHRAGMATIC RESPIRATION

Correct breathing involving the use of the diaphragm is a very difficult action, requiring many months of training. This type of breathing is derived directly from Pranayama, the discipline of yoga that is occupied with the dynamics of breathing.

The diaphragm is the flat plate of muscle between the stomach and lungs and plays a fundamental role in breathing. Our lungs can be visualised as two pyramids: the widest and therefore most capacious and important part is at the bottom. But this is also the part that we seldom use during normal respiration.

The type of respiration that we will be conducting at any given time during the day is most definitely 'thoracic', in so much as it is localised in the upper middle area of the lungs at the height of the ribcage. At the end of a normal expiration, when we presume to have completely emptied the lungs, if we pull the diaphragm upwards we will find that we are able to blow out still more air. This occurs because the diaphragm succeeds in pushing upwards the air that remains in the base of the lungs (where it would normally not be involved in a typical respiration). The action of the diaphragm allows for a greater quantity of air to flow in and out of the lungs.

The diaphragm can be likened to a cylindrical piston moving in the inside of a syringe. If the syringe is positioned needle upwards then when the piston is raised it expels air and when it descends it unloads the syringe of air. When used correctly the diaphragm should create the same effect inside our lungs.

Diaphragmatic respiration is the best method for the preparatory phase of apnea, whether from a point of view of economy (greater quantity for a lesser force) or mentality, as it induces a more favourable relaxation. Each complete diaphragmatic respiration is composed of three phases:

- abdominal (diaphragmatic)
- thoracic
- clavicular

In an inspiration the diaphragm moves first, extending downward towards the stomach. Air entering through the nose will fill the lowest part of the lungs (abdominal phase), then little by little the middle part (thoracic phase), and finally the top of the lungs (clavicular phase). An expiration occurs in the reverse sequence, starting at the top and finishing with the diaphragm, which moves gradually upward towards the bottom of the lungs. All these movements must take place uniformly and homogenously, without provoking the intervention of other muscles.

The duration of the expiration must always be double that of the inspiration. This ratio is fundamental to diaphragmatic breathing. Furthermore it is important that the band of abdominal muscle immediately below the navel is fixed, whether in the phase of inspiration or expiration.

It can be difficult, especially at the start, to conduct a diaphragmatic respiration with continuity and uniformity. The most complicated part is definitely the end of the expiration, when the diaphragm must be brought upward to empty the maximum amount of air out of the lungs. It can be simplified by dividing the expiration into two parts. In the first part, exhale completely from the top and moving downwards, but without moving the diaphragm. At the end of this phase pause the expiration to flex the diaphragm upwards, and then exhale the additional air that has been displaced upwards with this movement.

When beginning it is advisable to concentrate solely on the abdominal phase of the respiration. The first and most important step consists in increasing awareness of the diaphragm, isolating it, relaxing it and moving it in the right direction. The eight exercises that follow are directed at this objective. During these exercises it is important to always be conscious of the respiratory act, visualising the air in movement.

It is difficult to change techniques of respiration and preparation, especially if you have been using hyperventilation for many years. Initially you may have the sensation of starting an apnea without being ready for it, or of feeling short of air immediately upon putting the head under the water. It is important to have faith in the technique and be predisposed mentally; in time we will see that this softer approach gives remarkable benefits. The principal advantage obtained by a correct diaphragmatic respiration is a superior relaxation in the preparatory phase. In the case of a deep freedive there will be the extra advantage of being able to displace a greater quantity of air at a greater depth to compensate the ears and mask.

Another myth must also be discredited: when bodily development is complete it is *not* possible to increase lung capacity neither with aerobic exercise or techniques of respiration. Lung capacity is developable only during the growing years, by practicing aerobic sports like swimming, cycling, cross-country skiing and running. Thereafter it is only possible to improve the efficiency with which we utilise the air we succeed in loading into our lungs. The technique of diaphragmatic respiration is the best tool for this.

EXERCISE 1

Note: *relaxation must be as complete as possible, the breaths executed with the involvement of as few muscles as possible*

The base exercise for training diaphragmatic respiration is executed starting from a supine position with the legs bent. If we do the first session in this position then we can pass to a sitting or standing position, moving our attention to different aspects.

Execution

- Lie supine, with legs bent and feet flat on the ground. Place one hand on the thorax and the other on the upper abdomen.

Inspiration.

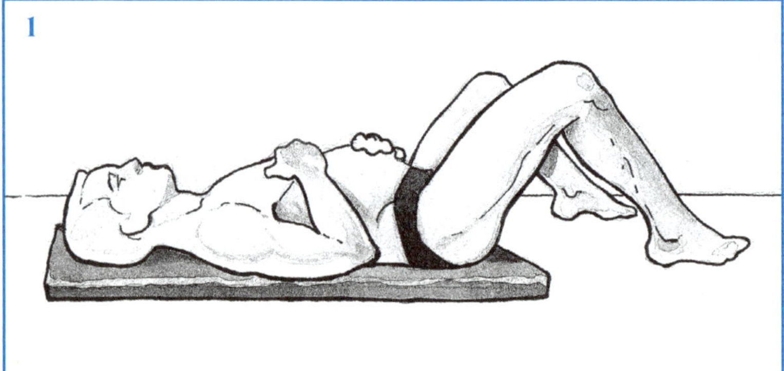

Expiration.

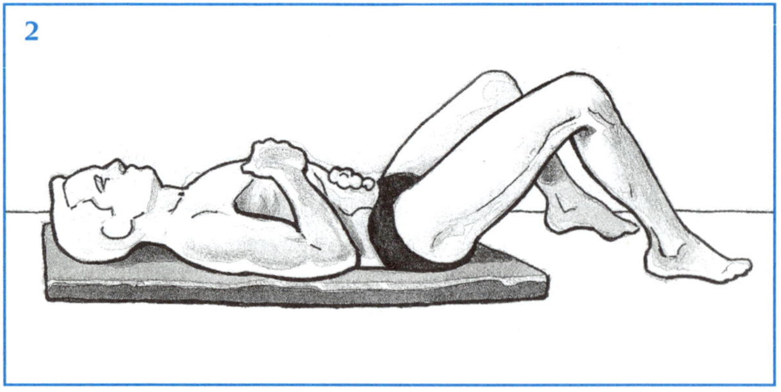

- Execute a long and slow inspiration, using the thorax as little as possible (the hand on the thorax should not move) and using the diaphragm as much as possible to inflate the abdomen (the abdominal hand feels its movement) (*Fig. 1*).
- Hold for an inspiratory apnea of 4-6 seconds.
- Execute a slow and deep expiration, 'deflating' the abdomen, which flexes inwards at the end of the expiration (the lower hand feels its movement) (*Fig. 2*).
- Hold for an expiratory apnea of 4-6 seconds.

EXERCISE 2

Execution

As for the preceding exercise, but in a seated position (gravity makes it more difficult both to raise the diaphragm and to contract the abdominals during expiration).

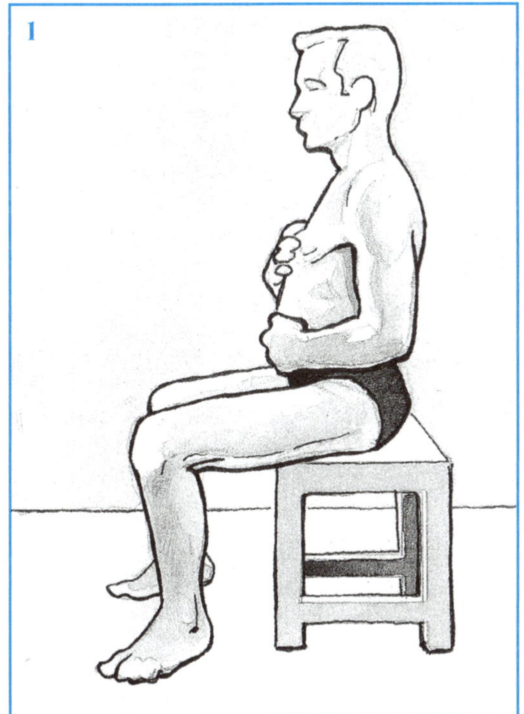

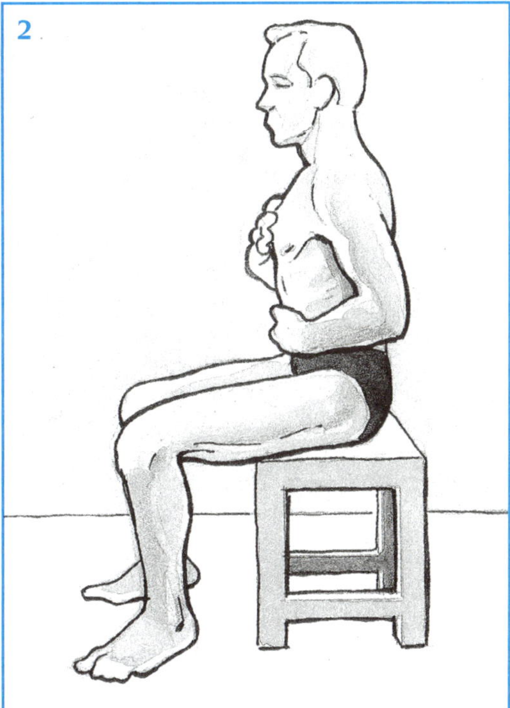

EXERCISE 3

Execution

As for exercise 1, but during the expiratory apnea execute long contractions of the diaphragm and the abdomen, bringing the latter up and then down over the longest time-course possible. Avoid developing muscular tension in the thorax or other parts of the body.

EXERCISE 4

Execution

- Place the hands on the belly just above the pubic bone so that you will be able to feel abdominal movement during the exercise. The movement of the pelvis that is attached to this bone should increase the depth of the respiration and the amplitude of abdominal movement.
- Raise the pelvis as much as possible during the inspiration and lower it during the expiration.
- The inspiration and expiration will always be diaphragmatic and therefore the movement of the pelvis up and down will always be accompanied by the outwards and inwards flexion of the diaphragm.

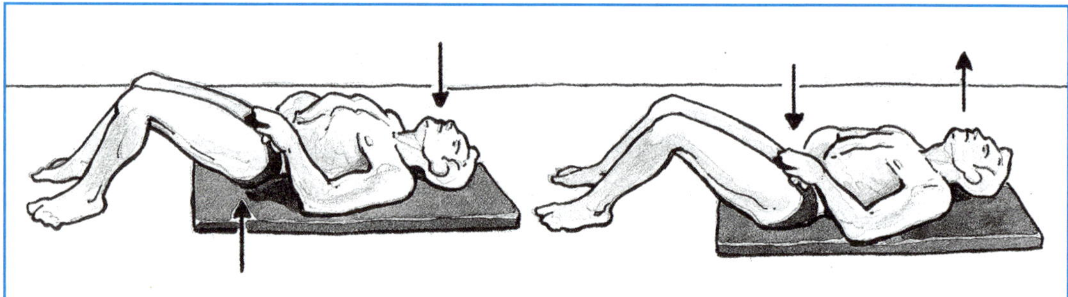

EXERCISE 5

Execution

- Assume a seated position with legs crossed and hands placed on the knees in order to better feel the extension of the vertebral column.

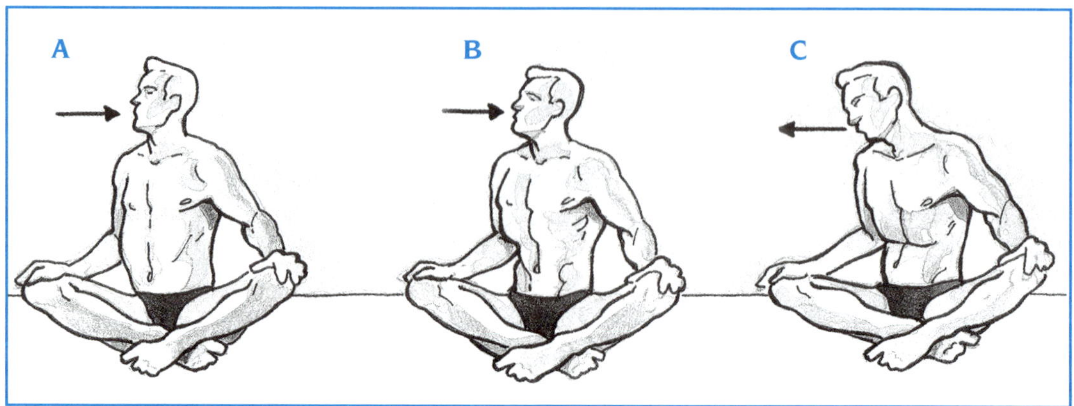

- Start the exercise inhaling slowly through the nose and directing the air into the abdomen, lowering the diaphragm as much as possible (*Fig. A*).
- Without interrupting the breath, try to expand the ribcage, and therefore the upper part of the chest (*Fig. B*).
- The expiration is executed using firstly the air from the thoracic cage and then contracting the abdomen, bringing the diaphragm upward. To facilitate maximum emission of air, you can involve the vertebral column with the respiratory movement, relaxing it to bring the head forwards (*Fig. C*).

EXERCISE 6

Execution

- Lie supine with legs bent and hands holding the knees.
- Execute a long and slow expiration accompanied by a flexion of the thighs, to bring them onto the abdomen and to compress the base of the thorax. The diaphragm is raised, flexed inwards into the thorax (*Fig. 1*).
- At the end of the expiration use the hands on the knees to repeatedly squeeze the thighs into the thorax, enabling an additional expiration.
- Execute a long and deep inspiration, returning the knees to the original position and flexing the diaphragm back outwards (*Fig. 2*).

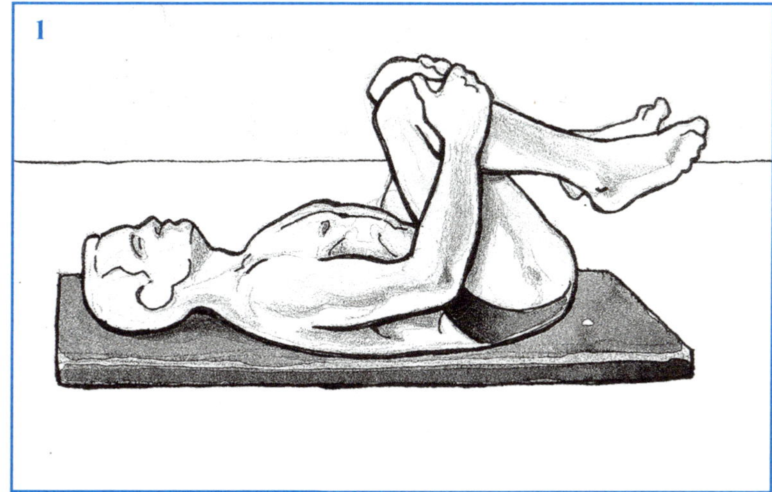
1

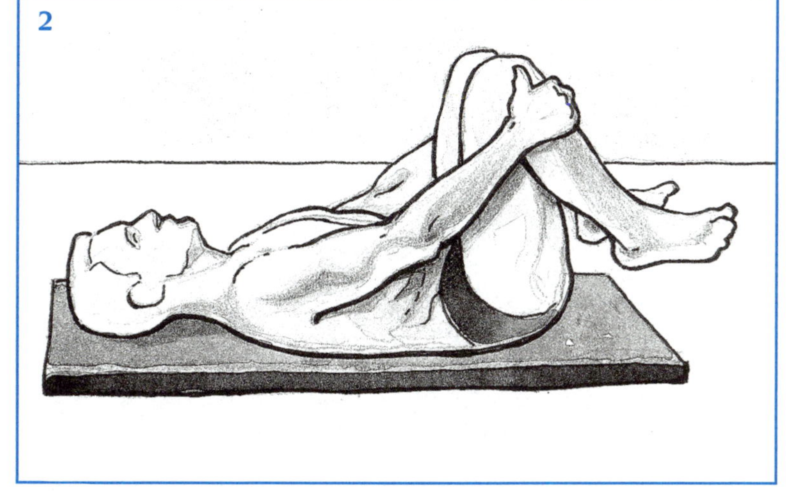
2

EXERCISE 7

Execution

- Kneeling on all fours, execute a long, slow inspiration (with consequent lowering of the diaphragm), hyper-extending the vertebral column and the head (*Fig. 1*)
- Brief apnea of 5-6 seconds.
- Execute a slow expiration, recalling the diaphragm. Exert pressure on the hands to arch the back upwards, and bring the head forwards until the chin makes contact with the sternum (*Fig. 2*).

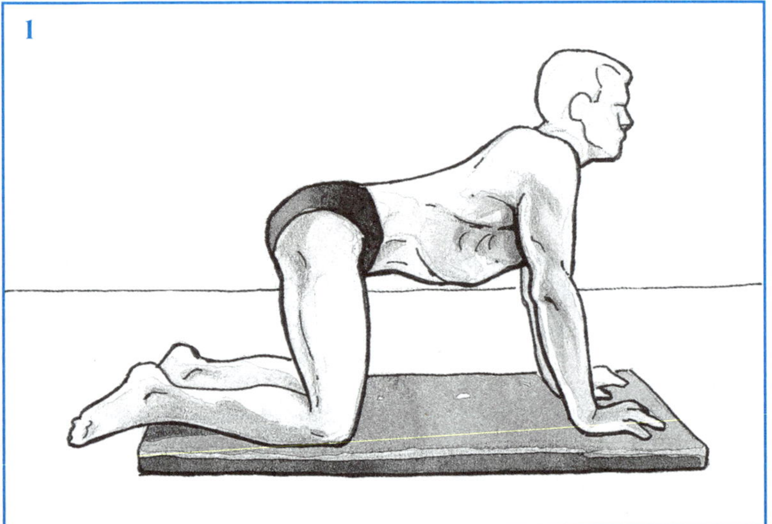

EXERCISE 8

Execution

- Close the right nostril with the right thumb and perform a long and continuous diaphragmatic inspiration through the left nostril (*Fig. 1*).
- When the inspiration is completed, move the same hand across to close the left nostril with the ring finger (*Fig. 2*).
- Perform a long and continuous expiration through the right nostril.
- At the end of the expiration, perform a diaphragmatic inspiration through the same nostril, without moving the fingers. When this inspiration is completed move the hand back across to close the right nostril with the thumb and complete the expiration through the left nostril.
- Begin again from the first step.

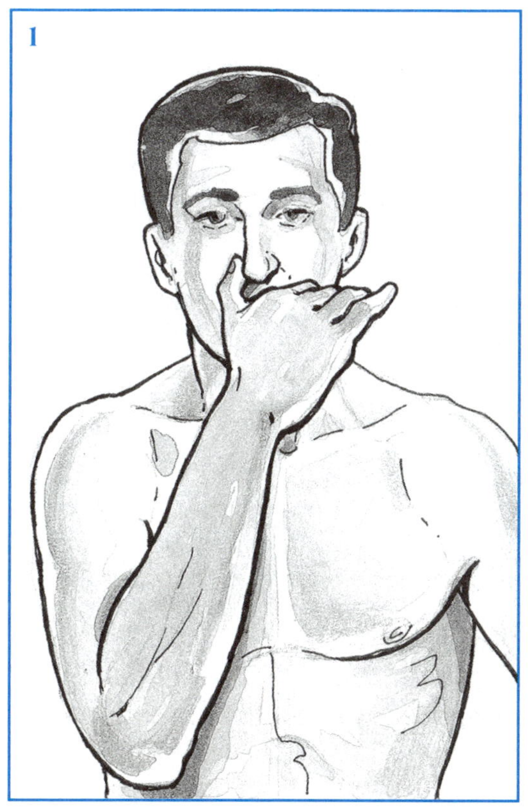
1

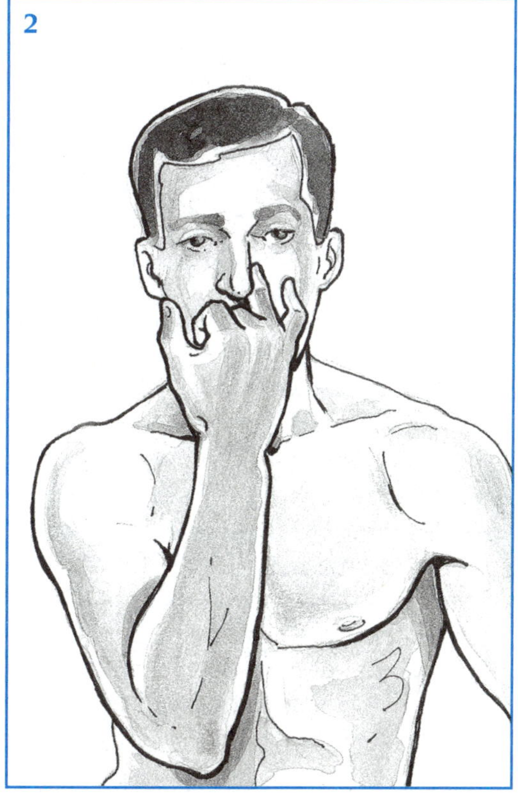
2

The variation to these eight exercises is to insert an apnea after each phase of respiration. First add a pause after the inspiration, then another after the expiration. The expiration must always be twice the duration of the inspiration, which is in turn twice the duration of the apnea. For example with an expiration of 8" the exercise should be organised in the following way:

8" inspiration – 4" apnea – 16" expiration – 4" apnea...

THE CARPA

This term is used to describe a manoeuvre of respiration performed in the moments immediately prior to diving.
It is a technique used by a small number of athletes, who are all very experienced. However there are many top apneists that insist that they can find no benefit in this manoeuvre, and there are even those who claim the manoeuvre causes complications that reduce performance.
The aim of 'carpa' is to fill the lungs as much as possible at the end of the last inspiration. This is achieved by using the mouth like a pump, opening and closing it in sequence to force residual air in the mouth towards the lungs. In this way air becomes compressed to a maximum in the lungs, allowing the athlete to begin the apnea with a greater quantity of air to that supplied by a normal maximum inspiration.
The advantage can be that there is a little more air at one's disposition, for the apnea and for the compensation of eardrums and mask in a deep dive, but in order for it to not produce contraindicative effects it must be executed with maximum caution and without any errors. A rigidity of the musculature of the thorax will create negative effects!
The disadvantages are: loss of physical relaxation pursued in all the preceding phases of respiration; the freedive is initiated some time after the start of the manoeuvre, an interval which in some athletes has been known to last as long as 16 seconds; used in the preparation for a static apnea, the over-tension of the thorax produces increased tension in the thoracic musculature with obvious consequences to relaxation.
This manoeuvre was born in France in the search for a solution to the limit imposed by compensation of the mask. However it remains a difficult manoeuvre, recommended only for expert apneists, and requires expertise and experience.

4.3 TECHNIQUES OF RELAXATION

A running or cycle race, a walk or a swim all produce concrete modifications, especially to blood circulation and respiration, that are easily verifiable by anyone. The benefits are also manifested as relaxing effects at a mental level. In spite of this, these exercises are not always sufficient to relieve the psychological tension from a normal working day.

Natural activity, such as work, social and family life, all influence the metabolism significantly. This effect has been proven by many experiments on subjects in the workplace and in families who have changed both physically and psychologically according to the hours, to people's opinions and to the rhythms of the environment. This will all happen regardless of the participation of the subject: it is sufficient merely to be present physically or mentally.

Thus it is against our wishes that we undergo habits of metabolic adaptation that clash with the autonomy and self-control every one of us would like to display.

On the other hand it is possible – as has been testified by scientific research on subjects in a state of relaxation – to reduce the heart rate, to voluntarily control metabolism, respiration and electrical conduction of the skin, without losing consciousness, but by simply reaching a state of profound physical and mental relaxation.

According to current terminology our behaviour is 'voluntary' when we do that which we want to do, and 'conscious' when we are entirely aware of what we are doing. This power of control is easy when we move a muscle of the locomotor system, but practically impossible when we wish to control the internal organs or glands. **Homeostasis**, the internal equilibrium of the body, is maintained by involuntary and unconscious mechanisms, and reacts automatically to external or internal stimuli according to predetermined models. The upper regions of the brain cannot modify these behaviours, except through indirect means: the stressed director can walk out the door of his office or take his mind off the job, but he is not able to get rid of an indigestion with a similar act of will.

Self-control by relaxation

When a person is scared or anxious some kind of action that reduces the fear or anxiety will tend to present itself, even if in the long run it turns out to be incompatible and damaging to the normal conduct of daily life. One example is given by the smoking of cigarettes to relieve tension, which leads to the many stresses of smoking itself. A neurotic personality is, in critical moments, manifested as a fit of anger, or it can be completely hidden, as in the repression of thoughts or emotions. In both cases relaxation can be a helpful tool of re-education, during which negative connections are overcome and replaced with positive, ameliorative connections.

We receive different physiological, psychological and social benefits from the technique of relaxation that make it a legitimate tool for personal health and therapy. The deep alienation of our body and its intimate processes can be significantly reduced by this technique, affording us the fascinating experience of control over our body's equilibrium.

Hence there is a definite value in mastering techniques of relaxation, which without doubt improve performance in apnea.

RELAXATION

When people discuss methods of relaxation each person will inevitably think that their method is the best, their technique is the most efficient etc. The real problem is not the technique, but the personal mind-set and the methods adopted with respect to one's own psychological profile and psychophysical characteristics. There are many techniques of relaxation: Autogenic Training, Mental Training, Yoga, and Pranayama. Each of these is efficient and has a long tradition.

With the exception of yoga, relaxation exercises are normally performed lying supine with a soft support under the head, or seated in an aerated zone. They should always be conducted on an empty stomach. The sequences of exercises are more mentally engaging than they are physical.

In order to relax we must assume an **attitude of open receptiveness** to our body, whilst maintaining a passive observation of ourselves. The aim is to listen to the 'messages' that the body sends us; we must learn to 'sense' ourselves. The fundamental rule then, is to be open with oneself: we must succeed in immerging into such a state of total introspection that we nullify external stimuli and all mentally distractive comings and goings.

The awareness: here and now

To know exactly what is entailed by relaxation one must be aware of how rarely we are actually *present* in daily events. We normally only witness the tendency of the mind to wander when we are trying to complete a mental task that is dis-

PHYSICAL EFFECTS OF RELAXATION

- Reduction of metabolism
- Reduction in concentration of lactic acid in blood
- Significant decrease in respiratory rhythm
- Increased skin tone
- Reduction of heart rate with an increase in cardiac reserve
- Stabilisation and normalisation of sleep
- Normalisation of arterial blood pressure
- Optimisation of physiological equilibrium

MENTAL EFFECTS OF RELAXATION

- Greater emotional stability
- Stabilisation and optimising of memory
- Intellectual enrichment
- Increased concentration and duration of attention
- Reduction of anxiety and of neurotic or depressive tendencies
- Greater sensitivity in the perception of other people's experiences
- Reinforcement of ego and greater acquaintance, trust and control over oneself
- Greater introspective capacity
- Increased social skills
- Less inhibitions towards self-communication and towards one's own thoughts and sensations
- Easier to communicate openly with others
- More open to physical contact
- Greater creativity and energy in social exchanges.

rupted by this wandering. In reality body and mind are seldom strictly coordinated.

We must therefore be able to calm and control the mind and develop an understanding of its nature and function. The aim is not only to create states of beatitude or to control attitude and behaviour, but most importantly to grasp the nature of reality beyond conditionings. In a certain sense we achieve a 'reawakening' with respect to anything that happens to us. We are made aware of how often we are disconnected from our own experiences, how even the most simple and pleasant of daily activities (eating, talking, driving a car, reading, thinking, making love, making plans, drinking, reminiscing, expressing feelings) pass rapidly, with the mind projected on to the next task. This abstract behaviour, this 'not being present', becomes the habit with which experiences are kept at a distance.

However with practice awareness can become such a concrete action that it breaks the chain of thoughts and habitual opinions, unlocking alternatives to those contained in everyday routine.

The fact that mind and body can be disassociated, that the mind can wander, that we can be unaware of where we are and of what our body or our mind is doing, is a simple matter of experience.

Body and mind can be reunited.

We can develop habits to the extent where we become perfectly coordinated in them. The result is a conscious self-control that is evident also to others: a lively gesture made with complete awareness is easily recognised by the grace and precision that distinguish it. With exercise the connection between the intention and the physical act becomes stronger and stronger, until their separation disappears almost completely and is no longer perceptible. This awareness is revealed in a particular type of unity of body and mind that is completely natural and desirable.

HOW TO RELAX

To reach an effective relaxation we must learn to admit any bad mental habits, any unproductive ways of feeling, acting or reacting, and any commonplaces that we may have. To relax, therefore also means adopting precise psychological strategies to combat personal mental habits.

Techniques of relaxation help to rediscover the balance that is so easily lost in day-to-day life. Thus a good apneist is indeed the result of correct athletic training, but most importantly of a **mental training** that must define the entire athletic preparation.

The technique of **total relaxation** can be learnt in various ways, and with different methods according to the inclinations of the apneist.

Total relaxation

Total relaxation between basic functions and daily activities has the task of adjusting the reactions of the organism to the environment, giving place to that psychological and behavioural adaptation that defines the feeling of well-being in man. This adjustment and internal synthesis involves the processes of learning, memory and creativity, and guarantees continuity in personal development.

One of the main features of total relaxation is a strong relationship between muscular form and mental activity. Muscles learn to maintain posture (during static apnea) or learn a specific movement (finning during constant weight), influenced by psychological conditionings in which the muscle's basic function has been moved to the centre of a psychosomatic dialogue.

Mental control becomes determinate, and in order to increase safety it must effectively relax the body, making actions more efficient and the entire performance more economical. The attainment of this optimal condition is aided, as we have mentioned, by a preparation based on Autogenic training. The aim of total relaxation is therefore to assuage both body and mind with a single solution.

The practice of Autogenic training starts with basic physical relaxation, which consists in paying attention to each part of the body – from head to toe or vice versa – reducing muscle usage to a minimum. Upon completing this bodily relaxation we pass on to calm the emotions with an exercise of mental relaxation that consists in visualising 'a scene from nature'.

This involves immersing oneself into the visualisation of a real or imaginary place, focussing all the senses on each detail of the scene. The fragrances in the air, the smell of the sea or vegetation, seeing the most significant things in the place, feeling the contact of the body on what is around us, listening to the noises, allowing the mind to exist in a positive 'virtual reality' that calms and refreshes.

Control the mind to control the body

Relaxation training, whether dry or in the water, is fundamental for the apneist: it creates stimuli that train the mind to 'listen' to the body as well as to manage it.

During relaxation, whether passive or dynamic, the level of self-consciousness decreases; in doing so it liberates numerous physical automatisms and underlying emotions. With the power of control over the conscious, learning ability is expanded and self-awareness is promoted. Emotions can be modified at any moment by exploiting the appropriate mental associations. It will become more and more easy to reach a state of inner calm in a shorter time. States of mind that are beneficial to apnea can be recalled using simple gestures such as touching the thumbs and forefingers of both hands.

During a profound relaxation it is possible to experience, as in the visualisation of a scene from nature, distinct and intense sensations, whether tactile, olfactory, gustative or auditory. Even impressions of the body can undergo significant modifications; we may experience the sensation of having enormous hands or a swollen head. At times we can have the impression that the legs, arms or head are separate from the body, the torso is missing, or the body itself has become miniscule. At other times all these sensations can be replaced by passing irritations, intermittent pain, headaches or pins and needles in the hands, feet or elsewhere. The throat can tighten, or seem inflamed. Salivation can be so abundant that you are forced to swallow continually. Alternatively the mouth can be dry, the nose leaky, or you can have fits of sneezing or coughing.

At other times you may be plagued by sighs and yawns, or involuntary sucking movements with the lips, or the stomach may gurgle incessantly. In rare cases you may feel nausea, or an urgent need to urinate or defecate. The body may even be subjected to small muscular contractions, or images may be 'seen' such as spirals, whirls, geometric forms, vivid colours and sparkling lights.

The 'strange sensations' of relaxation

At times we may have the impression that the body is inclined, overturned or upside down. It is not particularly unusual to feel restlessness or strong emotions such as violent anger, pleasant sexual sensations, abandoned laughter or crying. This is only a partial list of the many ways that tension can be unloaded. These sensations are present only at the start of the practice of relaxation: in every case they are dispersed spontaneously in the space of a few minutes.

The ability to perform the following techniques and exercises correctly will mean that when they are repeated in water, during an apnea, the mind will be occupied, passing the time. We embark on a mental journey, a 'voyage outside time', that acts as a barrier to deflect all distractive thoughts.

Exercises for the mind

- **Mental repetition of particular words**, for example: 'my body is completely relaxed'. 'I am completely weightless'. Try to match these phrases with a dedicated pursuit of physical relaxation.
- **Passing through all the points of contact between body and floor.** In a supine position start with the bottom of the body (right heel, left heel, calves, gluteus), working your way upward (all fingers of left and right hands, elbows, shoulders, neck). Each time that we concentrate on a point of contact we must feel that our whole body is resting solely on that spot. Only after reaching this sensation do we pass to the next point of contact.
- **Listen to surrounding noises** and imagine a possible scene, starting with the source of the noise. For example, if you hear a child's voice, imagine the child dressed in a certain way, intent on doing certain things, and with a certain expression on its face. If you hear a bird singing, imagine the bird in a tree, between the leaves, the wind that moves the branches, etc.
- **Concentrate on the beating of your heart** at particular points such as the fingertips, the solar plexus (just under the sternum), or the temples. Follow the heartbeat mentally, and imagine being able to slow its rhythm.

- **Concentrate on the rhythm of your breathing** until you can see it from the outside, as you would see it another person. Visualise the thorax moving up and down etc.
- **Concentrate on your forehead** and try to feel it as being fresh and light, as if it has been disconnected from the warm and heavy mass of the rest of the body. The sensation of freshness should be experienced as a state of calm and inner well-being.
- **Follow the flow of air with your mind**, thinking of it as a fluid that fills the body (changing its colour), then empties completely (returning the body to its initial colour).
- **Imagine harmonious and rhythmic movement.** For example the circular and concentric waves that are formed in a pool after a pebble is dropped into the water. Associate this with your own breathing.

4.4 MENTAL TRAINING AND APNEA

By **Mental Training** we mean any methodology that is capable of organising thoughts effectively and reaching individual objectives. It should train the mind to maintain concentration, optimise memory and to visualise: in short to perform all those activities that are typical of a clear and conscious mental organisation. There follows two basic techniques:

AUTOGENIC TRAINING

Autogenic training refers to the relaxation of mental concentration that allows modification of physical and mental conditions. The first approach to techniques of relaxation generally involves an instructor, who guides the apneist with their voice through a de-tensioning process. The apneist follows the instructions, preoccupying themselves with maintaining concentration and observing the effects.

True Autogenic Training will start later. When alone, the apneist will choose a time to dedicate to Autogenic Training by 'auto-instruction', choosing a programme with respect to psychosomatic characteristics and available time. Utilising specific exercises, the apneist may obtain spontaneous improvements of muscular tone, vascular function, cardiovascular activity, neuro-vegetative balance and level of consciousness.

Autogenic Training and Meditation, Yoga and Pranayama, Mental Training and Visualisation are all the bread and butter of top-level apneists: methodologies with a long tradition and proven value.

In this manual we have integrated the different techniques of relaxation with the aim of initiating the reader, and providing the stimulation that will enable further exploration. The first step is to recognize and confront any false and limiting opinions about yourself, such as negative thoughts or instabilities that might unfavourably influence learning.

Some of the most frequent are:

- I cannot control my body
- I feel helpless when faced with something I cannot control
- I will never be able to control my fear or anxiety
- I am scared of being punished or punishing myself if I make a mistake
- I believe I am 'omnipotent', 'perfect', and 'always right'
- I feel weak, and lethargic
- I am subject to psychosomatic syndromes
- I am not unable to turn ideas into actions
- I don't like myself
- I don't have the potential

Only through awareness can we use our potential of self-improvement to remove these disturbing thoughts that limit our existence. Only through inner discipline will we be able to increase our capacity. By increasing self-esteem and confidence we can make the most of favourable external factors. We must therefore learn to substitute negative attitudes or thoughts with positive and creative processes.

In our daily lives we each have many different levels of consciousness that are manifested through all sorts of codes of behaviour, whether social, cultural, emotive or perceptive. These states of consciousness that concern sleep, dreams and waking life, also concern the ability to influence bodily, mental, emotional, instinctual or creative consciousnesses in every one of us.

Through a program of daily relaxation we will first learn to deal with ourselves and with the world of water in a way that greatly enriches our quality of life. The brain has evolved to transform us and to learn, by contact with ever increasing stimuli, new potentials of action and reaction. Mental Training must follow several procedures that verify and make use of the different levels of awareness.

RELAXATION WITH COLOURS: KATABASIS

Level one: red

After having assumed the ideal position for relaxation – either lying supine or sitting comfortably in a chair – close the eyes and prepare to enter a state of **physical relaxation** visualising the colour **red.**

To relax physically, begin with the head and move down the body, identifying (without lingering too long) the sensations and images connected to each specific area. Use phrases and words that facilitate the process of de-tensioning, such as "I am relaxed... I feel light... my body is loose...' The parts of the body to focus on are the scalp, forehead, nape of the neck, eyes, jaw, face and the tongue (which is a very important organ). Next proceed along the shoulders, the arms, the back, thorax, abdomen, internal organs, pelvis, legs and feet.

In this way we can locate any areas of tension, flux, and internal movements in the body. This occurs by listening attentively to the body parts, to the signals from the peripheral nervous system, and dispersing small and large tensions with a simple mental command, phrase or sound. This phase is the most practical and fundamental of the whole process.

Level two: orange

Orange is the level of **emotional relaxation**, which is achieved by concentrating on positive emotions such as joy, happiness, content, receptiveness, and all other constructive feelings.

This second level has the aim of evoking a contented state of mind and a positive emotional balance. Personal equilibrium is consolidated, allowing for control over mood shifts. This equilibrium can be felt tangibly and easily maintained.

Level three: yellow

We then pass to visualising the colour **yellow**, or a yellow-coloured object. Yellow is the colour of **mental relaxation** and is engaged by bringing into focus or remembering serene and relaxing images from nature. This orientation of the mind towards natural images aims to dissociate the mind from the problems and preoccupations of daily life, leaving any negative thoughts or worries outside of the place in which we are relaxing.

This third level of relaxation permits the **slowing of thoughts**, with an expansion of imagination and visualisation. We all know how difficult it is to concentrate the attention on creative or associative higher mental function for a reasonable period of time. In fact subjective time, which refers to thoughts and normal mental courses, is generally connected to the past (resolved or unresolved plans) and the future (attempts to form plans). Too often these mental strategies serve only to manage anxiety and to give the ego maximum scope of action and control. Instead, the subjective time that we require is tied to the present time of here and now, to transformation and the power of destiny.

Level four: green

From yellow, having relaxed mind, body and emotion we then pass to **green.**

If we have achieved optimum relaxation and de-tension of the body, feelings and mind then it is possible to feel at peace with the world, as if you were on the roof of a house, observing in total tranquillity what is happening inside. This phase is especially useful when daily problems are experienced with too much involvement.

The fourth level then is the plane of **inner peace**, or mental calm, and the absence of thoughts, or at least those that entice and draw us into the plane of stress and pressure. It is a state of mental emptiness, the capacity to live 'here and now' in our space and time. In the 'here and now' there are no problems, there exists only the body, that moves and pulsates, living according to a condition of pleasurable abandonment. There are no expectations or involvements of the rational ego.

When we relax we often experience thoughts, emotions or physical states that sneak in the back door to disturb us. We must learn to relax ourselves with a certain method, where such thoughts, worries and fears are left 'outside', creating a mental vacuum within. This emptiness is not passive; it is simply the restraint of the ego that wants attention as well as control over our entire vital system.

Instead the ego should be seen as a psychological tool that needs to evolve and have an ever-improved dialogue with the more developed psychological structures – the self and its foundations. The mental vacuum is therefore understood as an opening of sensory channels and is achieved through the stimulations of energy vibrations connected to the development of our 'sensitivity'.

Level five: blue

From the colour green we then pass to **blue**, and we move in a natural progression to concentrate on more genuine feelings and affections that we either experience or would like to experience. The aim is to experience the most potent emotion: **love**.

The sensitivity is thus extended to the fifth plane of existential levels, that of love. This is the plane that allows us to involve ourselves entirely in what we are doing. Our body is experienced with a participation; an extraordinary expansion that translates into an emotional and psychological fluidity of energy where the elements in which we are immersed become substance for the nutrition of the soul.

Level six: indigo

From blue we pass to visualise the colour **indigo**. In doing so we **reflect** on our personal and collective aspirations, which are manifested as the ultimate purpose of our deepest ego or inner self.

The sixth level is connected to the objective, and therefore also the capacity, of comprehending reality. The capacity of being beyond past and future to perceive in the here and now a profound contact with the nature, rhythm and movement of things.

Level seven: violet

We complete the scaling of the existential levels by passing to the colour **violet**, where we stabilise a contact with our most intimate reality, that which we call the **spiritual dimension**.

Reaching the highest level of the existential plane we will have obtained a profound state of relaxation in which the conscious becomes 'subjugated' and calmed, while the soft and quiet voice that arises from the unconscious is able to express itself in sensations and images.

The seventh level proves the possibility of living by the highest experiences, transpersonal, a superior dimension to that which we inhabit, where our potentiality unfurls to perceive the pulsating vitality of the personal universe.

Repeating this technique systematically we will quickly become able to concentrate with length on the waves of colour (Katabasis). Once the sequence of colours is learnt it should be repeated, allowing each of the colours, sensations, images and different mental connections to take control. With every successive repetition of the exercise these factors will become more evident, individual and more internal.

UNDERWATER RELAXATION

CHAPTER 5

The scuba diver dives to look around. The freediver dives to look inside.
- Umberto Pelizzari

After having studied the dry preparation for apnea, both on the mental plane – with techniques of relaxation and autogenic training – and on the physical plane – with respiratory techniques – we now examine how these techniques are applied during apnea. We will then look at the three main disciplines: static apnea, dynamic apnea and freediving.

It is important to take your time. The alternative techniques of respiration and relaxation that we have proposed will produce results; they may come more slowly, but they will come.

To enjoy the experience of apnea one must forget the tension provoked by the idea of having to do something at all costs. It is important to utilize all the sensory channels: visual (visualisation), auditory (listening to noises, the internal voice) and kinaesthetic (points of contact with the bottom, contact with the water). Apnea is 'a journey outside time', and this requires the employment of significant concentration to detach from the dimension of time that characterises our existence.

To be successful we must 'make an effort to not make an effort'.

For inexperienced apneists it will be essential to create mental handholds that

THE COCONUT, CORAL AND THE SEA: SMALL STORY, ALMOST ZEN

Brisby, the old Maldivian fisherman: "I saw you in the sea today. My compliments", he says, in uncertain English. "I really like how you move underwater. I am only an old fisherman, but allow me to give you a piece of advice. Remember that you can go underwater in two ways".

So saying, he takes out a small piece of coral and throws it into the sea; then from a coconut he pours the sweet, white liquid: "Look", he continues, "coral and coconut milk are now together in the water. But the coral is still coral, while the coconut milk is now sea: when you move underwater you must not be like the coral, but like the coconut. When you dive you must not go against the sea; it should not be you, your body, your skin and the sea, but each part of your body must become at one with the water".

HOW TO PREPARE FOR A STATIC APNEA

The answer to this question should by now be obvious – breathe and relax! The problem remains how, for how long, and up until what point?
Body position in the water is critical, and there are different solutions that may depend on the topography of the pool where the attempt is being made: deep/shallow with a border that is level to the water or above it. The vertical body position is usually the most suitable, considering the natural erect posture in which we spend most of our time. However some apneists prefer being horizontal and prone, breathing with the snorkel, or supine and extended, with the face above water and the feet on the edge of the pool. In any case the aim is to unload all muscular tension. Remaining standing on the feet means using the muscles of the lower limbs, and therefore not being able to relax the legs.
The important point is to assume a relaxed position that exploits the flotation force of the water and the structure of the pool. For example if the edge of the pool is level with the water then it allows support of the shoulders. This takes the weight off the spinal column and allows for an expansion of the thorax that favours respiration. In short adopt the strategy that best suits the context of the breath hold.
Breathe using the techniques described in chapter 3; by concentrating on the air flowing inwards and outwards the mind will also become relaxed. Continue with a screening of the body, from head to toe or vice versa, ensuring that any tensions accumulated during the day are released. When you feel ready, begin the apnea. The apnea starts with the final breath, which, contrary to what one might imagine, needn't fill the lungs entirely. In general the lungs take on about 80% of their maximum capacity, and no more. This avoids acquiring muscular tension in the thorax. The final movement before starting is to take position in the water. This doesn't require actually making a dive. The correct action is no more than relaxing into the water, allowing it to support the body.

can bring us quickly into an ideal psychophysical state. For example it is as important to share and celebrate with comrades the joy of achieving a new personal best as it is to experience the emotions intensely for oneself and memorise the event; in future the memory will be an excellent point of reference for the preparation of new performances. This will contribute to increase self-esteem and to motivate the apneist for further progress.

5.1 STATIC APNEA

The fundamental condition for this discipline is that the position assumed is one of total relaxation, irrespective of whether you find yourself floating on the surface or sinking to the bottom of the pool.

We often believe ourselves to be relaxed when in fact several bands of muscles may still be contracted. Because of this we must check off each body part using a special technique that we will describe in detail in this section.

Ignoring the time

Static apnea is definitely the most difficult discipline from a psychological point of view.

Ours will be a battle against time, or more precisely against our perception of time.

A very simple example: suppose we breathe normally and at the same time fix our attention on the second hand of a clock. In this condition five minutes is an interminable length of time. Imagine the same thing without breathing! If instead we read a book, listen to good music or have an interesting conversation with a friend, the same amount of time (five minutes) passes very quickly.

This is the mental condition that we must reproduce underwater in apnea. When we hold our breath we must try to free the mind from any disturbances such as thoughts about time; our mind must be occupied in some way, in an attempt to 'deceive' time. The exercises that were trained on dry ground supply the 'motive': the subject with which we keep our mind occupied.

STOPWATCH: PROS AND CONS

The use of a stopwatch in static apnea has given rise to discussion and controversy. Apnea is something extremely personal, "a look inside oneself"; therefore it is necessary to understand for yourself whether the presence of a timing device can help psychologically. Some people are limited by the use of a watch, since the passing of time slows and becomes more urgent. What we can do instead is flow with it, moving our attention elsewhere.

Other apneists use the stopwatch as a kind of psychological support to the act, a sort of 'guardian angel' over performance. If you lose your concentration in the relaxation phase, the first question that is instinctively asked will be: "How much time has passed?" Without a watch it would be impossible to supply an answer and thereby return to the condition of relaxation that had been present until that moment. The mind is now occupied with the time factor and cannot be directed back to an effective relaxation.

Instead, by opening the eyes, and with a minimum movement of the wrist, you can take a glance at the watch. In this way the question can be answered and the lost concentration recovered.

Techniques of underwater relaxation

The principal aim of all these exercises is to keep the mind occupied, avoiding thoughts of the time that passes so slowly. Only by deceiving time with the mind can we obtain substantial static apneas.

Remember that it is important to surface upon feeling the need to breathe: apnea should not be a sacrifice, but rather a sensation of pleasure and well-being.

1. Points of contact

Of the different techniques of concentration and relaxation underwater the most easily applied is that of *points of contact*.

Execution

- Kneeling on the bottom of the pool, with the head supported on the wall, identify the points of contact (the forehead, knees, toes and if necessary the fingers).
- Isolate a single point, losing sensitivity to all the others.
- Once this sensation is achieved pass to another point of contact.
- Repeat the exercise for all the points of contact.

With practice you should achieve a unique sensation in which the body has sensitivity in a single spot; the body senses the external world through that point only, and all the other points of contact will vanish. It will seem as if the body rests only on that point and the rest of its weight is lifted and floating in an oblique position in the middle of the water.

If we use 30" to find the desired sensation in one point of contact, then the entire exercise will take about 3'. The mind of the apneist will be completely occupied with the pursuit of total concentration on oneself and time will fly past.

2. Screening each part of the body

Another effective technique consists in *reviewing each body part*, from toe to head, to verify that each muscle is in a state of deep relaxation; by listening to and inspecting each muscle group with the mind you can obtain a profound lowering of muscular activity, a state of psychophysical de-tensioning and a complete well-being.

Execution

- In static apnea, visualise each single part of the body and analyse its state of relaxation. Starting from the bottom with the toes, feet, heels, calves, knees, thighs, gluteus, the back, ab-

dominals, chest, shoulders, arms all the way to the fingers, the neck, forehead, eyelids, cheeks, jaw, lips, teeth and tongue.
- Repeat mental phrases, such as: "I am relaxed", "my body is loose".
- Once the perfect state of relaxation is reached it can be stabilised by the visualisation of a change of colour. The colour red, already used in Katabasis (see *Chapter 4*), will be very helpful.

The apneist will thus 'see' the colour red in each part of the body from toe to head as it is progressively relaxed by the passing of thoughts and the force of mind. If you feel that the body part is tense or not completely relaxed, then you must concentrate on that specific zone, seeking to relax it totally. Once relaxed we recommence the 'mental journey of the body' to search for other points of tension nesting between the muscle fibres.

A point of critical importance is the tongue, which is like an on-off switch for the rest of the body. The tongue must be relaxed and fall completely downward and backward, depending on the position of relaxation. **If the tongue is not relaxed then neither is the rest of the body.**

3. Relax with sounds and noises

Even *sounds and noises* can be utilised for relaxation. At times a potentially disruptive noise can be transformed into a genuine stimulus of concentration. We need only to visualize the images that represent the sources of the noise.

Execution
- Identify and isolate a sound or noise.
- Try to envisage the origin of the noise that we are hearing from underwater (for example: isolate the voice of a child and visualise the face; imagine the child's costume, hair colour, facial expression and so forth).

In this creative attempt the mind will have been occupied on something other than thoughts of time, which will therefore pass much more rapidly. This technique can transform an annoying situation into an actual aid for the apneist. When we are in the pool, practicing static apnea on the bottom, the people swimming above us can be bothersome. However we can concentrate on the noises of their arms and legs swimming, and from this visualise the movements, styles, body shapes and colours of swimming costumes.

4. Concentration on the heartbeat

Execution

- Identify and listen to the heartbeat in the temples, fingertips or at the base of the sternum.
- Slowly move the attention from one point to another in succession.
- The transfer from one point to another should happen very gradually, only after the pulse has completely pervaded this part of the body.
- Control the pulse with the mind, accompanying it with a gradual reduction of its frequency, due to relaxation.
- Rhythmic repetition of words and phrases can be used for this exercise too.

5. Relive pleasurable moments

This exercise activates the memory, or the imagination of a situation that one would like to live, i.e. to dream, and to let oneself wander through a particular fantasy. This is an excellent exercise for concentration of the mind and to deceive time with pleasure.

6. Numbers

It can also be helpful to *repeat numbers*, in a particular rhythm. It does not have to correspond to the number of seconds elapsed underwater, but can rather follow a casual sequence on which the mind is concentrated.

7. Landscapes

Imagine finding yourself in a world of total peace and tranquillity: a mountain pass, hill country, an enormous green meadow, in drifts of white snow, in the dunes of a desert, on a beach where the waves are breaking… Immerse yourself in the environment, sensing its colours and smells as if they were nearby.

All these exercises of relaxation in water are applicable to the beginning and middle phases of an apnea. Towards the end, when the urge to breath is most compelling, it is practically impossible to utilise these techniques. In this phase it can be much more advantageous to 'play'.

The following exercises are helpful in the finishing seconds of an apnea:

- rub the hands together slowly

- touch the fingertips together, one by one
- observe a fixed point in the pool
- move the fingers and toes in unison
- follow with the eyes the movement of a particle suspended in the water

5.2 DYNAMIC APNEA

For the preparation of a dynamic apnea, do not undervalue the period prior to immersion: relaxation and respiration are still of fundamental importance, even if underwater finning involves physical force. Dynamic apnea is a less difficult trial than static apnea from a mental point of view as it presumes a point of arrival. Static is a struggle against time, whereas in dynamic the meters pass while the athlete is engaged with underwater movement.

With optimisation of finning style, body position and buoyancy, it will be easier to dedicate the mind to planning the dynamic apnea itself. The most delicate phase is obviously the final stretch of the dynamic apnea, where the craving to breath and the onset of contractions instinctively bring a sudden increase of velocity in an attempt to arrive as soon as possible at the finish.

Controlling speed

This situation must be categorically avoided, as it is both counterproductive to performance and dangerous, since it increases the risk of blackout. In the final stages of a dynamic apnea the increase of velocity brings a loss of control of the situation: the athlete is no longer in command of rhythm, position or technique. The most urgent impulse is to reach the end of the performance and breath as soon as possible; there is a single thought in the apneist's brain: to arrive. In this way it is easy to lose touch with the bodily signals that give warnings of safety limits. Remember that the keystone of all the different apnea disciplines is **self-control**.

In the final part of a dynamic apnea we must seek to be in total control: the instant that the mechanism that would cause us to speed up is activated it is necessary to intervene mentally, imposing a **reduction in the rhythm of finning**, a general relaxation, and a psychological lucidity that allows control over the entire action. Constant velocity should be enforced even more strictly than in the preceding stages. Only by imposing this reduction in rhythm can we control every movement of the body.

A helpful exercise that allows us to distinguish whether the finishing stage of the attempt was 'clean' consists in carrying out a simple action at the exit of each and every repetition or attempt. Bringing the hand to the head or checking the time of the apnea are examples of simple but effective actions that allow verification of the lucidity of the exit. If the ultimate stage of the dynamic apnea is an ordeal then during the first breath afterwards the apneist will easily forget to repeat this conventional action, which demonstrates the incomplete mental control of the freediver.

5.3 FREEDIVING

Just as for the other disciplines, performance during freediving will also depend directly on surface preparation before the dive.

The technique of pre-dive respiration varies slightly. In contrast to dynamic and static apnea in a pool, before a freedive respiration is conducted through a snorkel, with the nose closed off inside the mask. Thus the apneist is constrained to inhaling and exhaling through the mouth. Despite this, **the rhythm must be slow and homogenous** with a time of expiration greater than that of inspiration.

The 'virtual descent'

On the surface, just before the dive, **visualise the entire freedive**: duck-diving, descending meter-by-meter, compensating, feeling the position of the body, turning at the bottom and the ascent. To this end the techniques of visualisation that are learnt with mental training will be invaluable. After completing this 'virtual descent' constructed of images, sensations and noises, and after having de-contracted the body, the athlete will be focussed and ready to start the attempt.

Then comes the ultimate breath, the duck-dive, the intense finning of the first several meters, and the fall towards the bottom. During the descent, and especially in the phase of freefall, the apneist must remain completely relaxed and self-aware in each instant. He or she must verify that there are no contracted muscles or other tensions.

It can often happen that during the descent we start grinding our teeth together, with strong contractions of the jaws – this must be avoided. The eyes stay closed, in the pursuit of maximum relaxation, and open only every 4-5 meters to verify that our direction of fall is still parallel to the down-line.

Reaching the bottom, we reverse direction with a quick and agile tumble turn. Here begins the hardest phase, the ascent. We look neither upwards or downwards, but only at the rope in front.

The ascent

We relax, and while we rise with vigorous finning we repeat in our minds the stimulatory words: "I am loose, I am relaxed. I am flying towards the surface. The distance between me and the air is less with every stroke..." It can be helpful to close the eyes in the ascent also, so as to 'melt away' the distance.

In terms of mental effort the last part of the ascent is the most demanding. In this stage oxygen reserves are beginning to run out. We must be able to restrain instinct with reason.

At about 15 meters from the surface, it is quite normal to experience **diaphragmatic contractions**. The most common error is to look towards the surface. Doing so brings the sensation of still being very far away, and there will be an overwhelming urge to speed up the ascent. The idea of reaching a place where we can breathe becomes the priority, but in doing so the little remaining oxygen is burnt uselessly, and this error at the end of a strenuous apnea can cost a blackout.

We must cover the final meters whilst still mentally controlling the rhythm of finning and the width of the stroke, maintaining good muscular relaxation and taking advantage of the positive buoyancy to draw us to the surface. A positive attitude will help to overwhelm the instincts that could lead to the loss of control.

Mental control of the finning

Close the eyes, and control the finning, maintaining its width and fluidity. After three or four fin-strokes say to yourself: "I am already half way there, a little more and then I will be able to breath".

The secret of overcoming suffering and fatigue is to think positively; we convince ourselves of the simplicity of what we are doing. And again: "one more fin-stroke and I will be positively buoyant... the worst is behind me".

Part three

BECOMING AN APNEIST

THE FINSTROKE

CHAPTER 6

For someone approaching apnea for the first time it is most important to first master swimming across the surface, breathing and finning with the appropriate equipment.

Formulating and improving finning technique on the surface, breathing well through the snorkel, and making a correct duck-dive to submerge in the most efficient manner should all be prime objectives for the beginner apneist. The pool constitutes the ideal environment to take the first steps in this experience: propelling oneself forwards with a pair of fins is simple, but correct finning is a complex technical action that requires coordination.

Therefore in this chapter we will describe the different modes of **finning; that it is to say swimming – on the surface and at depth – whilst wearing a pair of fins**.

The recognition and understanding of one's own errors is fundamental to improvements in performance. At the end of the chapter we have listed the most common errors, subdivided into three groups: **errors of the lower limbs, of body position and of inadequate fins**. This analysis of the errors, and their comparison with personal ways of interpreting the exercises will help the reader both to understand better what is 'ideal finning', and most importantly to recognise the effects of incorrect biomechanical actions.

6.1 BIOMECHANICAL ANALYSIS OF FINNING

Finning is the diver's principle means of locomotion in the liquid element.

Finning style differs from person to person depending on many factors: anatomical dimensions (height, relation between various body segments, distribution of mass and its development, flexibility); functional qualities (muscular tone, posture); type of fins (length, rigidity); desired effect (greater velocity, less disturbance of the water for spearfishing).

The corollary of this is that **there does not exist a standard finstroke**, valid for all individuals and possible situations. That said, for ease of explanation we have tried to define a 'model' finstroke, which will be referenced in the analysis of dynamic apnea and the correction of possible errors.

In the interests of understanding better the biomechanics of finning, during scientific research a video was made of an athlete swimming with fins. The video was then slowed down so as to distinguish which parts of the body contribute to the movement, and in what way. Reference signals were positioned at the hip, knee, ankle, foot and fin, and a timekeeper on the side of the pool recorded lap times.

The footage revealed the relative angles that describe the kinematics of finning and the behaviour of the fin itself in the sagittal plane, as well as the frontal and transverse planes (*see boxes on pages 152-153*). In particular for each of the two lower limbs there is a distinction between a phase of 'down-kick' (*Fig. 1*) termed the **advance** and a phase of 'up-kick' (*Fig. 3*) termed the **return** (*Fig. 4*).

The phase of advance involves:

- the plantar flexion of the foot
- the extension of the leg
- the flexion of the thigh
- the clockwise rotation of the pelvis

The phase of return involves:

- the dorsal flexion of the foot
- the flexion of the leg
- the extension of the thigh
- the anticlockwise rotation of the pelvis

1

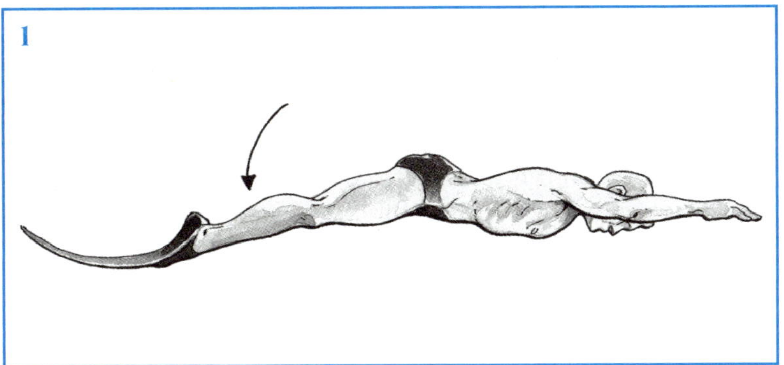

2

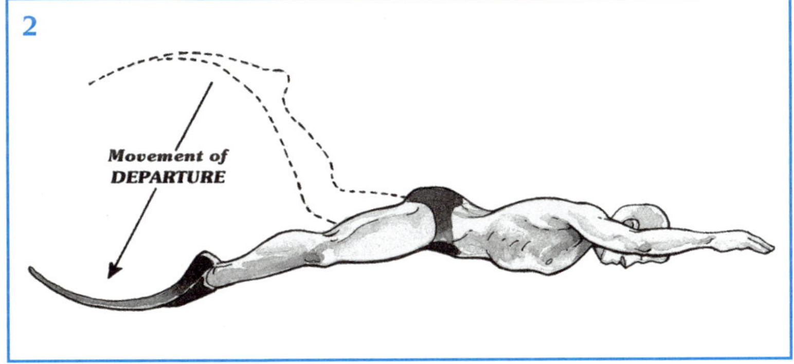

3

4

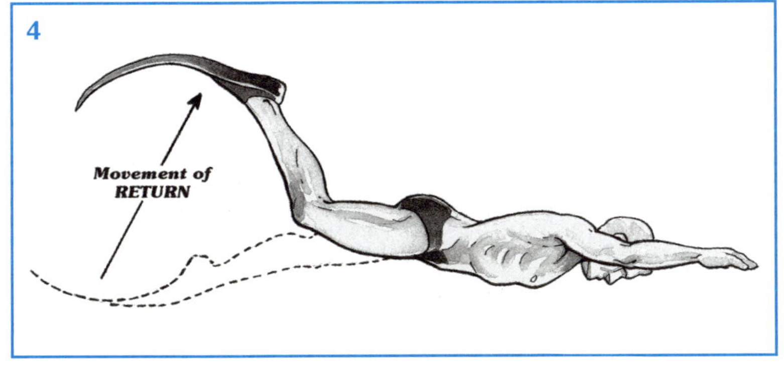

AXES AND PLANES OF THE HUMAN BODY

For a better understanding of the relationship of the limbs with the fins and with the apneist's torso, we have summarised in this table the definitions of 'axes' and 'planes:' in practice these are coordinates that allow us to trace a three dimensional map of the body.

Imagine that the human body is crossed with three axes and cut into three plains.

Longitudinal axis: traverses the body from the top of the head to the point of union of the heels.

Transverse axis: across from one shoulder to the other.

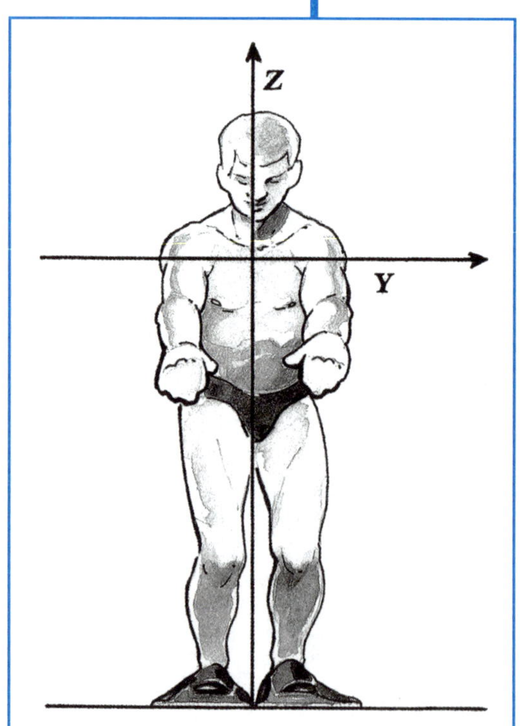

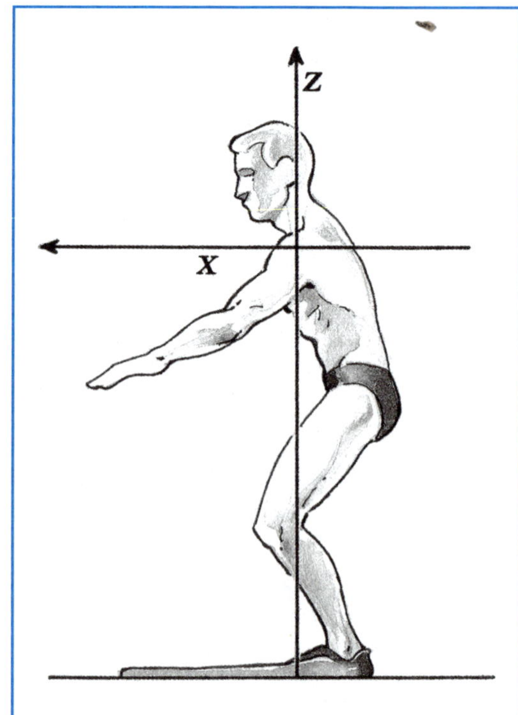

Sagittal axis: from chest to back (anterior to posterior).

The said axes define the following planes:

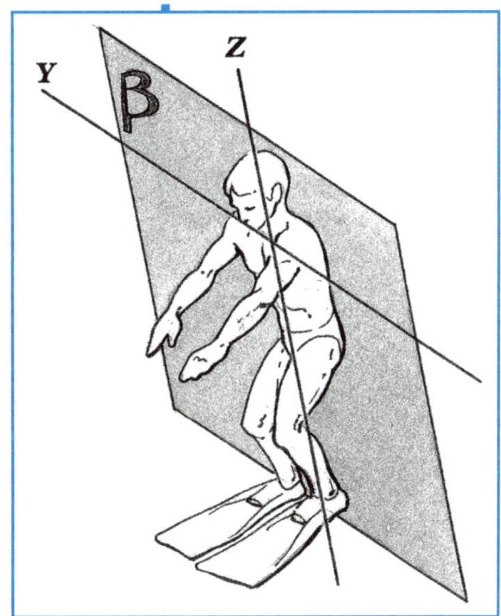

Frontal plane (β):

divides the human body into two asymmetric sections: an anterior and a posterior (z-y).

Sagittal plane (α):

divides the human body into two symmetric sections: a left and a right (z-x).

Transverse plane (γ):

divides the human body into two asymmetric sections: an upper and a lower (x-y).

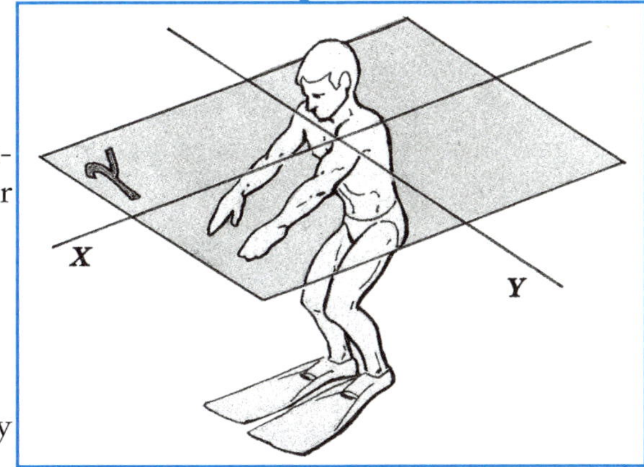

Axis of rotation:

the imaginary line around which a body rotates.

For the entire cycle, use the following table:

Table 1
Intervention of the various segments of the lower limbs in a finstroke with a period of 2.5 seconds.

<table>
<tr><td></td><td colspan="7">Period of finning
0 1 sec 2.5 sec.</td></tr>
<tr><td>Foot</td><td colspan="2">F.D.</td><td colspan="4">F.P.</td><td>F.D.</td></tr>
<tr><td>Leg</td><td>F.</td><td colspan="3">E.</td><td colspan="3">F.</td></tr>
<tr><td>Thigh</td><td colspan="3">E.</td><td colspan="2">F.</td><td colspan="2">E.</td></tr>
<tr><td>Pelvis</td><td colspan="7">R.A. R.C. R.AC.</td></tr>
<tr><td colspan="8">where:</td></tr>
<tr><td>F.P.</td><td colspan="7">= Plantar flexion</td></tr>
<tr><td>F.D.</td><td colspan="7">= Dorsal flexion</td></tr>
<tr><td>F.</td><td colspan="7">= Flexion</td></tr>
<tr><td>E.</td><td colspan="7">= Extension</td></tr>
<tr><td>R.AC.</td><td colspan="7">= Anticlockwise rotation</td></tr>
<tr><td>R.C.</td><td colspan="7">= Clockwise rotation</td></tr>
</table>

To properly interpret the features of a finstroke it is necessary to define the following parameters:

- **amplitude of finstroke:** the transverse distance between the boundaries of ankle movement with respect to the vertebral column; at normal velocity it is a function of the subject's body height and the type of fin.
- **period of finstroke:** changes depending on velocity and amplitude of the finstroke; generally it is between 0.5 and 2.5 seconds.
- **stroke frequency:** the number of finstrokes executed in one second, equal to the inverse of the period.
- **average velocity:** is the mean velocity of the entire body in the direction of motion.

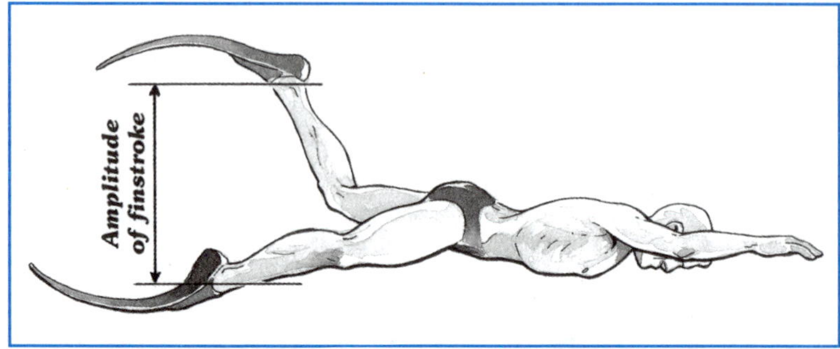

We will now look at the biomechanical behaviour of the limbs and joints, listing the principle muscles involved in the movement of finning. **The experimentally revealed maximum and minimum angles are given as limits of articulation at the joints.**

Behaviour of the foot and ankle

In the phase of advance:
- consists in the plantar flexion of the foot, which reaches maximum angle of rotation from the line of the vertebral column, measured experimentally as 57°;
- principle muscles involved are: sural tricep, posterior tibial, long and short peroneals, long flexor of the big toe, long flexor of the toes.

In the phase of return:
- consists in the dorsal flexion of the foot, reaching a minimum rotation of 10.5° experimentally;
- principle muscles involved are: anterior tibial, long extensor of the big toe, long extensor of the toes, anterior peroneal.

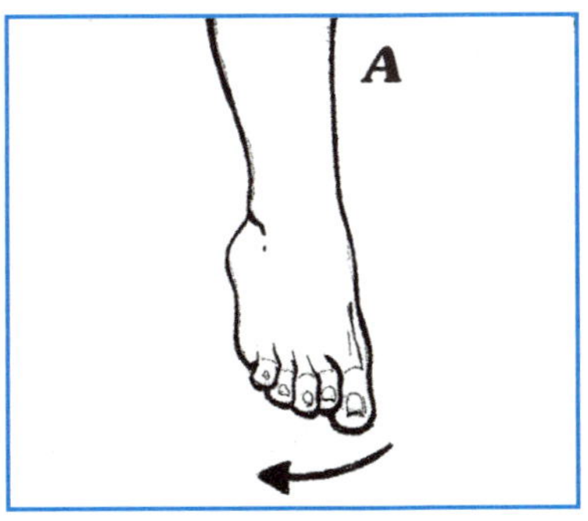

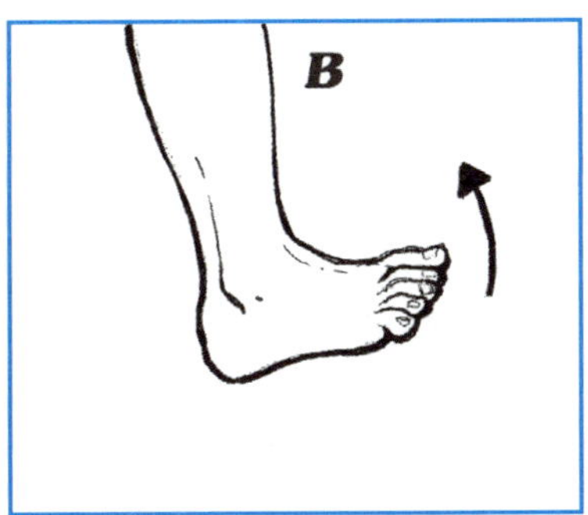

A - Plantar flexion of the foot.
B - Dorsal flexion of the foot.

Knowing these angles of articulation that mediate the action will allow you and your trainer to plan the angles of the chosen machine for muscular development at your gymnasium.

Behaviour of the lower leg and knee

In the phase of advance:
- consists in the extension of the leg and the arrival at a maximum rotation of – 5.8° experimentally;
- principle muscles involved are the quadriceps.

In the phase of return:
- consists in the flexion of the leg, with a maximum rotation of 76.1° experimentally;
- principle muscles involved are: gastrocnemius, semitendinous, semimembranous, femoral bicep, slender muscle, popliteal, sartorius.

A - Flexion of the leg.
B - Extension of the leg.

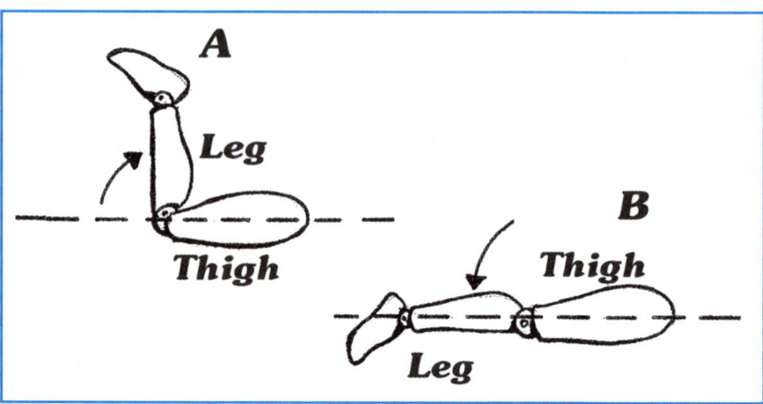

Behaviour of the thigh and hip

In the phase of advance:

- consists in the flexion of the thigh, with a maximum rotation of – 39.6° experimentally;
- principle muscles involved are: ileum psoas, straight muscle of the thigh, sartorius, tensor of the fascia lata, anterior fascia of the medial gluteal, pectineus, short and long adductor, slender muscle.

In the phase of return:

- consists in the extension of the thigh, with a maximum rotation of 21° experimentally;
- principle muscles involved are: long head of the femoral bicep, semitendinous and semimembranous, greatest gluteal, posterior fibres of the great adductor.

A - Flexion of the thigh.
B - Extension of the thigh.

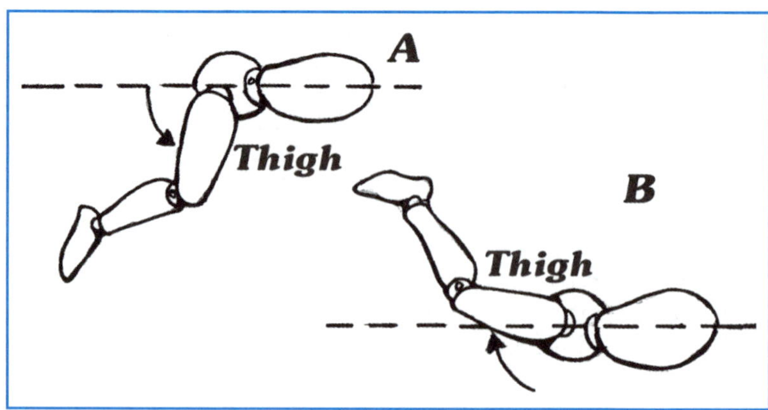

Behaviour of the pelvis and vertebral column

To simplify the description we have assumed that it is the pelvis that rotates, when in actual fact the pelvis is connected rigidly to the vertebral column, and the vertebral column rotates about its longitudinal axis.

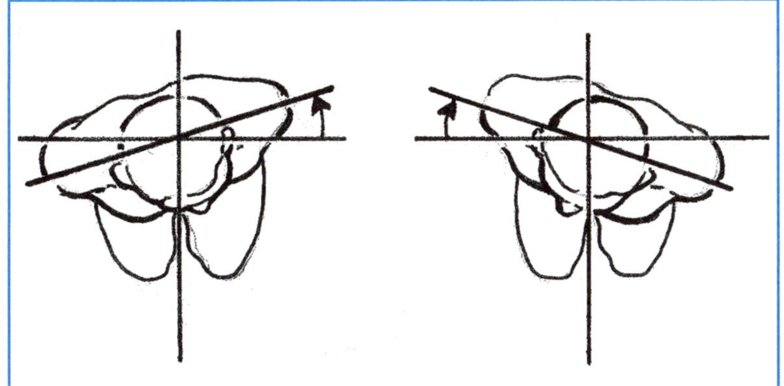

Rotation of the vertebral column on its longitudinal axis.

In the phase of advance:

- consists in the clockwise rotation of the pelvis, with a maximum rotation of 39.3° experimentally;
- principle muscles involved are: left internal oblique of the abdomen, right external oblique of the abdomen, left transverse muscle of the abdomen, left sacrospinal, right transversospinal.

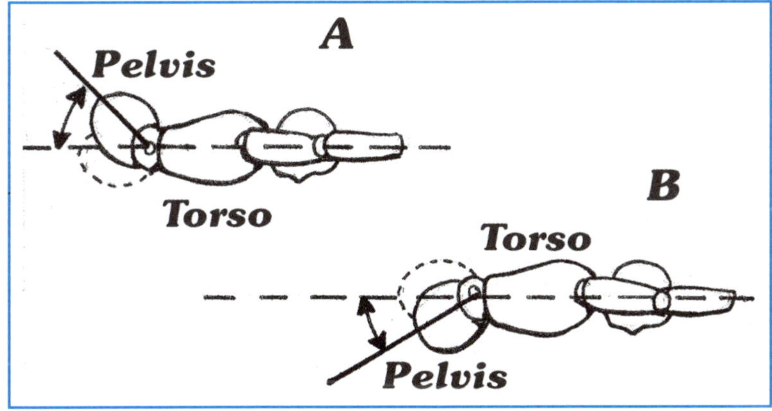

A - *Clockwise rotation of pelvis.*
B - *Anticlockwise rotation of pelvis.*

In the phase of return:

- consists in the anticlockwise rotation of the pelvis with a maximum rotation of – 39.4° experimentally;
- the principle muscles involved are: right internal oblique of the abdomen, left external oblique of the abdomen, right transverse muscle of the abdomen, right sacrospinal, left transversospinal.

6.2 IDEAL FINNING TECHNIQUE

Even if technology has contributed remarkably in recent years to the development of materials, apnea remains a sport in which physical preparation, athletic movement and technique are crucial. The athlete must work to improve finning style and efficiency underwater, irrespective of which fin is chosen.

Finning technique is fundamental to freediving: it dictates velocity of the descent, hydrodynamics, directionality and consumption of oxygen.

Furthermore the type of finning determines the style of the apneist and is the most noticeable characteristic to observers. There are two very different schools of practice in apnea: **European** and **South American.**

Of the many differences between the two, that of finning technique is easily the greatest: the classic European style is completely contrary to the 'pedalling' of South American athletes. The latter push with the lower part of the fin in the return phase: in this way the knee bends to almost 90 degrees, pushing the column of water downward, and the finstroke looks very similar to a pedalling action, especially in the ascent. However trials in ergonomic pools have shown that the classical style of finning has a superior efficiency.

Finning style is personal

All apneists will have their own type of finstroke that is **a function of their anthropometrical characteristics**, and determines their style: the stroke can be quick and light or wide and powerful. **The musculature of the athlete usually influences the movement of the leg:** a powerful physique tends to impress an elevated and more open push, which allows a significant advance with less finning. On the other hand, a lanky apneist will generally have a quick, light stroke, which may be more harmonious, but is definitely less profitable.

In apnea one must first and foremost consider the consumption of energy: it is true that velocity and hydrodynamics are important, but it is also true that they must be obtained with the minimum possible oxygen expenditure. To achieve this we must find the right balance between these two techniques: a high amplitude of finstroke, but not at the limits of maximum width, and a good rhythm – not excessively fast. It isn't difficult to make your own **compromise between amplitude and frequency**. With an exaggerated amplitude it is practically impossible to maintain an elevated rhythm, and vice versa.

In the light of all this, we can confirm that **there is no absolute best finstroke,** but there is a most efficient one. The ideal finstroke is basically defined by:

- characteristics of the fin
- technical ability of the apneist
- anthropometrical characteristics
- quality of training
- quality of the water (fresh or salt)

Each of these variables contributes in a different way to the efficiency of movement; they are related to each other, but can be analysed individually to facilitate corrections to technique.

A badly executed duck-dive wastes energy only once in a dive, but if finning is incorrect then precious energy is lost with every meter. In terms of propulsion this is by and large far more limiting than any other component.

The expert apneist exhibits elegance in the use of the fin; even if at times basic errors are encountered that – due to the fact that the movement has become automatic – are the most difficult to correct, especially in people who have taught themselves.

Freediving courses often ignore the instruction of correct finning technique, since anyone with fins on their feet will succeed in moving through the water with a reasonable velocity. Quite often the only indications of how to use this equipment regard the position of the legs (straight), the width of the stroke, and a pause at the maximum width of the fins, which is very counterproductive to efficiency.

When using long fins, the technically correct finstroke requires an action that – from the abdominals to the toes – involves all the muscles of the lower trunk and legs, whether in the movement of the push forwards or return backwards. The advancing leg bends slightly at the knee and then extends; however in the return backwards it remains extended all the way to the foot, which is kept in complete plantar flexion. The action must be continuous; there should not be any pause. **The action should therefore be fluid and unbroken, characterised by a rhythm that is a function of the changing activity.** In a sense, displaced water must be compensated by an equal force in the opposite direction.

It is evident that the foot plays a crucial role and that the fin must be perceived as an extension of the lower limbs to the point where the water displaced by the blade of the fin feels like it is instead being displaced by the naked foot.

VELOCITY AND CONSTANT WEIGHT

A very important consideration for constant weight freedives when we are striving for a good performance is the velocity of the descent and ascent, which determines the total time of immersion. The optimal velocity is 1m/sec, which means that if the maximum depth reached is –40m then the ideal dive time would be 1'20".

Velocity depends on:

1. rhythm of finning
2. hydrodynamics of the body
3. buoyancy
4. quality of the water

1. Rhythm of finning

Rhythm is conditional on amplitude. However it must be steady; the ideal action is continuous, without interruption or pause. Departing from the surface, or taking off from the bottom, the finstroke is wide, and the rhythm fairly quick. As the resistance due to hydrostatic force decreases and the velocity of the apneist increases, the amplitude is reduced and the rhythm diminishes. The velocity of descent is sustained by a more relaxed rate of finning until, at 60% of maximum depth, the legs stop moving altogether. This is the freefall phase, where the body assumes the most hydrodynamic position so as to take advantage of the acquired velocity.

2. Hydrodynamics of the body

A hyper-extended position of the head (*see Chapter* 9), having the compensating arm in the wrong position (*see Chapter* 9), an arched body, or wide legs are all factors that offer resistance to the water, reducing the velocity of descent.

In order to take maximum advantage of the freefall we must exploit the momentum gained in the preceding phase of the dive.

3. Buoyancy

Weighting is critical for the distribution of effort between the descent and ascent. A heavy weight belt in constant weight freediving favours the velocity of the descent, but subsequently, when one must return to the surface, it becomes a burden that fatigues the legs. Remember to be neutrally buoyant at –10 m.

4. Quality of water

Fresh and salt water have different densities, and thus different resistances from the hydrostatic force. A dive in a lake will involve a quicker descent but an exhausting ascent, whereas in the sea to maintain a good velocity in the descent the action must be stronger, but during the ascent the apneist will feel 'lighter'.

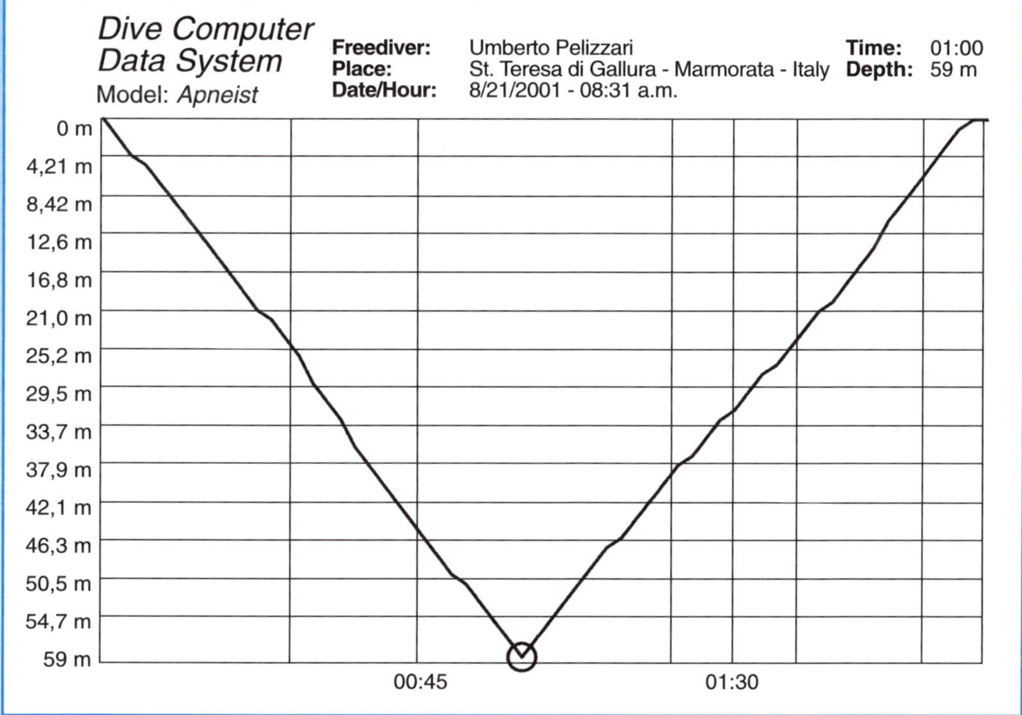

The graph demonstrates that the ideal velocity of a constant weight freedive in optimum conditions of finning, hydrodynamics and buoyancy is 1 m/sec, whether in descent or ascent. It also shows that the maximum depth of 59m was reached in a time of 1' and the ascent was also made in 60".

The rhythm of finning, determined by the frequency and amplitude, **depends on the situation:** descent, ascent, short or long dynamic, etc. For example **in dynamic apnea** it is recommendable to **never vary stroke frequency**, seeing as it is best to move at the maximum velocity permitted by economy of oxygen consumption. Only training and great sensitivity, consequent of experience or time spent finning, will enable the student to discover and develop their rhythm. This does not mean we should stop training at variable velocities, which can often resolve problems with technique as well as prepare muscles to support a greater load of lactic acid.

In constant weight freediving, the finning of the descent after the duck-dive is very similar to the phase of the ascent after the turn at the bottom. The distribution of force is equal, but inverted. At the start of the descent flotation force tries to retain the apneist on the surface, while after the first few meters and beyond the threshold of neutral buoyancy the freediver becomes negative and falls towards the bottom without effort. Ascending, the apneist must oppose their weight and push against the negative force to reach the surface. Hydrostatic pressure will gradually decrease and buoyancy increase, allowing for reduced finning and taking the load off the lower limbs.

6.3 DIFFERENT WAYS OF FINNING

It is sometimes enjoyable to fin-swim a distance lying on your back. The speed that can be reached is exhilarating for the neophyte, even if it may distract the attention from controlling the movement. In short, even an improper finning style produces satisfactory propulsion. By using diverse modes of finning the student can experiment with different systems of propulsion that recruit varied muscle groups. It is a fantastic experiment in propulsion, as it tends to re-equilibrate muscular work, especially in a subject with little experience.

Initially, **finning in different positions can help define the movement** and prevent errors, or at least acquire the self-awareness that facilitates auto-correction. Later on these exercises will be indispensable for the development and balance of the relevant muscle mass, and therefore for structuring an effective training schedule. Furthermore, the diverse body positions in water determine different conditions of equilibrium and perception that help reach a more refined awareness of the action.

In the end, using different methods of finning during long transfers on the surface will mean that through working diverse muscle groups we can avoid physical exhaustion and improve safety.

Vertical finning

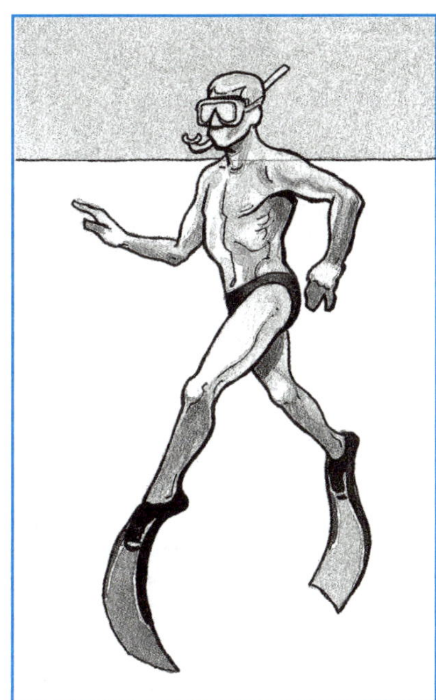

In this exercise **the position is erect; the amplitude** of the finstroke **is normal**, but the **rhythm is slow**. At first it will be difficult to keep the finning symmetrical, therefore the student will need to use the hands in opposition to remain oriented in the chosen direction.

With time, the muscles that control finning will start to become trained, and the technique of the action will be corrected; at this point an appropriate weight can be used, in such a way that the technical movement is always becoming more effective. Two pieces of advice to avoid the most common errors: **when the leg moves backward the foot must remain extended; be careful not to bend the knee excessively when the leg is moving forwards in the advance phase.** A lateral movement on the surface is indication of an asymmetry of action.

Finning on the surface

This involves finning in a prone position with the arms straight out in front and the hands on the surface, palms downward.

The position of the body is not relaxed, but slightly arched in the lumbar part of the back, since with effective finning this will push the chest on a diagonal plane respective to the surface, raising the body and thereby favouring respiration. If the position of the body is not perfect and

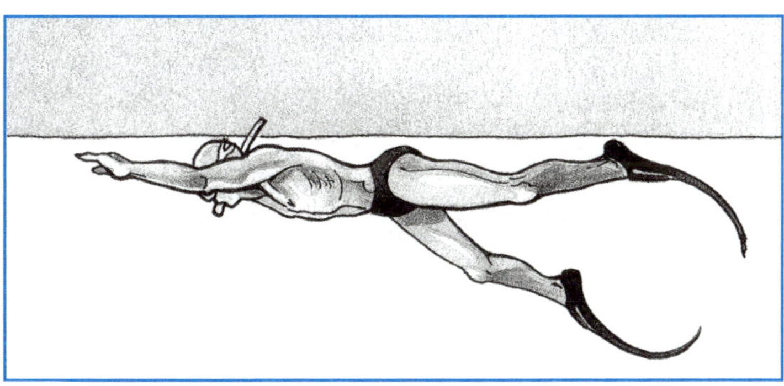

the finning is not efficient, the mouth will not emerge enough to breathe, and execution will become impossible.

In the beginning there may be a few difficulties, such as an arched body position, which will cause the fins to break the water excessively, losing propulsion.

A good exercise **to improve body position** is to **keep the hands on the back, holding one wrist with the other hand, and then force the arms backwards into an arc** so that the elbows come as near as possible to each other. At the same time it will be necessary to hyperextend the head upward as if looking up at the sky. This exhausting drill should be used for short distances to ensure correct position in the water. When this purpose is achieved return to the normal exercise with the arms straight out in front. This is the most common mode of surface finning when using a mask and snorkel.

Dorsal finning

In this mode of finning the face is emerged from the water and turned upwards, so breathing is simple. The advantages of this position are that it favours a general relaxation of the body, which can completely recline under the water, enjoying the force of flotation. Furthermore, when finning on the back **the body maintains a more relaxed position**, making it easier to keep the fins constantly immersed.

The supine position is completely natural, with the groin angled almost into a seated posture. In this posture it will be the back, not the chest, which breaks the water, on a slightly diagonal plane that promotes the emersion of the upper torso. **The head**, as always, **acts to regulate depth.** Bringing the head towards the chest sinks the legs, enabling finning to become wider. Be careful not to go too far though as the body can tend to move from the correct diagonal to a vertical position. In this case the greater resistance offered to the water would slow down the planing movement. On the other hand, if the head is brought too far backwards the fins tend to break the surface of the water.

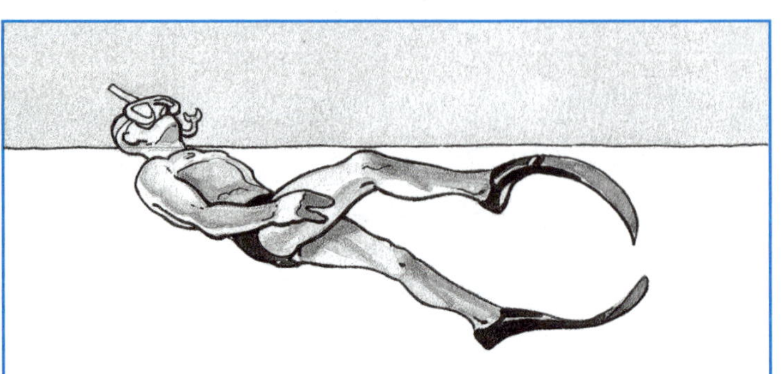

An **excellent point of reference** to verify correct execution is the **eddy on the surface that is created by the fins, which approach the surface without emerging.** The hands, kept on the thighs, can accompany the movement of the lower limbs so as to sense their amplitude and rhythm. Be careful not to keep the head tensed between the shoulders – this contraction costs energy and is of no profit.

Dorsal finning allows the relaxation of muscle groups utilized in the preceding actions and is often used for crossing large distances. For complete relaxation lie back on the water without tensing any part of the upper body, head included. Contraction of the neck muscles is a common fault, and is not easily noticed.

Finning on the side

If dorsal finning is the most relaxed position, especially when a snorkel isn't used, then side finning is not far behind. Breathing is more difficult because the head must be raised and turned slightly upward. The diagonal of the body that is required to keep the fins immersed can be minimal, since the fins move on a plane almost parallel to the surface.

This allows **unlimited amplitude of finning, with the fins constantly immersed to avoid breaking the surface.** Side finning has the advantage of enabling the apneist to look in the direction of movement, or to observe the movement of the lower limbs and notice any errors in their action. The lower arm is stretched forward, with the palm of the hand facing down, while the upper arm remains along the flank.

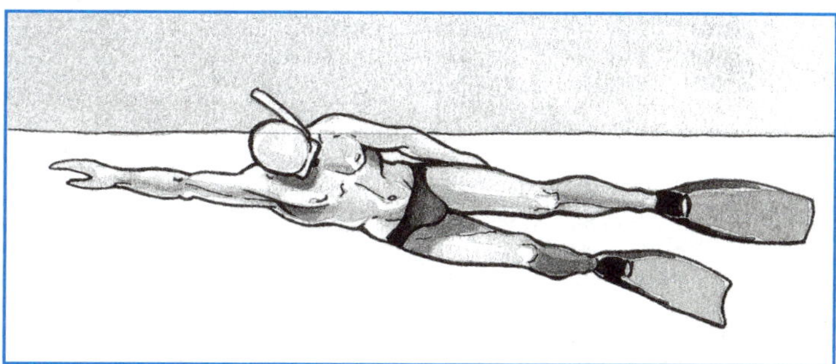

6.4 ERRORS OF FINNING

It is possible that you may not find your particular error from amongst the following described, since incorrect finning is often characterised by a combination of several errors. A good instructor will help to understand the origin of the problem, to correct the problems and help to change technique.

However it is very important to keep in mind one's own anthropometrical characteristics, and not to try and copy the correct finning of someone who is, for example, ten centimetres taller, and has a completely different musculature.

To facilitate the identification of personal technical problems we have organised the errors into three groups defined by the cause of the problem: actions of the lower limbs, body position and inadequate fins.

A – Errors due to incorrect action of the lower limbs

1. Stroke is too wide
2. Pause at maximum width
3. Forward flexion of thighs
4. Flexion of the leg under the thigh
5. Extension of leg
6. Incomplete movement in advance phase
7. Flat feet in return phase
8. Divaricated legs
9. Movement is too narrow and quick
10. Valgus feet

B – Errors due to body position

11. Hyperextended head
12. Arched body position
13. Raised shoulders and retracted head
14. Inversion of the rolling of the shoulders
15. An error of hydrodynamics

C – Inadequacies of fins

16. Loose foot pocket
17. Soft foot pocket
18. Lack of lateral railing
19. Junction between blade and foot pocket
20. Inefficiency of blade

We will now analyse the errors, describing first the dynamics, then the causes and effects, and lastly suggesting corrections.

A – Errors due to incorrect action of the lower limbs

1. Stroke is too wide

Description: Incorrect opening of the lower limbs. The advancing leg is excessively flexed, while the returning leg is excessively hyperextended.

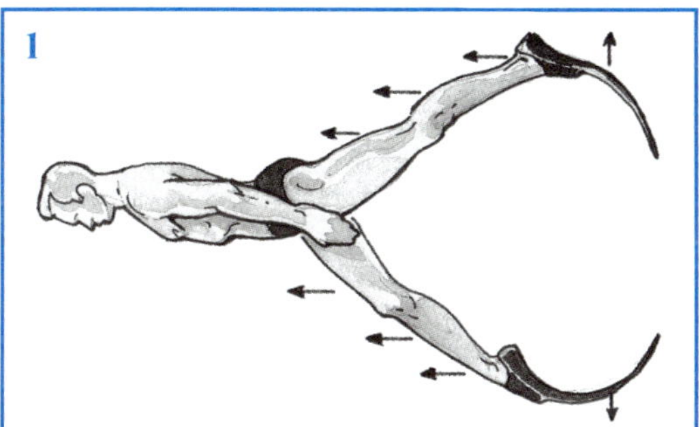

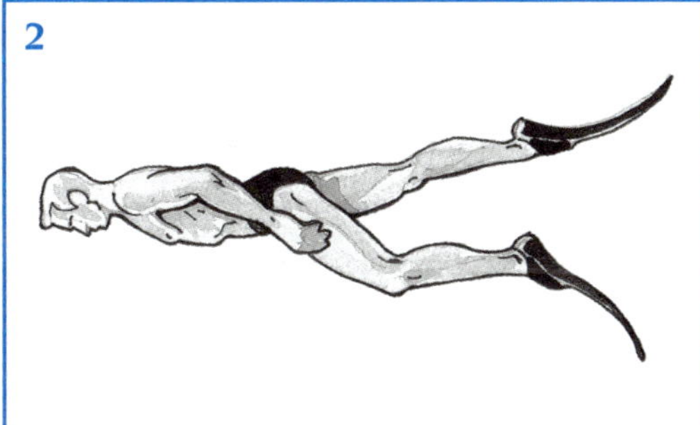

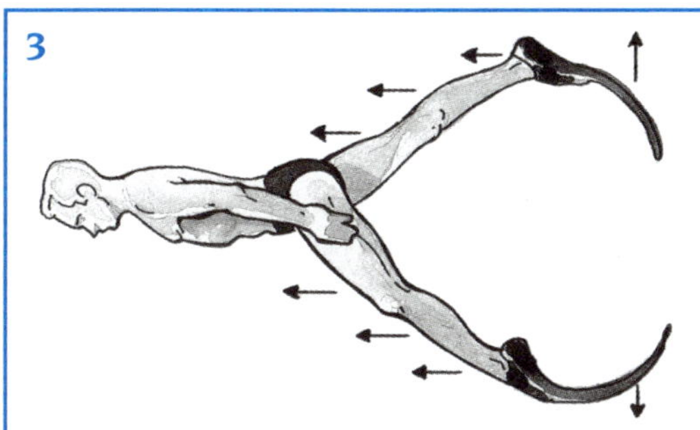

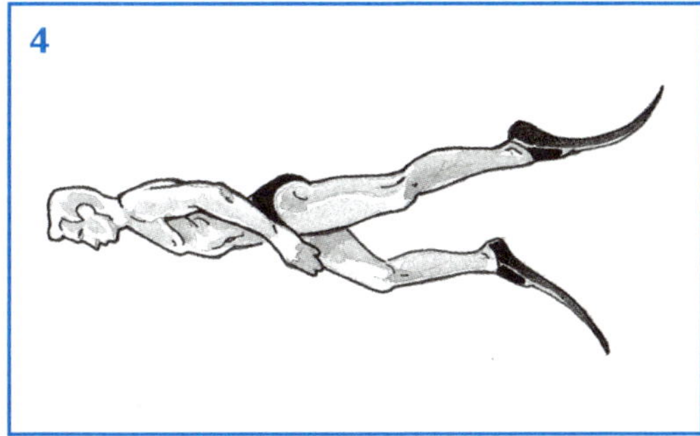

Causes:

- **False interpretation of the idea that progress should be slow and calm.** The subject believes that this action is more effective and has more style.
- **The action is 'hyper-controlled'**, evidence of a level of psychological tension in the subject, who must dominate the action.

Effects:

- The open lower limbs offer greater resistance to forwards movement.
- Discontinuous forwards progress. Alternates between fast moments and slow moments.

Correction:

- A more rapid execution of the finstroke, besides being narrower, will support the sensation of progress through the water.
- Practice finning in different positions to control the action of the legs. For example: on the left and right side or in a supine seated position.

2. Pause at maximum width

Description: **The apneist makes a pause of variable period when the fins reach maximum width.**

The rhythm is interrupted, and the action is not continuous. This error is often associated with the excessive amplitude described in the previous error.

1

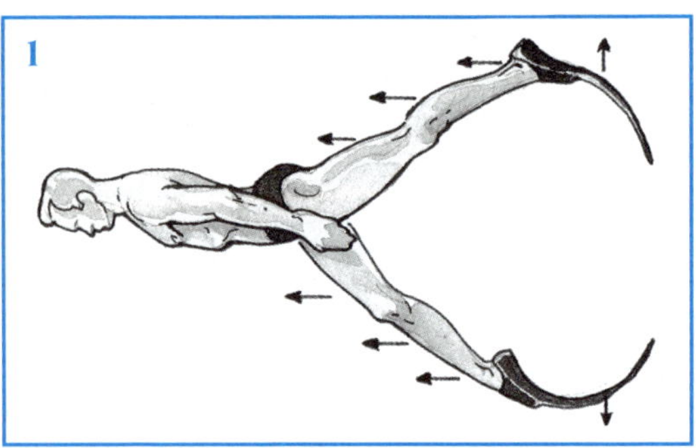

2

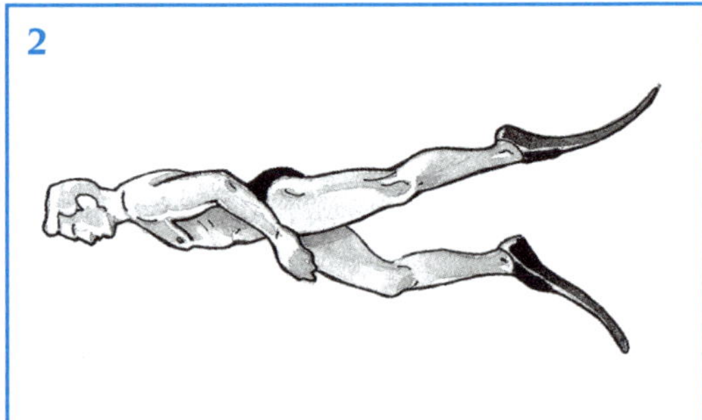

3

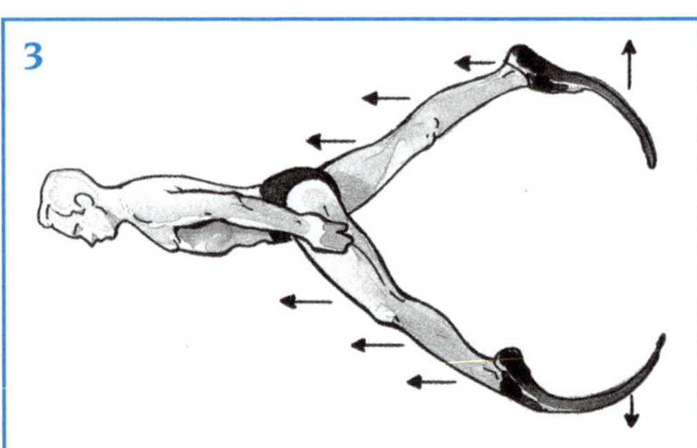

4

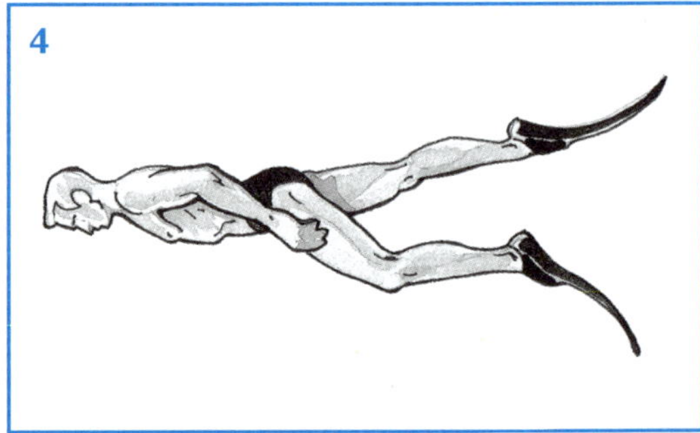

Causes:

- Sensation of security and balance given by the stabilising action of the fins, comparable to the flaps on an aeroplane's wings.
- The action is 'hyper-controlled', evidence of a level of psychological tension in the subject, who must dominate the action by making a pause.

Effects:

- The lower limbs offer a greater resistance to forwards movement.
- Forwards velocity is compromised by the pause.
- Progress alternates between fast and slow moments.

Correction:

- A more rapid execution of the finstroke, besides being narrower, will support the sensation of progress through the water.
- Subsequently, effective finning can be achieved by progressively reducing velocity, without lengthening the stroke.

3. Forward flexion of thighs

Description: **In the advance phase of the stroke the knee is brought forwards with a flexion of the thigh**; the fin 'cuts' the water rather than displacing it.

1

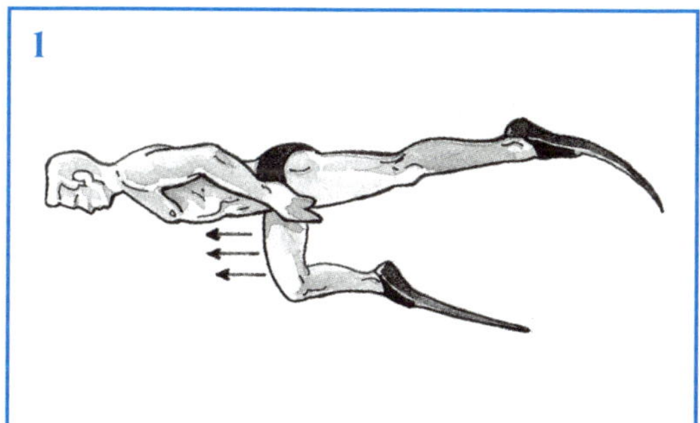

2

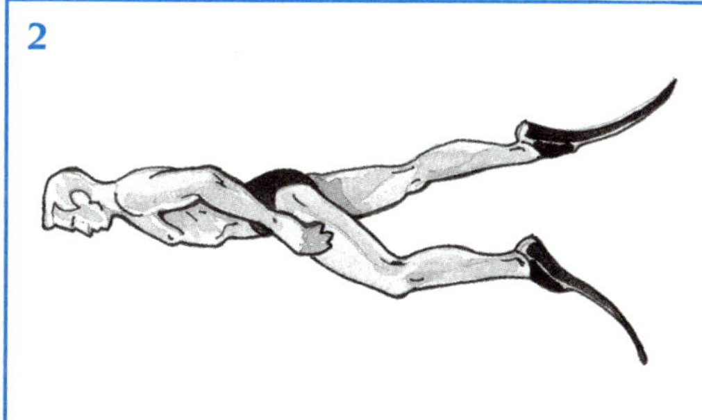

3

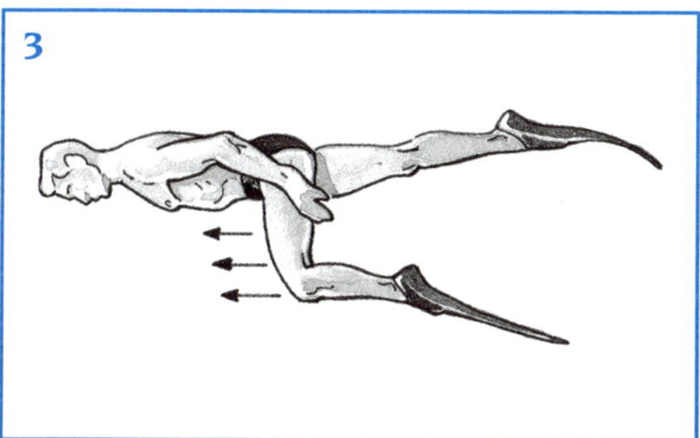

4

Causes:

- Little training; insufficient muscular tone of thigh flexors. The apneist may accuse water resistance to the foot/fin system and avoids it by slipping the leg.
- Fin is excessively rigid or long.

Effects:

- The thigh bends to as much as 90°, which pushes water forwards, braking forwards progress. In the advance phase the upper part of the fin does not displace water.

Correction:

- Vertical finning, initially without weight, then with successively increasing weight.
- Practice finning in different positions to control the action of the legs. For example: on the left and right sides, in a supine seated position, or with a flutter-board on the surface.
- Finning keeping the hands on the hips to feel for the forwards flexion.

4. Flexion of the leg beneath the thigh

Description: **In the return phase** of the finstroke the apneist **flexes the lower leg under the thigh.** The foot/fin system 'cuts' the water without exerting any pressure to displace it.

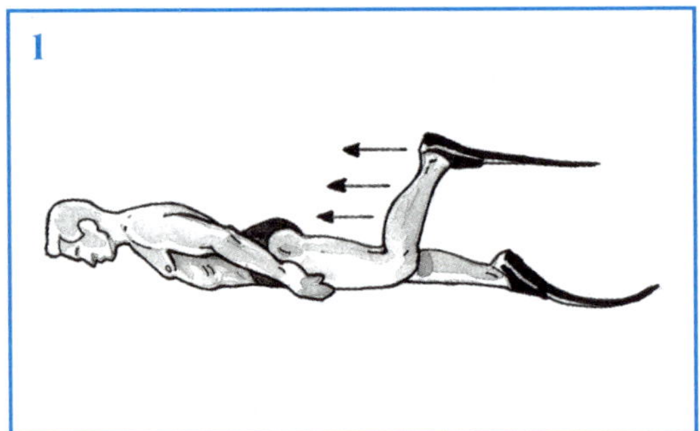

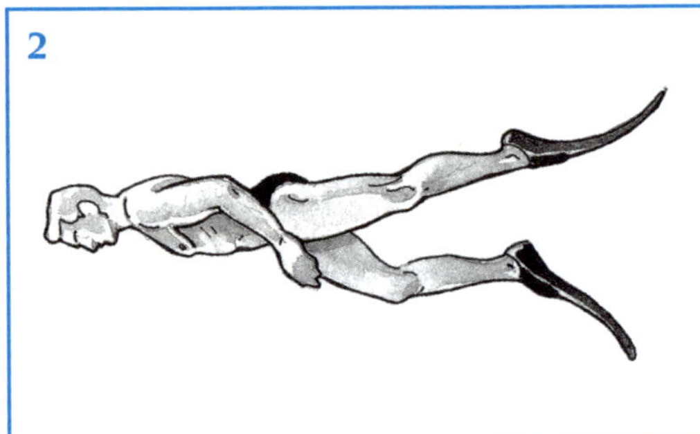

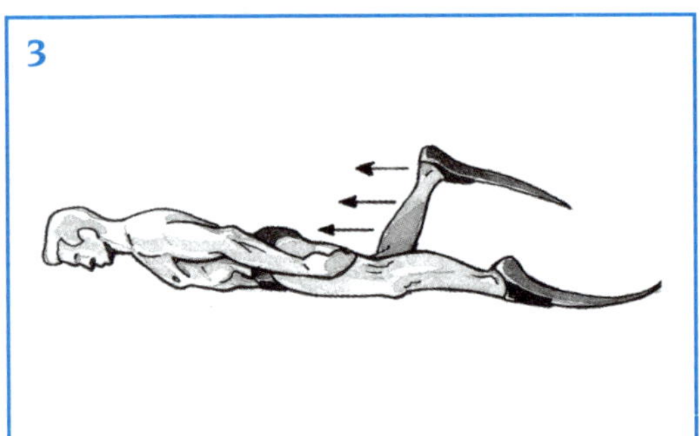

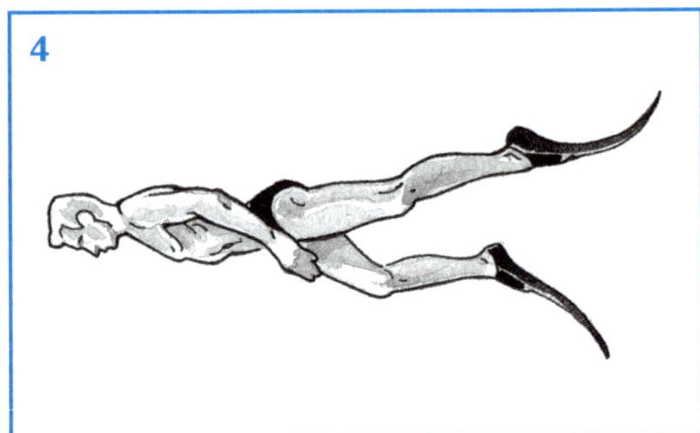

Causes:

- Little training; insufficient muscular tone of thigh extensor.
  The apneist may accuse water resistance to the foot/fin system and avoids it by slipping the leg.
- Fin is excessively stiff or long.

Effects:

- Inefficiency of propulsion. In fact the underneath of the fin does not displace any water, and its propulsion is therefore negligible.
- The resistance offered to the water by the surface of lower leg slows forward progress

Correction:

- Vertical finning, initially without weight, then with successively increasing weight.
- Practice finning in different positions to control the action of the legs.
  For example: on the left and right sides, in a supine seated position or with a flutter-board on the surface.

5. Extension of the leg

Description: The advance phase of the finstroke is correct; the limb advances with the knee partially flexed, but **the error is in the finish.** The incomplete extension of the leg favours the beginning of the return phase with a firm extension of the thigh until the limb is completely aligned.

1
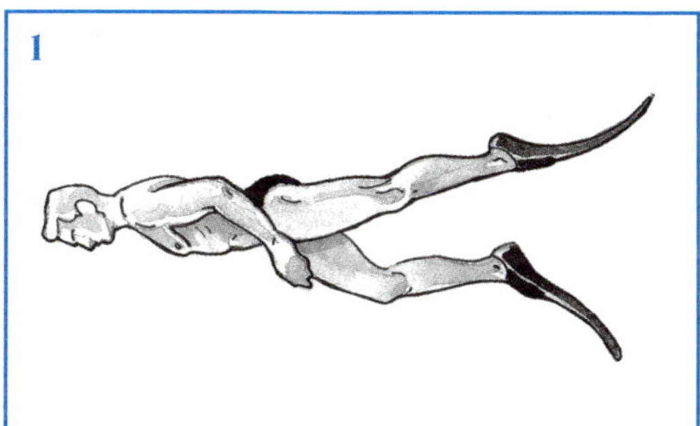

2
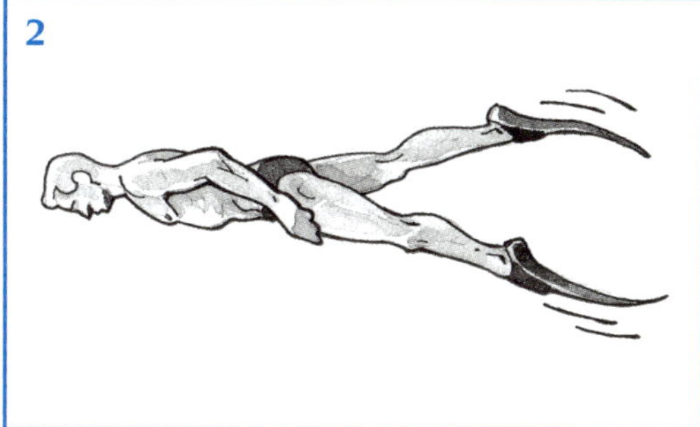

3

4
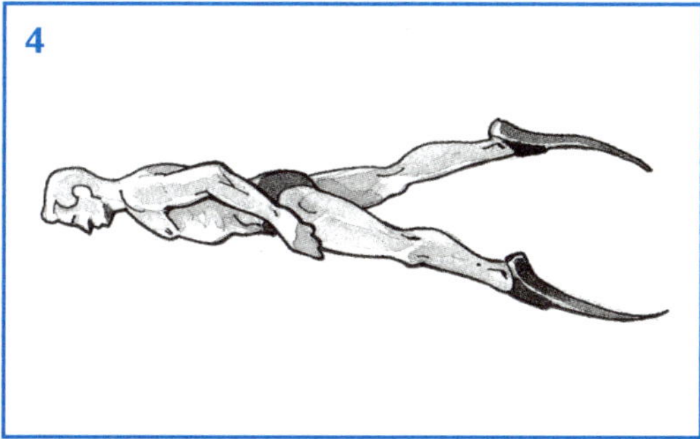

Causes:

- Little training; insufficient muscular tone of thigh extensor: weak femoral quadriceps.
- Fin is excessively stiff or long.

Effects:

- Partial inefficiency of propulsion in advance phase.
  The apneist may accuse water resistance to the foot/fin system and avoids it by not completing the action of reversing direction.
- Loss of force in the final part of the advance phase of the stroke.

Correction:

- Improve capacity of the quadriceps; in the gymnasium use the leg extension machine, calibrated to operate between 10° and 70°, to increase the strength of the thigh.
- Focus all concentration on the contraction of the quadriceps, feeling the complete extension of the leg. Be careful not to make a pause at the end of the movement.

6. Incomplete movement in advance phase

Description: **Finning is not symmetrical with respect to the frontal plane,** and develops exclusively in the posterior half (behind). The advance phase is incomplete; the limb never passes the frontal plane, with reference to the abdomen, to complete the stroke. In the prone position assumed by the apneist during dynamic apnea, the action is always above and upward.

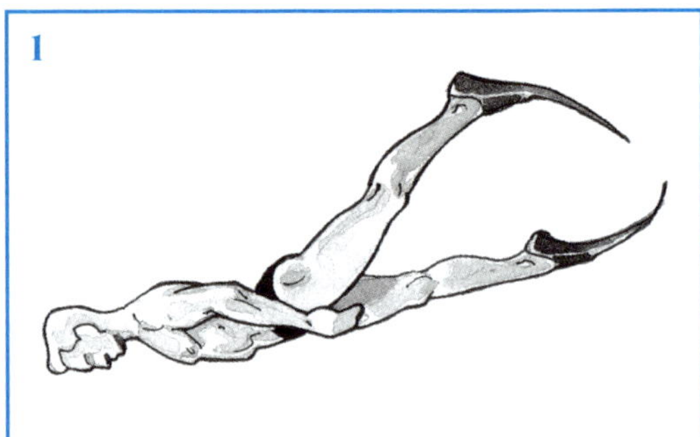

1

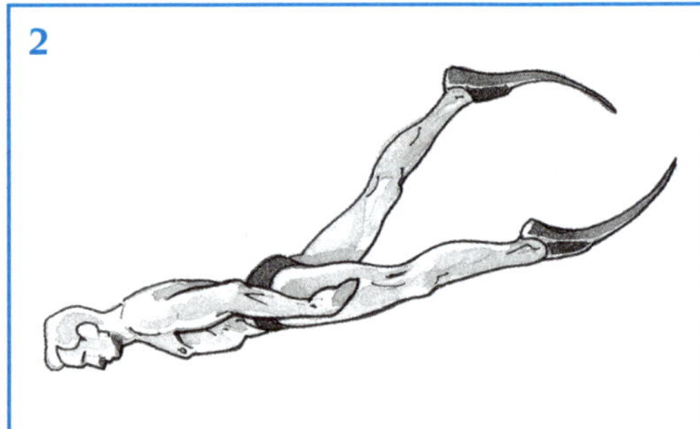

2

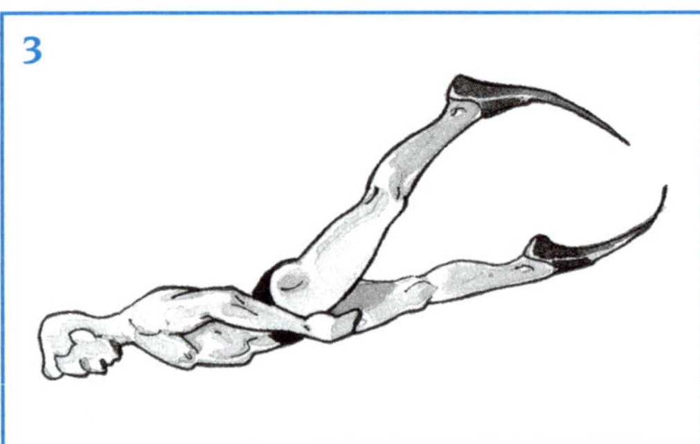

3

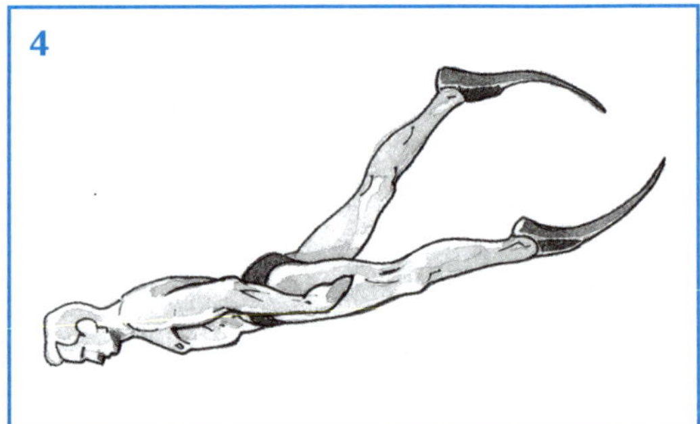

4

Causes:

- Lack of perception of movement and posture. Extensive muscular tension. Generally manifested in subjects with little aquaticity, and/or great positive buoyancy.
- Incorrect body position may cause hyperextension of the head, in which case the hyperextension of the lower limbs in the return phase is an attempt to correct the hydrodynamics of the body.

Effects:

- Little hydrodynamics of body position.
- Oblique position with respect to forward movement has bad hydrodynamics.
- Little endurance, due to considerable accumulated muscular tension.

Correction:

- Swim on the bottom.
- Decrease weighting, or reduce the quantity of air in the lungs
- In dynamic apnea, push the feet towards the bottom

7. Flat feet in return phase

Description: The foot is in complete flexion, or at a right angle with respect to the lower leg.
This error is generally associated with **flexion of the leg beneath the thigh.**

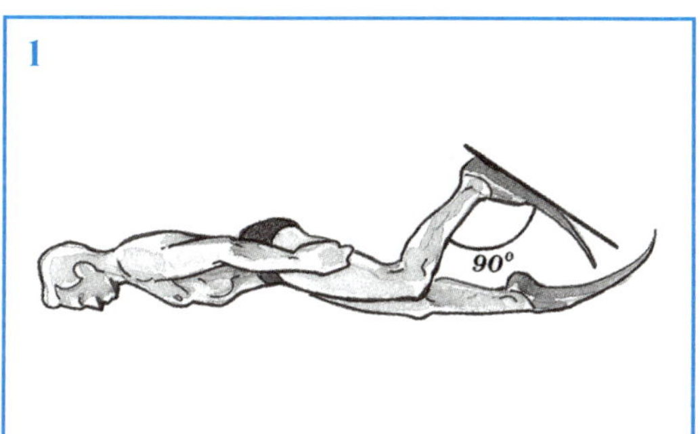

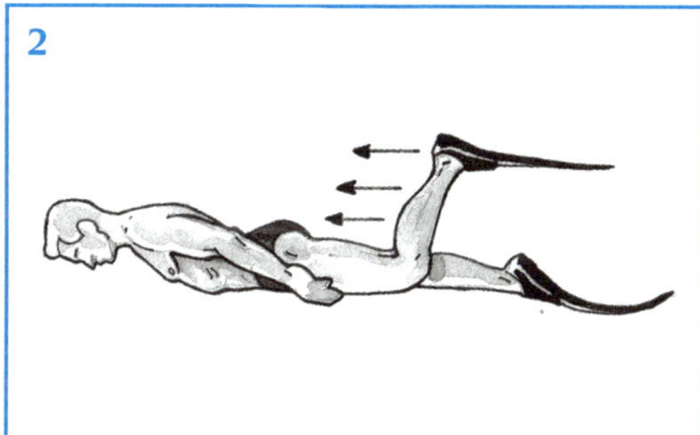

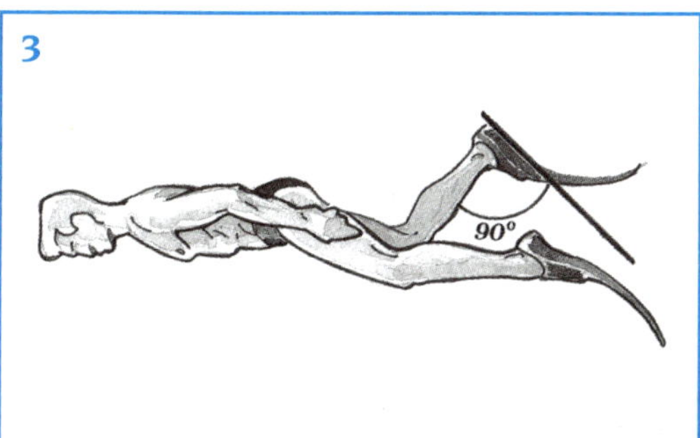

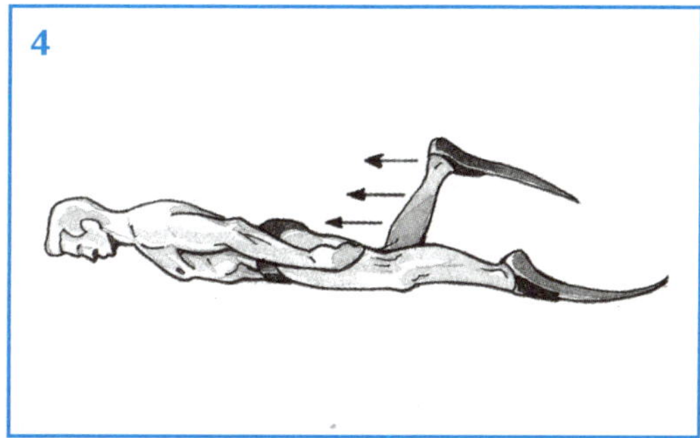

Causes:

- Little strength in the relevant muscular structure of the leg.
- Great muscular tension of the anterior tibials and foot.
- Problems of articulation of the ankle, knee or hip.
- Foot pocket or blade of fin is too rigid.

Effects:

- Total inefficiency of propulsion in the return phase.
- The foot cuts the water and the blade of the fin does not displace water.
- Coupled with a correct movement in the advance phase it will produce a rotation of the chest on the longitudinal axis, inducing continuous variations in body position.

Correction:

- Rapid vertical finning.
- Dorsal finning, visually controlling the action of the feet.
- Exercises to increase articulation of the ankle: stretching.

8. Divaricated legs

Description: The lower limbs are not parallel to each other or the axis of the body. With respect to the longitudinal axis of the body they are divaricated.

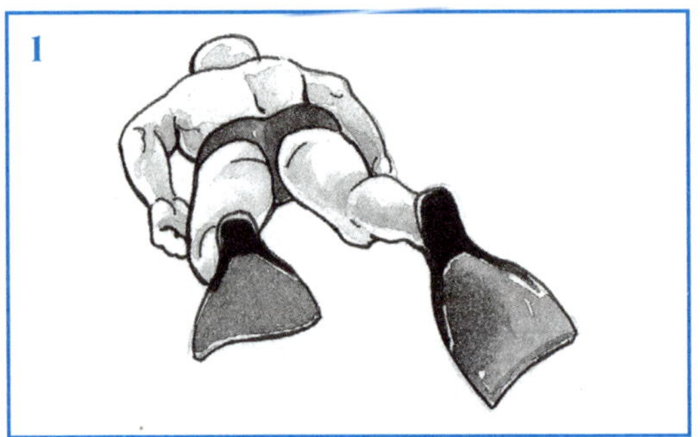

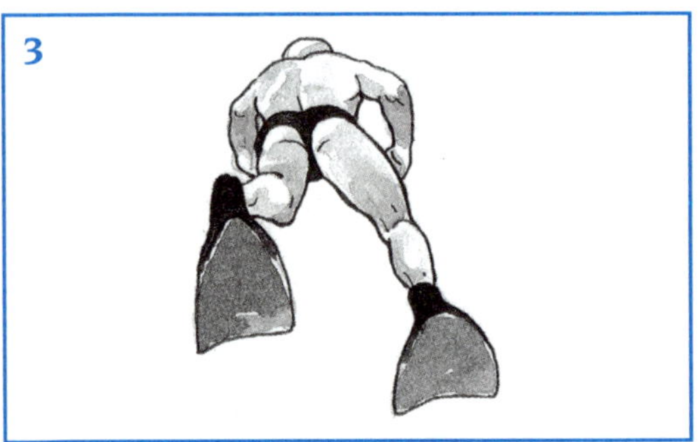

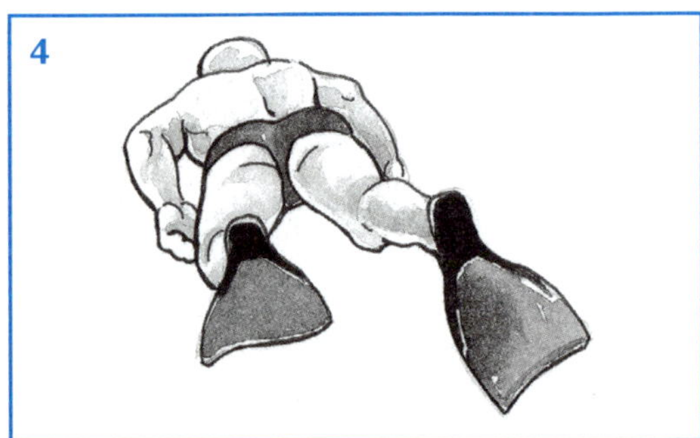

Causes:

- This error is generally associated with Valgus feet, where the fins bump into each other during finning, and to compensate the apneist tends to widen the knees so that the fins don't touch.
- General muscular tension of the legs.

Effects:

- Considerable dissipation of energy; although the action is efficient it is not economic.
- Excessive rolling of the chest.
- Associated muscular tension contributes to incorrect body position.

Correction:

- Fin whilst seated on the edge of a swimming pool (legs in the water), controlling the alignment of the foot with the rest of the leg.
- Increase the associated musculature of the legs and feet.
- Mobilize the ankle. Reinforce the stabilising muscles of the ankle.

9. Movement is too narrow and quick

Description: The frequency (number of finstrokes in a unit of time) is too high, and compromises an economic velocity.

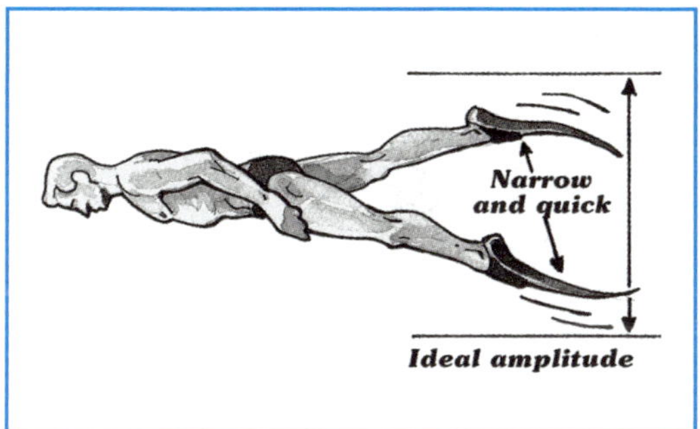

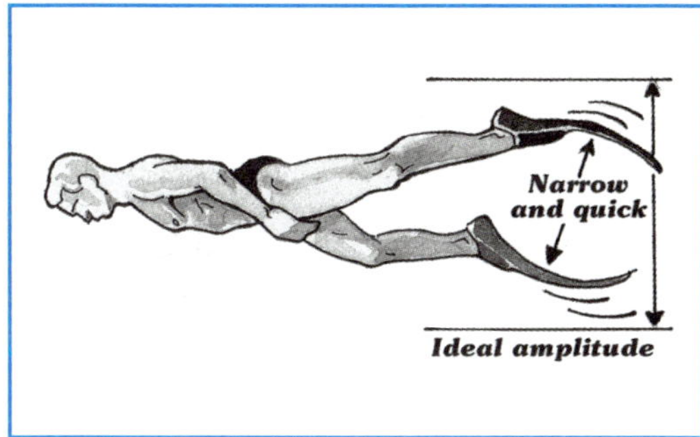

Causes:
- Excessive nervous tension. Loss of control of the situation.

Effects:
- Elevated consumption of oxygen.
- Lack of relaxation and difficulty in integrating into the environment.

Correction:
- Prepare well mentally for the dive.
- Visualise a slow execution, with a wide stroke.
- Mentally control the frequency by counting.

10. Valgus feet

Description: Valgism of the feet will have the effect of aligning the blades of the fins inwards towards each other. The axis of the foot/fin is not aligned with the axis of the lower limb.

1

2
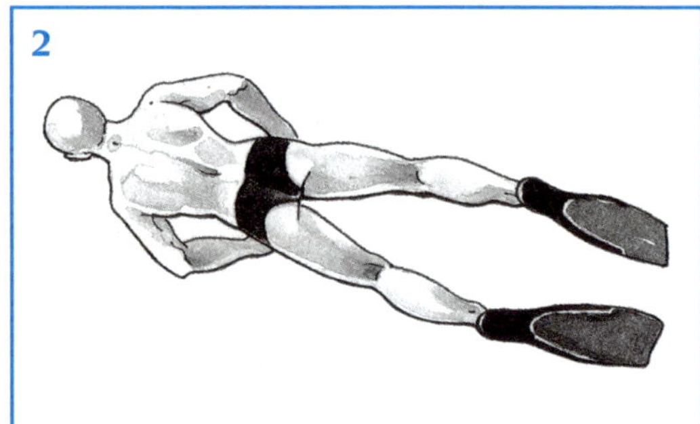

3

4
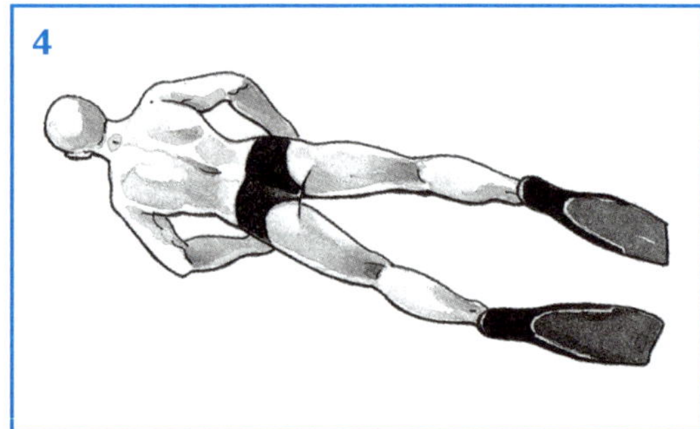

Causes:

- Lack of musculature in the ankle/foot structure.
- Lack of muscular tone of the anterior and posterior tibial, anterior peroneal, and short and long peroneals.
- Lack of control of a fin with a blade that is too long and/or too rigid or without lateral railing (*see page 215*).

Effects:

- The blade of the fin turns inward, so the apneist tends to correct by widening the knees (*see page 204*).
- The power of the blade is inefficient and uneconomic.

Correction:

- Actively control the action.
- Swim stretches on the surface dorsally, observing the action.
- Mobilize the ankle, and improve the tone of the muscles mentioned above.
- Fin whilst seated on the edge of a swimming pool (legs in the water), controlling the alignment of the fin, foot and lower limb.

ASYMMETRY OF THE ACTION

Description: Errors 3, 4, 5, 6 and 7 can also be manifested monolaterally, or on the left or right side only.

Causes:

- Less strength in one of the two legs.
- Lack of sensitivity that prevents recognition of the imbalance.
- Problem of flexibility in the hip, knee or ankle.
- Muscular tension on left or right side.

Effects:

- Incorrect body position.
- Forwards progress is oblique: to the left or right, and not in a straight line.

Correction:

- Vertical finning watching and controlling the movement.
- Improve the musculature on the weaker side.
- Finning on the surface on the left or right side.
- Analytical relaxation of the contracted areas.

B – Errors due to body position

11. Hyperextended head

Description: On land a person will look in the direction they are moving and at everything they are doing. In the same way an apneist when freediving will tend to look in the direction in which they are moving. It is instinctive, and this position, considered the prone position, implies a hyperextension of the head necessary to look forwards.

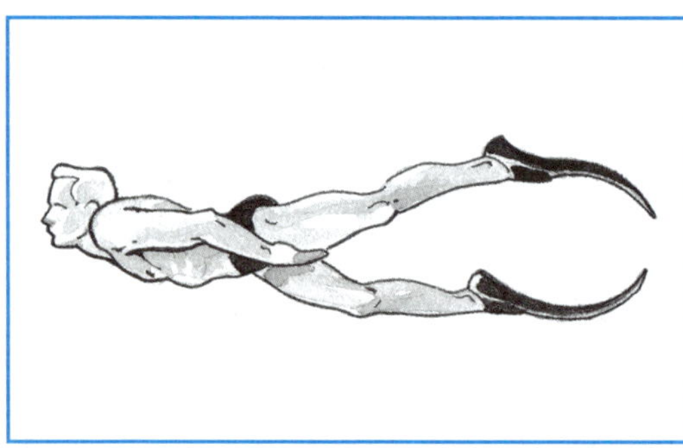

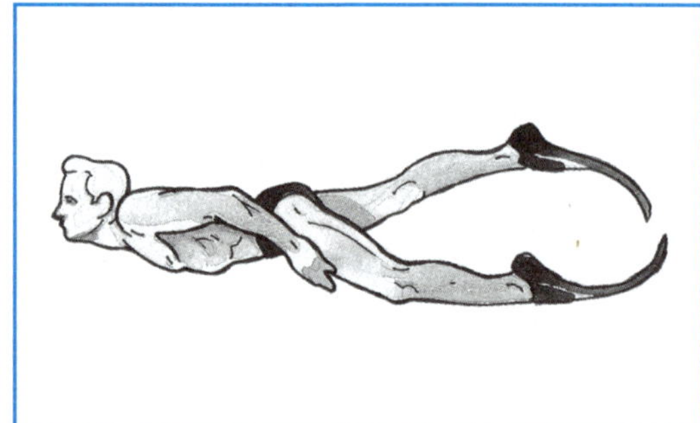

Causes:

- Psychological factors: anxiety generated by fear of colliding with obstacles or fear of the unknown.
- Rigidity of the neck.

Effects:

- Contraction of cervical muscles and trapeziums. Consumption of O_2.
- Contraction of trapezoids.
- Variation of body alignment in water.

Correction:

- Keep the chin close to the sternum.
- When freediving watch the down-line, keeping the head between the arms.
- Perform dynamic apneas with the arms stretched forwards, keeping the head in the middle between the arms; the ears should be touching the arms.
- Look at the abdomen.

12. Arched body position

Description: The body position in the water is curved. The head and the vertebral column are hyperextended and the chest is arched backward.

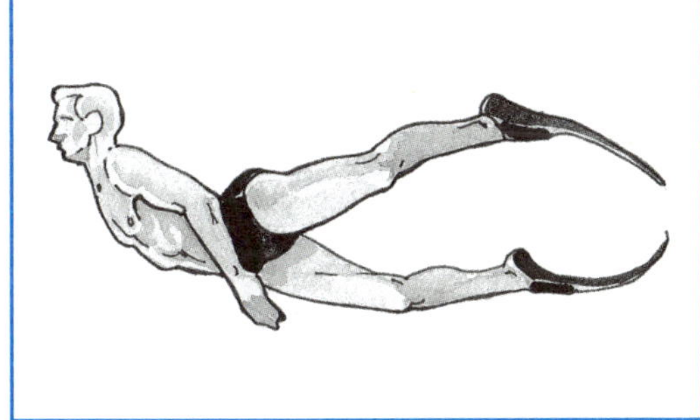

Causes:

- Hyperextension of the head.
- Muscular tension of the torso due to insecurity or anxiety.
- Rigidity of the pelvis and shoulders.

Effects:

- Little hydrodynamics of body position.
- Difficulty in maintaining depth in dynamic apnea. Body position causes lifting force.
- Distancing from the down-line in constant weight dives.
- Rapidly fatiguing, little efficiency.

Correction:

- Fin on the surface, aiming for maximum length of the body in the water.
- Dynamic Apnea with the arms extended, keeping the head between the arms.
- Stretching of the spine.

13. Raised shoulders and retracted head

Description: The shoulders are elevated and the head has a 'retracted' posture; there is visually noticeable muscular tension in the upper torso, especially bearing on the shoulders.

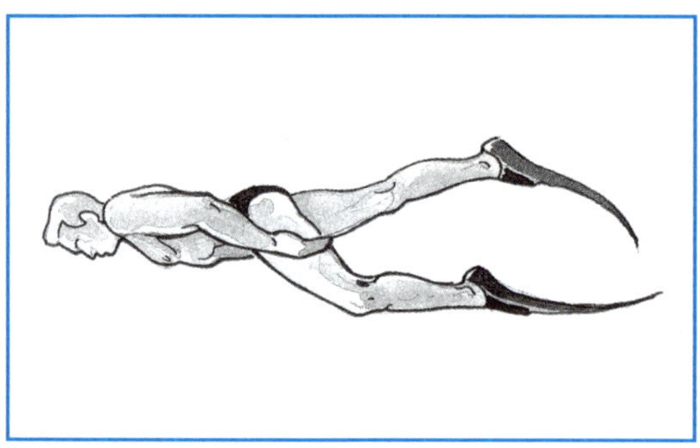

Causes:

- Nervous tension and anxiety.
- Muscular tension in the upper back.
- Problems of flexibility in the scapulo-humeral belt.
- Cold.

Effects:

- Reduction in the roll of the chest, and therefore less penetration through the water.
- Unrelaxed body position and possible difficulty in maintaining depth in dynamic apnea.
- This posture coupled with correct finning in the advance phase will produce a rotational movement of the chest on the longitudinal axis, inducing continued variations in body alignment.

Correction:

- Swim short stretches.
- Maintain the arms aligned to the sides: they should be relaxed.
- Make small, visually imperceptible movements with the head and shoulders to verify that there is no tension in the cervical muscles, trapeziums or scapulo-humeral belt.
- Feel the force of the water on the shoulders and allow them to assume a natural position.

14. Inversion of the rolling of the shoulders

Description: Normally, as in the action of walking, when the lower limbs move forward (for the finstroke the equivalent is the advance phase) there is an opposite movement of the shoulders: left shoulder-right leg and right shoulder-left leg. However in this error the action is inverted, so that movement of the right leg is coupled with movement of the right arm.

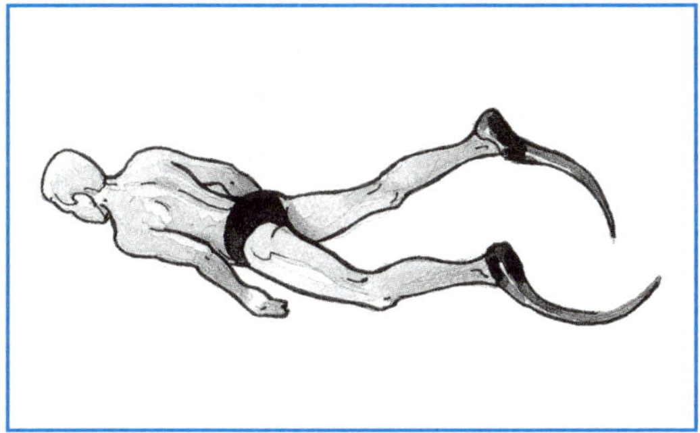

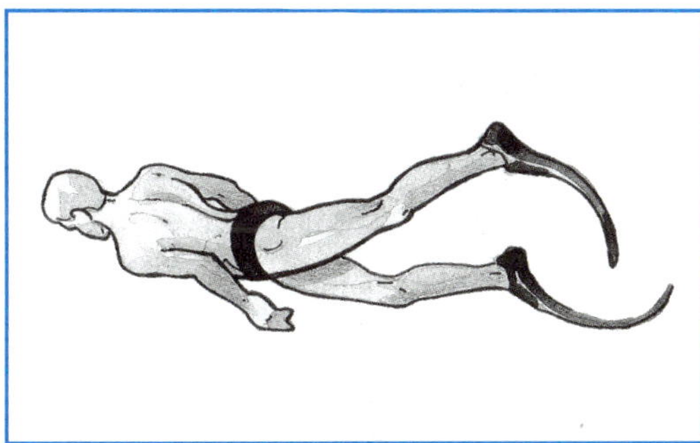

Causes:

- Lack of control of the action. Difficulty of coordination due to stress.
- In constant weight, an excessive relaxation; losing control of the action.

Effects:

- Inversion of the rolling movement of the shoulders and torso. When associated with the movement of the lower limbs this constantly alters position and alignment in the water, passing from a position on the left side to one on the right.
- In constant weight this error is evidenced by a rotation of the body on the longitudinal axis and continued oscillation of the body from left to right.

Correction:

- Vertical finning, keeping the shoulders out of the water or level with the surface. Utilize progressively heavier weighting to increase the load on the lower limbs and improve capacity of control over stress.
- Vertical finning, in front of the side of the pool, keeping both hands on the edge. With the arms tense, feel the force on the left hand in the advance phase of the right finstroke and vice versa.

15. An error of hydrodynamicity

Description: During the descent in constant weight, the apneist, who must compensate using the Valsalva method, brings the hand to the nose but keeps the elbow out at a distance from the body.

Causes:

- Nervous tension and anxiety.
- Lack of control of the action.
- Problems of flexibility in the scapulo-humeral belt.

Effects:

- Slowing of the descent due to the resistance of the arm.
- Loss of hydrodynamic body position.

Correction:

- Concentrate attention on the elbow.
- The relaxed movement of the hand to the nose must follow the median line of the body.
- Adopt the Marcante-Odaglia technique of compensation (*see Chapter 7*).

C – Inefficiencies of the fins

After having examined in detail the errors and the consequences of erratic movement of the body we now analyse the problems that can be attributed to inadequacies of the fins.

16. Loose foot pocket

Description: One of the greatest causes of a loss of efficiency in the fin is the imperfect compatibility of the foot with the foot pocket.

Causes: There aren't many models of foot pocket on the market, and therefore we are almost always restricted to choosing fins that at times may not fit perfectly. The compromise between comfort of the foot and efficiency of the transmission of movement to the blade is almost always made at the expense of the latter.

Effects: The 'play' of the foot in the foot pocket has repercussions on the passage of muscular impulses created in the lower limbs, with a consequent loss of power due to imperfect transmission of force from foot to the blade. Many apneists avoid this problem with the use of booties or socks of appropriate thickness.

In effect, this will homogenously reduce the 'play' of the foot in the foot pocket, but will not significantly reduce the gaps between the two, which are usually situated under the arch and above the joints of the toes.

It isn't easy to correct this problem, and it requires careful attention; a detailed analysis of the finstroke will help detect any energy loss in the foot/foot pocket system, but then only the personalisation of the foot pocket will resolve the problem.

Correction: You can attempt to reduce the play of the foot with thicknesses of neoprene, which if arranged correctly can restrain the movement of the foot without limiting it too much. In the sport of fin-swimming athletes use a type of sock that caps the toes, and in so doing forces the foot towards the heel. Others glue pieces of neoprene onto the inside of the foot pocket, as internal padding. It is easy to remodel a neoprene insole that can be fixed to the inside of the foot pocket.

17. Soft foot pocket

Description: The softness of a foot pocket depends on the structure and blend of the rubber with which it was constructed. It is only recently that manufacturers have begun to carefully evaluate technical features other than comfort. In particular, they are re-evaluating the importance of a foot pocket that favours the efficient transmission of force.

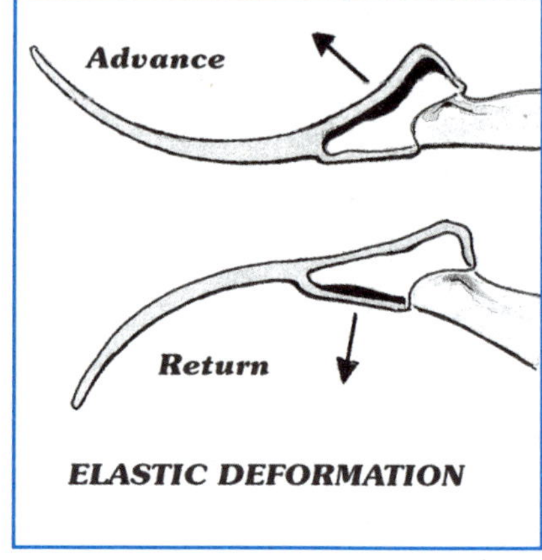

The parts in black show the 'play' between foot and foot pocket.

Causes: Excessive softness of any blend of rubber in the foot pocket, justified only by excessive pursuit of comfort. Inadequate form of the foot pocket. The thicknesses and reinforcements with which it was designed are not sufficient to maintain uniformity of the force produced by the apneist.

Effects: When the fin is flexed it is subjected to an important elastic deformation, in a particular way and in limited conditions, such as in the take off from the bottom or the first few strokes after the duck-dive, when hydrostatic resistance is greatest. In these moments the deformation will result in a loss of 'adherence' to the water. In the advance phase of the stroke the foot pushes against the instep, creating a space under the sole, whereas in the return phase the foot is pushed against the sole, causing a lengthening of the heel of the foot pocket. If the sole is too soft it will not remain uniform with the side spars and there will be a flexion due to the arch of the foot, exactly where the base of the blade is inserted between the side spars under the sole, producing an additional elongation of the heel of the foot pocket. The movements produced by the actions of the apneist will be dispersed due to the excessive softness of the rubber of the foot pocket, causing a great waste of energy.

Correction: Avoid overly soft foot pockets. It is better to forfeit comfort in favour of a greater adherence to efficiency.

18. Lack of lateral railing

Description: Experimental trials have demonstrated that long fins, even if they have strengthening spars that finish halfway down the blade, disperse about 20% of displaced water.

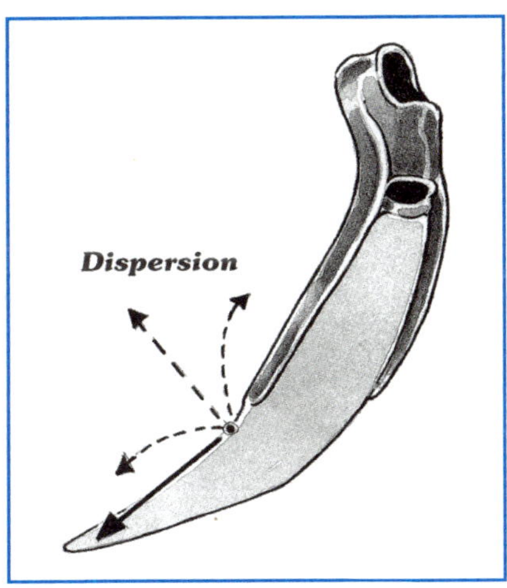

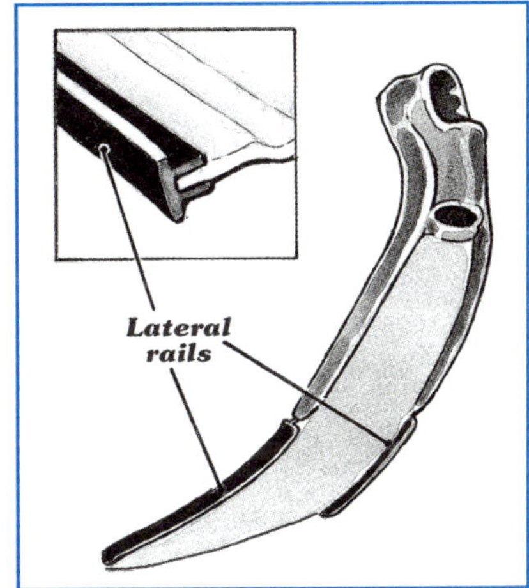

Causes: The lack of lateral rails that channel the flow of water produced by finning.

Effects: The fins skid laterally and the finstroke is often incorrect: the feet become Valgus (*see page 176*).

Correction: To reduce lateral dispersion, which actually flutters the fins, making them instable, it is sufficient to apply simple L-shaped profiles of rubber to the blade, like those used for sealing windows. However they cannot be too heavy, or the modification will become counterproductive by dampening the elastic response of the blade and reducing its return to the initial position after being bent, nor too light, or they will not channel the water enough.

Be careful not to confuse the railing with the ribbing present on the surface of the fin, which serves mainly to increase the rigidity of the blade for the same thickness, and not to channel the flow of water.

19. Junction between blade and foot pocket

Description: A drawback to fins with interchangeable blades is the junction between the blade and the foot pocket. If the two parts don't match well then there will be a degree of 'play' between them.

Causes: The reason is that the blade is held in place only by screws; essentially its assembly is inadequate.

Effects: Hence there is a certain amount of energy dispersion, even if it isn't to the same extent as with a loose or soft foot pocket.

Correction: This drawback can be simply resolved by sealing the spaces between the blade and the foot pocket and spars with silicon.
Remove the screws, take of the blade and remount it with silicon.

20. Inefficiency of the blade

Description: With time and use the blade's elasticity will change, and the materials will generally weaken, making the fin more liable to breakage.

Causes: This is especially true for plastic materials. Carbon has a greater resistance to use.

Effects: It is not easy to notice the diminution of performance of one's own fins.

Correction: To do so it is a good idea to regularly try other models, so as to understand the differences in terms of strength and snap (return).

6.5 THE MONOFIN

Man's history is strewn with examples of revolutionary technological solutions inspired by observations from nature. One need only watch a modern Boeing jet and think of Leonardo da Vinci's first dream of flight to understand the long and laborious road. The idea of flight was born from observations of birds, watching a log floating inspired boats, and while following marine mammals Jacques Mayol found the answers to the questions of *Homo Delphinus*, or the bond of the apneist with his aquatic origins. Forced by a weight into the abyss and by a balloon back to the light, Mayol and Maiorca began a struggle for conquest of the blue that lasted two decades. Neither of the two was ever offered an alternative to classic fins that could give underwater man a more effective system of propulsion. The solution could have been the monofin.

This tool had been used for years in fin swimming, and was designed specifically for this sport, where the action is horizontal and the athlete is not subjected to any variation of pressure. It was not suited to use at depth, where the force required to overcome hydrostatic pressure deforms its shape significantly during descent and ascent. However it gave rise to a new era for apneists, who started to modify their technique, adapting to the new sensation of having a single fin – a tail – instead of two independent extremities. This involved a completely different movement, more involved both in technique and sensation. A new way of moving underwater, of expressing and performing apnea, of liberating oneself in immersion. The movement is analogous to that of a dolphin's, using a greater number of muscle groups that, unlike the bifin action, aren't localised entirely in the lower half of the body. In equal conditions, the work seems less fatiguing and is more profitable in terms of velocity and therefore dive time.

The first to use the monofin in constant weight freediving was none other than the oldest daughter of Enzo Maiorca. On the 4th of July of **1992, Rossana Maiorca** was the first monofinning apneist to break a record: –58 meters in 1'48", sixteen seconds quicker than her –56 of the previous year. A decade later apneists have adopted this method as a more natural way of diving. Nature, in this case the cetaceans, has once more supplied us with a new and entirely different approach to the depths.

The final testimony to monofins is that a constant weight monofin dive is both quicker and more economical than with two fins. Compensation even seems easier, due to the action of the chest, ribcage and abdomen, which don't remain immobile, but accompany the wavelike movement. You might expect that since the total time of immersion is 30% shorter than a bifin dive to the same depth, compensation should be more difficult – or at least more hurried – but in reality the opposite is true.

The experience of many freedivers is that the undulating action of the body favours compensation, especially if the rhythm is fluid. This could be attributed to the pleasure and relaxation induced by the movement. However the chief reason is that as the wave of movement passes through the body it applies pressure to the diaphragm. In particular, this is caused by muscles in the abdomen, which, together with the glutei and leg abductors, participate in the closing movement of the stroke. In the down kick the arching of the chest exerts a pressure on the diaphragm, which displaces air from the lungs towards the head, i.e. to clear the ears. This has been demonstrated in many athletes.

Choosing a monofin

Most monofins on the market have been designed to satisfy the movement of fin swimmers. The blade will have certain properties of flexion and elasticity (Kg of force) in relation to the discipline (speed, depth, etc) and the anthropometrical characteristics of the swimmer. There are four possible materials: plastic, fibreglass, carbon fibre and carbon mix (a mixture of fibreglass and carbon fibre). Each of these materials has particular physical characteristics that favour performance to different degrees. Footage of monofin freedivers has shown that the lateral wings can bend out of shape, losing efficiency in the push of the blade. To correct this defect many athletes proposed a monofin design with bracing that allows it to bend in the centre whilst maintaining rigidity on the external edge in order to convey the flow of water into the centre. This is the so-called 'spoon effect' and is very beneficial to the advance phase of the kick. Once more the idea is born from observation of the caudal fins of cetaceans such as dolphins. This design has been experimented in Russia, but trials are always orientated towards fin swimming.

From our underwater vantage point we sometimes see the propellers of passing boats, and will notice that they are not all the same – they depend on the size of the engine and the purpose of the boat. The same applies to the fin, which is our body's propeller.

In choosing fins, and in particular monofins, we must make a compromise between required performance and how much we are willing to spend. In this field cost is often synonymous with highly researched materials, and production by manufacturers who are almost artisans. In general the carbon fibre used for the blade is produced in the form of a tissue, with a weave that is orientated to give resistance and elasticity in the right directions. The fin can be composed of as much as 60% fibre and this imparts optimal mechanical properties to the material. The fibres are set in a matrix that protects the fibres as well as redistributes force uniformly. Carbon fibre blades frequently contain fibreglass in the middle.

Most monofins are made from fibreglass or glass/carbon mixes fixed with epoxy resin. The advantage is that they are cheaper than pure carbon fibre fins, but maintain the same mechanical qualities.

In analysing a monofin's elastic properties, we assume that deformation (bend) is directly proportional to the force applied, and define rigidity as the constant of this proportionality. In other words, for an equal deformation of a blade that is twice as rigid you will need to double the force. Several models of monofin come classified with a number expressed in kilograms of force, which defines their rigidity by describing the amount of weight that must be applied to a point on the fin to obtain a particular deformation. The more rigid the fin, the more weight is necessary to bend it.

The type of rigidity is defined by the type of force applied. For our purposes we will be interested in rigidity in the sagittal plane (Figure 1), i.e. how much the blade bends when force is applied from the side of apneist. This property depends both on the material and the cross-section of the blade. A blade made with plastic polymers will have a lesser rigidity than a composite fibre blade of the same thickness.

It is necessary also to evaluate torsion and flexibility in the plane orthogonal to movement (transverse plane). The great advantage of composite materials, whether fibreglass, carbon fibre or a mixture, with respect to the traditional materials, is that by changing the order of layering we can obtain variable elasticity using the same base materials. We can create fins that are rigid in the centre and flexible at the edges, and fins with the opposite arrangement that produce the spoon effect (convex curve). An elevated resistance to torsion is always recommended to avoid S-shaped deformations along the free edge.

However the most important property is flexibility in the

direction of movement. As we have mentioned, elasticity depends also on thickness, so that to keep the fin flexible requires reducing its thickness. A fin that is flexible but resistant at the right places (at the junction between blade and foot pocket, and at the end of the spars) adopts a changing profile at different sections, thinner where flexibility is required and thicker where resistance is required.

Deformations of the blade

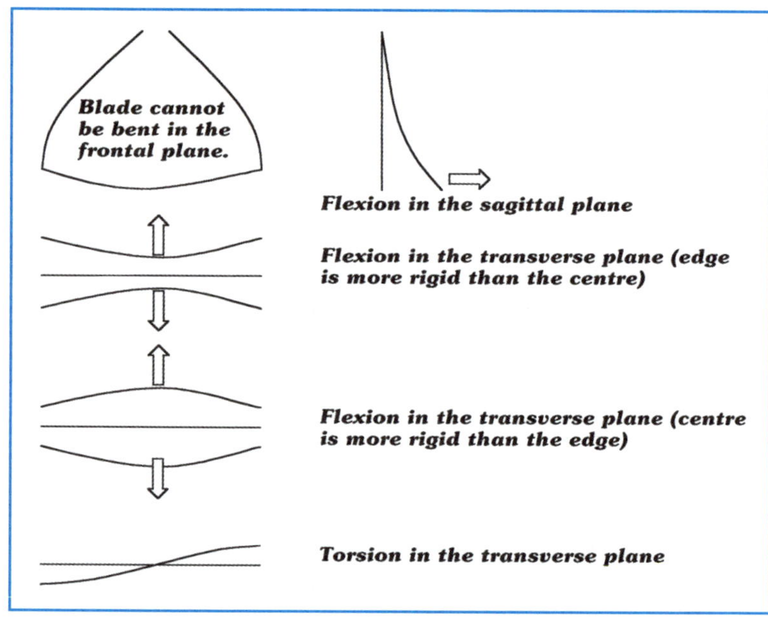

PRELIMINARY MONOFIN EXERCISES

Finning underwater is more complex with one fin than it is with two. Despite its advantages the monofin requires a flexibility of the spine and a greater coordination.

Experience has taught us that the weak point in an imperfect action is almost always dependant on the lumbar area and the flexibility of the shoulders. Partial stiffness or rigidity of the joints in these areas will limit the fluidity of the action. An inflexibility that prevents the arms lengthening forwards in line with the back makes it difficult to achieve a good body position in the water, and increases resistance to forwards movement. Little or no mobility of the vertebral column will impede the passage of oscillatory movement (which is intrinsic to the action) along the biomechanical chain of joints from head to foot. In an attempt to generate a force that compensates for this inflexibility, the knees are often bent excessively, reducing the efficiency of the action.

In the light of these considerations the following exercises are aimed at increasing sensitivity to the movement in water and therefore:

- mobilise the relevant joints;
- improve muscular elasticity, strength and endurance;
- improve coordination of the actions that compose the specific technique.

The exercises apply a precise learning progression that gradually develops the whole monofin action. This principle should be applied to any training session, and therefore it is best to start with free body, followed by bifin exercises and finishing with the monofin. In this way the resistance to the propulsive action in water is gradually increased.

Free body exercises

The following progression of exercises are performed first with free body and subsequently with equipment. They involve different positions that increase sensitivity to the oscillatory movement of the pelvis, which generates a wave of energy that propagates through the body until it unloads itself on the monofin and hence the water. All the relevant muscular groups must work in synergy and this can only be achieved by sensing their movement. The aim of the exercises is to increase this sensitivity.

1. Perform dolphin kicks in a dorsal position, with arms by the sides and the head in line with the spine. The action must involve the whole vertebral column. To control the movement it will help to concentrate on the pelvis, which must follow an oscillatory motion of rising and falling.
2. Perform dolphin kicks in a prone position with the arms still by the sides. The head is in line with the spine, meaning that the face is immersed. In order to breath, raise the head at intervals of a certain amount of kicks. The point of reference in this exercise is still the pelvis, and we must continue to focus on its oscillatory motion.
3. In a lateral position (first on the left then on the right side) perform dolphin kicks, whilst maintaining the head in line with the spine. In this position it will be easy to visually control the movement of the legs and correct any bending of the knees.
4. All of the above exercises can be executed with the arms extended past the head. The alignment and closure of the forearms above the head will be extremely beneficial to mobility of the shoulders and elbows. This position will also improve hydrodynamics in the water.

Exercises with short fins

The following exercises are the same as proposed for the free body. The use of short fins increases resistance to movement of the feet, producing a more effective advance. There will also be a greater load on the muscles involved in maintaining a hydrodynamic position. These exercises represent a small step towards the correct use of a monofin.

5. Positioned dorsally, perform dolphin kicks of the legs with short fins attached. Arms should be by the sides and the head in line with the spine. As for the analogous exercises performed with free body, concentrate on two parts of the body: the pelvis and the knees. The first must oscillate freely while flexion of the latter must be restrained.
6. Perform dolphin kicks in a prone position with the arms by the sides, and the head aligned with the vertebral column. A correct position of the head will mean that the face, and therefore the airways, are immersed. It will be easiest to perform this exercise using a fin-swimming snorkel (which are positioned centrally). Otherwise the head can be raised forwards to breath at regular intervals.
7. In a lateral position (first on the left then on the right side) perform dolphin kicks, whilst maintaining the head in line with the spine. As for the exercise with free body you will be able to visually control the movement of the legs out of the bottom of your eyes.
8. Another step forwards will be the execution of the above exercises with the arms lengthened past the head. This body position will favour the hydrodynamics of the movement, making it more efficient and more similar to the final movement with the monofin.

Exercises with freediving fins

To further approach the techniques of the monofin, whilst respecting the criteria of gradual progression, we can substitute the short fins for the long bladed variety used in freediving. Once again there will be a greater displacement of water and therefore a more effective advance. The feeling of resistance to the feet will also increase, which is the purpose of the exercises.

9. Positioned dorsally, perform dolphin kicks of the legs, maintaining the head in line with the spine. The gaze is directed up towards the sky whilst concentration is focussed on body position in the water. The oscillation of the pelvis is still critical and the wave that this produces must travel uninterrupted from the shoulders to the fins.
10. Perform dolphin kicks in a prone position with the arms

by the sides, and the head aligned with the vertebral column. In order to breathe you can raise the head forwards or, for greater continuity in the action, a centrally mounted snorkel can be used. Remember to concentrate on the movement of the pelvis through the water.

11. In a lateral position (first on the left then on the right side) perform dolphin kicks, whilst maintaining the head in line with the spine. Together with the sensations of the action it will be easier to have a more precise idea of the wave movement and to correct any errors. Remember that the action starts from the pelvis with an oscillatory movement that, due to the position, develops in an anterior – posterior direction, i.e. from head to toe.
12. As for the exercises with short fins, all the above exercises can be performed with the arms lengthened past the head. In this position the whole of the body will act against the water, unloading the wave energy created by the oscillation of the pelvis.
13. Fin with dolphin kicks in a prone position, with the hands placed one on top of the other in the middle of a flutterboard. The head must be aligned with the vertebral column – do not hyperextend it! Exert pressure on the flutterboard, pushing it forwards, not towards the bottom. This will have the effect of lengthening the body in the water, extending the shoulders and arms into an even more hydrodynamic position. The use of a fin-swimming snorkel will allow easy breathing without having to raise the head.

EXERCISES WITH THE MONOFIN

After having tried, felt and understood the oscillatory movement of the pelvis with different levels of resistance to the feet we can now move to the use of the monofin. To start with we recommend using a very soft blade, possibly with a reduced surface area. The initial sensations will definitely be pleasurable, but be careful not to get carried away with the speed and the ease of movement that can be obtained, even with an incorrect knee action – an error that once engrained will be difficult to put right.

14. Position yourself dorsally, and with the arms along the sides move the legs with dolphin kicks, keeping the head aligned with the vertebral column. The monofin will offer a greater surface of resistance with respect to the bifins, and will give a sensation of flight. Don't let yourself be

overcome with the feeling of the water sliding past the body without force; the knees are the weak point in which we generally lose control of the movement and end up bending excessively without oscillating the pelvis correctly. Remember that the wave action starts from the pelvis and passes uninterrupted through the body from shoulders to fins.

15. In a prone position with the arms by the sides, move the legs with dolphin kicks, maintaining the head in line with the vertebral column. A fin-swimming snorkel will allow easy breathing without needing to raise the head, meaning that the action can be more fluid without annoying interruptions.
16. In a lateral position (first on the left then on the right side) perform dolphin kicks, whilst maintaining the head in line with the spine. The monofin should still be totally immersed in the water, and using goggles or a mask you will be able to control the action of the legs and the oscillation of the pelvis without changing the position of the head.
17. All the above exercises can be performed with the arms lengthened past the head. This is the final position that characterises the movement of the monofin. All of the preceding preliminary exercises with the arms extended have the aim of mobilising, reinforcing and increasing sensitivity in the joints and muscles used to maintain body position and propagate the wave action initiated in the pelvis. We thus finally put to the trial the techniques that we have learnt in the progression towards a complete movement for the monofin.

COMPENSATION

CHAPTER

7

"Today I just couldn't seem to equalise". "With these ears of mine I'll never be able to go underwater". These are some of the most common phrases of apneists who have an exasperating sensitivity for the health of their ears. Their apprehension is more than justified; any kind of problem with the auditory apparatus has but one consequence: no diving.

Compensation means preventing inwards squeeze of the eardrums due to the increase of hydrostatic pressure during diving; to do so it is necessary to introduce air into the middle ear with the 'compensatory manoeuvres' described in this chapter, restoring the eardrum to its initial position.

During the descent the increasing ambient pressure causes a compression on our body. The tissues that compose the human body are for the most part constituted of liquid and bone, and can therefore be considered incompressible. Nevertheless there are cavities that must be equalised to the ambient pressure.

As we descend into the depths we will need to practice appropriate manoeuvres that facilitate the flow of air into these cavities (ears, frontal and paranasal sinuses), in order to compensate the variations with external pressure. If this doesn't happen then the organs and anatomical structures in question will undergo damage (barotraumas) due to the uncompensated pressure. During freediving, compensation doesn't just involve the ears and sinuses, but also the mask. This piece of equipment constitutes another important airspace – connected to the nose – that is subjected to the ambient pressure variations, and which therefore must be compensated. In this chapter we propose techniques and manoeuvres of compensation that, if followed correctly, will help the apneist to overcome problems of pressure.

7.1 COMPENSATORY MANOEUVRES

Compensation is a completely subjective manoeuvre. It is impossible to give definite answers to the questions: "How often should I compensate?" and "How many times do you compensate in the first twenty meters?" There is no precise physical law – it depends exclusively on the sensitivity of the eardrum and the capacity of the apneist.

However the first fifteen to twenty meters is certainly the most delicate zone, since the frequency of compensation is greatest. This is due to the fact that the pressure at –10 meters is double that of the surface, but with successive increases of ten meter's depth the extra atmosphere of pressure will have a proportionally lesser effect. Translating this into practical terms, the first 10 meters of depth require the greatest number of compensations. Problems of compensation due to pathologies will almost always arise in the first ten meters of depth, and rarely deeper.

The first compensation must be executed immediately after the duck dive, at less than a meter's depth. There are basically two techniques: the first, simpler technique takes the name of Antonio Valsalva; the second technique, which is a little more complex, was discovered by, and is named after, Marcante and Odaglia.

Valsalva Manoeuvre

This is executed by shutting the mouth and squeezing the nostrils closed with the fingers. **It is the easiest and most spontaneous technique.** It is sufficient to blow out, whereupon the air, unable to exit through nose or mouth, will be forced into the middle ear and therefore against the eardrum.

Marcante-Odaglia manoeuvre

Compensation is effected by particular movements of the jaw and of musculature connected to the movement of the tongue, which exerts pressure on the soft palate.

The Marcante-Odaglia manoeuvre is slightly more difficult to perform: one may succeed in executing it normally out of the water, but when diving the chance of success is less. The ability to compensate in water with this technique depends, especially at the start, on natural gift and a particular disposition, but it is possible to acquire these with training and with tubular exercises.

Other manoeuvres

There exist other techniques of compensation that are effected with particular movements of the tongue, soft palate and jaw.

Correct movements of these structures act on the muscles that control the opening of the Eustachian tubes and the reduction of pharyngeal volume, thereby forcing air into the middle ear.

The arguments in favour of compensating using manoeuvres of the tongue-jaw-palate, or the Marcante-Odaglia manoeuvre are obvious:

- **it is more comfortable**, and less traumatic for the ear;
- **it allows both hands to be kept completely free**, since in well trained apneists the pressure of the mask against the nose is enough to allow compensation;
- **it does not require the intervention of pulmonary pressure**, nor does it have any repercussions on the lungs, avoiding the cardiocirculatory alterations and inconveniences attributed to the Valsalva, and making it particularly advisable for the apneist;
- **one can perform the manoeuvre even in conditions of expiration**. For this reason, it is not just advisable but almost imperative for very deep freediving;
- although it requires a more complex execution and particular abilities, **one can obtain a pressure even greater than with the Valsalva**, without requiring an exceptionally muscular physique;
- other than increasing the pressure, it simultaneously **activates a movement similar to swallowing**, but more intense and localized near to the orifice of the Eustachian tubes, favouring their opening and enabling compensation with pressures inferior to those required by the Valsalva;
- **it uses muscles that are far smaller than those required by Valsalva**, and this is of obvious value to economy of oxygen use;
- **it is more rapidly executed** and can be repeated continually with minimum force and great ease.

VALSALVA TECHNIQUE

Antonio Maria Valsalva (1666-1723), celebrated anatomist and author of the study *The Human Aura*, gave his name to the compensatory manoeuvre that is today used by millions of divers. At the beginning of 17th century Antonio Valsalva used this manoeuvre to expel, by puncturing the eardrum, the purulent substance of otitis media. The Valsalva was successively used in immersion, and his correct expression of Pascal's law was coined to describe it: **"A pressure created in a major cavity will diffuse uniformly into all the connected minor cavities."**

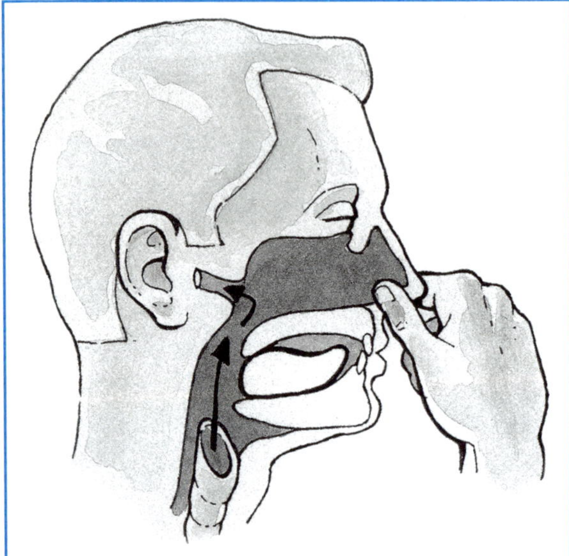

The manoeuvre consists in exerting maximum expiratory force during an inspiratory apnea and maintaining the mouth and nose firmly closed. Since thc natural exits are blocked, the expiratory force causes an increase in intrathoracic pressure, which, in these conditions, finds its way toward the external air in the direction of the eardrum.

Given that the pressure was created by an expiratory force, i.e. a decrease in endothoracic volume, **Valsalva must be practiced during inspiratory apnea to give the maximum effectiveness.**

From what has been said thus far it should follow that a subject cannot execute the Valsalva after a maximum forced exhalation, and thus an apneist at maximum depth will not be able to obtain the maximum force, or rather the maximum pressure, since the volume of air has been reduced in relation to depth. In reality many apneists that descend to great depths will initially use the Marcante-Odaglia or other compensation techniques involving the tongue, before passing to Valsalva in the very last part of the descent. The result doesn't depend merely on strength, but most importantly on ability to remain relaxed and to behave at depth with the same fluency and control as that displayed on the surface.

To conclude, the Valsalva is useful when it is difficult to compensate the middle ear. In these cases it is necessary to compensate much more often – the delay between compensations should be short, as the suction effect of the Eustachian tube will compromise the action. Some apneists use the strategy of keeping the tubes constantly open in the first ten or twenty meters of the descent. A good ability of compensation, whether with Valsalva or Marcante-Odaglia, allows the tubes to be kept open, favouring a continual passage of air to equalise the pressure in the middle ear.

MARCANTE-ODAGLIA TECHNIQUE

Duilio Marcante, one of the founders of Italian diving, and the professor Giorgio Odaglia, pioneer of hyperbaric medicine, gave their names to the compensatory manoeuvre termed the Marcante-Odaglia, which in some countries is more commonly known as the 'Frenzel manoeuvre'.

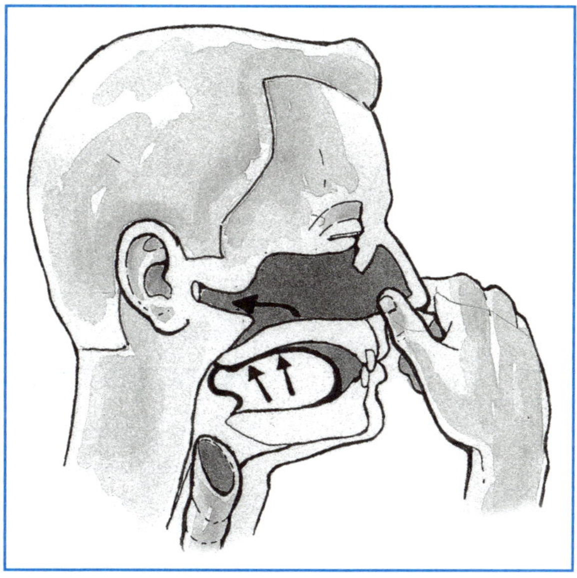

The principle that inspired this technique is simple: **it is much more advantageous and less energy expensive to pressurise a smaller air space, like that of the nasopharynx, than a larger space, like that of the lungs.** The trick, therefore, is to completely isolate the region of the nasopharynx – where you will remember the Eustachian tubes begin – from all other internal and external air cavities. The separation of the external environment happens through closing the nose: either squeezing it shut with the fingers or exploiting the pressure exerted by the mask. Separation from the respiratory airways is achieved by forcing the soft palate upwards and closed. This causes a reduction in the already small space of the naso-pharynx, and therefore a reduction of the volume of gas contained. Given that volume is inversely proportional to pressure (Boyle's Law), the latter increases.

The soft palate is forced upwards by a retraction of the tongue, which fills the oral pharynx and pushes against the soft palate in a position similar to that assumed when swallowing. Acting upwards like a piston, it thereby compresses the air contained in the little cavity. Furthermore the action of the tongue is associated with the contraction of pharyngeal muscles. These muscles are close to the orifices of the Eustachian tubes and assist in their opening, and therefore the passage of pressurised air towards the middle ear.

Expert apneists often claim to use compensatory manoeuvres identified as Valsalva, but which with further analysis turn out to be variations of the Marcante-Odaglia.

To ascertain which is being used, one need only try to compensate repeatedly with the mouth open after an expiration, whilst keeping one hand on the upper abdomen. If you feel the classic 'vibration' of the eardrum, which is a symptom of the increase in pressure, and the upper abdomen remains immobile, then the manoeuvre executed is the Marcante-Odaglia and not the Valsalva. However there is an exception. Sometimes in order to execute this manoeuvre correctly the respiratory apparatus moves at the same time, perhaps out of force of habit or reflex; you will therefore need to try to keep the ribs and diaphragm completely still.

As has been mentioned, the Marcante-Odaglia will be successful when the hand on the upper abdomen doesn't feel any movement, when there is a feeling of the tubes being opened and the two eardrum membranes flex outwards from the pressure that acts on their internal face.

PERSONAL TECHNIQUES

The compensatory manoeuvres cited above will help to develop a technique that better suits individual characteristics and requirements. However it will be more difficult to acquire the necessary proficiency to manage the various techniques in extreme conditions.

It is important never to wait for the pain when equalising – always anticipate it slightly. Remember that the best compensatory manoeuvre is the one that requires the least amount of force.

Rather than understanding all the techniques without knowing how to perform them, **it is better to adapt yourself to pressure with a personal manoeuvre that is effective for you.** It is very important for safety that the apneist understands his or her compensatory manoeuvre. At times, personalised manoeuvres turn out to be a compromise between those cited above, and adequately complement the characteristics of the apneist. Ignoring this simple but critical aspect can be a great risk for the safety of the ears. In the deep end of the pool you can experiment with all the different techniques of compensation – firstly head-up, then head-down – to put in place your own method of compensation.

Some ideas for exercises are: compensating head-up while attached to a weighted rope, a pole, or a deep enough ladder, or practicing compensation in the extreme condition of maximum expiration, in the deep end of the pool.

During the descent try to move the jaw forwards or backwards. You can move the tongue in an almost caressing movement of the palate that reaches the softest part at the back. You can also bend the tongue completely backwards as if you intended to push it down your throat. Actively swallowing may also assist in equalisation.

7.2 USING THE DIAPHRAGM TO COMPENSATE

As we have seen in Chapter 2, the diaphragm is a plate of muscle situated between the lungs and the stomach. Essential for respiration, it favours the use of the lower part of the lungs, which is the most important area for capacity since it moves the greatest quantity of air, whether inhaling or exhaling.

If this muscle is well trained it can be of major value in the most difficult phase of compensation. **An apneist that effectively controls the diaphragm will benefit from a greater reserve of air for compensation.**

As we know, the volume of air in the lungs reduces with an increase of pressure (Boyle's Law). Therefore at a certain depth, taking into account that some of the air inspired on the surface will have been utilized to compensate the mask and ears, the reserve of air will be at a minimum, and compensation will be most difficult. When a freediver nears this depth limit it becomes essential to take air from the lower part of the lungs to compensate.

Correct movements of the diaphragm will allow us to transcend that critical threshold where we normally have the sensation of not being able to continue, and think: "I've run out of air to compensate with!"

When we feel that it is impossible, due to the depth, to force more air toward the eardrum, then the only air still available will be that which we can move from the lungs to the ears using the diaphragm. To make matters worse, in normal freediving and in constant weight record attempts the body is upside down, meaning the ears are positioned beneath the lungs.

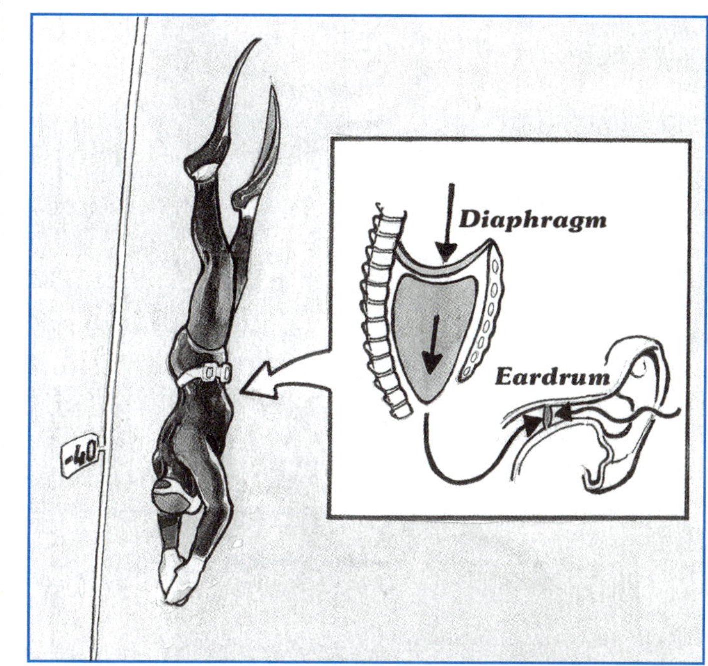

It is important not to 'tense up', and to keep all the muscles of the thoracic cage and neck completely relaxed. With correct diaphragmatic movement the manoeuvre will be effective, with a displacement of air in the direction of the head and therefore towards the ears: air that is over and above what a traditional compensation allows the apneist. After this diaphragm contraction a normal compensatory manoeuvre should equalise the air-spaces as per usual.

Therefore a good flexibility of the thorax and an accomplished control of the diaphragm will allow more efficient use of air resources for compensation. As we have seen in chapter 4.2, exercises that train diaphragmatic respiration and stretch the ribcage will rehabilitate correct function in this part of our body. Training the diaphragm is as important as training the legs, fitness or static apnea.

7.3 TUBULAR AEROBICS

The exercises that are proposed in this section constitute a new approach to the activity of compensation. They are aimed at **training all the structures of the nasal-pharyngeal-tubular area that are directly or indirectly involved in the mechanics of the Eustachian tube**, with the goal of creating a smooth and efficient system, ready to confront compensation at depth.

We have divided these exercises into two categories: **muscular exercises** that reinforce and synchronise the structures of the nasal-pharyngeal-tubular area; and **manoeuvres of autoinsufflation** that specifically train the Eustachian tubes. These exercises must be executed out of the water.

THE PURPOSES OF TUBULAR EXERCISES

The exercises that we propose in these pages are helpful to:

1. reinforce and synchronise the structures of the nasal-pharyngeal-tubular area;
2. impart an awareness and competency aimed at obtaining an effective and appropriate compensation;
3. protect the auditory structures from lesions of any kind, safeguarding their auditory function;
4. allow anyone to discover, and be able to apply the best technique of compensation, tailored to suit personal capacity and objectives.

MUSCULAR EXERCISES

Each time you perform one of the proposed exercises try to achieve a better coordination, without forcing the structure.

WHAT, WHEN AND HOW MUCH TO EXERCISE

Tubular exercises, like all muscular training, should be executed daily for the first 20-30 days. During this period perform all the proposed exercises and manoeuvres for at least 10-15 minutes per day, sitting comfortably in front of the mirror and automating the proper movements without following them blindly, which won't bring the results desired. Subsequently, it is enough to maintain the exercises once a week and to intensify the activity the day before diving, in order to prepare the structures.

Tongue exercises

Bring the tongue as far as possible out of the mouth, towards the chin, then retract it and force it all the way back, keeping the tip of the tongue on the floor of the mouth.

Brush the roof of the mouth with the tongue, moving from front to back and trying to reach the soft palate. The correct execution of this exercise is often accompanied by a vomit reflex.

Trace the perimeter of the lips with the tongue, rotating clockwise then anticlockwise.

Jaw exercises

Repeatedly open and close the mouth.

Move the jaw laterally, from right to left and back again, without contracting the lips.

Rotate the jaw on the frontal plane, clockwise then anticlockwise.

Repeatedly protrude and retract the jaw, keeping it on a transverse plane.

During the execution of these exercises, if one or the other of the ears contains mucous in the middle ear cavity it is quite likely that the subject will hear a noise like paper tearing. If the middle ear is free the only possible noise will be the sound of mandibular articulation.

Soft palate exercises

These exercises are very important, as the muscles of the soft palate play a primary role in the dynamics of the tubes. If possible watch and analyse the quality of movement of the soft palate in a mirror.

Pronounce a series of three quick and powerful /ah/ sounds, then close the mouth for a few seconds and recommence.

These vocalisations provoke a firm and complete contraction of the soft palate; if this does not occur then it is necessary to continue with this type of exercise until successful. The pause is recommended because a longer series can cause an uninterrupted contraction of the palate, making the movements imperceptible. In the same fashion pronounce successive series of /ee/, /eh/, /oh/, /oo/, /eek/, /ak/, /ok/, /ook/.

Contract the soft palate without emitting a sound (this corresponds to the enunciation of a silent /ah/ sound).

Using an tongue depressor or a spoon, you can touch the soft palate and stimulate a reflex contraction. For some people this exercise is not appropriate, as it stimulates the vomit reflex.

Breathing exercises

Blow out a candle from an increasing distance, inflate balloons, and exhale through a straw into a container of water. Breathing exercises assume a perfect closure of the soft palate, so no air should escape from the nose at all.

Emit vowel sounds with varying intensity and pitch. This exercise involves displacements of the larynx and soft palate.

Tongue-soft palate exercises

Slide the tongue over the palate from front to back, keeping it well in contact until it falls, producing a characteristic clicking sound. Usually we tend to produce this sound by striking the tip of the tongue quickly and repeatedly on the back of the bottom teeth; note that the correct exercise instead involves the top surface of the tongue, and the tip falls further backwards.

Keeping the mouth open, move the tongue like a piston towards the soft palate, and at the same time contract the soft palate, without emitting a sound. The tip of the tongue is kept in contact with the floor of the mouth.

Tongue-jaw-soft palate exercises

Try to induce a yawn by means of a deep oral inhalation, followed by a 2-3 second apnea, during which the mouth is kept open and the palate contracted without making a sound, then release the air with an oral exhalation. Yawning is an important physiological mechanism as it involves many muscles and causes an active opening of the Eustachian tubes.

Execute the following succession of movements:

- Extend and lower the jaw.
- Push the tongue out of the mouth as far as possible towards the chin.
- Retract the tongue, brushing the palate from front to back, keeping the mouth open.
- Emit an /ah/ sound.
- Close the mouth and gently retract the jaw.

Swallowing exercise

Take a gulp of water into the mouth, pinch the nose closed and swallow, whilst lowering the head. This position sends the air displaced by the liquid towards the tubes, and protects the airway, avoiding inhalation of water and coughing.

The swallowing exercise can be performed using any type of drink (fruit juice, milk, fruit shake etc). The greater the volume and density of the water in the mouth, the more air will be mobilised. The tubes are also opened by belching, so it is also possible to use fizzy drinks, closing the nose at the moment when air rises back up.

Single and double airway expiration exercise

This exercise favours nasal respiration, opening of the tubes (due to the pressure changes created during this type of respiration), aeration of the nasopharynx and nasal cavities and stimulation of movements of the soft palate. At first one nostril is used at a time – the second is closed with the simple pressure of a finger – but subsequently both nostrils are used together.

- Nasal inspiration and oral expiration
- Calm and comfortable inspiration and expiration
- Short and forced inspiration followed by a calm expiration
- Calm inspiration followed by a short and forced expiration
- Short and forced inspiration and expiration.

AUTOINSUFFLATION

The term 'autoinsufflation manoeuvre' is used to identify an exercise useful for the training of the Eustachian tube. Optimal condition of the Eustachian tube – critical for compensation – is based on a continued and balanced muscular training.

In this section we will examine in detail several exercises of autoinsufflation: these are basically compensatory manoeuvres performed 'dry'.

The tubular exercises must always be performed in the way indicated in the following pages; however during immersion they can be modified according to freedom of movement and requirements of the individual. Whether

WARNING

The opening of the Eustachian tubes during autoinsufflation manoeuvres is evidenced in most people by a 'click' inside the ear.
There may be a bothersome sensation during the initial session of autoinsufflation manoeuvres and in the first exercises with the balloon and nose-piece, but this is not cause for concern. It is caused by the repeated introflexion and extroflexion (due to the movement of air) of a hypo-mobile eardrum, and will disappear as soon as the condition of hyper-pressure is interrupted.
However if the annoyance becomes painful it is advisable to discontinue autoinsufflation and receive an otoscopy exam in order to prevent the acute, light or initial phase of middle ear inflammation.

diving or training out of the water, it is necessary to remember that **these manoeuvres should never be performed if the ear is inflamed or in cases of bad colds**. This is to avoid pathogenic agents climbing the tube and the movement of air and liquid in the middle ear that could cause pain and damage to the structure. Instead, in these cases the muscular exercises are very helpful, as they favour the aeration and cleaning of an inflamed ear.

Compensatory manoeuvres can protect the ear and make a dive more pleasurable, provided that they are perfectly understood and executed at the right time and place. Their success is based on a correct and constantly stimulated activity of the Eustachian tubes.

As we have emphasised, these exercises are aimed at allowing anyone to obtain maximum mastery of the structures involved in compensation. In doing so it can happen that, possibly during training in a pool, and when the physical and surrounding conditions allow, the Valsalva and Marcante-Odaglia manoeuvres can be substituted by movements targeted at single muscles, obtaining the same result, but with a lesser expense of air and energy.

Valsalva manoeuvre

1. Execute a moderately deep oral inspiration.
2. Close the mouth, lower the head, and gently pinch the nose with two fingers.
3. Breathe out powerfully into the closed nose, without inflating the cheeks or opening the mouth.
4. Maintain this condition for 3-4 seconds.
5. Free the nose, allowing the air to exit.

The manoeuvre must be short and it is advisable to allow a moment's relaxation between one execution and the next, so as to avoid hyperventilation.

The Valsalva manoeuvre is effective if the momentary state of hyper-pressure created in the nasopharynx during the exercise is sufficient to cause the opening of the tubes.

In fact, if a more elevated pressure is required then a possible sudden opening could cause great damage.

To reduce the thoracic hyper-pressure that is created during the manoeuvre, it is a good idea to pronounce two vowel sounds in succession, after the oral inspiration and before proceeding to the autoinsufflation.

Mysuria manoeuvre

1. Execute a moderately deep oral inspiration.
2. Inflate the cheeks with the inspired air and pinch the nose closed with two fingers of a hand.

3. Place the thumb of the second hand on one cheek, the palm on the mouth and the fingers on the other cheek.
4. Place the base of the tongue against the soft palate, and push lightly backwards.
5. Squash the cheeks with a light pressure of the fingers, without allowing the air to escape from the mouth, and at the same time lower the head and swallow.

The Mysuria manoeuvre combines the hyper-pressure of the nasopharynx with a contraction of the entire pharyngeal zone, caused by the act of swallowing. There is a reduced amount of pressure required to open the tubes with respect to that required by the Valsalva manoeuvre.

Marcante-Odaglia manoeuvre, or Frenzel

The nasopharynx is turned into a closed cavity full of pressurised air that is easily forced towards the middle ear through the Eustachian tube.

We have discussed this at length in the preceding section, but it will help to be reminded that this manoeuvre requires the most coordination.

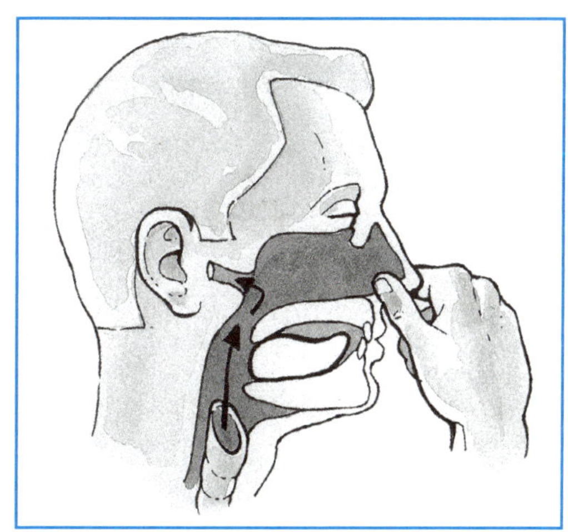

1. Draw air up into the oral cavity by a pumping action of the base of the tongue.
2. Maintain both the nose closed and epiglottis closed for the entire duration of the exercise.
3. During the exercise the soft palate must be repeatedly contracted.

Using an instrument of autoinsufflation

There are instruments available that, if used correctly, allow for the compensation of the middle ear, guaranteeing proper function of the transmission system of the eardrum and ossicles and a suitable ventilation of the cavity behind the eardrum. With these instruments, air may be injected through the nostrils towards the cavity of the nasopharynx, where the orifices of the Eustachian tubes are located.

The success of the exercise is only guaranteed under normal anatomic and physiological conditions of the tube, on the basis of which the instruments were designed. If these conditions are not present, and the pressure alterations and functional problems of the middle ear are derived from a prolonged state of insufficient activity or inactivity of the tubes, then for a complete and specific treatment it is necessary to precede the exercise with a program of 'tubular aerobics'. These are then continued while the autoinsufflation exercises are gradually introduced.

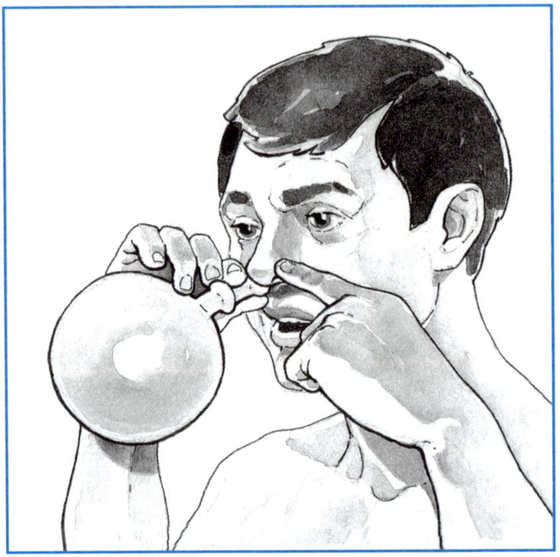

Most autoinsufflation instruments consist in a plastic toggle that is inserted into a nostril and connected to a balloon. They are used as follows:

1. Place the round part of the toggle in contact with a nostril, and close the other nostril with a finger.
2. Perform a deep oral inspiration and close the mouth.
3. Breathe air out through the nose to inflate the balloon.

We now suggest several exercises with this instrument. Don't forget that for a complete execution the exercises should be performed through both nostrils!

Exercise A

1. Inflate the balloon to the required dimensions.
2. Breathe the air from the balloon into the nose.
3. Swallow.

The swallowing exercise associates the active opening of the tubes caused by the swallowing to a passive mechanism of opening created by the air from the balloon. Coupled with the constant airflow, this combination allows an optimal aeration of the middle ear and an effective tubular cleansing.

Exercise B

1. Inflate the balloon to the required dimensions.
2. Pronounce the following phrases with sustained intensity, articulating and stressing each phoneme.
   "The geese with golden galoshes"
   "This gelato is gustatory"
   "Alana bred a jaguar and a llama"
   "A pyjama rotter"
   "Frodo's dodo got in a grotto"
   "A duo of rude two-timing ghouls"
   "Catch the cadet"
   "Two teens guard an apartment"
   "Claire ate an iguana"
   "Tomcat, tomcat, tomcat…"

"The gang joked with a go-go girl"

3. With the jaw lightly protruded, pronounce:
   "Aug, aug, aug..." (like an Indian)
   "Ghi, ghi, ga/goh/geh/ghi/goo"
   "Kee, kee, ka/koh/ke/kee/koo"
   "Glug, glug, glug"

When air rises into the nasopharynx cavity and the trunk of the Eustachian tube the voice acquires a distinctive tone. It can be defined as intermittent, monotonous, 'course', and resonant. At the same time as the vocal emission you may have a sensation of open ears, of air moving or rising towards the ears, of confusion or feeling dazed, or of cleanness and freshness.

The phonation exercise has the same aim as those preceding: to open the Eustachian tube by means of the production of precise phonic sequences. Generally the phenomena that cause the tubes to open are those in which correct articulation requires distinct movements of the soft palate, but everyone should find the most effective phrases for themselves.

7.4 COMPENSATING THE MASK

Descending into the depths, we feel the pressure squeezing on the eardrums. To avoid the pain or a ruptured eardrum that this inconvenience can cause, we perform a manoeuvre of compensation, with the techniques already described.

However there is another 'air cavity' that is subjected to this phenomena: the mask. As described in Chapter 1, **the best mask for apnea has the smallest** volume. The more the internal volume is reduced, the smaller the volume of air that needs to be introduced by the apneist to equalise the internal pressure with the external, avoiding the uncomfortable suction effect.

The increase of depth and therefore hydrostatic pressure causes the squeeze of the mask against the face, with a consequent suction action. This experience must be prevented to avoid bursting capillaries in the eye due to the 'vacuum' effect between the mask and face.

Mask volume

Compensating the mask is very simple: it requires only the exhalation of air through the nose into the mask during the descent, maintaining a constant mask volume and thereby keeping it from squeezing on the face.

COLDS, SINUSITIS AND OTHER OTORHINOLARYNGOLOGICAL PROBLEMS

The middle ear, and in particular the eardrum cavity, the Eustachian tubes and the complex of the paranasal sinuses and nasal cavity constitute the functional system on which a normal compensation depends. In diving – and in particular freediving – we must pay great attention to any pathologies in this region, in order to avoid damage that can be difficult to amend, or even permanent.

For example a banal rhinitis, the common cold, may create an obstruction of the tubular recesses of the nasal cavity and a hypertrophy of the upper and medial turbinate, which would impede a normal compensation of the paranasal sinuses. Generally this is the effect of inflammation and the subsequent mucous that limits drainage of the sinuses.

Blockage of the sinus openings that occurs without variation of ambient pressure leads to several alterations in the sinuses. For example, the absorption of air with decrements of pressure in the sinuses; the emission of liquids, oedema and inflammation of mucous. When a problem of this nature is present during the descent, the decrease of pressure in the sinuses always exacerbates it, and the mucous can rupture blood vessels, leading to haemorrhage and nosebleed. These episodes are often distressing to the freediver, even though nosebleeds aren't a particularly serious symptom.

The reverse block is instead suffered in the ascent. This obstruction, which impedes the natural outflow of air, can be due to the blockage of the sinus openings by inflammation of mucous, by a cyst or by a polyp inside the sinus. For this reason the pressure balance that is correct during the descent is not necessarily likewise for the ascent.

Chronic sinusitis can expose a diver to barotraumas of the paranasal sinuses and middle ear during immersion. It is therefore inadvisable to expose oneself to pressure variation. The most common causes are allergies, chronic irritations due to smoking, prolonged use of local vasoconstrictors and vasomotor rhinitis.

Acute barotraumatic otitis arises almost exclusively during the descent in the phase of external compression, when the forced opening of the tube occurs partially or not at all; at this point if the descent is continued there will be a relative decrease of pressure inside the eardrum, which develops into the so-called 'tube block' that brings a simultaneous closure of both the tubular opening to the inside of the eardrum and the opening into the nasal walls. This generates bleeding inside the eardrum, but if the dive is continued then the greater risk is rupture of the eardrum membrane itself.

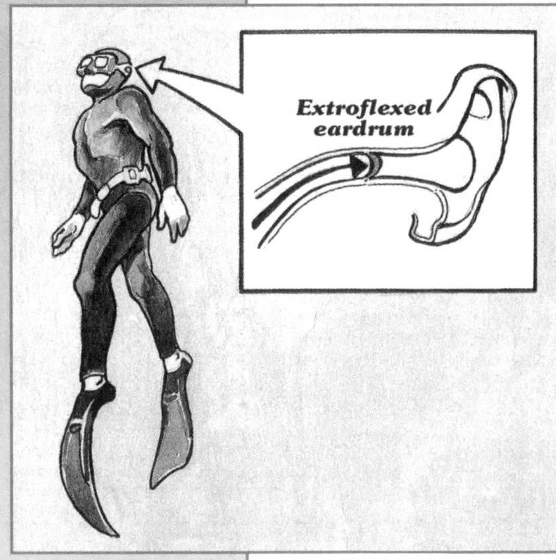

Acute labyrinthitis is a pathology that can arise during either the descent or the ascent. In the former, the sudden increase of pressure of an excessively quick descent can cause the so-called piston effect of the footplate of the stirrup, with a rupture of the cochlear opening and possible fistula labyrinthitis (with the eardrum still intact). Velocity can cause a piston effect in the ascent phase also, but the rupture would be of the vestibulum, due to the explosive increase of pressure inside the ear.

Alternobaric vertigo is a labyrinthitis dysfunction of short duration – only a few seconds. It generally disperses in the course of the ascent, and is related to an insufficient or incomplete opening of the tube on one side with respect to the other. Therefore the monolateral vestibular stimulation is the result of a delay in pressure equalisation of one middle ear with respect to the other.

Inflammation of the eardrum (acute otitis) and damage to the eardrum and/or vestibular complex are disorders caused by the lack of, or inefficient opening of the Eustachian tube, which puts the middle ear in touch with the throat, and in normal conditions is closed. This closure is ensured by the elastic pressure of the cartilaginous portion of the tube, and by the surface tension of the coating of mucous. The periodic opening of the tube allows air at ambient pressure to enter the cavity of the eardrum, allowing compensation and correct functioning of the middle ear. The lack of opening or inefficient opening can be caused by: a) inflammation of the eardrum (acute otitis), which occurs in conditions of normal external pressure; b) damage of varying severity to the eardrum and/or cochlear/vestibular complex, which occurs during the course of a changing external pressure.

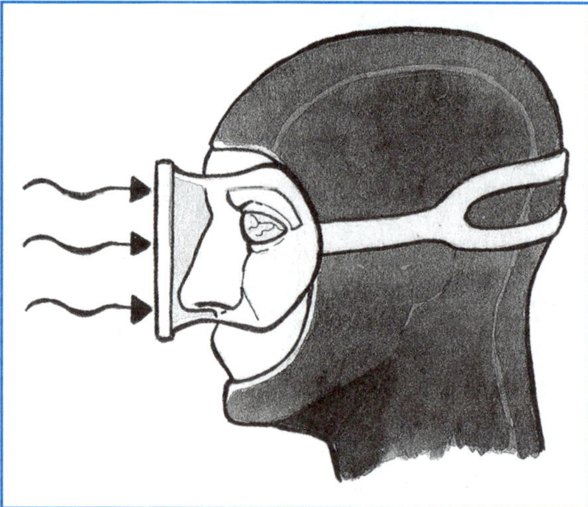

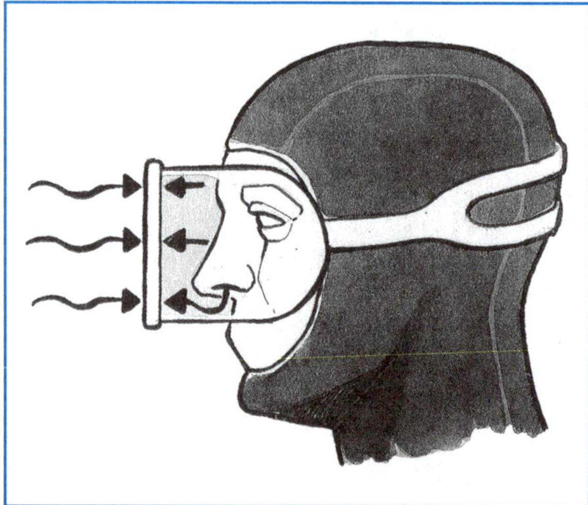

This explains why it is impossible to descend to depths with simple swimming goggles: the nose is not connected to the goggles, so the squeeze effect cannot be prevented.

An apnea mask has a reduced volume specifically so that it can be compensated with the least amount of air. The air committed to the mask will no longer be at the disposition of the eardrums.

The limit imposed by the impossibility of further compensation of the mask exists mainly for advanced apneists, as it usually occurs at depths greater than 20 meters.

Don't give up at the first failure in compensating the mask – the manoeuvre can very easily be trained. It is important to improve personal sensitivity to compensation in order to understand when to equalise, and exactly how much air to emit into the mask.

It is advisable to anticipate mask squeeze: several meters before the first occurrence, even if there is no obvious need, expel a small amount of air into the mask to keep it partially compensated. This prevents the need of a forced discharge of air from the lungs to overcome the pressure of the mask on the face when approaching the limit of compensation.

Be careful though: the air should not be given out any old way – the apneist is not a scuba diver and doesn't have enormous reserves of air: his air tanks are his lungs. Thus it is important to economise the air, exhale the minimum amount necessary, whether for the eardrums or for the mask. Above all, when compensating the mask avoid at all costs letting air escape from the mask itself and going to waste.

A very useful trick is starting the dive with the mask already completely compensated. You might think that this is the default condition, but it is not always so. When we are breathing on the surface, other than taking air into the mouth through the snorkel, we also inhale through the nose without realising it, taking air from the mask. This will mean that in the moment in which we start the dive the mask will already require partial compensation. To avoid this, during the last phase of ventilation before the duck dive the expiration must pass out of the nose as well as the mouth, completely replacing the air inside the mask. The mask fills to its limit and air begins to escape only after its maximum volume is reached.

An error that is commonly performed at depth is to rob air from the mask in an attempt to compensate the eardrums. This causes the mask to be totally crushed onto the face, before the critical depth is reached. The remedy of this inconvenience is to contract the diaphragm, as has been described: if this muscle is used correctly it will allow the use of residual air that would normally be inaccessible.

7.5 COMPENSATING AT THE DEPTH LIMIT

Many apneists, including experts, refer to a depth limit in freediving, expressing their unshakeable certainty about the impossibility of exceeding a certain depth. The apneist is forced to stop the descent due to a complete lack of air with which to compensate the mask or eardrums, but during the ascent the apneist still has a surplus of oxygen.

If you watch closely, towards the end of the descent, near the maximum depth, their descent position will change completely: from hydrodynamic, tapered and loose, the body becomes suddenly rigid, the back arches, the legs bend, and in particular – the most serious error – the head hyperextends forwards to look for the bottom. When the head is in this position it is practically impossible for air to pass from the lungs to the eardrums, and thus compensation is impossible.

The problem is even more evident in the case of compensation of the mask, where the quantity of air required and the pressure difference to overcome are further elevated.

Therefore the most important piece of advice is to always keep the head in line with the body, between the arms – never hyperextended forwards in the ultimate phase of the freefall.

Consequently, even the neck will return to a relaxed state, and the back will lose the contracted, arched position that has so little hydrodynamics. The loss of the looseness and relaxation that characterise the first part of the descent can be due to two factors: nervous problems (fear of a certain depth) or physiological problems (lack of bodily adaptation to the depth).

The inability to compensate becomes almost a mechanism of defence of the organism, which knows it is not perfectly integrated into the environment and therefore sabotages the descent. The solution to this problem is simple: to solve a difficulty compensating at a depth you must go to that depth!

At this critical profundity the position of the head must be controlled, and the tongue, neck, shoulders etc must all be relaxed. To be able to do this we must use equipment that allows us to reach the depth without force. In order to train compensation at this depth there's no need to descend finning, in constant weight, when we can be pushed by a weight, or pull ourselves down the guide rope with our arms. In this way we will arrive at the critical depth without a fear of having to return quickly, and we can dedicate time to our compensatory manoeuvre. In the meters preceding the maximum profundity the descent can be slowed, braking with a hand on the cable.

When the pre-determined depth is reached the apneist breaks the fall, keeping close to the cable. At this point the apneist must confirm that he or she is completely relaxed and the head is in line with the body. Then, with a fluid and harmonious movement, the diaphragm is brought upward, towards the base of the lungs, as indicated in chapter 7.2. All these actions must be mentally controlled, ensuring maximum decontraction. Subsequently the apneist proceeds to the manoeuvres of compensation of the eardrums and mask. This pause on the bottom will last a few seconds, after which the ascent will be initiated.

By repeating this dive and these procedures to the critical depth our body will habituate both psychologically and physiologically to the pressure.

FORMATION IN CONFINED WATER

CHAPTER **8**

The objective of this manual is to accompany the reader in the safe and enjoyable practice of apnea in lake or sea (open water): places where the ambient variables (water temperature, visibility, current) require a good capacity of adaptation and an accomplished technique.

The road that leads to open water starts with acclimatisation in the pool, a confined space of water with constant ambient factors (water, visibility and depth). In short, a 'sheltered' environment. In this constant setting it will be easier for the neophyte to evaluate and understand the sensations produced by the exercises: feeling, listening to and observing the body to analyse its psychophysical reactions. The first step is to learn to be at ease in the water and to be in control of every action – in short, to acclimatise and feel safe.

On the *physical level* this means making every action effective: controlling all movements, reducing muscular work to the bare essentials for a minimum consumption of energy.

On the *mental level* it means maintaining a condition of relaxation and concentration effective for apnea.

In each and every moment of training in the water remember the 'three **E**'s':

- Effective movement in relation to;
  - equipment used.
  - physical capacities: strength, endurance, speed and flexibility.
- Economy of O_2 and energy consumption, which depends on psychophysical stability.
- Efficiency of personal physical and mental conditions.

In this chapter we will propose exercises that improve coordination, respiration and control of movements in an environment that produces a whole range of modifications of the organism.

The swimming and 'free body' (without equipment) exercises are aimed at improving the physical ability of the athlete, the efficiency of movement in the water, and the combating of stress. They will teach the aspiring apneist to relax in the water, to feel the contact of the body with the liquid element and to abandon oneself in the water, feeling the weight of the immersed body and therefore also the flotation force. We will learn to move with awareness, and hence with economy, exploiting all the advantages given by the physical and chemical characteristics of water.

Subsequently, with equipment, we will be able to acquire specific techniques of freediving that complete the training necessary to safely conquer the underwater world.

8.1 SWIMMING

Swimming is an activity of fundamental importance to apnea since it improves aquaticity; the coordination required to swim freestyle and breaststroke gives the capacity to be comfortable in the water, with both relaxation and awareness.

To coordinate a complex movement means considering and controlling different actions and sequences of movement. This is only possible if we can manipulate the body with appropriate mental commands; it is necessary to coordinate thoughts with actions until, after they have been repeated with awareness dozens of times, they become automatic. Only with this process will the apneist become **effective, economic and efficient.**

FREESTYLE (*see figure on page 217*)

To swim any style efficiently it is essential to **visualise the water as a fulcrum on which we 'turn' or 'push' the body** with the use of the arms. The more profitable the fulcrum, the more water we will succeed in moving.

If this visualisation is seen clearly then it will be easier to sense contact with the water and sliding on the surface, and to correct any possible errors.

The body Assumes a **horizontal position** face downward in the water, which presents minimum resistance to forwards movement.

The head Must be **'reclined' on the surface** such that the water level reaches the eyebrows.

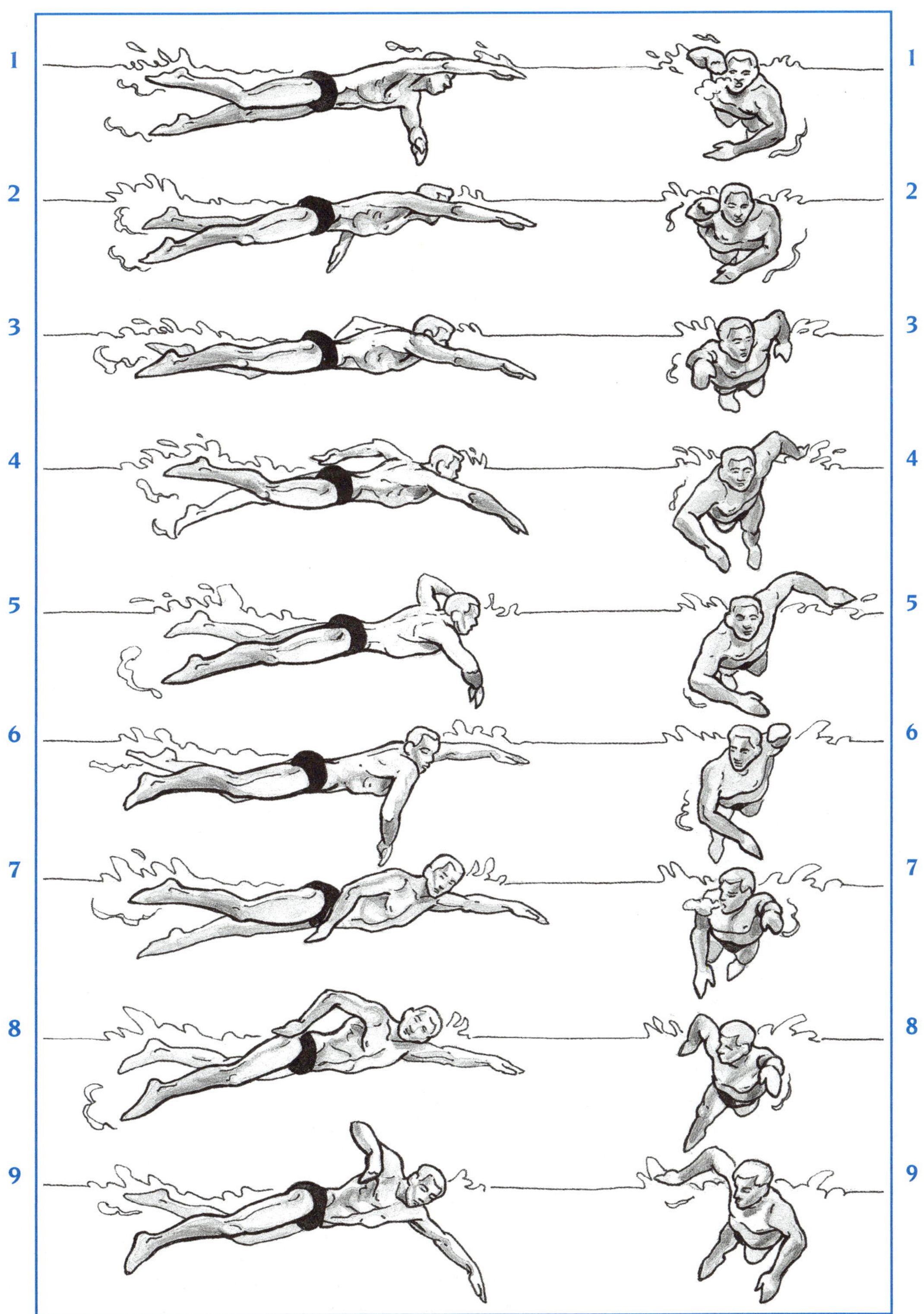
1
2
3
4
5
6
7
8
9

The arms

In freestyle, **the armstroke** holds a great importance since it **contributes over eighty percent of the force.**

The movement of the **armstroke** is conventionally divided into two phases: one through the air, called the **recovery** (*Fig. 8, 9 right arm*), and one underwater, called the **pass** (*Fig. 1, 2, 3, 4, 5, 6, 7, right arm*).

The **pass** is again subdivided into four parts: in reference to the right arm there is a **placement** (*Fig. 1*), **catch** (*Fig. 2*), **pull** (*Fig. 3, 4, 5*), and **push** (*Fig. 6, 7*).

The **first phase** is represented by the distance that the arm must complete beneath the surface of the water before arriving at the **'catch'** – the profitable phase of the armstroke; the **second phase** brings the arm from the catch to a perpendicular position with respect to the surface of the water; at this point the ultimate part of the pass, the **push phase** is initiated: the arm, and in particular the hand, pushes the water backwards towards the feet.

After having made this trajectory underwater, on the orthogonal projection of the median line of the body, the arm completes the aerial **phase of recovery**, to submerge once more in front, in line with the shoulder.

The recovery of the arm must be performed as close as possible to the body. To achieve this the arm must be bent at the elbow, which **follows a semicircular trajectory above the surface of the water, without touching it.** Furthermore, during the recovery the arm must be relaxed, for conservation of energy. Don't forget the fact that superfluously **contracted muscles** in associated movements produce a **considerable consumption of oxygen.**

There will be propulsion in the first phase of the pass, even if it is in small amounts, on the condition that the hand maintains the correct angle of catch. Without doubt the most profitable technique is an **'S-movement':** the hand describes a double curve, the first outwards, the second inwards, ending at the same height as the centre of the shoulder.

The least profitable method for this phase consists in describing a semicircle, perpendicular to the longitudinal axis of the body. This is a very common error that nullifies some of the propulsive force; in so much as the result of this action is a **worthless lifting force.**

It is not easy to assimilate the 'S-movement' and, especially for beginners, it is good to reach a compromise: when the arm is extended and the hand is already immersed, maintaining a firm elbow, use the hand as a kind of spoon, forming a perpendicular angle to the median axis, which 'collects' the water to bring it to the level of the head. At this point not only the hand, but also the forearm is 'leaning' on the water. The arm and forearm, with the help of the elbow, push a significant quantity of water ('fulcrum'), backward in the axis of the body, causing a substantial forwards propulsion. The higher the elbow, the less the arm will be displaced outwards, meaning a shortening of the interval before the catch and the active phase of the pass is initiated.

The two arms follow a continuous, alternate movement, so that while one is in the recovery phase the other is active in the pass, maintaining constant propulsion, and eliminating 'dead time'.

The legs

The movement of the legs starts with the articulation of the femur-coccyx joint (hip), and also incorporates the articulation of the knee and foot. The latter in particular must be very flexible and loose.

The legs **alternate with a continuous movement** from up to down and down to up, in such a way that the feet follow, under the surface of the water, an arched trajectory of about 30-40 cm; this action is therefore very similar to the finstroke described in Chapter 6. The downward movement is a result of the articulation of the knee, while in the upward phase a maximum extension of the leg is recommended.

The chest

The rolling of the chest on the longitudinal axis of the body produces great advantages to the mechanics of swimming. Whilst one arm is performing a recovery, the head rotates towards that arm to breathe. The roll is achieved **with a torsion of the chest**, which raises the shoulder, facilitating respiration (*Fig. 7, 8 page 217*). The roll brings other benefits: most of all it avoids the forced articulation of the shoulder. Furthermore it brings better penetration through the water, a better lengthening of the arm and lessens the negative effects of the arm recovery.

Respiration

Breathing is effected by **rotating the head, whether to the left or to the right**. Make sure that the slight rotation of the head doesn't influence the position of the chest. Remember that an exaggerated torsion of the head brings an excessive torsion of the chest, which is an obstacle to forwards progress and coordination in general.

Forwards movement through the water produces a dip in

the water just below the chin, which makes the **inspiratory phase** easier without having to force the rotation of the head. For this reason **the expiration must be completed beneath the water** (*Fig. 7 page 217*) so that the subsequent inspiration can be performed quickly, without interrupting the rhythm of the armstroke.

The decision of when to turn the head is very important for harmony of style: in modern freestyle the breath is inserted in the moment when the arm on the side where the breath is to be taken is beginning its recovery phase.

The **stroke-breath relationship** will influence the efficiency of the swimming. One can be lead to believe that a high-

SOME ADVICE TO IMPROVE BREASTSTROKE

In breaststroke the legs contribute greatly to propulsion by kicking the water with the point of the foot. However they can increase their effectiveness by pressing with the inside of the leg on a diagonal plane, thus obtaining a positive reaction similar to that achieved by opposition of the hands.

The leg kick doesn't explode from the start, but instead slightly after it. In the leg recovery the heel approaches the gluteus without forwards flexion of the thigh and without widening of the knees. These movements would expose the surfaces of the thigh to the water, slowing forwards progress.

The pass of the arms on the surface in breaststroke has both the task of pulling the body forwards and lifting the head up for the inspiration. Its movement, which is reduced to a pull only, is executed with the palms of the hands pressing backwards. In contrast to freestyle the arm recovery is made underwater. The arm and especially the leg recovery must both be executed gently, or else they would in effect become a 'negative' pass.

The head must not be lifted excessively but only so much as to allow for the inspiration; otherwise it would represent an excessive weight that would produce further sinking.

In contrast with the other styles, the body assumes a less horizontal position with respect to the surface of the water. This is because the pelvis tends to sink with respect to the line of the shoulders, facilitating the movement of the legs. However the body recovers its horizontal position in the moment of maximum extension of legs and arms.

An error that frequently hampers beginners is the excessive raising of the pelvis in the moment of maximum recovery of the legs and the start of the push, exactly when it should be lowered; this error changes the body position in the water and reduces the economy of the swimming.

The movement of the legs requires a lot of attention in order to gain maximum efficiency in this style.

ly elevated number of leg kicks together with a proportional number of armstrokes can produce an elevated velocity, but there are limits, determined especially by the ability of maintaining physical coordination. For this reason, even if an emergency might require a quick intervention, an apneist should **never swim with an excessively elevated velocity**.

On the other hand, a competitive swimmer spends their energy solely against the clock, and it is compulsory to reach the finish completely exhausted. In our sport this is not acceptable. Obviously, in apnea training the velocity of the swimming doesn't represent a definite objective.

In the sea we almost always need to cross considerable distances, with the added complication of waves. We must try to attain maximum efficiency with minimum wasted energy. Therefore we must work on training endurance, with two, three or four leg kicks for each armstroke. For beginners in particular, **a coordination of six leg kicks per armstroke** is recommended.

BREASTSTROKE

This style of swimming includes movements that, especially in the legs, are analogous to those of the frog. **Breaststroke is the slowest but most natural style**, and for this reason it is often used by instructors in the introduction to swimming. **Breaststroke is the only technique of swimming with a free body that is also effective underwater**.

Breaststroke receives a very different force from the arms, which pull the body, and the legs, which push. Thus, in contrast to freestyle, progress is not continuous and fluid, but instead altered by a rhythmical slowing and accelerating.

While there are different ways of swimming breaststroke underwater, on the surface it is swum in a very particular fashion – coordinating the movements of the limbs to enable an opportunity to breathe. In *surface breaststroke* the necessity of synchronizing the movements of the limbs with the breath doesn't allow for complete development of the armstroke; *in underwater breaststroke* there is no such difficulty.

All breaststroke, whether competitive or revised to suit the apneist underwater, requires symmetrical and perfectly coordinated movements.

The body

All movements are symmetrical, and the body floats in a prone position in the water. The body does not need to oscillate laterally, and neither is breathing lateral, as it is for freestyle, but rather frontal and facilitated by the fact that the mouth doesn't breathe on the waterline (let alone below it, as for freestyle), but emerged completely. To enable this the head must be lifted rhythmically to a considerable height, and this requires that the feet sink and therefore act well beneath the surface. The expiration occurs while the head is underwater, during the pause that the swimmer inserts after the legstroke with the aim of exploiting in repose this most profitable part of the push.

In breaststroke the legs commence the recovery while the arms are finishing the pass (*Fig. 4 page 223*). The kick is finished with the arms already extended forwards, having finished their recovery (*Fig. 6 page 223*). Thus the impulse starts with the pull movement of the arms (*Fig. 1, 2 page 223*). The pause occurs only at the finish of the two pushes. The freediver, who struggles not against the clock, but against their energy consumption, must take advantage of the conclusion of the legstroke by being relaxed, with arms, legs and feet all extended.

Breaststroke has three fundamental characteristics: the recovery happens underwater; there is no push phase, and all the movements must be symmetrical.

The arms

The arms are extended forwards, with palms facing downwards, after having made a slight outwards rotation of the palms (*Fig. 1 page 223*). They then follow a trajectory outwards and slightly down, bending slightly until they are in line with the shoulders and perpendicular to the surface of the water (*Fig. 2, 3 page 223*). At this point the hands and elbows move back towards each other, returning to the initial position (*Fig. 4, 5 page 223*).

The pass is thus divided into two phases, the *catch* and the *pull*; there is no push since the arms do not pass the line of the shoulders. To reiterate, the recovery occurs under the surface of the water and is represented by the forward extension of the arms.

The legs

In the **legstroke** the push phase is clearly distinguishable from the recovery, and as for the armstroke the movements of the legs must be symmetrical and simultaneous.

To describe the movement we start from the extended position. While the **pelvis lowers slightly**, the legs are flexed, bringing the calves back onto the thighs and the heels back towards the gluteus muscles (*Fig. 2 page 225*). The feet are then rotated so that the toes are facing outwards ('hammer feet' *Fig. 3 page 225*). The legs are extended with an almost semicircu-

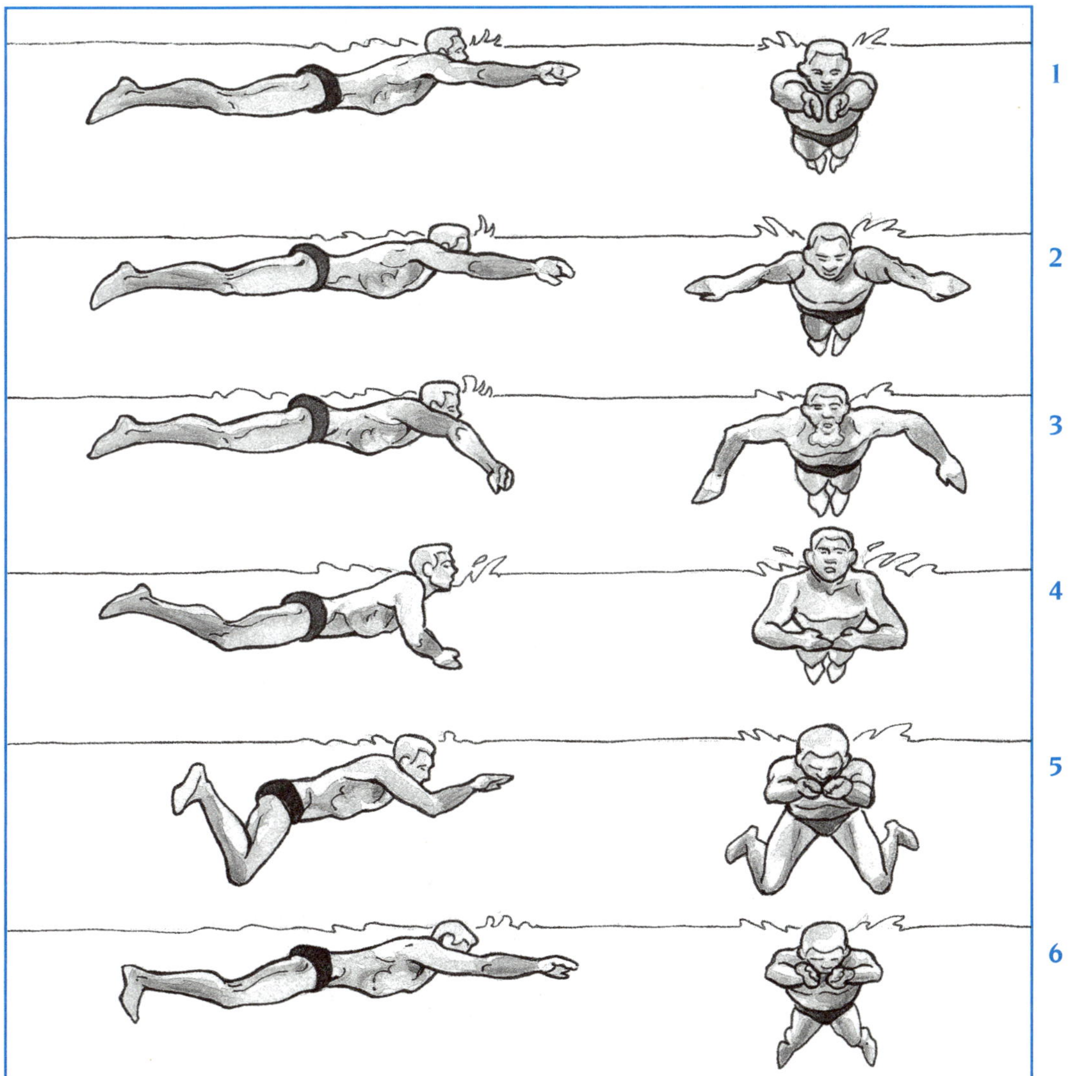

lar movement to return to the position of maximum extension, with the legs together and the feet naturally lengthened.

These movements must be performed without widening the knees excessively. Another serious error is **the loss of 'hammer position' in the feet:** some swimmers do not push the water with the sole, but with the top of the foot, in a form of dolphin kick. The best exercise to correct this defect is to execute legstrokes only, with the arms stretched along the sides in such a way that the points of the feet (in the hammer position and rotated outwards) touch the fingertips.

Another exercise that can be performed dry or in the water involves an instructor pressing with the palm of the hand against the ball of the students foot, forcing its movement so as to create the necessary neuromuscular sensitivity.

An equally common defect is the recovery of the legs with the knees bent forwards. This flexion of the thighs offers a greater resistance, to such an extent as to nullify the push produced by the closure of the legs. An excellent exercise to improve this aspect of technique consists in executing the leg movements of breaststroke vertically, at about 10 cm from the edge of the pool. In this way any possible errors will be easily revealed since the knees will strike the wall of the pool.

Respiration

Theoretically one can swim keeping the head constantly above the water and therefore not have any problems of respiration, but this is absolutely counterproductive to the economy of swimming. It was noted many years ago that swimming with the head immersed provided a more hydrodynamic position and was a quicker style.

This led to the birth of underwater breaststroke, but this was subsequently abolished by the regulations, which now state that the head cannot be immersed completely, but must always break the surface of the water. In this case we must look for a compromise: the head remains beneath the water, but with the crown just above the surface, according to the prescription of the rules.

The inspiration is inserted when the arms are at their maximum width and the legs are still closed. It must be effected with minimum backwards extension on the frontal plane, as well as trying to avoid any lateral movement that could compromise the symmetry of the body with respect to the surface of the water.

Coordination between arms and legs

It is essential to coordinate the arms and legs in order to optimise the dynamics of the style.

Starting from the horizontal position with the arms forward and legs extended, the arms initiate movement first, and only at the end of their pull phase do the legs start to flex. The legs perform the push phase at the same time as the recovery of the arms, in such a way that the body assumes as horizontal a position on the water as is possible, for the most effective glide.

An incorrect coordination between the upper and lower limbs is a serious defect that compromises swimming to the point where in extreme cases forwards progress is practically

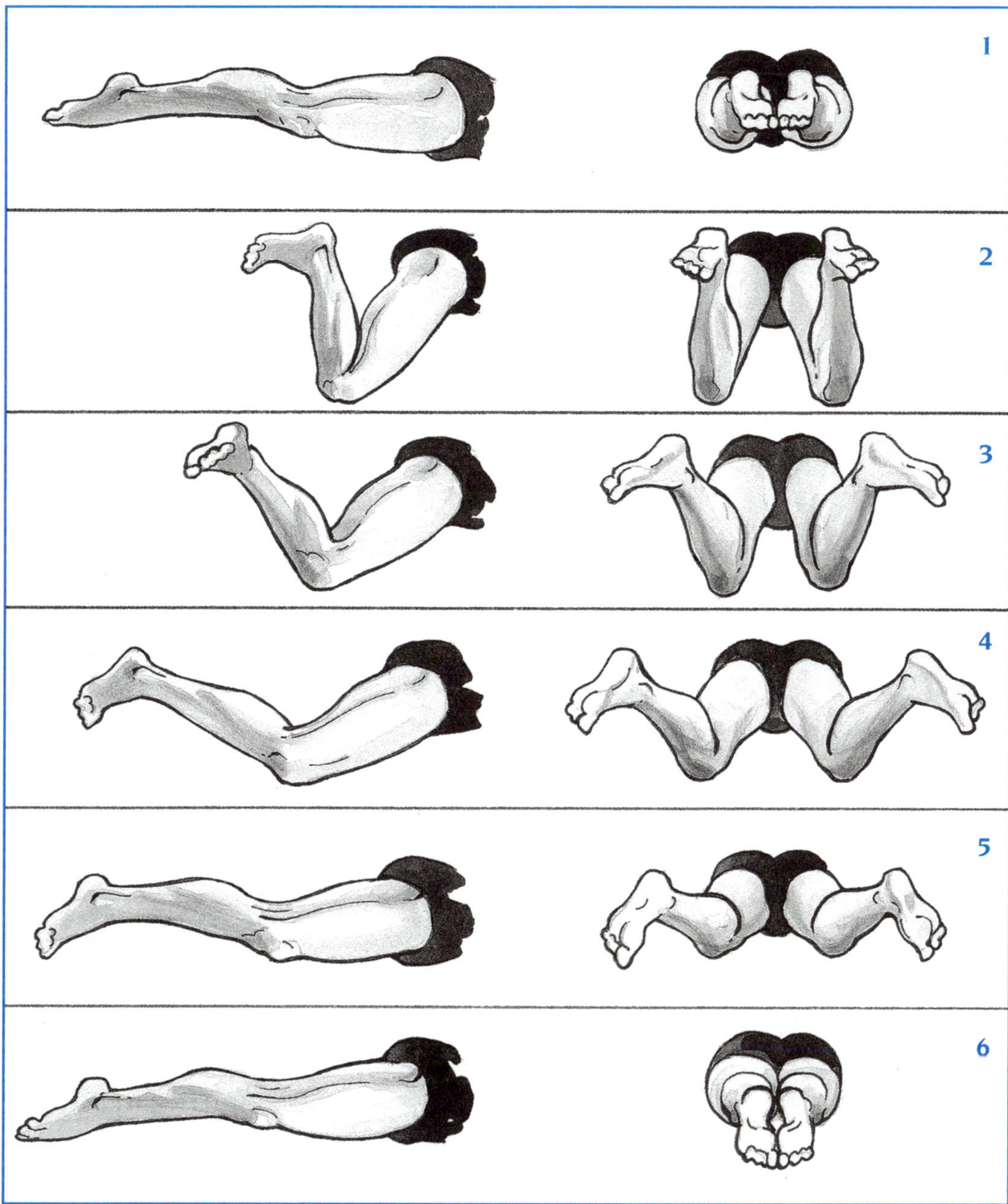

halted. These problems of coordination can be resolved with the following exercise: **beginning from the horizontal position with arms and legs extended, perform first a complete armstroke, then the legstroke after the arms have returned to the starting point. Then gradually reduce the dead time until optimal coordination is reached.**

8.2 EXERCISES WITH FREE BODY

The exercises proposed in these pages serve to improve **general aquaticity** and increase sensitivity to contact between body and water. Operating in challenging situations in terms of co-ordination and endurance to apnea will stimulate **self-control**.

The awareness of actions whilst in apnea underwater is a good indication of the level of security acquired by the apneist. All the exercises that follow are performed without equipment. The only gear that may be used is swimming goggles, wetsuit and weight, and only when absolutely necessary. Mask and fins are not used. The free body exercises are:

1. Breathing exercises in water
2. Compensation during an assisted descent
3. Underwater breaststroke
4. Folding duckdive
5. Dolphin diving
6. Recovering objects
7. Buoyancy with free body
8. Static apnea
9. Partial exhale apnea
10. Full exhalation apnea
11. Forced compensation
12. Exercises of displacement
13. Flotation exercises

BREATHING EXERCISES IN WATER

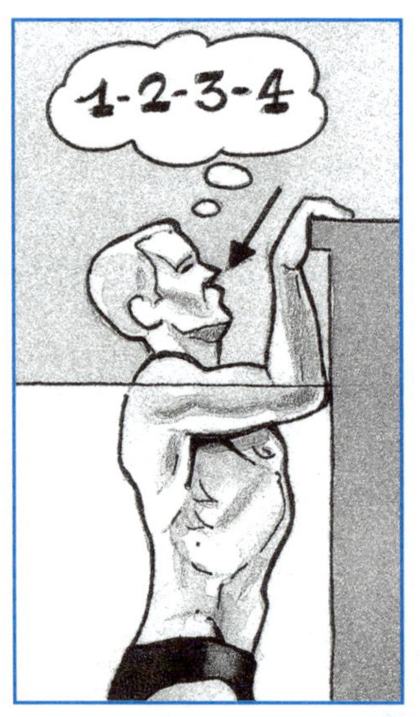

Breathing in the water is an elementary exercise that constitutes the base of everything that follows.

Execution

1. Place the hands on the side of the pool and if the water is shallow, kneel on the bottom
2. **Inhale deeply**, preferably through the nose.
3. **Exhale through the mouth, with the face immersed.**

In this exercise one should maintain **a continuous rhythm:**

the time of expiration should be at least double that of the inspiration (for example inspiration 4 seconds, expiration 8 seconds). *(For the description of the mechanics of the act of diaphragmatic respiration see Chapter 4.)*

With training, one should try to increase the time of the respiratory cycle, arriving if possible at a total time of one minute (20" inspiration and 40" expiration). This exercise can be applied also to **swimming laps with a flutter-board**, in which the respiration described above is performed with accompanying leg movements.

COMPENSATION IN ASSISTED VERTICAL DESCENT

This is a fundamental exercise to improve sensitivity to variations of pressure on the eardrum.

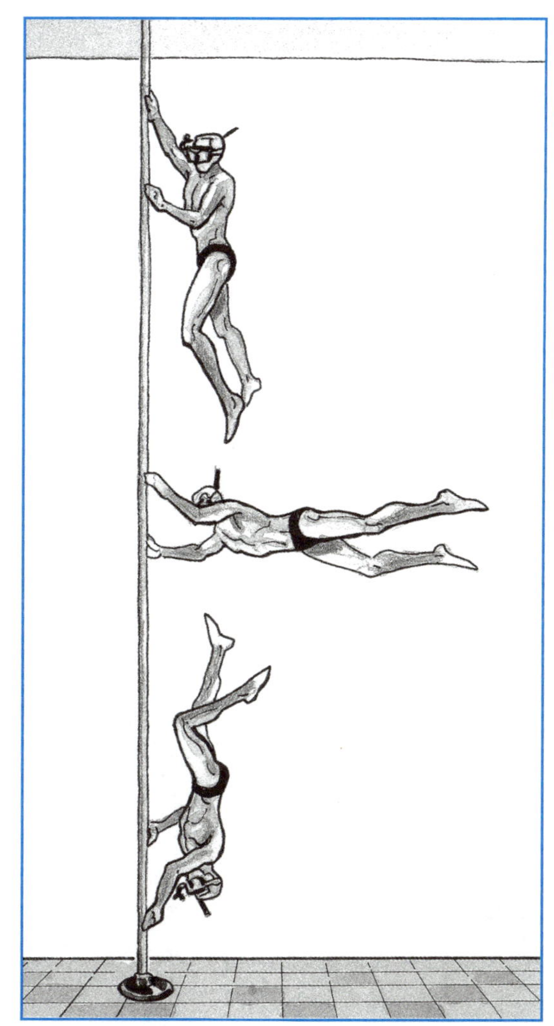

Execution

1. Using a pole appropriately placed on a bottom of at least 3 meters **pull yourself downwards using the hands**.
2. Compensate with care and regularity (*see Chapter 7*).
3. Sense and evaluate the physical reactions of the body while compensating.

Initially it is advisable **to descend head-up**. Once compensation technique is correct and there is no pain or irritation, start the descent horizontal and then **head-down**.

For the success of this exercise it is important to always maintain maximum relaxation.

UNDERWATER BREASTSTROKE

This exercise can start with a dive from the side, or – if we are in a shallow pool – directly from the water, with a powerful leg push after having placed the feet flat against the wall.

Execution

1. The arms are extended forwards; the legs are together and extended backwards.

2. Maintaining the prone position, start with a complete pass of the arms. This will give a considerable force, which if exploited by a hydrodynamic position will allow substantial advance: remember to keep the head relaxed and aligned with the vertebral column – not hyperextended.
3. The arms pause briefly, resting alongside the thighs where they have finished the pass.
4. The legs recover, and at the same time the arms also recover, being brought back in front of the head. The successive kick of the legs finds the body in a hydrodynamic position ideal for exploiting the resultant momentum.

We have therefore two very distinct passes separated by a pause: one for the legs and one for the arms: two pauses, and therefore two phases. This technique can be easier learned by starting in an extended position. For a better coordination it can be useful to repeat the following orders in your head during the execution:

a) **arms, pause;**
b) **legs, pause;**
c) **arms, pause;**
d) **legs, pause.**

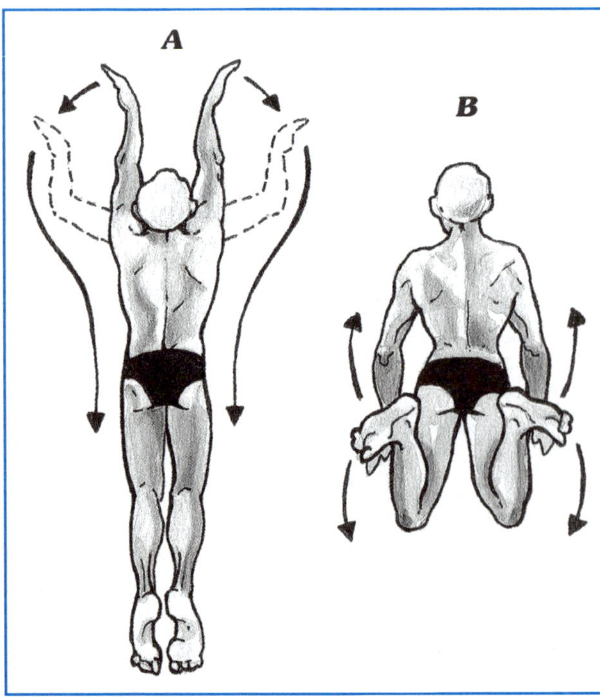

Do not be in a hurry whilst learning this technique: **perform the exercise slowly – the limb movements should not happen explosively, but be guided by mental commands.** The objective is to reach a relaxed but efficient action that uses the minimum number of muscles and is therefore economical.

In contrast to surface breaststroke, in underwater breaststroke the arms can perform a complete pass, in which the hands move well past the line of the shoulders to finish on the sides of the legs. We will therefore have both a pull and a push phase, which makes underwater breaststroke much more successful. If we consider that one of the most common errors in surface breaststroke is an inefficient legstroke, the armstroke in underwater breaststroke will be able to make up for this error, favouring advance even in the absence of an effective leg push.

As for breaststroke on the surface, dry execution will help the coordination of movements of underwater breaststroke.

FOLDING DUCKDIVE

The **duckdive** is the technique that allows the passage of the body from a prone to a vertical head-down position. The aim is to leave the surface to start the dive in the most efficient way, which means using the least amount of energy to descend as far as possible.

There are different ways of duckdiving: the technique described here requires folding the legs against the thighs, together with the upper limbs against the trunk. For this reason it is called **the folding duckdive**.

This duckdive is used by anyone diving without equipment: preparing themselves on the surface without a snorkel, they will need to respire with head above the surface, and the body is hence in an almost vertical position.

Execution (*see figure on page 230*)

1. The body starts in a position slightly oblique with respect to the plane of the water surface, sustained by vertical breaststroke and opposition of the hands. Movements will be minimum, but sufficient to maintain the head above water, allowing for breathing (*Fig. A*).
2. The first action is to lengthen the body across the surface with a breaststroke kick.
3. The arms extend and make a complete semicircular pass finishing at the hips. The hands are perpendicular to the surface and the palms are rotated towards the feet. At this point we will have a forwards displacement due to the pass of the arms (*Fig. B*).
4. Bring the knees to the chest and at the same time bend the head and shoulders downwards (*Fig. D*).
5. As the body is folding up into this 'egg-like' position the last phase begins with a downwards extension of the arms (anti-pass), which gives a resistance to the forwards movement gained by the armstroke, inducing an easy turn of the body towards the bottom (*Fig. E*).
6. The upward extension of the legs (*Fig. F*) will push the body downwards, submerging it further below the surface (*Fig. G*).

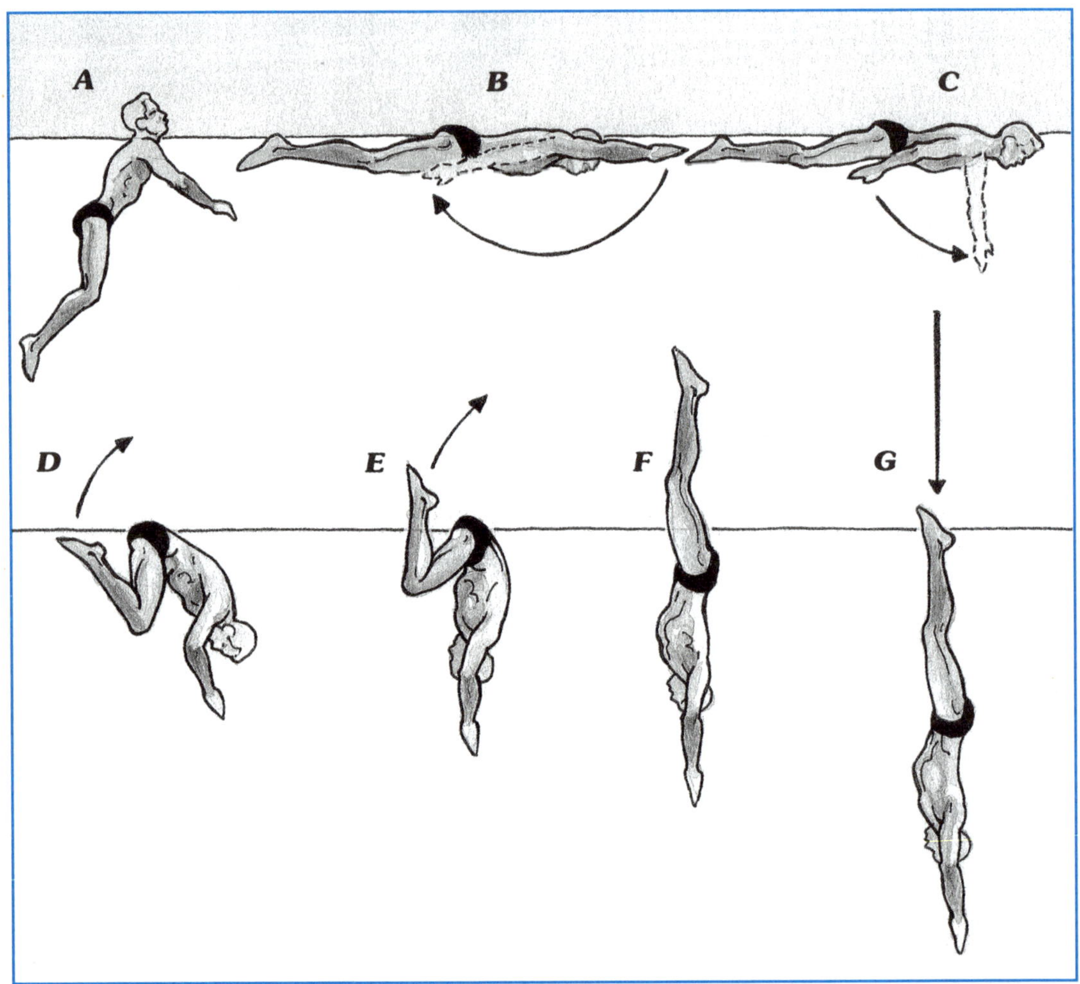

To make it easier the three phases can be attempted first separately, then in sequence, with a slow execution that favours awareness of the movements. If practicing in shallow water where the depth is less than a meter and a half, place the hands on the bottom at the end of the duckdive, and it will be easier to sense if the body is in the required vertical posture. Subsequently pass into deeper water.

The efficiency of the duckdive, and therefore the depth obtained, is dependant on **perfect vertical position**, hydrodynamics of the body, the amount of weight that you succeed in putting above the surface (i.e. the portion of the legs emerged), and the efficiency of the initial breaststroke pass. If the folding duckdive is performed correctly, it will, for example, allow the freediver to fully submerge in fresh water after a maximum inspiration, to a depth of about four meters.

There are several difficulties the beginner may encounter: overcoming the positive buoyancy of an inspiratory apnea, imperfect or uncoordinated movements, uncontrolled leg throws, lack of a sense of position, general difficulties in turning the body the necessary angle of almost 180°, inability to rotate without using the lower limbs (which must submerge without futile agitation of the surface). All these can be resolved through much practice, calm, and coordination. It may be useful to identify the **most frequent errors.**

The most common error is caused by an **insufficient breaststroke kick** or armstroke. If the arms are not well coordinated they will limit the forward rotation of the chest; consequently the legs may be elevated, but won't reach the vertical.

The opposite error is also very common: **movements executed with excessive force** and frenzy, coupled with an initial throw of the legs that is too forced. In this case the legs easily exceed the vertical.

An analogous problem is encountered when the legs are elevated too late. After the breaststroke kick and the armstroke the body will be in rotation, and if the upward extensions of the legs is delayed then they will continue to fall past the head. Ultimately the lower limbs must remain extended vertically upwards, firmly together, until they are completely immersed.

DOLPHIN DIVING

This is an extremely effective exercise for relaxation and is a good activity for recovery after intense training. Although the first attempt will probably be difficult and tiring due to lack of coordination, with confidence it will become pleasurable and especially relaxing.

The exercise can be performed with an expiration either during the descent or the apnea. The folding duckdive determines the success of this exercise.

Execution

1. Execute a folding duckdive towards the bottom.
2. Upon reaching the bottom, prepare for the ascent, placing the feet well and assuming a crouched down position with the legs bent.
3. Extend the arms upwards and return to the surface with a strong push of the legs.
4. Reach the surface in an extended posture and in expiration.
5. Inhale, perform a breaststroke armstroke, and perform another duckdive to start the cycle again.

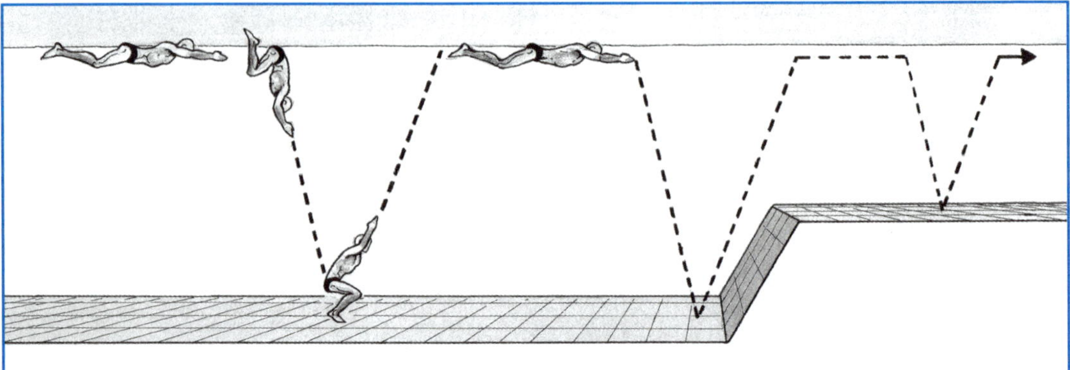

Complete one or more lengths of the pool, coordinating the respiration, duckdive, descent, the positioning on the bottom, the push off and the return to the surface. These steps are all performed whilst in search of the best conditions of relaxation.

RECOVERING OBJECTS

The objective of this exercise is to create a **complex situation**. It deals with the coordination of many consecutive actions to recover a certain number of objects from the bottom of the pool. In this exercise the return to the surface is critical, requiring coordination between respiration and duckdive. You will need some objects that are visible on the bottom.

Execution

1. Submerge with a folding duckdive.
2. Reach the bottom and recover the first object.
3. Prepare for the ascent, placing the feet firmly on the bottom and crouching down with the arms extended upwards. The object is kept in the hand closest to the edge of the pool.
4. With each dive a single object is recovered and placed on the side of the pool without touching the side.
5. After placing the object, dive again with a folding duckdive, without pausing on the surface.
6. Collect another object and repeat the exercise.

With the repetition of this exercise the following sequence of actions will become automatic:

a) **respiration**
b) **duckdive**

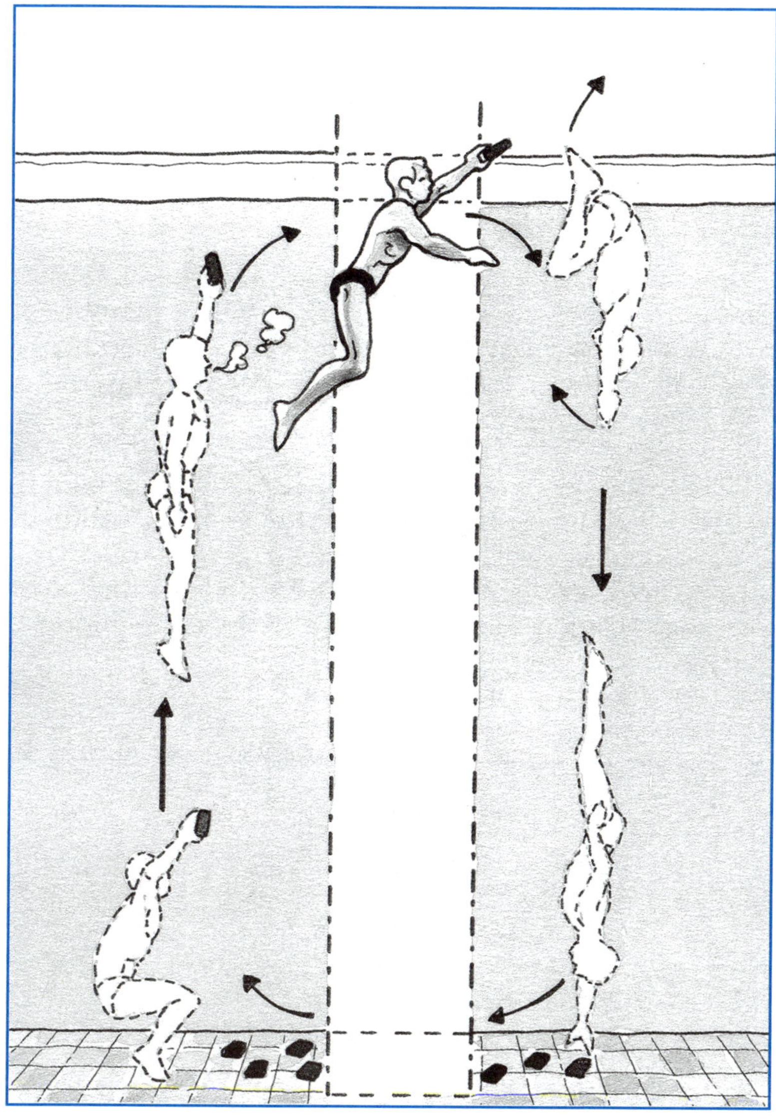

c) **descent**
d) **push from the bottom**
e) **ascent**

Understanding and being in control of this sequence is essential in emergencies, for example in a case where the apneist must perform a search on the bottom. A good control of the execution and a suitable sense of timing will help overcome any emotional factors that could inhibit the action of the rescuer. It will be easy to evaluate self-control while the attention is concentrated on collecting the objects.

BUOYANCY WITH FREE BODY

The perception of the flotation force (buoyancy) of our body is integral to the pursuit of relaxation in the water and to security. Begin on the surface, counterbalancing the air in the lungs with weights of different sizes. This will help recognise the different levels of buoyancy at different depths when we take our first dive.

Such an awareness will impart a greater calm and a reduced muscular activity. To encourage this condition, start the exercise without a wetsuit. Subsequently, when we put on the wetsuit, we can experiment with different amounts of weight until weighting is optimised.

Knowing precisely how much buoyancy is obtained at various depths – and most importantly being habituated to 'sensing' it – will aid the freediver greatly, whether on a psychological level, favouring peace of mind, or by reducing muscular movement and thereby economising energy.

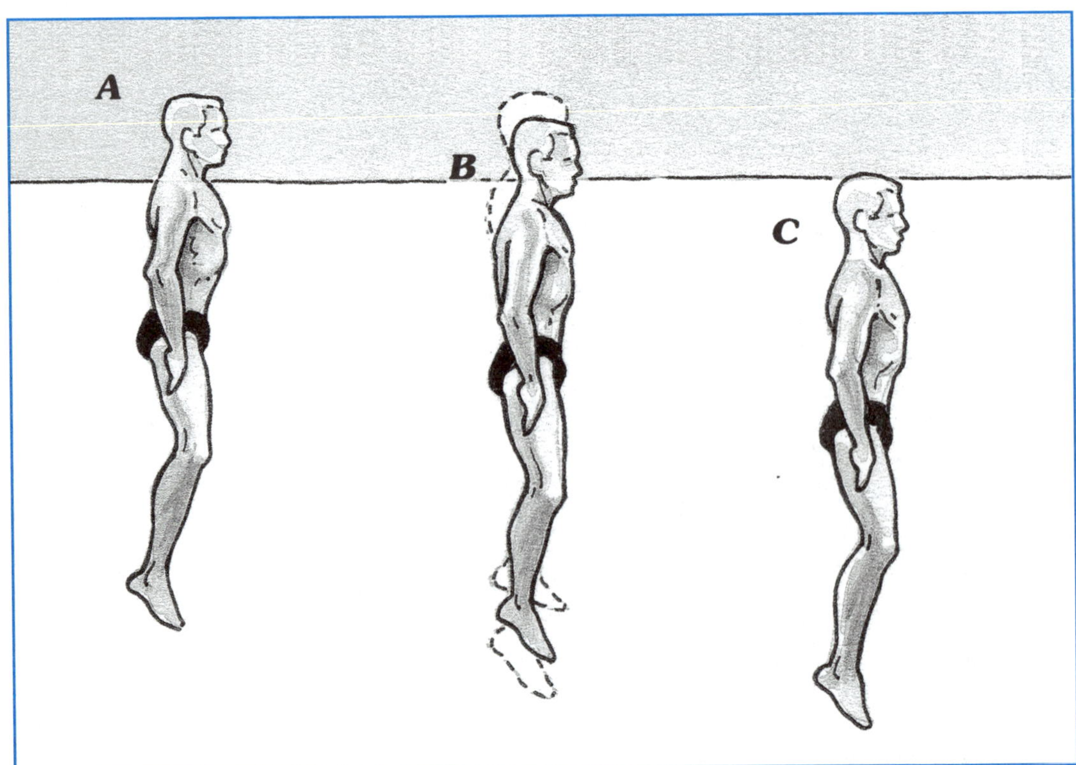

STATIC APNEA

The fundamental component of this exercise is total physical relaxation in the water, whether floating on the surface or resting on the bottom. Relaxation begins in the preparatory phase, coupled with correct respiration, and is completed after having assumed the desired position on the surface or bottom.

It is more important to pursue comfort and the pleasure of physical contact with the water rather than elevated performance.

ANALYSIS OF A STATIC APNEA

There are three critical moments to the success of an apnea: before, during and after. It is essential to be mentally and physically predisposed to the static apnea.

Before

The first step is to assume position in the water: whether next to the side of the pool or the ladder, try to support yourself with the arms in order to take the weight off the vertebral column, allowing the body to abandon itself in the water. We seek a condition of physical relaxation by exploiting the partially immersed position, and the supportive action of the water on the immersed part of the body.

In this first phase of muscular decontraction it is important, as we have seen in Chapter 5, to be breathing effectively. Respiration and relaxation (Chapter 4) are inseparable. A complete diaphragmatic respiration will help predispose the body to static apnea. The 'mentality' must also be prepared. A positive attitude must generate a desire to 'occupy oneself with oneself', to 'make an effort to not make an effort', and to 'look inside'. In a nutshell, to discover how far the mind is capable of controlling the instinct to breathe.

During this phase respiration is regular, favouring relaxation, and alternates between drawn out inspirations and expirations that empty and fill the lungs as much as possible. This breathing is necessary to prepare the lungs and ribcage to receive the right amount of air in the final respiration, without accumulating muscular tension; the breathing is a means of stretching the ribcage.

Upon reaching the optimal mental and physical conditions, we will be ready to make the final respiration and assume position in the water. Remember that the last inspiration should not exceed 70% of the total lung capacity.

During

The static apnea starts after the last respiration, upon taking position in the water. Whether floating on the surface or resting on the bottom, the entire body must be perfectly relaxed. To be certain that each muscle is decontracted, we use the mind to check if any harmful tensions have accumulated. Whether from head to toe or vice versa is irrelevant; what matters is that we exploit the relaxing action of the water, which acts on the body to decontract it as much as possible.

Experience has shown that some zones of the body are particularly delicate in terms of physical relaxation: the spine, shoulders and tongue. We are often unaware of contractions that accumulate in these areas and are extremely detrimental to apnea.
After having obtained a good physical relaxation, the best mental condition that can be achieved is that of travelling outside of time. Time is the dimension that characterises our existence and against which we must indirectly struggle. The techniques to help you on this voyage can be found in Chapter 5. To know when to terminate the apnea we must listen to the body's signals, first and foremost the diaphragmatic contractions.
At the end of the apnea it is important to maintain a position suited to the exit, close to the edge of the pool or the ladder. Your training partner will be there to assist you if needed.

After
Upon concluding the apnea, place the hands on the side of the pool or ladder, or on the forearms of your training partner. Lift the head first out of the water, remembering to continue to control your actions, in particular respiration, for a few moments. Do not exhale forcefully, but rather exhale half the air, inhale completely, and only after exhaling again resume normal respiration.

PARTIAL EXHALE APNEA

Also called a **hanging apnea**, this exercise favours habituation to the evaluation and perception of buoyancy and position in the water, both critical for the security of the apneist.

The purpose of this exercise is to regulate the volume of air in the lungs in order to be neutral at about 1.5-2 meters from the surface, or at least at a relatively shallow depth, as demonstrated in the diagram.

Execution

1. Assume a vertical position under the surface of the water and maintain the position, without making any movements; only the hands may be moved (as little as possible) to stabilise the body.
2. Reach neutral buoyancy at the anticipated depth.
3. Stay orientated towards the wall, with as much air in the lungs as is necessary to maintain neutral buoyancy at the desired depth. (It will be easier to maintain depth if there is a visible point of reference on the wall).
4. Upon reaching the position, remain for a 30" apnea, at

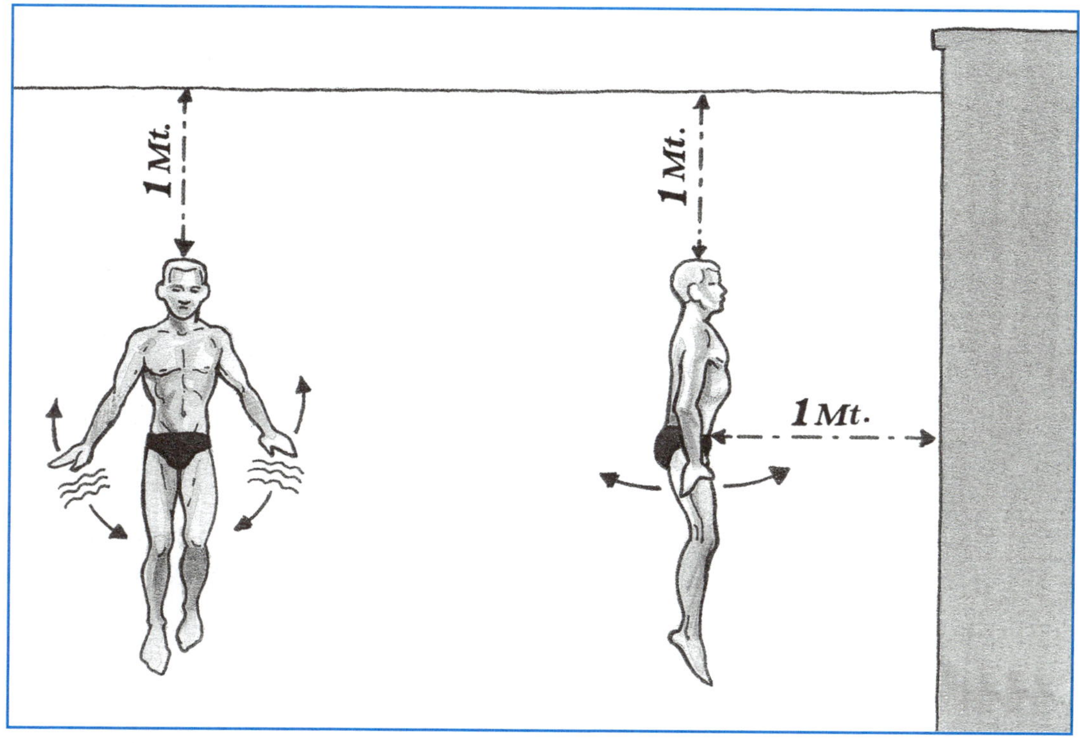

about a meter from the surface and one meter from the wall of the pool.

5. During the entire exercise the position is erect, with arms extended along the sides, legs straight and together, and feet extended. A rhythmic and continuous movement of the hands in opposition will help to maintain position.

The benefit of this exercise is an improved sensitivity to orientation and buoyancy in an apnea that is all but expiratory: depth and distance from the wall must be maintained with maximum composure and without the use of a mask. Success is contingent on buoyancy being completely neutral at the depth reached.

Performing this exercise with or without a wetsuit will familiarise the use of a weightbelt and different amounts of weight.

This exercise improves sensitivity to variations of buoyancy and body position at different depths, enabling greater serenity of mind, a deeper relaxation and a reduced muscular activity in the water. It will make it easier to regulate the actions of the finstroke and exploit the freefall whilst saving precious energy.

Being aware of the weight of the body in the water is indispensable to the pursuit of maximum tranquillity; it allows the reduction of necessary movements, and therefore the economisation of muscular activity and O_2 consumption.

FULL EXHALE APNEA

This exercise consists in performing an apnea underwater after a complete expiration. We recommend, especially for beginners, staying within a maximum depth of three meters.

Execution

1. Exhale.
2. Submerge with a 'candle dive', continuing the exhalation until it is complete (*Fig. 1, 2*).
3. Arrive at the established depth (in general the bottom of the pool) and compensate (*Fig. 3*).

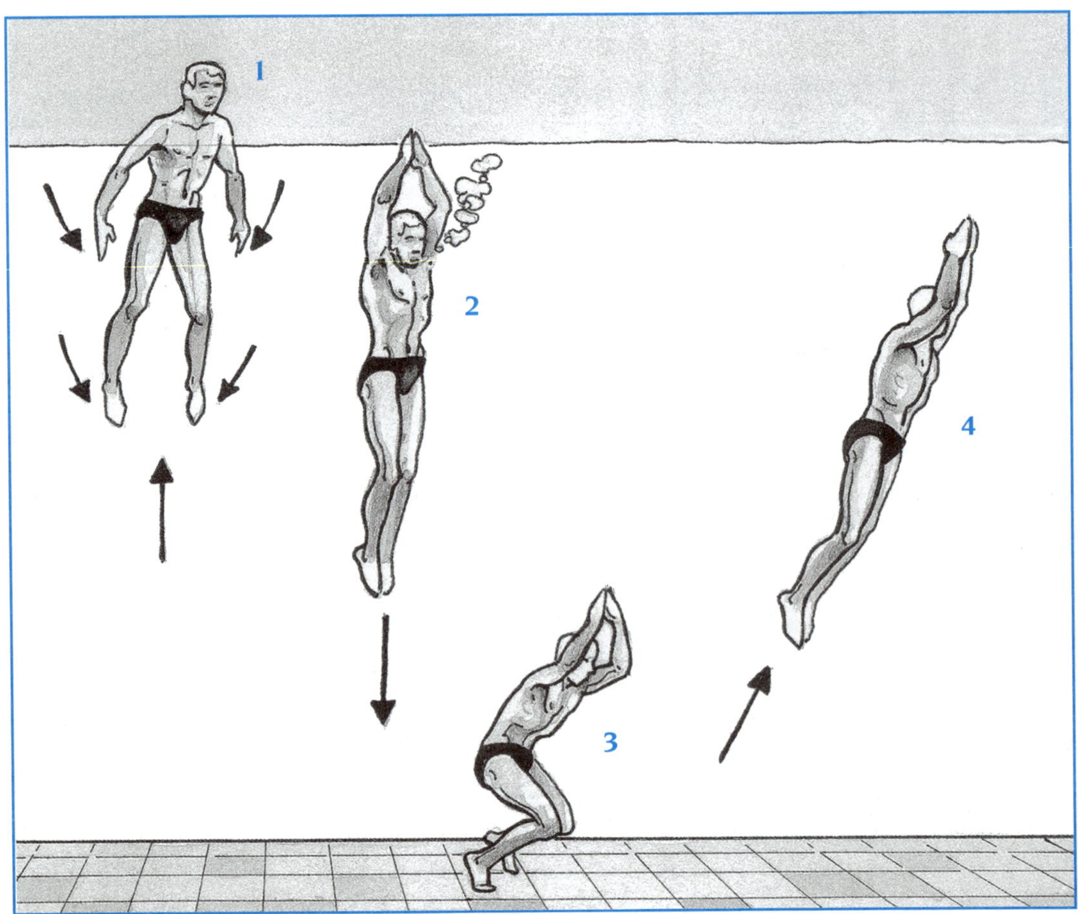

4. Prepare for the ascent, extending the arms upwards and assuming a crouched position with the feet placed well on the bottom (*Fig. 3, 4*).

This exercise trains self-control: an immersion with 'empty lungs' inflicts acute sensations, in extreme (if artificial) conditions.

Note: if possible perform the exercise with bare eyes (no goggles), to improve aquaticity and self-control.

FORCED COMPENSATION

The purpose of this exercise is to train the manoeuvre of compensation in extreme conditions.

Compensating with very little air in the lungs is a great deal more complex, and requires a greater sensitivity and the correct use of the diaphragm to push air into the Eustachian tubes. It is an excellent exercise to train elasticity of the diaphragm.

Execution

1. Perform an apnea underwater after a complete expiration (as described in the previous exercise).
2. Compensate with the diaphragm (*see Chapter 7*).

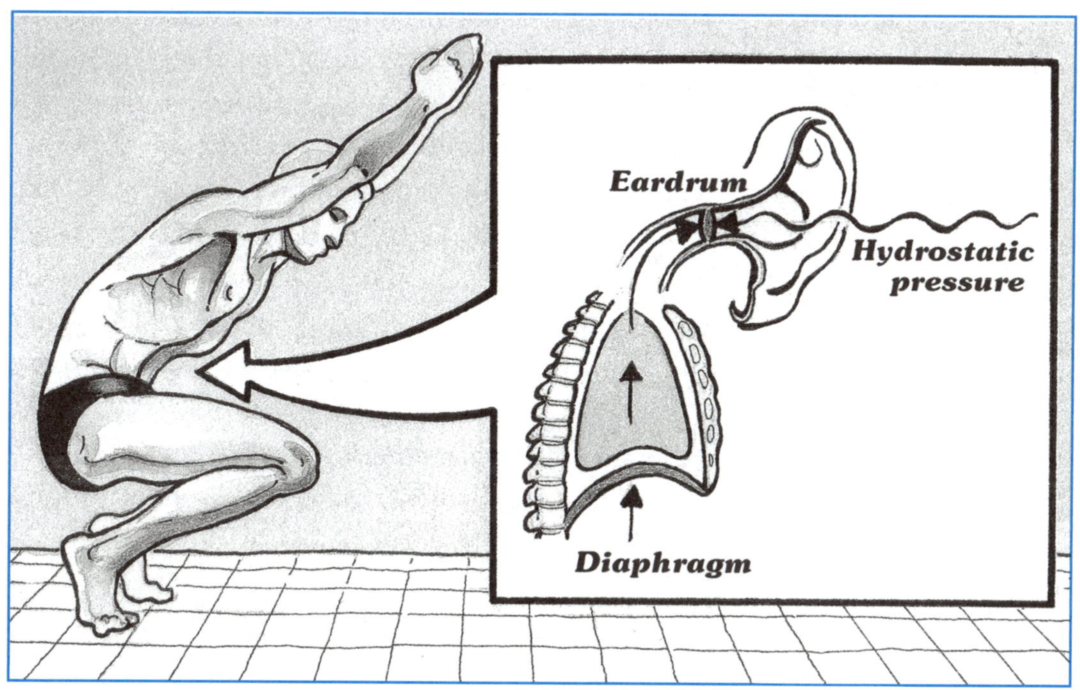

To start with, you can descend with the lungs not completely empty, so as to adapt gradually to the situation; subsequently, empty the lungs fully to encourage diaphragmatic compensation. The effect of this **forced compensation** is the introflexion of the abdominal walls, with consequent **compression of internal organs**. A training partner can easily observe the event, also at a shallow depth.

Note: the greater the depth reached in this exercise, the more effective the training. Therefore practicing in a pool with a 4-5 meter hole will help the apneist to add meters to their security depth in freediving.

Perform this exercise **gradually and with caution.**

EXERCISES OF DISPLACEMENT

During free body immersion the movement of breaststroke, with some variations, and the use of the arms represent the only means of moving effectively.

In this section we will see that several **exercises of displacement** prescribe wide and slow movements, even when we require the greatest efficiency. Opposition of the arms has the function of moving the body on the sagittal plain.

Opposition of the arms on the surface

This is the same movement used on the surface during the duckdive. In immersion however it can produce a forward rotation that we will call 'roll'.

Execution

1. From a prone, floating position, with the arms extended forward (*Fig. A page 230*), start the action with a complete breaststroke arm pass.
   The arms finish at the sides (*Fig. B page 230*). This produces a forward glide of the body through the water.
2. The arms then rotate inwards, and are extended downwards with cupped hands, reaching a plane perpendicular to the surface of the water (*Fig. C page 230*).
   With this second action there will be an opposition to the forwards movement of the body previously created by the breaststroke arm pass on the surface.
3. At the same time as this second arm movement, bring the torso forwards until it is aligned with the arms, and thus pointed towards the bottom.

Opposition of the arms in immersion. 'Forward Roll'.

Execution

1. After sinking feet-first in a vertical position with arms by the sides (*Fig. 1, 2 page 238*), rotate the arms inwards. With cupped hands, extend the arms forwards (*Fig. 1 below*).
2. The torso bends forward until it is parallel to the bottom (*Fig. 2 below*).

This action induces a rotation of the whole body about the transverse axis, called a 'forwards roll'. In the forwards roll the body is bent to 90°, but it is possible to proceed with such arm actions to complete a full 360° turn back to the starting position.

When the hands reach a position in line with the torso and above the head, they must change their position from 'palms backward' to 'palms forwards' i.e. the forearms must be rotated outwards.

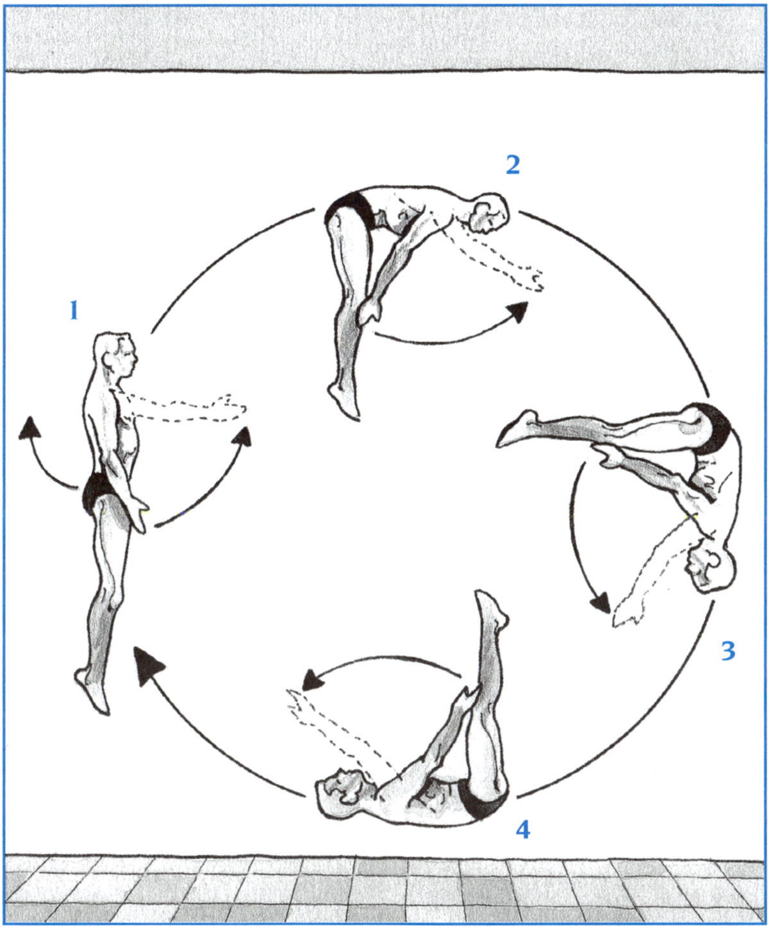

1

2

3

4

Opposition of the arms in immersion. 'Backward Roll'

This action is performed in immersion after sinking feet-first (*Fig 1, 2 page 238*). From the vertical position, use the arms and hands in the following way to produce a 'backward roll' on the sagittal plane (*Fig. 1, 2 below*).

The capacity of the vertebral column to arch backwards will determine the radius of the roll. Greater flexibility of the vertebral column will allow the back to arch further, tightening the radius of the circle described by the apneist's rotating body.

The roll is produced by lowering the arms in opposition. The arms are extended upwards from the sides, with hands facing forwards. The forward and downward rotation of the arms will then produce the backward displacement as illustrated in the diagram.

After the arms have returned to the sides they can extend again above the head to recommence the action of opposition towards the feet. The movement is slow. It is not easy to maintain rotation on the sagittal plane, especially in this type of roll; to succeed there must be a great force on the palms of the hands.

Having the arms slightly apart will make the exercise more straightforward, as it will be easier to use both limbs simultaneously, avoiding lateral movement.

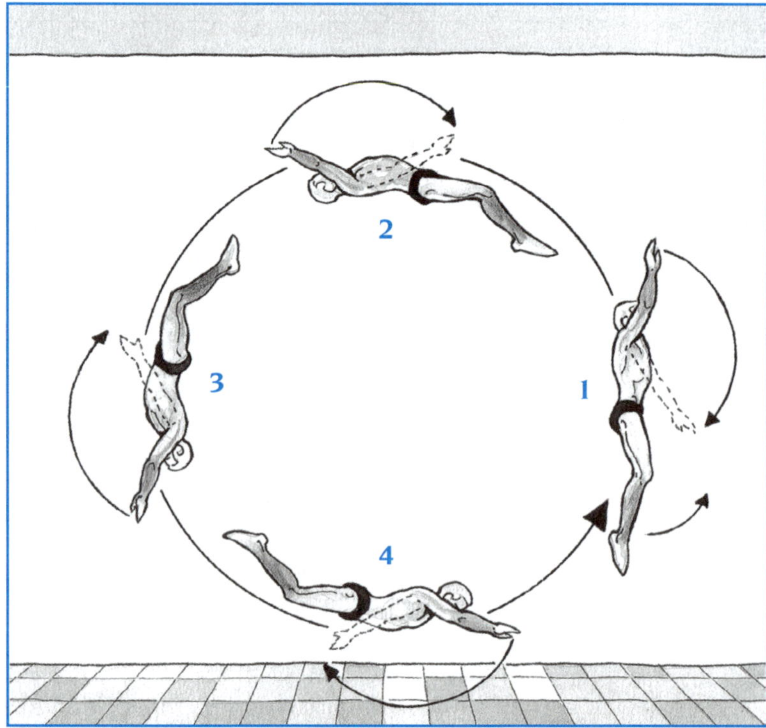

Displacement with the hands

This is often a useful exercise when operating close to the bottom. It is typically used to lift off from muddy, delicate or dangerous seafloors (inside a cave or wreck, on top of coral etc) above which the apneist is placed or in transit. Being able to lift off or move solely with the use of the hands is indicative of a superior level of technique and aquaticity.

The movement consists in more or less symmetrical opposition of the hands on the side that one wishes to move towards. In some cases a breaststroke armstroke can be more effective, even with a single limb (lateral displacement).

Swimming upside down

The execution of underwater breaststroke in a horizontal supine position (belly-up), using the extended arms to steer the body, will substantially increase aquaticity. The difficulty is in the lack of a clear point of reference such as the bottom. The labyrinthine system of the middle ear will be trained by the change of reference and equilibrium due to the reversed body position.

Furthermore, this exercise allows for the correction of several errors: if the legs are overly flexed during their recovery then the thighs will come too far forward and movement will not be horizontal. The use of a mask or noseclip is recommended for this exercise to avoid flooding the nose.

Dancing in Immersion

This exercise consists in performing a genuine underwater ballet, imagining music that accompanies the progression, or if possible listening to a hydrophone. The movements of legs

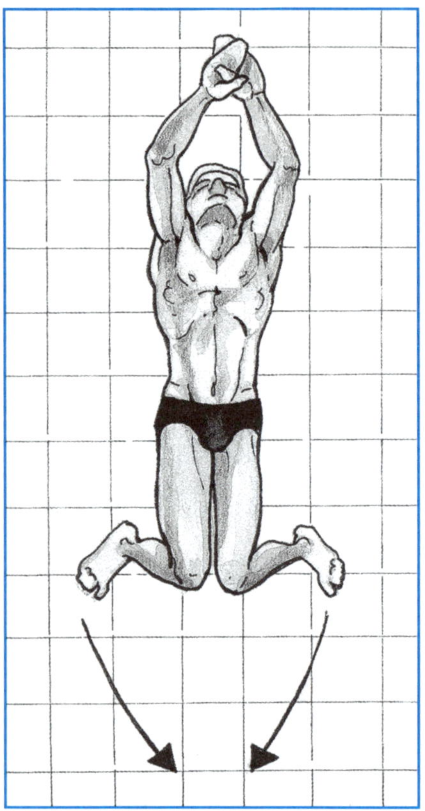

and arms should be slow, harmonious and continuous, based on the displacement exercises described above.

This exercise is undoubtedly beneficial for aquaticity; it stimulates creativity of movement, supports the perception of the body in water, and increases the elegance of underwater movements, favouring the acquisition of a personal style. The actions are not choreographed, but rather evolve from the possibilities of movement underwater in relation to the capacity of self-awareness in immersion.

When the face is looking upwards it is important to exhale to prevent water entering the nose; however for someone with good self-control it is sufficient to increase the air-pressure in the nose. If the apneist discharges air from the nose then at the end of the exercise they will find themselves with negative buoyancy.

FLOTATION EXERCISES

These exercises have the aim of improving general aquaticity. The use of the hands and arms to float instead of the legs means using smaller muscles and reducing the consumption of O_2. The efficacy of movement and the economy of the exercise both improve efficiency in water.

Symmetrical vertical breaststroke

The aim of this exercise is **to maintain the airways completely above the surface**, staying in a fixed position, with an erect posture. The movement of the legs is the same as in normal breaststroke on the surface. This imposes a rhythmical variation of vertical position, and only the opposition of the hands partially compensates the sinking effect. The hands are aligned with the forearms and move on the transverse plane together and apart, as described in the 'opposition of the hands' exercise. The variation in vertical position can be further reduced by moderating the power in the leg push, while taking their recovery slowly and with looseness.

An exaggerated power in the legs will emerge too much of the body above the surface, and this weight will have a subsequent effect on the sinking. An optimum angle in the groin will allow the feet to push downwards – not on a diagonal – which will help maintain position in the water.

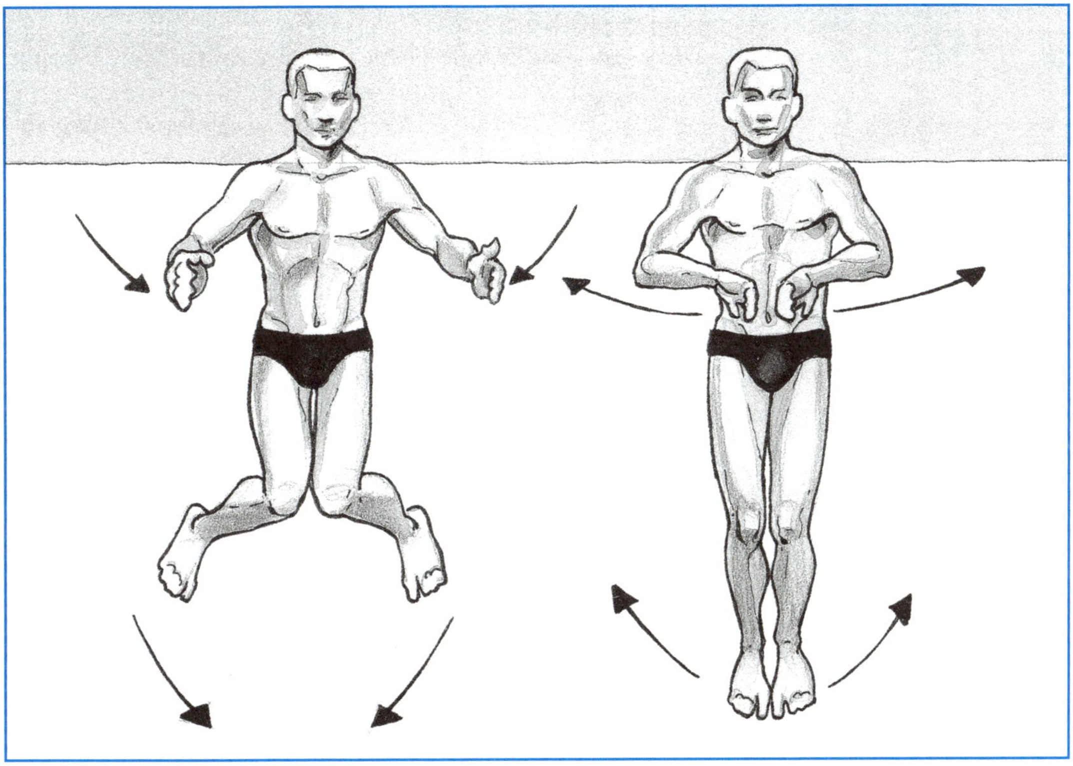

Alternate vertical breaststroke

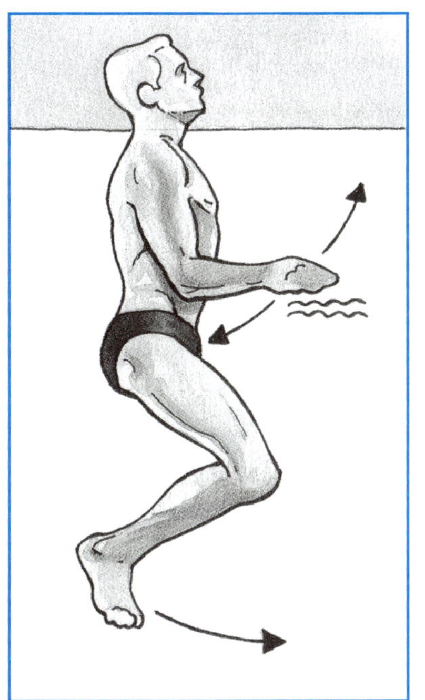

The objective and execution are the same as for the preceding exercise. **The action of the legs changes.** Their movement does not have the power of the symmetrical vertical breaststroke, which takes advantage of the force obtained by bringing the legs together, but it does combine a passive and active action simultaneously, favouring a stable flotation. Furthermore the alternate breaststroke allows the execution of very rapid movements of the legs that are more effective than those of the symmetrical breaststroke, in which the recovery must be slow. However it is an inferior technique in terms of economy.

Opposition of the hands

The forearms are bent to 90° at the elbow and stay as close as possible to the sides, trying to maintain the elbows slightly further back on the frontal plane. The hands are open, with fingers together and aligned with the forearms, but rotated to an angle of 45° on the transverse plane, thanks to the semi-rotation of the forearms. The wrist joint remains immobile.

The action consists in moving the hands together on the transverse plane, inclined at 45° and then moving them apart after having rotated them to 45° in the other direction.

8.3 EXERCISES WITH EQUIPMENT

Fins, mask, snorkel, wetsuit and weightbelt represent the base equipment. After having improved aquaticity with the free body exercises, it is now time to acquire the techniques of immersion in apnea that allow efficient movement through the water.

Correct use of the mask, breathing through the snorkel, finning, protecting from cold, and choosing a suitable buoyancy for the chosen activity are the principle objectives of the exercises that follow.

1. Weighting
2. Quick release of the weightbelt
3. Clearing the mask
4. Duckdives
5. Putting on equipment underwater
6. Simulated recovery of a victim
7. Ascending with difficulty
8. Vertical finning apnea (hands on the bottom)
9. Transition on the bottom
10. Horizontal finning apnea (hands on the wall)
11. Mixed underwater swimming legs/arms
12. Stop and go

WEIGHTING

This is a technique of defining the quantity of weight needed to neutralise, at a predetermined depth, the positive buoyancy given by equipment.

For safety reasons it is important to remember that the last few meters of the ascent from a difficult freedive are the most dangerous in terms of the risk of blackout. Furthermore, in

the last phase of the ascent we will be the most fatigued, hence being 'lighter' will help our legs save on oxygen. For this reason it is critical to be positively buoyant.

For example top-level athletes that dive past forty meters, moderate their weighting to be neutral at a depth of ten meters. In this way they will be positive in the last ten meters of the ascent. However during training in the pool it is sufficient to balance the positive buoyancy of the wetsuit on the surface.

Weighting in the pool is evaluated as follows: remaining motionless in a vertical position one should float with the water level at the neck during inspiration, and sink during expiration. Neutral buoyancy at a predetermined depth is evaluated by descending to the depth and assuming a horizontal position, arms and legs open, like a parachutist. If the weighting is correct the position will be maintained without sinking or floating back to the surface.

It is essential that the final inspiration is as consistent as possible.

QUICK RELEASE OF THE WEIGHTBELT

This manoeuvre is critical in emergencies. The aim is to establish positive buoyancy immediately, in order to ascend rapidly and safely, with a guarantee of floating to the surface. It is important then to observe some rules.

- **when the belt is closed on the waist the tail should not be greater than 10-15 cm;**
- **never fold the tail under the belt.**

The technique is very simple; both hands are placed on the thighs and slide towards the waist until they meet the belt. From here, following the strap, it is easy to locate the quick release buckle, and activate it.

This manoeuvre could seem mechanical; nevertheless one must remember that often when diving, and especially if the strap is nylon instead of elastic, the weightbelt can rotate, making it more difficult to find the release buckle. With this technique even the beginner can avoid the unpleasant surprise of not finding the buckle after bringing their hands straight to the abdomen.

CLEARING THE MASK

The mask can flood in two situations: on the surface and in immersion. In the first case the mask need only be taken off the face to let the water out. It is important to be confident in the mask, and to learn to reposition it well on the face, making sure that there is no hair or seam of the hood resting inside its edge.

In immersion the situation can be more complex. Flooding of the mask, especially the first few times it happens, is annoying due to the water entering the nose and eyes. With a small amount of experience this can easily be adapted to.

The exercise in the pool is aimed at habituating the student to this inconvenience. Water can be kept out of the nose by emitting a small amount of air at the moment when the mask floods.

The exercise gives a solution to the problem in case it happens during immersion. Mental lucidity and control of the situation can be maintained, whilst passing from an inspiratory apnea to a condition of expiration to clear the mask.

The mask is taken off the face whilst looking downwards, flooding it completely. It is then cleared whilst the head is kept hyperextended, i.e. inclined at 45°. It will be easy to find the right head position by simply looking toward the surface.

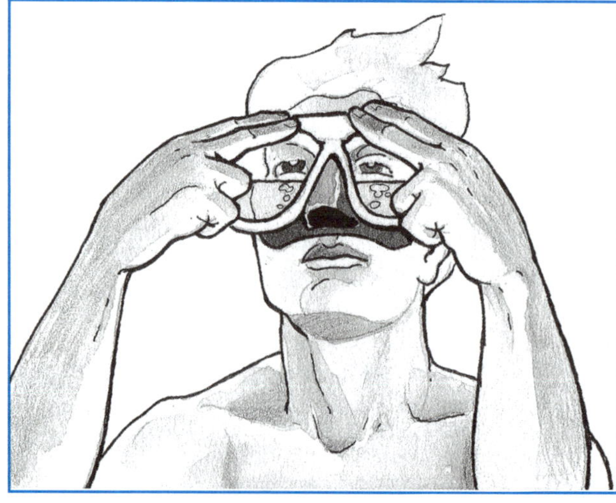

The air exhaled from the nose will fill the mask completely, expelling all the water. Air naturally rises upwards, and, not being able to escape, occupies the internal space of the mask, expelling the water downwards. It is critical for the success of the operation to keep the edge of the mask pressed against the forehead; in this way the only possible exit for water is underneath the lower edge.

The position of the hands is also fundamental. When the hands keep the top of the mask well closed and the emission from the nose is continuous, it will be easier to control the clearing, and not waste air by dispersing it outside the mask. To this end, the emission of air must be continual but not forceful. At first it may help to produce a faint but continuous hum with the mouth closed. In this way you will be able to discharge the right quantity of air from the nose, and most importantly in a continuous stream.

DUCKDIVES

The transfer from a prone position on the surface to a vertical head-down position, and more generally, the transfer from swimming on the surface to immersion, is facilitated by the use of precise techniques: the square duckdive, spearfisher's duckdive, or the feet first submersion.

Duckdives and technically correct finning demonstrate the abilities of a good apneist on the surface. The personal interpretation, and therefore the perfect style in the execution of this technique, will instead express the total adaptation to the environment and to the situation.

This isn't to say that its value is purely aesthetic: in fact style implies effectiveness, economy and efficiency of movement and therefore the maximum return. **Style has considerable practical value.**

Someone who executes the duckdive mechanically may reach the bottom quickly (time in apnea is precious), but with movements that are tiring despite being controlled. With a good style the same action will also be economical and efficient, avoiding superfluous muscular work that in apnea is detrimental.

Square duckdive

A correct duckdive is characterised by precise actions. With naturalness and with an almost imperceptible movement of the fins, one can maintain the basic horizontal position from which any type of duckdive can be executed.

The legs, immobile from start to finish of the exercise, are extended together with feet also extended. The gaze is directed always straight down, towards the bottom. The snorkel allows respiration with the face and mouth immersed – a convenient position in which to prepare for immersion. We can rest like this for as long as we like, relaxed, immobile, and supported only by hydrostatic force whilst we behold the deep blue.

The action begins with the movement of the arms, which are initially relaxed by the sides. From here they extend downwards until they reach a perpendicular position with respect to the surface. The action in opposition of the hands is essential to help direct the torso downwards to follow the upper limbs, while the lower limbs are raised.

In the square duckdive the legs are completely straight as they are lifted, and pass from a right angle position to the vertical, aligning themselves with the torso and arms. Pay attention to the position of the head. Looking downwards will involve hyperextension and offer greater resistance to the water, spoiling the efficiency of the duckdive. The head must be kept aligned with the torso until just before the bottom of the descent.

This type of duckdive is the most common and the most effective, especially for deep dives, since it allows straightforward sinking by exploiting the weight of the legs above the surface.

Spearfisher's duckdive

This type of duckdive may not be as effective as the square, but it is more fluid, and allows an excellent downwards glide with very little force and without the use of the hands to stabilise the descent. Very simply, from the horizontal position, while the torso bends 90° downwards, one leg is raised and the other remains immobile on the waterline.

The weight of the raised leg will submerge the body in the direction held by the torso, and the two legs reunite as the fins are immersed. From the head-down vertical position it will be easy to start the dive in the most efficient and smooth

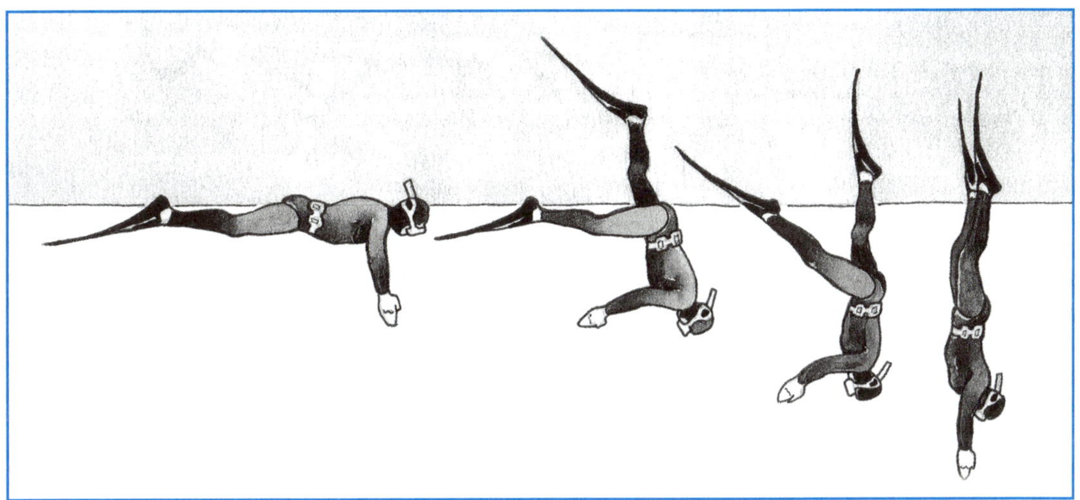

manner, with an appropriately moderated leg throw. This type of duckdive is the quickest, most fluid and elegant: a 'smooth and silent dart', used especially by spearfishers for a stealthy approach to their prey.

Feet first submersion

This technique, despite how bizarre and uneconomical it may seem, is an excellent solution for restricted spaces where the surface does not permit ample movement.

The apneist is supported by finning in a vertical position; the arms are widened outwards, placed on the surface of the water. The action starts with a vigorous finstroke at the same time as the arms are brought down to the sides. The aim is to

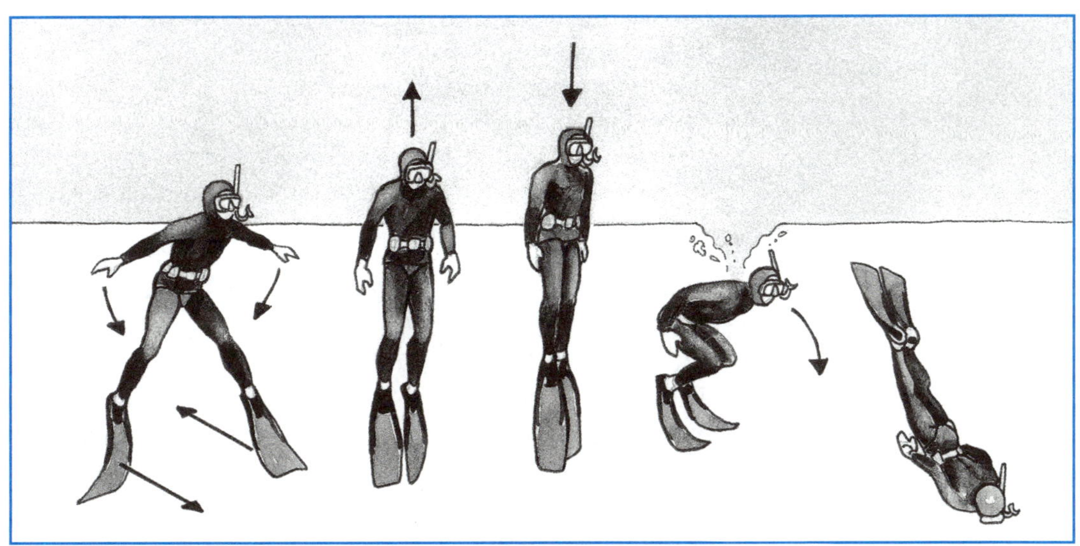

bring the body as far as possible out of the water, so that the apneist may be sunk by their own weight. Therefore it is necessary, after having executed the push upwards with the upper and lower limbs, to be as hydrodynamic as possible, keeping the arms by the sides and the legs together with the feet pointed down, i.e. with fins extended towards the bottom.

To assist the immersion the apneist can move the arms upward from the sides to further push the body downward. Upon reaching a certain depth – even one meter is sufficient – it is easy to rotate into the horizontal position and start finning in the desired direction.

PUTTING ON EQUIPMENT UNDERWATER

This exercise is intended as a simulation that requires considerable skills of coordination and aquaticity.

It involves diving without equipment – using a folding duckdive – and putting on fins, mask and snorkel, which are already positioned on the bottom of the pool, all before resurfacing.

Execution *(see figure on page 253)*

1. Effect the folding duckdive directly above the equipment on the bottom, reaching the fins, mask and snorkel in a few seconds.
2. Collect each piece of equipment and put on first the fins, then the mask, position the snorkel under the mask strap – if it is not already fixed – and finally clear the mask of water. Starting to clear the mask whilst still on the bottom will make the operation easier, economising on both air and energy. The volume of air emitted into the mask at depth will expand with the ascent due to the decrease of hydrostatic pressure, emptying the water completely, and saving on air.
3. Arrange the mask on the face and the snorkel under the strap and start the ascent head-up.

This exercise requires a good level of self-control and is therefore considered a good indicator of concentration and of the technical level reached.

The technical components that determine the success of the exercise are **the duckdive, the order in which equipment is put on and its correct use, the clearing of the mask, the replacement of the snorkel mouthpiece only after the first inspiration, the maintenance of a fixed position and mental calm.**

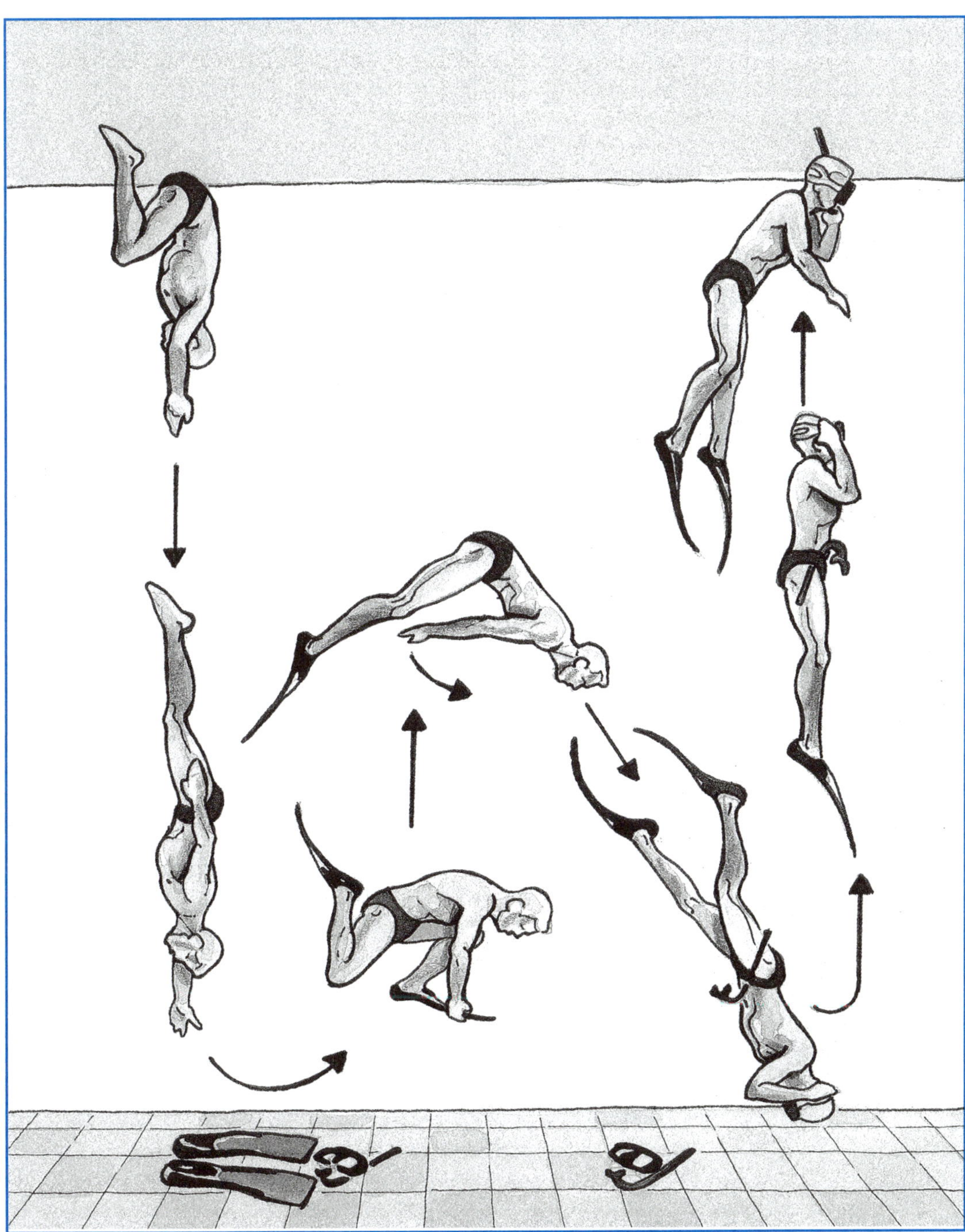

The mask must be cleared before surfacing. Upon reaching the surface and after having inhaled a single breath, the mouthpiece of the snorkel can be reinstated in the mouth and cleared to resume normal breathing.

The prospect of having to complete many tasks in a single dive can often arouse apprehension, due to an inability to evaluate the time required. With slow movements and calm actions the entire exercise can be completed in a maximum time of 40" and with a low consumption of energy. Positively buoyant apneists definitely have a disadvantage: it is critical that they have the right quantity of air in the lungs.

Some people may even surface whilst putting on the fins, especially if the pool is not very deep. In this case it is important not to fight against the ascent, but to allow yourself to be transported to the surface by the positive buoyancy in the position that the body naturally assumes while putting on the fins, trying to avoid unnecessary movement, which would only accelerate the rise and waste precious energy. For this reason it is important not to completely fill up with air before beginning, but instead to carefully regulate the size of the inspiration so as not to be too positive.

Very slow finning with the head down will help to maintain contact with the bottom until the mask is in place on the face, ensuring that there is no hair between the rubber skirt and the skin and that the strap is well adjusted. Only at this point can you position the snorkel tube under the mask strap. Position it well towards the back to avoid it moving laterally when the mask is cleared and having to be rearranged on the surface.

SIMULATED RECOVERY OF A VICTIM

This lifesaving exercise deals with the skills that a good apneist must possess in order to master an emergency situation, in which it is necessary to address complete attention to the victim.

Execution

1. 'Rescuer' and 'victim' face each other at a certain distance. Both are equipped with wetsuit, fins, mask, snorkel and weight.
2. At an agreed signal the rescuer swims rapidly to cross the distance to the victim as quickly as possible. The first part of the distance is completed finning on the surface; the rescuer then immerses with a duckdive and reaches the victim after a distance underwater that may be lengthened with training.
3. The moment the rescuer dives, the victim, wearing equal gear to the rescuer, sinks to a prone position on the bottom.

4. After completing the last part of the distance underwater, the rescuer finds the victim lying on the bottom.
5. The rescuer detaches the weight belt of the victim as well as their own.
6. The rescuer exploits positive buoyancy to ascend to the surface, bearing the victim with one of the techniques illustrated in *Chapter 9.4*.
7. Upon reaching the surface the rescuer must remove the victim's mask and keep the victim's face constantly above the surface, whilst transporting him or her to the starting point, finning dorsally.
8. Upon arriving at the edge of the pool, the victim's head is kept well above the surface while they are removed from the water, completing the exercise.

A satisfactory execution is characterised by: a good velocity in the approach to the victim, a rapid and efficient recovery from the bottom, transport on the surface with the victim's head at all times above the surface, correct transport of the victim out of the water and a correct lateral recovery position.

This exercise is very important and formative: a good apneist must know how to execute each action in sequence without interruption. It requires a good technical preparation, but also considerable physical preparation to be able to support the load of the victim in transport.

The rescue in water must become automatic, for which it is necessary to frequently repeat the simulation. In order for

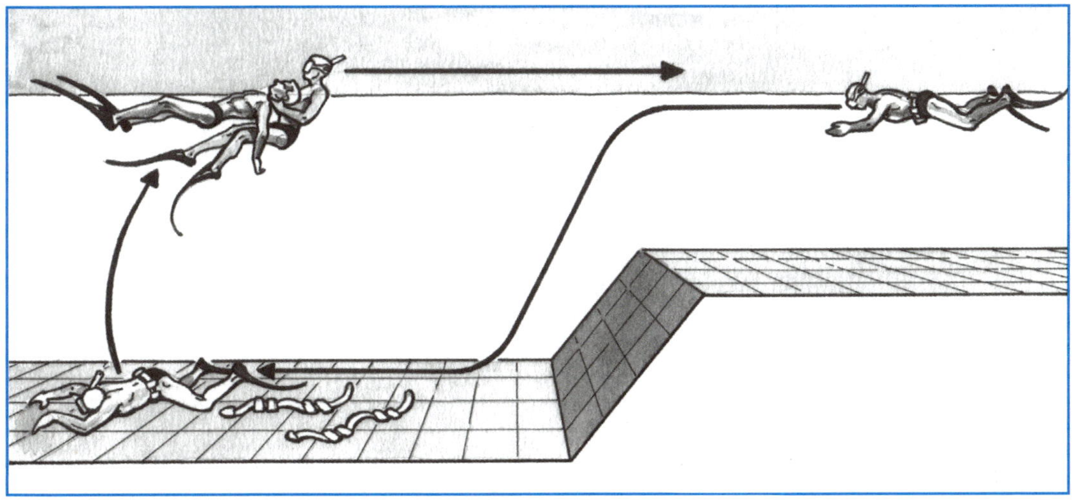

the attention of the rescuer to be always addressed to the victim, the execution of the exercise may even be imperfect. However the absolute necessities of keeping the head correctly above the surface and transferring the victim out of the water and straightaway into the lateral recovery position should never be undermined.

This is an excellent exercise for learning to coordinate the actions required in 'victim recovery', and can be performed in open water for a more realistic simulation.

The rescuer in a simulated emergency should always complete the procedure with 'first response', but this requires training in CPR (cardiopulmonary resuscitation). To administer CPR a course in first aid is imperative, and completes the training of the apneist.

ASCENDING WITH DIFFICULTY

This exercise may be performed in **the 'hole' or deep end of a pool.**

Execution

1. Departing from the surface with a duckdive, reach the bottom where two heavy weightbelts have been placed in advance.
   The weights should be chosen in relation to the equipment worn and therefore buoyancy in water.
2. Put on the two weightbelts and start the ascent.

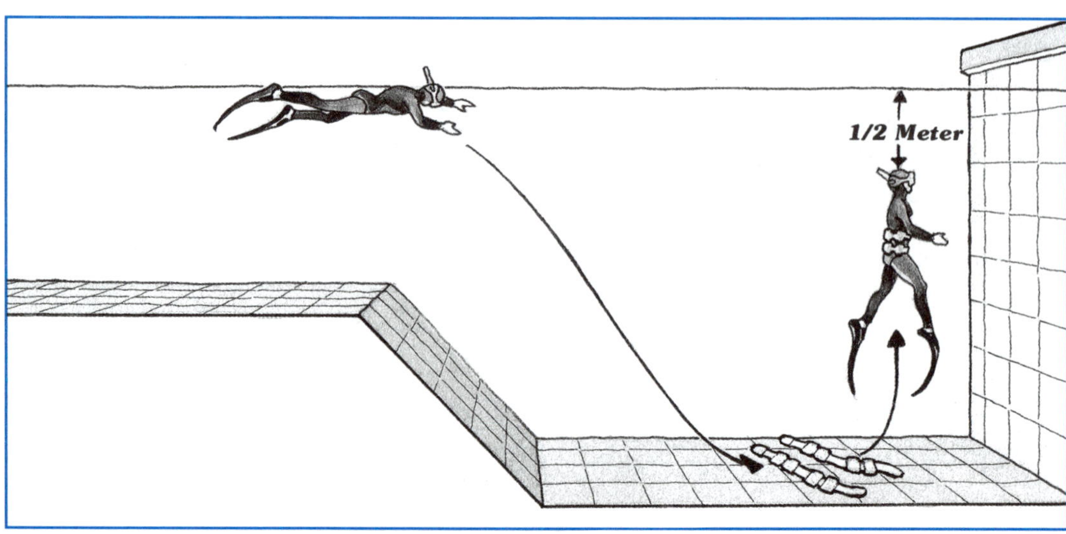

3. Stop at about halfway to the surface, finning to maintain vertical alignment.
4. Remain like this for sufficient time to verify correct finning technique and self-control, and then resurface after having abandoned one or both of the weightbelts using the quick release.

DYNAMIC APNEA

This discipline involves crossing as great a distance as possible in apnea, at a more or less constant depth. The phase immediately before departure is of fundamental importance: its two main elements are physical and mental relaxation and correct respiration. Having already dealt with the psychological aspect and relaxation in this discipline in Chapter 5, we will now analyse the technical components. The last inspiration doesn't have to be complete. The bottom of the pool is usually three meters at the deepest. To swim with completely full lungs gives us an elevated buoyancy, and as a consequence the force of the finstroke is not only working to advance our body but also to maintain it in immersion. In short we will have a dispersion of force. It is better therefore to start with lungs filled to 80% of their maximum. The departure must be smooth and relaxed, with a duck-dive that will take you to the bottom after an oblique translation.
The body must maintain the relaxation during wide and homogenous finstrokes. In order for dynamic apnea to be effective, economic and efficient it is important that technique is without the errors illustrated in Chapter 6.
It is impossible to maintain as complete and wide a finstroke as is used in a free-dive descent: the presence of the bottom of the pool inevitably limits the amplitude of movement downwards, unless we are able to swim at least a meter above it. In the interests of physical relaxation, it is advisable to keep the arms along the sides for the entire duration, as this avoids great muscular tension in the shoulders and back. The arms can be stretched forwards to increase hydrodynamics in the case of specific training, such as apnea sprints at maximum velocity. The head must be aligned with the body. Lifting the head to look forwards, other than being of considerable detriment to relaxation, also increases the resistance of the body to the water. Lane markers drawn on the bottom of the pool are an excellent point of reference to maintain the correct bearing. Another component of technique is the turn. Upon reaching the end of the pool, if we are turning to the left then the right arm is placed on the wall to facilitate the rotation, while the left is already turned to point in the new direction. If the pool is shallow, and finning is therefore close to the bottom, then the left arm is placed on the bottom and acts as a pivot upon which the whole body turns. If we turn to the right then the opposite orientation is used. The dynamic apnea must finish with a constant and linear finstroke, avoiding an increase in rhythm in the attempt to breathe sooner (see Chapter 5.2). Remember not to exhale forcefully or with violence at the end of the apnea (see Chapter 10.1).

Note: in falling to the bottom the weightbelts may damage the floor of the pool, so it is best to use weights with a plastic coating, or better still a belt with neoprene pockets. Ideally one makes use of two assistants, giving them a weightbelt each, rather than letting them fall to the bottom. This exercise is a close simulation of a difficulty in ascent.

Considering the strength required, it is important that there be constant surveillance in this exercise.

A longer execution is helpful to simulate real situations in training. Apneists with low CO_2 tolerance will become fatigued maintaining the halfway position, but the aim of the exercise is also to test the effect of an unanticipated physical force, such as can happen in an emergency ascent from depth.

VERTICAL FINNING APNEA (hands on the bottom)

The aim of this exercise is to put the apneist in the same head-down position that is assumed during a constant weight freedive. In doing so, the movements and forces of a deep descent can be reproduced in the swimming pool.

Obviously the effects of pressure and the consequent compensation are dependant on the depth of the pool.

Execution

1. After having performed the duckdive and reached the bottom, the apneist assumes a vertical position, with the arms extended and the hands placed on the bottom of the pool.
   The head, depending on preference, can be kept hyperextended as demonstrated in the diagram, or relaxed and aligned with the torso between the arms.
2. Maintaining this position, begin finning with wide and homogenous finstrokes that reproduce the rhythm, intensity and amplitude as well as body position of a freedive descent.

In this position the vestibular complex – nervous centre for the sense of equilibrium – receives the same stimuli to which it is subjected in a constant weight freedive; by gradually increasing time of immersion and varying amplitude and rhythm, one can also create hypoxic stimuli.

TRANSLATION ON THE BOTTOM

This is an aquaticity exercise, excellent for improving the efficiency of finning, self-control and especially **sense of equilibrium** and orientation whilst head down in the water. It involves 'walking' on the hands, trying to maintain adherence to the bottom with a suitable finstroke.

Execution

1. After reaching the bottom with a square duckdive, assume a vertical position with the hands placed on the bottom.
2. The head should be perfectly aligned with the vertebral column (exactly halfway between the arms) to maintain the right position during the course of the exercise.
3. Upon assuming the position, begin finning to maintain adherence to the bottom and to advance, moving first one hand then the other.
4. Walk backwards on the hands, in the opposite direction to where the eyes are looking.
5. Finish the movement, turn and resurface.

The finstroke must be wide, slow and most importantly symmetrical to guarantee a constant vertical position and a

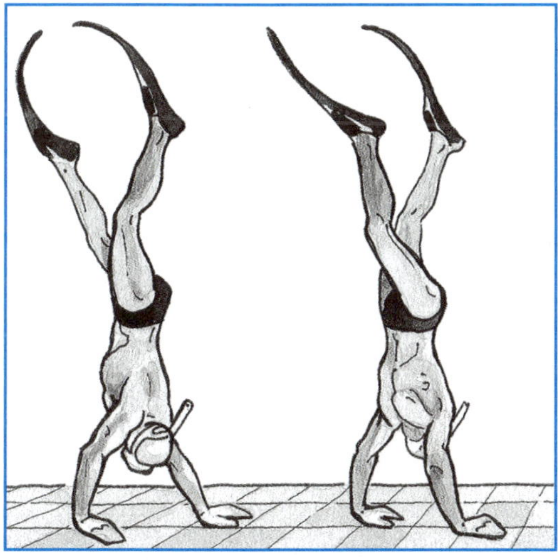

Correct execution

Incorrect execution

reasonable advance. The exercise is performed in deep water initially with a mask, and successively without to improve perception of the body in relation to the water as well as equilibrium and general self-control. A good execution is characterised by the **a maintenance of vertical position**, amplitude of the finstroke, coordination in the movements of the arms, and most of all by composure and personal style, which are indicative of calm and harmony.

HORIZONTAL FINNING APNEA (hands on the wall)

This exercise is practically identical to the preceding, with the difference that **the position of the apneist is rotated by 90°** – i.e. perpendicular to the wall – to give a horizontal position that simulates dynamic apnea.

Execution

1. The hands are placed on the wall, the arms straightened, and the head in line with the body.
2. The legs move with regular and uniform finstrokes. Specific training stimuli can be produced by gradually increasing the time of immersion, amplitude and the rhythm of the finstroke.

MIXED UNDERWATER SWIMMING LEGS/ARMS

This involves swimming **mixed laps** underwater in apnea. If one direction is swum finning, then the return can be made using the hands to pull along an opportunely placed rope. The exercise can be performed in a pool or in open water at a constant depth.

Execution

1. Correct finning.
2. Slow and regular movement of the arms.
3. Composure in immersion.
4. Absence of muscular contraction in inactive areas of the body.

This exercise is **preparatory for diving with a down line**, which will be used in open water for constant weight. By adopting different techniques for the length with fins and the return using hands, the apneist will acquire, lap by lap, the ability to decontract the muscular sectors that aren't required.

STOP AND GO

After having placed weights at one end of the pool, depart from the other end finning underwater. Upon reaching the weights, perform a static apnea, using the weights to remain on the bottom for an opportune amount of time, which can be increased with training. Without resurfacing, depart to complete the return leg.

A valid variation of this exercise consists in completing a static apnea before departing and then performing a second at half way or at the end of the distance.

Devising variants of 'stop and go' creates training situations above all on a mental level. Evaluate the following components: correct and regular finning, correct and relaxed position in the static apnea (which is not too long and not too short), control of the action in both underwater lengths.

This exercise employs a 'waiting apnea', combining the dynamic apnea with the static. It is therefore important to fin in a relaxed manner, with the least amount of force possible, then pass the time stationary and absolutely relaxed, before completing the return to finish in total calm.

8.4 AND NOW, APNEA GAMES

Playing in apnea; we can and we should, and not only because games – as demonstrated by dozens of studies – are the best way of learning (the young of any species learn by playing), but also because a fun period at the end of a training session is the best way of relaxing, being at ease with companions, and entering into a healthy dimension of recreation.

After a hard training session **games** favour the **recovery of attention** that is brought back to the environment around us, relieving the tension that may have accumulated. In the first dive in open water, games can become a **useful device for increasing aquaticity** in an exposed environment. Not to mention that during games the apneist forgets about time and performance. The attention is focussed on achieving playful objectives. **Not thinking about the apnea** is one of the best ways of realising a good time, a good depth, or a good length. Furthermore, games will enhance motivation.

The introduction of a game into the practice of apnea allows a more collective spirit to be bought to a sport that can appear very individual, and satisfies that natural propensity of any individual to socialise. All of which is very gratifying, and reduces tension.

However recreation does not mean irresponsibility. Playing doesn't entail disregarding safety. All the games are played with two or more people, and so imply a level of surveillance.

We now propose several games to play together with apneist friends. Some require accessories, such as a plastic whiteboard, a pencil and eraser, balloons, several different coloured strings, an opportunely weighted draughts board with pieces slightly modified for underwater use, obstacles and ropes of various types.

GAMES FOR STATIC APNEA

All the games that we propose are played with constant reciprocal surveillance. With a friend or in a group, safety is a matter of watchfulness and attention: the pressure of a hand gives sufficient information on the state of well being of a person.

Paper, scissors, rock

This game that is a popular arbitrator of disputes can also be played underwater. The game is very simple: each player uses their hand to simulate one of three objects:

Paper – open hand
Scissors – extended index and middle fingers
Rock – hand closed to a fist

The two apneists position themselves facing each other, and at the judge's signal show their hands – which have until that moment been kept behind their backs. The rules are:

- **scissors beats paper**
- **paper beats rock**
- **rock beats scissors**

And naturally the winner is the person who succeeds in playing the most games underwater.

Electric shocks

A group of three or more apneists hold hands in a circle. A predetermined player (the power station) sends out an electric shock, or a light squeeze of the hand, which is passed from hand to hand until it returns to the power station. The objective of the group is to pass the shock around the circle as many times as possible.

Morse code

Dots and dashes! The transmitter in our case is represented by the fingers of the apneists. One person sends a message, the next transmits it, and so forth.

The difficulty is in conserving the message in its original form and in enduring apnea for as long as possible.

At the end of the chain the receiver can write the message on a small underwater whiteboard for the final check of the judge, and comparison with other competing teams.

The longest expiration

On the surface, or on terra firma, attempt as long an expiration as possible. It is an excellent exercise for training and warm-up. A stopwatch and a companion with whom to compete are all that's necessary for an animating challenge.

Bubbles

Create the most beautiful bubble or bubble ring of air from the bottom of the pool while a second person watches from the surface.

The clock

A judge establishes a time of apnea, and the competitors must stay underwater for this predetermined time without having a watch to consult. Everybody starts at the same time, and the winner is the player who surfaces closest to the time announced by the judge.

A possible variation: everybody is started together by the judge, who supervises the players, and at a command everybody stops their apnea. The winner is the player who makes the closest guess of the time of the static apnea just completed.

Buddha From the lotus position to standing on the head, let the imagination run wild, and hold the poses for as long as possible in immersion.

Empty lungs Make a stop on the bottom of the pool in complete expiration. The winner is whoever remains the longest in apnea with empty lungs.

Draughts A game of draughts with a difference: each move is made on the bottom in apnea. On surfacing the competitor must remove the mask. Only after the opponent has surfaced can they replace the mask and dive to study the countermove and play their own. An adjudicator on the surface guarantees the rules are followed.

The flea race Each player has a coin (flea). The race takes place on the bottom of the pool; the aim is to be first to the other end. The flea must be moved without touching it, and therefore only by the movement of water produced by the hand, or – on a higher level of difficulty – by jets of water from the mouth.

Each player may surface for air at any time, knowing that it will slow their advance to the finish.

GAMES FOR DYNAMIC APNEA

Snails Establish an underwater course: the winner is whoever finishes last. The participants cannot stop, but only moderate the frequency of their finning.

Relay race This is a good means of developing ability of propulsion. Establish an easy or complex course, organise teams composed of two or more apneists and place them at the extremes, or at the same end of the pool, depending on the length of the pool and the level of ability of the apneists.

The batten can be a snorkel or a simple pat on the hand of the next team member. The underwater course can have different difficulties depending on the availability of material.

Undersea courses

In the sea, carefully considered underwater courses can aid discovery of the environment. These involve passages through open caves, or through equipment opportunely prepared and placed, such as circles, squares etc.

Swimming in pairs

After dividing into pairs, each half swims a certain distance. One of the two members of the pair pushes the other by the feet, which are placed on his or her shoulders. The partner in front controls the direction. Upon arriving at half way, the roles change, and the pair departs for the return.

Caterpillar

The game described above can be rendered even more amusing with the participation of other apneists. Together everyone forms an 'underwater caterpillar' that must cross a certain distance before reversing direction.

The blindman

Using a mask with its lenses obscured, the players must swim an obstacle course (ropes, circles, squares etc). The winner is whoever arrives at the finish in the shortest possible time.

Heavy feet

Appropriately weighted, without fins but with a mask, it is possible to run races, relays or games of tag. All underwater obviously – on the bottom of the pool or of the sea, but always in shallow water.

Underwater hockey

The puck can be a small half-kilo weight or a metal disc. Equipped with snorkels for hockey sticks, the players must score in the opponents' goal, conventionally represented by the wall of the pool.

Parachutes

On the bottom of the pool or sea, arrange small plastic bags, which are each numbered or have a different colour, and are held in place by weights. Each team must make their parachute take off by blowing air from their lungs into the bag, possibly after having first swum a short distance underwater. The team whose bag surfaces first are the winners.

FORMATION IN OPEN WATER

CHAPTER 9

When you look into the abyss,
The abyss also looks into you.
– Friedrich Nietzsche

The moment has arrived to confront the open water of seas and lakes; to put to the test everything that has been learnt in the pool.

Open water is introduced gradually and with prudence, knowing that from the very first dive the situation has changed, and that we must also accommodate variations in the environment: current, tides, waves, temperature and weather conditions. Hence in the first section we have summarised the most important information on the underwater environment (qualities and movements of water).

However we haven't included notes on the flora and fauna of different marine environments. Even though this topic represents for many one of the motivations of apnea, its enormity is such that it would require an entire volume to itself. We recommend the reader instead to the bibliography, where can be found information on specific texts.

For our part we will limit ourselves to a single observation: diving in the sea or lake denotes entering quietly and gracefully into a world that even today hides many fascinating surprises. One of the delights that makes freediving and snorkelling so fascinating is the observation of marine life. The waters form many biological environments that are very different to each other, and are host to a boundless variety of living creatures. During any dive the apneist must behave as a well-mannered visitor and courteous guest, not as a 'raider of the sea:' every lover of the sea must be aware of the potential damage that improper behaviour can cause.

9.1 THE OCEAN PLANET

Images received from satellites show that Earth is covered by water, an ocean planet: 71% of its surface is covered by sea, 55% of which is deep water.

Oceanography is a relatively recent science - it was developed at the finish of the 18th century. Until that time the movement of the masses of water and the geology of the sea-floor were studied only in relation to navigation. Only at the end of the 1700's the art of navigation and the science of the seas were separated to follow each their own courses.

Today geographers are inclined to sustain that there is only really a single ocean, even if it has three different names. The ocean represents only a part of the **hydrosphere**, which is comprised of all of the waters present on the planet in all the different states. In terms of volume, **97% of the hydrosphere** is made up of marine waters, while the other components are continental surface waters: the icecaps, watercourses and lakes, subterranean water and atmospheric water vapour.

The need of uniformity in the science has led to the definition of the **World Ocean** in a very schematic fashion, as constituted by a single body of water – distributed between

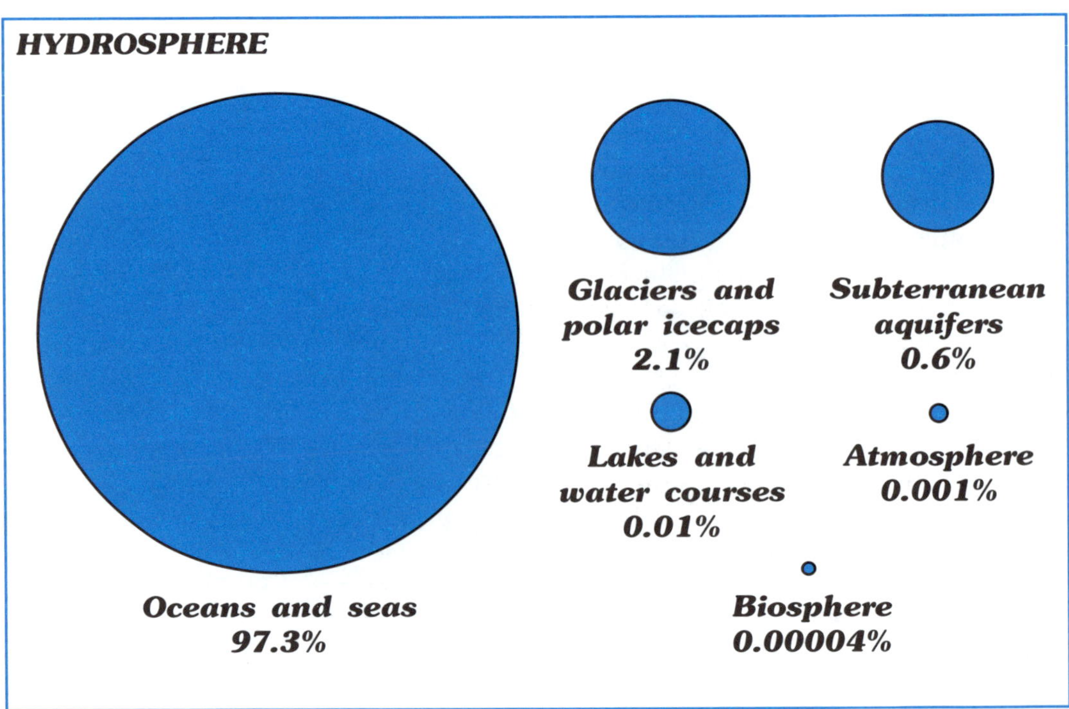

the poles and extending north through three main 'gulfs' contained between the continental masses. These 'gulfs' are the **Atlantic, Indian** and **Pacific** oceans.

It follows that the portions of the ocean enclosed between the continents are distinct, characterised by important physical and chemical differences that influence their climatic, biological and geochemical systems, and give them the name of **seas**.

The **physical properties of seas** depend on **temperature** and **density**, which is determined by the **concentration of salt** in the water. Temperature and salinity undergo changes primarily on the surface, where the ocean 'interfaces' with the atmosphere. The **interaction between air and water** produces changes in the gaseous qualities of the water as well as its heat and energy. This is why the seas have such different qualities at the different latitudes. The salinity of the North Sea is 0.9%, while the Red Sea has a concentration of over 4%.

There are different theories regarding the formation of the oceans, but there is a shared hypothesis that they were produced by the condensation of water vapour present in the primordial atmosphere, which, with the cooling of the planet, commenced to fall down on Earth in the form of rain. Over time this deluge collected in the lowest parts of the planet, until it filled the oceanic basins that now contain **1.5 billion km^3 of water**.

Before arriving in the oceanic basins, water that falls on land carries with it several mineral salts, which together with the products of intense volcanic activity are even today responsible for a good part of the salinity of the oceans.

Thermocline

Just like air, colder water is denser, and therefore tends to stratify beneath warmer water. In this way actual layers of water are created, with different temperatures at varying depths. The boundary of a band of water of the same temperature is called a **thermocline**.

In discussing the genesis of the oceans we have referred to the temperature of the water, attributing to this physical property an important responsibility in the determining of climate: changes in the state of water such as evaporation act on the Earth as a kind of giant thermostat.

The main **heat source** that warms the sea is **solar radiation**; the depth of penetration of solar radiation is proportional to clarity of the water and therefore the quantity of particles in suspension. In normal conditions in the middle of the ocean,

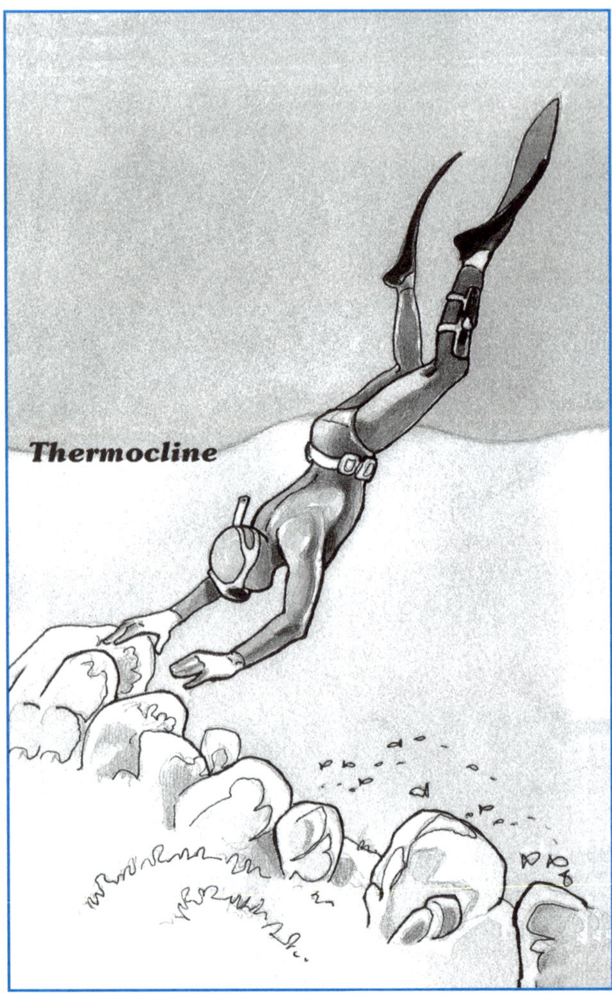

80% of heat energy is absorbed between the surface and a depth of 1 meter; while that absorbed beyond a depth of 100 meters is equal only to 0.45% of the total energy accumulated by marine water.

The warming of deep water can occur by **conduction**, which is transmission of heat from a hotter particle to a nearby colder particle; or by **convection**, which is of much greater importance in oceans and seas.

Convection is caused in the waters of the sea by means of the turbulent movement of masses of surface water. These are caused principally by waves and vertical motion due to differences in salinity, especially where there is great evaporation, or where the air temperature is very low such as close to the poles.

Even **marine life** is strongly conditioned to **water temperature**, and therefore man needs to follow suit with thick neoprene to provide an adequate thermal protection. In Chapter 1 we mentioned that **in water the apneist loses body heat 25 times faster than in air**; this is a good reason to wear a wetsuit of suitable thickness for the environs.

Thermoclines give further motivation for the choice of wetsuit. In fact this phenomenon occurs in both sea and lake, with **sudden changes of temperature between the surface**, which is generally warmer, **and the strata of depths**. These changes can at times exceed **10° C**, especially in lakes, which are generally smaller and shallower.

We must therefore keep in mind that when we dive in lakes and seas with temperature bands, **the difference between the surface temperature and the temperature at depth is considerable. Attire must be suitable for the conditions found at depth**, not on the surface. In tropical waters however, the difference in temperature between the surface and the depths is generally insignificant.

Salinity

The salinity of the sea has an average value of around 3.5%. This means that the total mass of solid substances contained in 1000 g of water (1 litre) has an average weight of about 35 g. In reality there are variations that in certain cases reach significant values, whether on the surface or at depth.

In the oceans the values of salinity are comparatively higher inside the **tropics**, where they are raised to as much as **3.7%. At the equator** – where precipitation is elevated and where the cloudiness dampens the action of solar radiation – **the salinity of the waters is generally less** than at the tropics.

In the higher and lower latitudes towards the poles the salinity decreases to reach values around **3.3-3.4%**. In these areas evaporation is not as intense, and there is a significant addition of fresh water from the melting of ice.

The whole of this discourse on distribution of salinity changes greatly if we move to the seas, or those parts of the ocean that are enclosed by a continent: here the salinity attains large variations with respect to the waters of the oceans.

While in the English channel the salinity is 3.5%, on the Danish coast of the North sea it decreases to 3.2%, and in the gulf of Finland, land of a thousand rivers, the salinity drops as low as 0.3-0.4% due to the substantial run-off of fresh water. The massive reduction in the salinity of this water raises its freezing point, so that in contrast to seawater, which freezes at around - 2°C, in this state it will freeze at 0°C, creating considerable problems for navigation.

Passing into the Red Sea, which is enclosed by deserts, the saline concentration is among the greatest of the open seas, varying from 4.1% to 4.3%, with an average temperature of 24°C as opposed to the 13°-14°C of the oceans.

In the Mediterranean the average salinity exceeds 3.6%, even if the value varies greatly according to the region; it passes from about 1.8% salinity in the Black Sea, due to a great inflow of freshwater from the Russian rivers, to 4.0% salinity in the Levant Sea, where the African coast is mostly desert.

Salinity and temperature together define the density of the water, which determines the **flotation force** (see the Archimedes' principle described in *Chapter 2*) that controls the buoyancy of the apneist.

Any good apneist and lover of the sea should know all of this in order to **calculate the correct weighting**, which will be very different in the Mediterranean as opposed to the Red Sea. The higher concentration of salt in the Red Sea requires an increase in weight to compensate the greater density and therefore the greater positive buoyancy.

Transparency

There was a time when measurements of seawater transparency were based on the visibility of a white disc of 30 cm diameter positioned in the water. With this method values between 30 and 60 m of depth were registered in subtropical seas, even if a flicker of reflection was registered up until pre-abyssal depths.

Today the **technique for measuring transparency** of marine water has been changed, and in place of the white discs are **photoelectric selenium cells** that allow the measurement of the range of a particular wavelength of spectral light to a determined depth. As we have seen in *Chapter 2*, due to the absorption of colours everything under 20 m appears blue. Nevertheless, a determinant factor in the level of transparency is the suspension of the particles, which render water more turbid, impeding the passage of light.

Light has a primary importance for marine life. The first link of the food chain is plankton, constituted by microscopic living organisms: animal (zooplankton) and vegetal (phytoplankton) that require light to complete the photosynthesis necessary for their existence.

It is easy to see from this small observation how physical pollution of the water can seriously modify the food chain, causing the rupture of the entire ecosystem.

9.2 THE MOVEMENTS OF WATER

The sea is continually subjected to the action of forces such as **wind and atmospheric pressure**, as well as forces generated by variations of several properties such as density, salinity and temperature.

These forces determine changes in areas of water that generate the **movements** of:

- **waves**
- **current**
- **tides**

These movements influence subaquatic activity: it is necessary to understand them to be able to better plan dives, making them safer and more enjoyable. The motions of the waves and the current often arouse fear in whosoever approaches the sea. By understanding them it will be easier to predict variations in the sea and most importantly to adopt suitable codes of conduct.

Waves

The most frequent cause of waves is the **wind**. Less common, but equally significant, are seismic activities, that sometimes produce tsunamis of enormous size.

Every wave caused by the wind is formed in the same way. To understand the phenomena that produce waves we can imagine the surface of the sea or lake as being calm, and the action of the wind that suddenly strikes the expanse of water. This initially provokes the formation of **small ripples**, and if the wind action continues, exceeding 4-5 meters per second, then the inclined sides of each ripple will present a greater surface on which the wind can press, with an angle of impact tending towards the perpendicular. Given the turbulent nature of airflow, they will first form small waves. Some of these, being more inclined than others, will break and yield part of their energy to other more stable waves that they have caught up to. As this continues, the action of the wind will intensify the wave motion, forming forced waves that increase in dimension and velocity until they reach the stage of stationary waves, which have the lowest dimension and velocity compatible with the force of the wind and surface tension.

If the wind becomes faster than the waves then the crests will incline greatly to fall and disappear in the troughs, giving place to an offshore breaker. The properties of the wind are thus determinant in the generation of waves.

There are three factors that determine the **size** that a wave can reach:

1. **Wind force (velocity).**
2. **Duration of wind (time).**
3. **The surface that the wind crosses without being obstructed (fetch).**

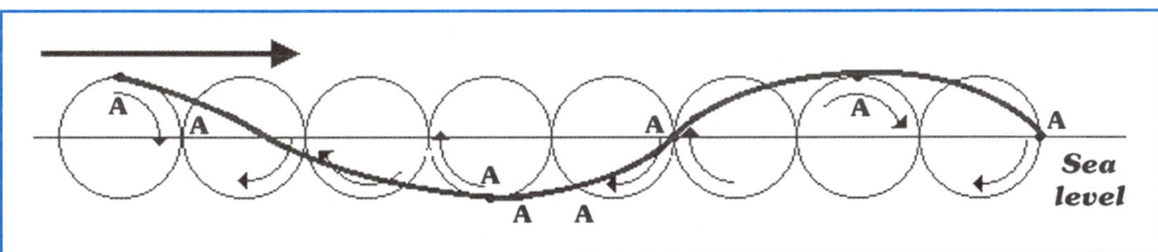

ANEMOMETRIC BEAUFORT SCALE

Beaufort grade	Classification of wind	Average velocity of wind at a height of 10 m above a flat and uncovered terrain		Description of the effects
		knots	km/h	On land
0	Calm	0-1	0-1	Calm: smoke rises vertically.
1	Breath of wind	1-3	1-5	The direction of the wind is revealed by smoke but not by wind vanes.
2	Light breeze	4-6	6-11	Wind is felt on the face; leaves rustle & an ordinary wind vane begins to move.
3	Gentle breeze	7-10	12-19	Leaves and small twigs are in constant motion; the wind extends light flags.
4	Moderate breeze	11-16	20-28	The wind lifts dust and sheets of paper; small branches move.
5	Fresh breeze	17-21	29-38	Small trees in leaf start to sway; crested waves on inland waters.
6	Strong breeze	22-27	39-49	Large branches are in motion; whistling in telegraph wires; umbrellas used with difficulty.
7	Near gale	28-33	50-61	Whole trees in motion; inconvenient to walk against the wind.
8	Gale	34-40	62-74	Twigs break from trees; very difficult to walk against the wind.
9	Strong gale	41-47	75-88	Slight structural damage occurs; chimney pots, gutters and slates removed.
10	Storm	48-55	89-102	Rare in interior land; trees uprooted; considerable damage to buildings.
11	Violent storm	56-63	103-117	Verified very rarely; widespread and serious damage.
12	Hurricane	> 64	> 118	

Description of the effects		Wave height
Off shore	Next to the coast	m
The sea is like a mirror.	Calm.	
Ripples are formed with the appearance of scales, but without foam crests.	Fishing boats just have steerage way.	0.1 (0.1)
Small wavelets are still short but more pronounced; crests have a glassy appearance but do not break.	The wind fills the sails of boats that then sail at about 1-2 knots.	0.2 (0.3)
Large wavelets; crests begin to break, losing glassy appearance; scattered whitecaps.	Boats begin to careen and sail at about 3-4 knots.	0.6 (1)
Small waves becoming longer; fairly frequent whitecaps.	Good working breeze; boats raise all canvas and sail clean and full.	1 (1.5)
Moderate waves taking a more pronounced, longer form; many whitecaps; chance of spray.	Boats shorten sail.	2 (2.5)
Large waves begin to form; white foam crests are more extensive everywhere; probably some spray.	Boats have double reef in mainsail; care required when fishing.	3 (4)
Sea heaps up; white foam from the largest breaking waves begins to blow in streaks along the direction of the wind.	Boats remain in harbour and those at sea lie to.	4 (5.5)
Moderately high waves of greater length; edges of crests begin to break into spindthrift; foam is blown in well-marked streaks along direction of the wind.	All boats make for harbour.	5.5 (7.5)
High waves; dense streaks of foam along the direction of the wind; crests of waves begin to topple, tumble and roll over; spray may affect visibility.		7 (10)
Very high waves with long overhanging crests; the resulting foam in great patches is blown in dense white streaks along in the direction of the wind; on the whole the surface appears white; tumbling of the sea becomes heavy and violent; visibility reduced.		9 (12.5)
Exceptionally high waves (small and medium sized ships might be lost for a time behind the waves); the sea is completely covered with long white patches of foam lying along the direction of the wind; everywhere the edges of the waves are blown into froth; visibility is further reduced.		11.5 (15)
The air is filled with foam and spray; sea completely white with driving spray; visibility extremely reduced.		14 (17.5)

Wave motion will not stop in concert with a drop in the wind, but will rather diminish steadily with dispersion of energy. The **long wave** is better defined as a **free wave**: with a more **regular and stable** appearance, it propagates for a great distance without apparent changes.

When observing objects that are floating during the manifestation of long waves, and in the absence of wind, it is easy to have the impression that the objects are moving forwards and backwards and up and down without advancing or receding. If the observer is transported by the water then the floating objects would also be carried in the direction of wave movement. In reality this is due to **oscillatory motion,** derived from the movement of particles of water. Each particle is subjected to wind action, the force of gravity and surface tension (dependant on the cohesive force of the molecules that constitute the liquid), and as a result follow circular orbits.

At the most elevated part of the wave **(crest)** the particles move in the same direction as the wave, while in the lowest part **(trough)** they move in the opposite direction. This movement is transmitted to the deeper particles, but the diameter of the orbit described diminishes rapidly to zero at a depth equal to half the wavelength. **Thus, although it may be rough on the surface, it will be calm underwater.** Each wave is characterised by **wavelength, amplitude and period.**

Wavelength is the distance between two consecutive peaks.

Amplitude is the difference in level between the crest and trough and is equal to the diameter of the orbit followed by the particles of water on the surface.

Period is the time taken for two successive crests to pass the same point of reference.

In open water when the largest waves break under their own weight smaller waves will be formed in the troughs. In this way waves are propagated even further than the fetch of

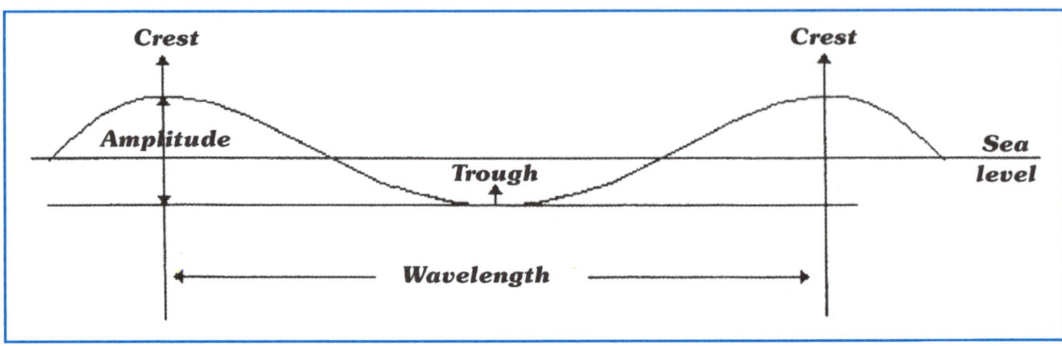

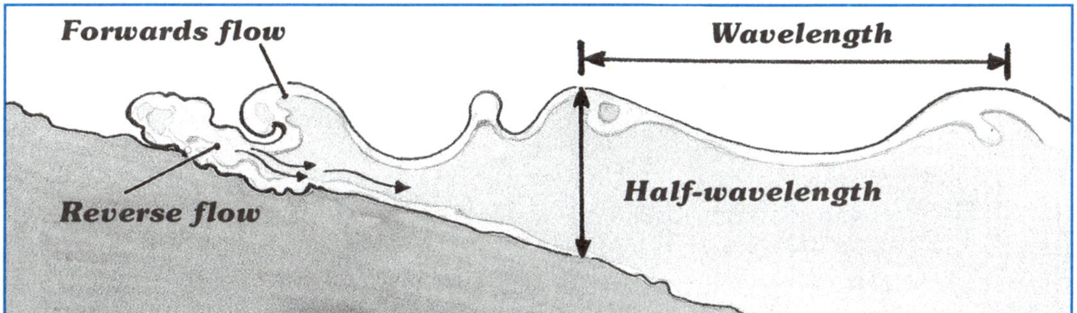

the wind, with a succession of large waves followed by ever-smaller series in an infinite reduction. Occasionally the rotation of the wind can cause propagation of wave energy in multiple directions, forming **confused water** that moves in two or more different directions.

When a wave nears the coast and reaches water that is shallower than half its wavelength, its velocity diminishes. The deeper particles of water that are in contact with the bottom are slowed by friction. **The bottom has a braking action**, that slows the base of the wave; however the crest proceeds at a constant velocity, tending to assume an acute form and increasing in height until it surpasses its limit of stability and falls into the wave trough. This is the origin of **surf** that follows the passage of oscillatory motion to transport the liquid mass.

Each breaking wave is characterised by the type of seafloor: when the wave encounters a steep seafloor its base is abruptly slowed and the water in the crest falls, tumbling and advancing with great energy; if the seafloor is gradual, with a gentle angle, the wave will form a breaker before reducing to a streak of foam.

When entering into surf it is imperative to observe the scene to determine the period of breaking waves and choose the most suitable moment and position to enter. Water that is dumped on the shore by surf must return to the sea. This return of water generates a **sucking current, or a rip.**

Currents

A Marine current can derive from a variety of causes; it is the tendency of water to stabilise the equilibrium of its physical and chemical properties, creating movements of water mass and thereby generating currents. In particular, differences of

- **temperature**
- **salinity**
- **evaporation of the surface**
- **inflow of fresh water**

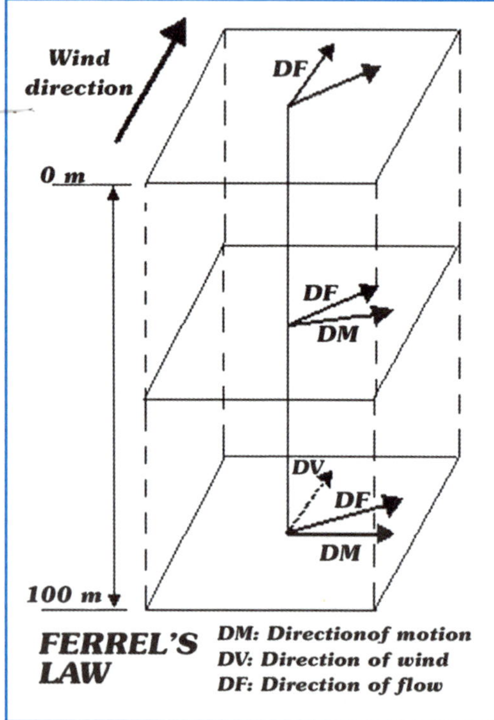

put the particles of water into motion, producing currents. In spite of this, the principal cause of currents is **wind action**.

When the wind acts on the water surface to cause wave action, some of the energy received by the water mass is transferred to depth. As the force is transferred to deeper levels friction will diminish its intensity until it is nullified completely.

During the downward transmission of motion there is an important change. The water on the surface, affected by the mass of air, does not move in the same direction in which the wind is blowing; the **Coriolis effect**, given by Earth's rotation, will cause it to deviate to the right or left of the wind, according to whether it is in the boreal or austral hemisphere **(Ferrel's law)**.

Supposing that the mass of water in question is divided into stacked layers, it follows that the deviation of motion is accentuated in the passage from one layer to the next.

The law that regulates the change of direction in the transmission of energy from the atmosphere to the sea applies also to any layer of water that transmits a force to the underlying layer. Thus a spiral is formed, and at a depth of about 100m an **Ekman current** is created whose direction forms an angle of 90° to the wind direction.

The triggering process of the wind and the dynamics of the mass of water combine with the effect of the Earth's rotation to generate and determine the direction of the great oceanic currents. These are incredibly important currents, which flow past entire continents, influencing their climates. One of the most well known is the **Gulf current**, a system of currents that flows from the **Sargasso Sea**, through the **Gulf of Mexico** and northwards along the **eastern coast of the United States** as far as Newfoundland.

It is of fundamental importance to freediving to know the currents that pass close to the coastline. Observations of the coast and the surface of the water are essential in the planning of a good session of freediving. If the dive site is not familiar it is best to collect information from **local diving centres or fishermen**.

Of the different forms of coastal current the most com-

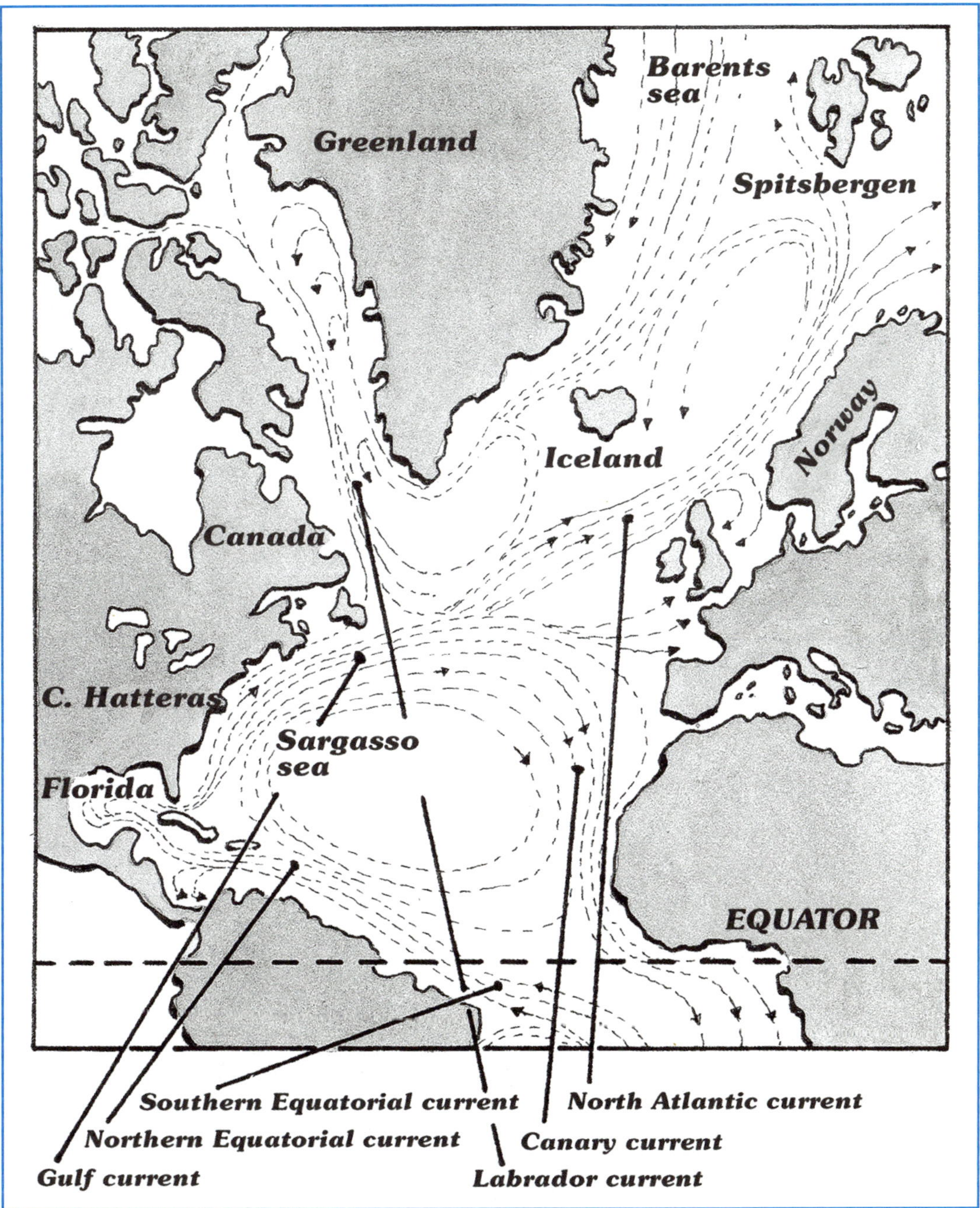

mon is the **shoreline current**. These are currents that run along the coast, and are generated by waves that meet the shore at an angle, impeding the regular return of seawater that breaks onto the land. In this fashion a current is generated that runs parallel to the line of the coast.

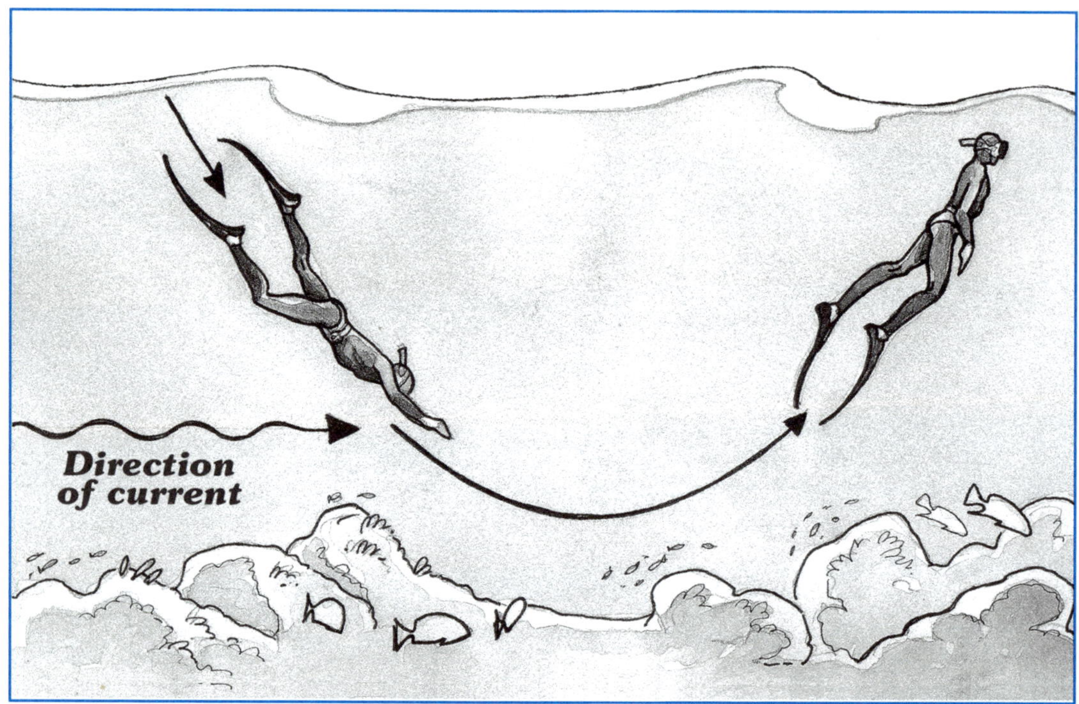

The other important type of current is the **rip**. A rip is normally generated by surf that dumps water onto a beach: this water must in some way return to the sea and therefore follows the course where it encounters least resistance. However a **rip current** is sometimes produced by the collision of distinct waters coming from different directions in particular coastal conditions such as a cave.

Setting off from land for a session of freediving, it is possible to take advantage of a rip to carry you out to sea, and use the waves to bring you back in. Hence it is a good idea to carefully evaluate the direction of the currents to be certain to exit on the coast at the predetermined point. If the **current is opposing** and strong in one place then **cut diagonally across it**: at the end of the session it will be easy to 'return to base'.

It is difficult and annoying to swim against a current whilst in apnea; therefore the apneist generally moves in the direction of the current during a dive.

With the use of a boat there are different possibilities of controlling the situation.

1. The boat drops the apneists at one point and picks them up at the end of the session in a predetermined approximate area.
2. The boat follows, watching the apneists or their signal buoy.

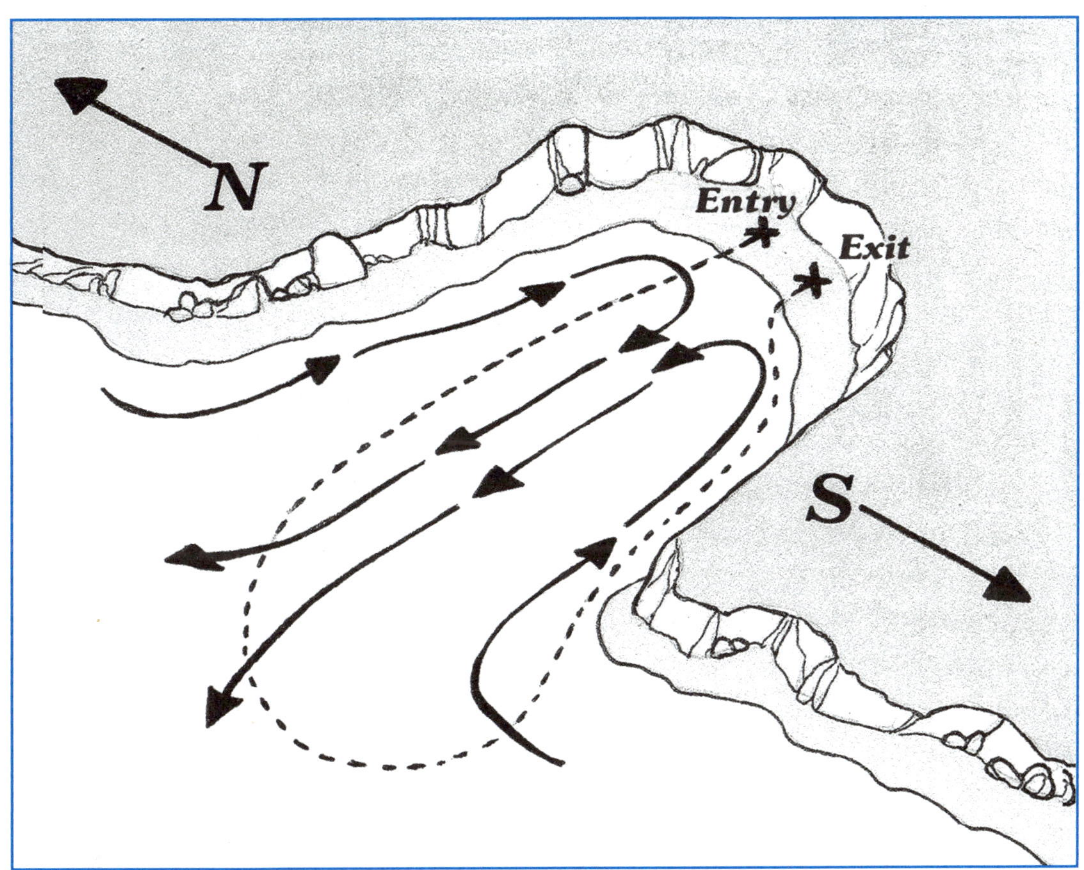

Freediving in the presence of a **strong current** is extremely tiring: therefore always start with a favourable current and let yourself be transported.

However it is important to remember that in the presence of **subaquatic currents** reaching a certain depth requires swimming further, both in the ascent and descent.

Tides

The periodic rise and fall of the level of seas and oceans due to the gravitational attraction of Sun and Moon on water mass is a phenomenon given the name **tide.**

The Moon is very close to the Earth, and the Sun has a huge mass that has a critical influence, despite being further away. The Earth-Moon system has a centre of mass M positioned on its axis of rotation S-S', around which the two masses rotate; the centre of this axis is 1,600 km underneath the surface of the Earth. When the two bodies rotate around the centre of the system two forces will be generated: the first is reciprocal action, the second is centrifugal force.

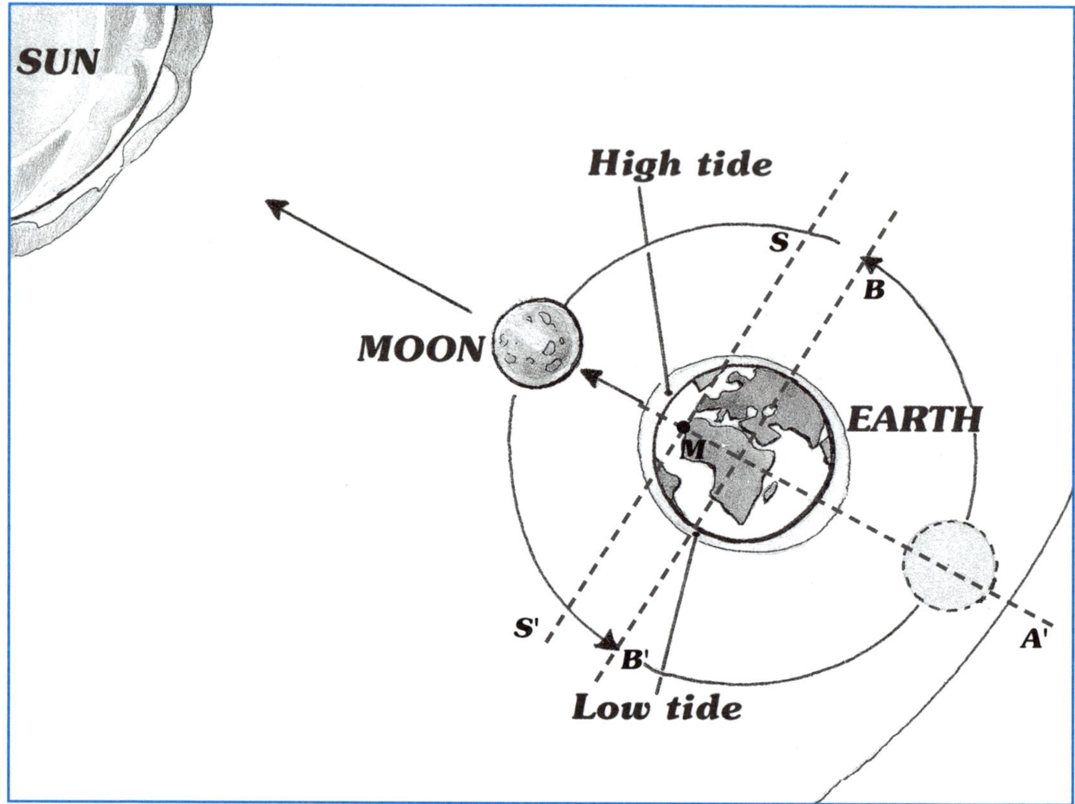

The moon exerts its maximum attraction on point A, which is the vertex of the hemisphere facing the Moon; the minimum attraction will instead be exerted at A', vertex of the hemisphere opposite the Moon. Rotating around the axis S-S', the system will have a centrifugal force that on planet Earth will be maximum at A' and minimum at A. This explains the accumulation of water along the A-A' axis **(high tide)** and a decline of sea level **(low tide)** along the B-B' axis.

Since the Earth rotates about itself once every 24 hours, and the Moon rotates about the Earth in about 27 days – i.e. a great deal slower – the **wave of tide** attributable to the Moon turns in the opposite direction to the Earth's spin, and with an interval between high and low tides of 6 hours, 12 minutes and 37 seconds.

In reality the phenomenon is not so regular, due to interference from landmasses, which combine with the different formations of seafloor and coast to create changes of tidal intensity and duration at different points of the globe. For this reason **tidal tables** are calculated and report precise information about the development of tides in the seas of the world.

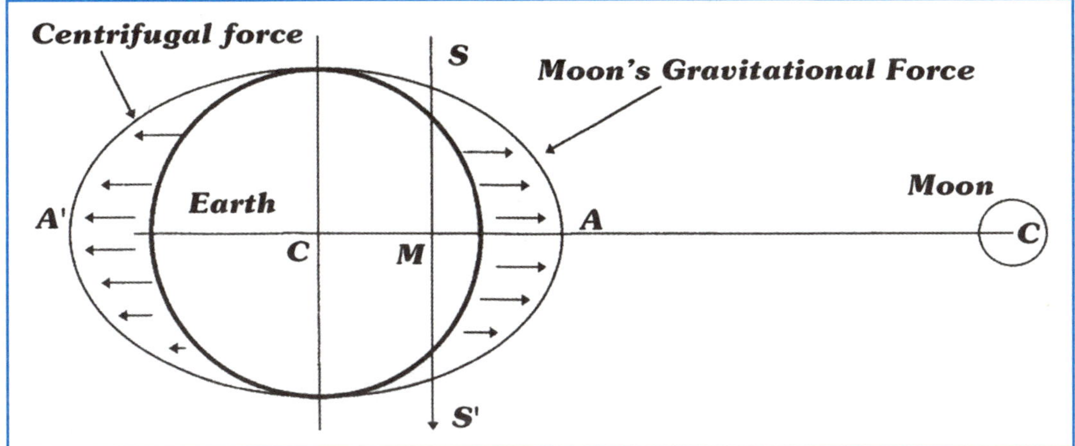

To be able to prepare well for an excursion in the sea it is important to know that between the movements from high to low tide and vice versa there is a period of calm called '**slack tide**'.

The movements of masses of water that cause the rise and fall of sea levels generate **marine currents.** When the tide meets land and the sea level rises, it follows a **flood current.** In the reverse scenario, when the tide retreats and water returns to open water, it follows an **ebb current.** These currents will interest us in a detailed way. As we have seen, currents move water both towards the shore and out to open water, influencing the entry and exit of a freediving session.

It goes without saying that the best period to freedive falls during the period of slack tide, when the waters are calm.

9.3 FREEDIVING IN OPEN WATER

The exercises that follow have the aim of helping the apneist to adjust to the new environment in conditions of maximum safety, and of instigating future experimentation.

The entries

There is no universal technique for entering the water. The most appropriate way is the easiest, safest and least disorientating. Each situation requires a suitable strategy, and for this reason various protocols were put in place that deal with the different possible circumstances.

Seated entry

This is the optimal solution for entering the water from an overhanging platform on a boat, from a rubber dinghy, or

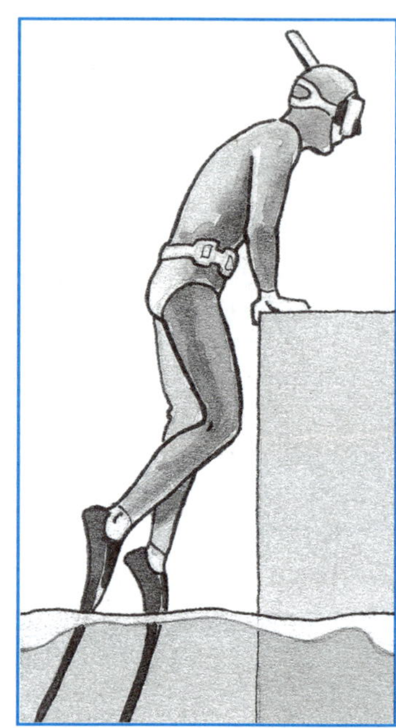

from a wharf, when the water is calm, and especially when the apneist is wearing fins with long blades.

Execution

- Sit down on the edge, with legs hanging over the side.
- The torso is rotated to the right (or left) until both hands can be put on one side, with fingers pointing away from the water.
- Keeping the hands on the edge, with the thumb hooked under to prevent slipping, push towards the water, rotating the body to enter slowly. With this technique the impact will be minimal.

Be careful with long fins! To insert them into the water without creating resistance the feet must be kept extended, with the fins pointed downwards.

The scissor jump

Also called the '**giant stride**', this is the most common entry if long fins are not worn.

Execution

- Standing on the wharf, on the platform of a boat, or on a point of entry from a boat that doesn't have too high a drop, position yourself with the fins close to each other on the edge closest to the water.
- Keep one hand on the mask and the other on the weight-belt.
- Step forwards, keeping the blade of the forward leg turned upwards and the heel down. In this way one enters the water with legs widened like scissors.

Backwards roll

Entry with a backwards roll is advisable only when there is reduced space (on small boats for example) and there is no other alternative. This type of entry can at times create problems of disorientation due to the fall backwards, which stimulates the vestibular centre responsible for equilibrium.

Execution

- Sit on the edge of the boat with the back turned towards the sea; keep one hand on the mask and the other, as is habit, on the weightbelt.
- Let yourself fall backwards.

Beach entry

When entering the water from the shore or from a beach we must still use the easiest and safest method; it is therefore essential to closely evaluate the conditions of the environment.

With rough and breaking sea: enter the water walking backwards, with the fins already fitted. Upon reaching a certain distance from shore, such that the surf is no longer bothersome, you can turn and stretch out in safety, finning on the surface.

With calm seas: enter walking, carrying the fins in your hands until the water is at knee or waist height. Then put on the fins, with help from your dive partner.

The best entry is:

- the easiest
- the safest
- the least disorientating

Finning

The finstroke is also a technique that, despite being performed correctly in confined water, can encounter some difficulty in open water, especially due to the greater distances that are confronted and the movements of the water.

Finning whilst wearing a wetsuit, with the consequent hydrostatic variations and lead weights, and in ambient conditions that are not always ideal, can be a problem. We must therefore train to adapt to these new, unstable conditions. It is vital to adapt strategies of behaviour that maintain a high level of safety. For example in **long transfers** it is important to use **different styles of finning** by changing position. In this way rather than using a single scheme of muscles, the work will be distributed between different fascias of the same muscle groups.

In open water the best finning style is the most effective, economic and efficient in relation to the ambient conditions and the type of activity. Therefore the amplitude and rhythm of the finstroke will vary according to requirements and to availability of energy.

Weighting

To weight correctly in open water we must consider not only equipment and water properties (fresh or salt), but also the intended activity. Here are some examples.

When snorkelling close to a coral reef a few meters deep, the main objective is observation of the environment in shallow water; in this case **the ideal weighting** must allow for positive buoyancy on the surface and neutral buoyancy at only

5-6 meters depth. This will make it easier to look around on the bottom, finning without excessive force. In contrast, negative buoyancy on the surface – too much weight – would make swimming difficult and needlessly tiring, while finning during the ascent would be considerably exacting, even putting the environment at risk of possible damage from an awkward clash of the fins on the bottom.

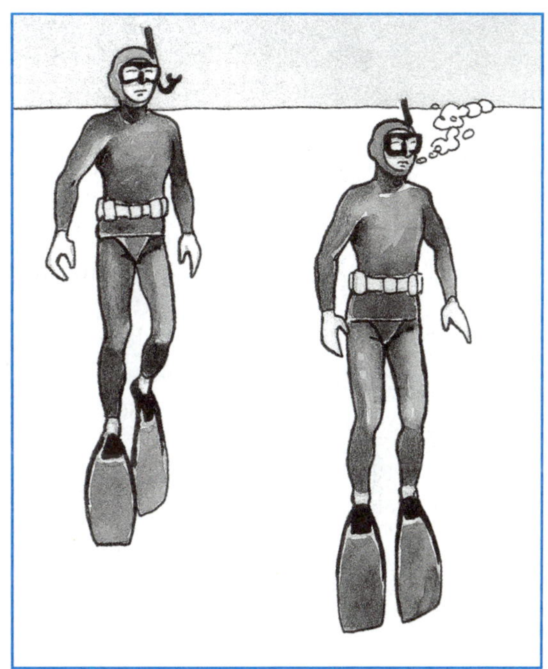

A **deep freedive** into open water requires different considerations. First of all it is necessary to know the **operating depth** in order to adopt a weighting that will give positive buoyancy in the last few meters of the ascent. This allows the apneist to have a favourable hydrostatic force when the legs are tired and oxygen is reduced to a minimum. In practice, if the operating depth is over –20 m, it is best to be neutrally buoyant at –10 m.

The duckdive

In open water the apneist dives towards the bottom in the presence of waves, currents, with little visibility, cumbersome wetsuits and weights: all factors that limit the freedom of movement obtainable in the pool.

The most disorientating aspect to the apneist is the total lack of visual reference points, especially in the 'big blue' or in a lake where the bottom isn't to be seen. The use of a **guide rope** will therefore be critical to trace a vertical line for the descent, which novice apneists might not otherwise follow, due to a lack of coordination. The rope becomes a sort of launching ramp into the infinite underwater world, and prepares the apneist to confront unfavourable ambient conditions in the future.

Technique is the same as for the duckdives described in Chapter 8. The difference is that weighting will completely change buoyancy. We depart for a deep dive with a more positive buoyancy (with little weight) and therefore the duckdive will be more demanding due to the flotation force that must be overcome.

Compensation

One of the first acclimatization exercises to practice in a freediving session in the sea is that of compensation. The temperature, colder than in the pool, will always creates problems, without mentioning the customary nervous and physical tension that accompanies the first few dives.

The following is a sequence of exercises that allows for a gradual approach to the problem, favouring an appreciation of the increase in pressure in relation to the times of compensation.

1. Descend head-up, pulling down the rope with the arms.
2. Descend head-up, pulling slowly with the arms along the rope, and pass gradually into a head-down position.
3. Descend head-down pulling along the rope.

We will never be able to emphasize enough the importance of maximum relaxation. Difficulties in compensation often depend on nervous tension of which we are unaware, not on technical problems with the manoeuvre.

From the first session in the sea it is helpful to try and move the diaphragm upwards, towards the lungs, to make compensation easier and to try and automate the coupling of the diaphragm with compensation. This ability will favour compensation at greater depths. Concentrate yourself therefore on compensation, or on the eardrum and the variations of pressure on it.

An important piece of advice: to facilitate the manoeuvre of compensation it is important **during the ultimate inspiration to compensate the ears and mask.** To do this we must briefly interrupt the inspiration to fill the Eustachian tubes, ears and mask with as much air as possible, then resume and complete a maximum inspiration. This additional air will be available for compensation.

Descent and ascent with arms along the down-line

This is a good exercise to approach depth and the use of the down-line in all open water sessions. It favours a gradual approach to deep freediving without excessive force and allows the neophyte (and the expert!) to acclimatise gradually. For beginners the contact with the down-line will help to keep stress and compensatory manoeuvres under control.

Execution

- In a head-down position, pull with the hands along the rope, finning and controlling the velocity of the descent.
- Pay attention to the width of the armstrokes. Don't be in a hurry to seize the rope after pulling; it is better to wait until momentum is exhausted, keeping your hands around the rope as a guide but without holding it – in this way you can feel the rope skim through the hands, and close the eyes.
- Relax, moving your attention to the point of contact between hand and rope. This technique helps for both descent and ascent.

For greater safety and to lower levels of stress the freediver can make some attempts without weight, using only the guide rope as propulsion. This allows the freediver to be completely positive during the ascent, and resurface effortlessly.

Constant weight descent

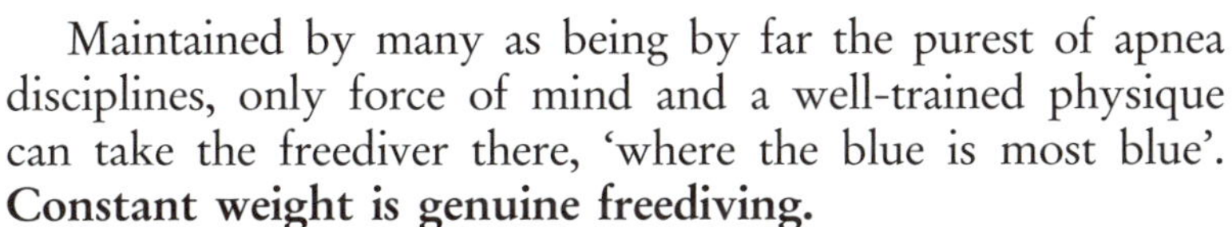

Maintained by many as being by far the purest of apnea disciplines, only force of mind and a well-trained physique can take the freediver there, 'where the blue is most blue'. **Constant weight is genuine freediving.**

Execution

- Prearrange **surface support** (*see Chapter 10*), **agreeing** with the companion on **depth, the pause at the bottom** (if anticipated), **dive time** and **the signals of communication.**
- Start the descent with a duckdive, taking a position next to the down-line.

- Fin downwards, keeping the guiding rope stretched in front of the eyes and within reach of the hands.
- Arrive at the established depth, calmly invert direction, and return to the surface without anxiety.

The fundamental components that determine the success of the exercise are: control of the situation, the calm with which the dive is performed, and the ability to 'merge with the blue'.

Variable weight

The use of a mobile weight enhances the descent velocity without compromising the buoyancy and therefore the security of the apneist during the ascent. It is called a variable weight dive because the weight is abandoned by the freediver on the bottom. The history of records includes diverse sled designs, created with many different materials and structures.

Mayol dived head down, dragged towards the bottom by a weight, with brakes to control velocity and facilitate compensation. In his last record Pelizzari used a sled shaped to a point so as to be more hydrodynamic and descend faster.

To start with, the simplest system is to use **a plain weight** fastened to a rope, which is set at the same length as the established depth so as to facilitate its recovery. Obviously a heavier weight will give a greater velocity of descent and it is therefore critical that the apneist is suitably adapted to compensation. On the surface the apneist prepares physically and mentally, breathing through a snorkel and keeping one hand on the weight, or on the line if using a mobile weight.

If a sled is available, take position on the apparatus. The head will be completely above the surface, and respiration can occur without a snorkel. Only upon reaching the necessary concentration, and after having effected the final inspiration, which in this case must be maximal, to allow for requirements of compensation, the apneist raises an arm to signal that they are ready to depart. The surface support free the weight or sledge to start the descent.

All attention must concentrate on physical and mental relaxation, and in particular on compensation, trying to anticipate each variation in pressure, and enjoy the **incredible sensation** that this way of diving confers. Upon reaching the target the apneist turns and starts the ascent, pulling with the arms along the rope as described in the first exercise in this section.

ANALYSIS OF A DIVE INTO THE BLUE

Preparation for the dive is performed in complete immobility and a position of absolute relaxation.

Control the breath with slow and calm diaphragmatic respiration, preferably performed with eyes closed – this will make it easier to find the necessary concentration and to visualise the forthcoming dive meter by meter (as explained in Chapter 5.3).

Before the duckdive, executing three complete and calm diaphragmatic respirations will help to discharge tension and to prepare the lungs to collect the greatest amount of air possible in the final respiration. In this case the thoracic tension that can be accumulated in a maximum forced inspiration is irrelevant. At just 10 m of depth the volume of air is halved and the ribcage returns to being elastic and decontracted, unloading any detrimental tension.

During the ultimate inspiration compensate the ears and the mask, putting as much air as possible at your disposal for compensation.

At this point execute the duckdive, powerful but calm, strong but neither extravagant nor hurried.

Remember that problems usually begin here: in haste to take off from the surface one can commence with rapid movements that will inevitably be tense and imprecise, increasing oxygen consumption without translating it efficiently into downwards movement. If the initial force is exaggerated then the apneist will find that energy reserves are already halved, with obvious consequences for concentration.

Particular attention must be dedicated to the finstroke and to the distribution of force. Straight after the duckdive the apneist must apply maximum force, with a wide and powerful finstroke to overcome positive buoyancy and descend, but a few meters later the force will already be greatly reduced.

Passing the point of neutral buoyancy, and with a now favourable hydrostatic force, the amplitude and rhythm, and therefore muscular work, are reduced to the point where the legs stop completely and settle into the freefall, trying to find the most relaxed and hydrodynamic position; in general we will fin actively to 60% of the intended maximum depth.

The ascent of a deep freedive is analogous to the descent in that the muscular work required to take off from the bottom and push towards the surface will be greatest at the start, but then diminish gradually, as the approach to the surface brings a more positive buoyancy.

Upon reaching maximum depth, the inversion or turn using the guide rope is critical. It involves passing from a head-down descent to a head-up position to begin the ascent towards the surface. The apneist grasps the guide rope with one hand to halt the descent, letting the legs fall past the body. When the position has been changed and the head is pointing up, the ascent can be initiated by pulling on the line with the same hand that arrested the descent. This hand therefore represents the pivot around which the rest of the body turns.

During the ascent the hands rest by the sides. The head is in line with the body with the eyes looking straight ahead at the rope. Upon reaching the surface it is important to resume breathing without exhaling forcefully, as described in chapter 10.1.

One aspect that must never be ignored during the descent is verticality, and the position of the body, in particular the head, which is a genuine rudder for the rest of the body. The head should not be hyperextended or with the face turned towards the bottom. In this case the spinal column would be contracted, in tension, impeding the relaxation necessary to deal with compensation in the critical moments. Many freedivers do not succeed in diving in a straight line, but turn in a slow, rather wide spiral, both in the descent and ascent. This is an unacceptable error, both for safety reasons and economy of the action. A correct vertical descent will avoid the loss of precious seconds (and even more precious oxygen) by proceeding in a straight line to the target.

The arms are also essential in the control of the line of descent and body position. Extended downwards they act as steering wings; in particular the hands modify the trajectory like genuine wing flaps.

As we have mentioned, compensation can considerably complicate the first experience. Therefore it is important to prepare oneself with Eustachian tube exercises (*see Chapter* 7) before entering the water. In this way the muscular structures involved in opening the tubes will be prepared, favouring compensatory manoeuvres.

If you feel an encroaching state of anxiety during surface preparation don't be afraid to allow more time to relax, and if the situation persists it is best to relinquish the dive. Knowing when to peacefully forfeit a demanding dive for personal reasons is an indication of responsibility.

The variable descent is an excellent way of training **adaptation to pressure** and the blood shift. It allows significant depths to be reached in short time and without exertion, leaving freedom for relaxation and total control of compensation. Small stops at the bottom allow the organism to adapt to the depth.

Dynamic apnea at depth

Technically this exercise would not be difficult if it wasn't for the fact that it ties together several very precise actions that each require good technique. A good execution demonstrates the capacity of the apneist to maintain control of the situation and their style, indicative of optimal aquaticity.

The exercise involves finning a certain distance in apnea underwater and at a constant depth.

Execution

- Immerse with a duckdive.
- Upon reaching the target depth, start finning with a rhythm suitable to the conditions and without scraping the bottom.
- After the duckdive, for safety reasons it is necessary to remove the snorkel from the mouth and not replace it until after resurfacing.

With time and training the difficulty of the exercise can be augmented by increasing length, time of immersion and the depth to create training stimuli and improve performance.

9.4 RECOVERY OF A VICTIM

This part of training involves the simulated rescue of an apneist who is unconscious at depth.

The objectives are **to bring the victim to the surface as quickly as possible and to aid the resumption of respiration.** For this exercise the pool simulation of this technique (*see Chapter 8*) will be extremely helpful. **It is a definite responsibility of every apneist to be prepared for an emergency.**

The following exercise can be practiced operating on a bottom of ten to fifteen meters, with a companion and an assistant on the surface. First establish who will play the role of victim and who that of rescuer, the third person remaining as backup.

Execution

- The victim leaves first, and upon reaching the bottom assumes a prone position, in static apnea. The same exercise can be performed close to the down-line. In this case the victim would maintain a stable depth by keeping one hand on the rope.
- After having checked from the surface, the second apneist – the rescuer – departs, and upon reaching the victim removes both the victim's and their own weightbelt and abandons them on the bottom
- With a now positive buoyancy the pair initiate the ascent to the surface.

There are different ways of carrying an unconscious apneist to the surface.

Arm under the shoulder

This method is the most simple (*Fig. A*). The rescuer passes an **arm underneath the armpit of the victim** and keeps the victim's head hyperextended with the hand of the same arm **placed over the jaw**. In this position the rescuer will be perpendicular with respect to the victim, allowing for all the space necessary for effective finning. To prevent the victim's body from creating extra resistance to the water during the ascent the rescuer should hold the victim close to their side.

With straight arms under the shoulders

The rescuer takes the victim under the armpits, and with arms extended upwards starts the descent with strong finning (*Fig. B*). The rescuer can be positioned in front of or behind the victim, according to the body shape and the contingencies

A

B

of the situation. In either case, the rescuer's legs will be lower than the victims and will have sufficient space to execute full finstrokes.

Upon reaching the surface, the rescuer must make sure to keep the head of the victim hyperextended and out of the water; the rescuer must then remove the mask and initiate mouth to mouth respiration at the same time as transporting the victim as quickly as possible to the safest point of exit. Techniques of first aid are detailed in *Chapter 10.*

9.5 APNEA GAMES IN OPEN WATER

These games must be supervised from the surface by someone who is well trained in handling emergencies.

Empty lungs

Involves descending for several meters with the lungs completely empty. A very useful exercise for training compensation.

Descent with positive buoyancy

Without any weight, practice moving freely in the three dimensions, leaving space for personal creativity. The positive buoyancy requires the practice of good freediving techniques to overcome flotation. The duckdive must be perfect to allow immersion.

Sprint to the surface

Several apneists dive to a determined depth, and then all together take off for the surface. The winner is the first to break the surface.

The blindman

Using an obscured mask, as described at the end of Chapter 8, the 'blindman' descends down an appropriately positioned rope to reach a disc from which a card is taken to bring back to the surface. After leaving the surface the player cannot hold the rope with the hand, but is allowed to brush against it.

Jump of the Orca

Involves resurfacing from a dive and trying to launch out of the water as much as possible.

Turn of the screw

Consists in descending along a rope to a predetermined depth, whilst making the greatest possible number of revolutions around the rope. The winner is whoever makes the most total turns in ascent and descent.

Writing

The aim of this game is to make a stop at a certain depth to write something, a task that requires a certain amount of lucidity and awareness. A simple whiteboard and pencil are enough to write the answers to questions of mathematics or other topics.

Treasure hunt

After an initial map has been drawn, with precise references to features above and below water, and after clues that lead to the treasure have been hidden, the teams must recover the clues at various depths and find the treasure. The first team to arrive at the treasure and recover it are the winners.

Freeclimbing

Obviously this doesn't involve scaling cliffs, but a freedive without fins, pulling oneself with arms along the rope both in the descent and ascent. The descent will be as slow as possible, and along its course the player may find small activities to carry out which have been placed there in advance: untie a knot, make a knot, respond to a quiz on a whiteboard, inflate a balloon, etc.

Elevator

Involves descending with a weight tied to a rope that is used to pull the apneist back up from the surface. Upon concluding the descent the rope and weight are recovered by an assistant on the boat. It is necessary to have a suitable vessel.

If an inflatable balloon is available and tied to the rope, then the ascent can be executed in the style of No Limits.

Pyramid

As in synchronised swimming, the *sincronette* who pose above the surface are held aloft by supporting action from the companions underneath. In this fashion many apneists can, with suitable finning, support their companions, who compose changing shapes and forms. A judge marks the teams' creative figures for originality and level of difficulty.

Group dive

Using a mobile weight fixed to a rope, a number of apneists descend together, turning progressively at their respective depths. The ascent is performed finning along the rope. It is important that the actions of the apneists are coordinated in the departure: they must all fin together to maintain contact with the weight.

Stop and go

Consists in making predetermined stops at different depths of the descent or ascent.

SAFETY

CHAPTER

10

Apnea is a discipline that requires great individual commitment, but this does not mean that it should be practiced alone. The system of pairs constitutes the primary rule of safety for apnea, as with all disciplines that are practiced in contact with the liquid element.

In this chapter several aspects of safety will be examined, starting with the study of the potential dangers of apnea: hyperventilation (a strongly contraindicative technique which is today superseded by breathing adapted to relaxation), the pre-blackout conditions, and the blackout itself.

We will discuss the rules of prevention that guarantee a safe and enjoyable apnea session: the system of pairs, diet, hydration and protection from the cold.

Safety also depends on state of mind; knowing oneself on a psychological level, being capable of listening to and judging one's own thoughts, knowing how to control any reactions and contain impulses. Therefore it is critical to learn how to untangle oneself from between conscious and unconscious internal actions, optimistic and pessimistic thoughts, decisions and doubts.

Finally, part of a good apneist's repertoire should be the ability to perform cardiopulmonary resuscitation (CPR), for which we recommend a specific course of theory and practice. Reading a book will not be sufficient. Seek instruction from a specialist and you will be certain to learn how to correctly manage an emergency procedure.

10.1 DANGERS OF APNEA

It is the precise responsibility of the apneist to **know the risks** of freediving, for two reasons: to cope with the possible emergencies of companions and to adopt behaviour that guarantees safe activity. In recent years sport medicine has made considerable progress, and in its evolution it has discovered risks connected to techniques that have been in use for years, as for example **hyperventilation**, revealed to be the cause of many blackouts.

Hyperventilation

About 40 years ago the precursors to the deep Italian freedivers started using a system of ventilation that seemed to be able to allow a man to remain in apnea longer. This technique was termed **hyperventilation**. Adopted by recommendation, it was also used by crowds of spearfishermen; some people employ the technique even today, unaware of its disadvantages and risks.

Before making the duckdive they would practice a particular pattern of respiration: the breaths would be **frequent, and protracted for several minutes**, but most importantly they paid special attention to the expiratory phase. **The movement was forced**; so much so that a rasping hiss like a moan would be heard coming from the snorkel – a death cry with each act of expulsion.

The success of the technique seemed to be dependant on the intensity of this asthmatic blasting. Many spearfishermen of years gone by would pump their chests like bellows, even using alternate movements of the arms, opening and closing them repetitively to inflate and deflate their ribcages in spasms. The objective was to eliminate all the 'used air', or at least the best part of it, and load up with as much oxygen as possible so that the organism could remain autonomous for a reasonable length of time.

After two or three minutes of continuous hyperventilation, and sometimes even less, the head begins to spin and the fingertips and the extremities of the limbs swarm with pins and needles.

Watching these athletes hyperventilating before diving, the professor **Mauro Ficini** – deceased in August of 1996 – realised that something was wrong, and begun tests on the true effectiveness of this technique, discovering that not only was it worthless, but that it represented an actual peril to the freediver.

During hyperventilation the lungs do not accumulate a greater quantity of O_2 in their alveoli. After two or three deep breaths the haemoglobin in the red blood cells that transport oxygen to the various organs is already saturated with O_2. To balance this, forced respiration will cause the lowering of CO_2 concentration, the 'waste' gas produced by the metabolic work of the various cells that respire, or rather that oxidise molecules of carbon to produce energy for use by the organism.

The disorientation, the dazed feeling, and the strange sensations that are suffered at the end of hyperventilation are not only therefore signals of hyperoxygenation, but also the unequivocal warning that the partial pressure of CO_2 has dropped to a dangerous level.

Our body is complex, equipped with sophisticated mechanisms that supply helpful signals, indicating in advance that something in the 'bodyworks' is not completely in order. When we hold our breath for a certain period, at the beginning we will feel well, without any need to replenish our air. This is due to the fact that vital intercellular exchanges continue normally with the two principal gases: O_2 taken from the pulmonary alveoli is directed to the cells while CO_2 is slowly accumulated as a waste product.

The state of well-being continues until the ultrasensitive receptors of the human body signal that the parameters of control are no longer within the established limits. The body is arriving at a critical phase and is put on its guard by further continuation of the breath hold.

O_2 has proceeded to decline from a reading of 100-105 millimetres of mercury (mmHg) measured in the pulmonary alveoli at the very first inspiratory phase, to a partial pressure of about 80mmHg. Cells of the various organs have continued to expel CO_2, which flows into the blood in the form of carbonic anhydrides and carbonic acids: from an initial partial pressure of 40mmHg it has increased to an approximate value of 55-60 mmHg.

The alarm bells set off by these concentrations immediately begin to ring: special nuclei of the nerve cells – carotid, aortic and bulbar chemoreceptors – especially receptive to CO_2 pressure in the arterial blood flow, to infinitesimal variations of pH, and to the shortage of O_2, order the respiratory system to immediately resume breathing.

What happens to the athlete that consciously holds their breath? Firstly there will be an increasing desire for air, which quickly becomes an irresistible need for oxygenation: **the so-called 'starving for air'.** Forcing on with the apnea the athlete will feel a discomfort spread through the stomach to the throat until they receive a sudden spasm of the respiratory muscles, the infamous diaphragmatic contractions.

In reality not everyone registers the same symptoms; this means that in a forced apnea an apneist may not feel any diaphragmatic contractions, due to lack of sensibility, or due to the absence of contractions themselves. Subsequently the subject reaches the point of breaking the apnea, and is obliged to resume breathing at once, so as not to run the risk of a blackout.

Hyperventilation deceives the bulbar centres appointed to stimulate the resumption of breathing. In fact it was verified that after several minutes of hyperventilation the pressure of CO_2 is lowered as far as 25-30 mmHg. Before feeling the stimuli induced by the increase of carbon dioxide, the organism risks going into 'tilt' due to the supervening poverty of oxygen: *O_2 break point*. In practice, when hyperventilating the apneist doesn't feel, or feels less, the starvation for air and the need to breath and is therefore more susceptible to blackout.

During a dive – where hydrostatic pressure enters into the game to significantly modify both pulmonary volume and pressure of respiratory gases inside the alveoli at depth – the problem is aggravated. O_2 passes from the alveoli to the blood flow with greater ease, helped by the increasing partial pressure, inducing the apneist to linger on the bottom, seeing as the available oxygen appears deceptively abundant. However during the ascent the values of lung volume and gases return to normal, revealing their deadly cards: the consumed oxygen will be elevated in measure, to the point where it is no longer sufficient to reach the surface.

During an apnea performed after hyperventilation, and therefore initiated with a lower concentration of CO_2, the arrival of the first diaphragmatic contraction is delayed, the interval between one contraction and the next is reduced, and the intensity of contractions is elevated.

Furthermore, hyperventilation provokes an increase in heart rate (values as high as 110 beats per minute have been recorded), an increase in blood pressure, and inevitable contraction of various muscles: three absolutely unfavourable conditions for apnea.

This is already sufficient to convince anyone of the fact that hyperventilation is worthless. "Whoever hyperventilates is cheating themselves", said Jacques Mayol. When the normal physiological conditions are re-established, as occurs during the ascent, a blackout can occur much more easily.

As we have seen in *Chapter 3*, each and every man and woman possesses the so-called 'dive reflex', which is manifested by a general

HYPERVENTILATION

Is nothing other than the technique of forced and rapid expirations and inspirations that, in terms of physiology, brings a reduction in the partial pressure of carbon dioxide; after hyperventilation our blood is not more rich in oxygen, as we are lead to believe, but poorer in CO_2.

muscular relaxation and a diminution of heart rate and blood pressure. Hyperventilation triggers reactions that are contrary to those that our body pursues when immersed in apnea.

Never hyperventilate before apnea.

Pre-blackout and blackout states

Normal cerebral function depends on an adequate transport of oxygen and glucose to the brain. The reduction of these two factors past a certain limit will rapidly bring a loss of consciousness or syncope, which is defined with the term **blackout**. Drowning is the most frequent result of a blackout in the water.

The majority of deaths are due not so much to the original causes of the loss of consciousness, but almost always to the fact that the diver isn't recovered immediately. Furthermore, drowning and the subsequent flooding of the lungs can disguise the real causes.

A blackout can also occur 'dry'; it can happen that the lungs are not flooded due to a series of fortunate reasons based on the position in which the diver settles on the bottom and on the concomitant lockjaw that seals the mouth, and prevents entry of water. Many divers have been saved in this condition after several minutes of not breathing. Cardiac and cerebral oxygenation are maintained by the increase in partial pressure of what little oxygen is still in circulation.

If we dive after hyperventilation then during the ascent, especially in the final meters, there is a collapse of P_pO_2 and a consequent hypoxic blackout.

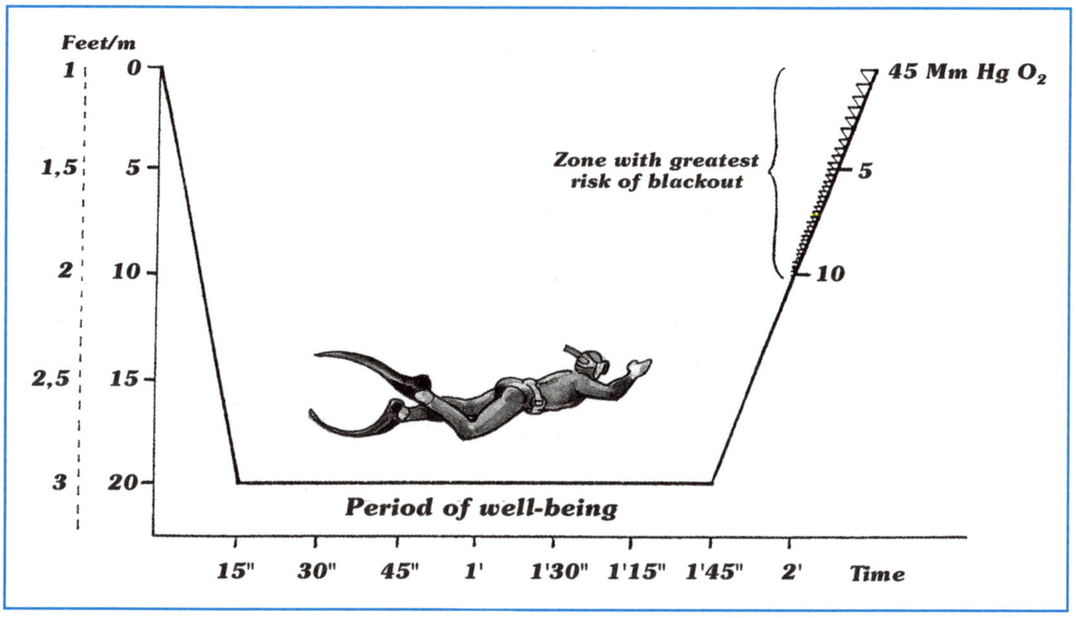

The most common sequence of events in a blackout incident is the following: the apneist performs a long hyperventilation to prolong the time and depth of immersion, in this way diminishing the concentration of CO_2 to as low as 15 mmHg, and increasing the partial pressure of oxygen (P_pO_2) as far as 140 mmHg.

During the descent the partial pressures of alveolar gases increase, until at a certain point past –20 m the alveolar CO_2 spreads into the blood, due to the inverted gradient; however the stimuli, the diaphragmatic contractions associated with starvation for air, are retarded. Blood O_2 will be maintained at elevated levels due to the effect of the hydrostatic pressure, giving the so-called 'feeling of well-being'.

The blackout: last defence of the body

The factors that contribute to blackout are simple if we consider that the principal criterion that governs any physiological activity is the conservation of life, even at the cost of permanent damage.

Holding the breath voluntarily to remain in apnea entails a gradual consumption of oxygen in the lungs, and therefore in the blood, as well as a corresponding increase in carbon dioxide in both areas. The receptors responsible for measuring concentrations of gases in the blood will constantly analyse these variations and communicate the state of things to the brain. As soon as carbon dioxide exceeds a certain level, the breathing reflex is triggered in the form of diaphragmatic contractions. The apneist ignores this stimulus, and so the levels of carbon dioxide and oxygen will continue to rise and fall respectively.

However the brain is uncompromising and strengthens its signals for a need of new air, transmitted in an increasingly eloquent language of many different stimuli; if the apneist continues to ignore these then they will come to a point where the brain takes control of the situation and terminates voluntary function. This is the blackout: a reaction aimed at reducing all metabolic activity to favour oxygenation (even if minimal) of the heart and brain.

We must therefore think of the blackout as the body's last attempt to save itself, not as the beginning of the end.

It is the apneist that communicates his wish (erroneously or out of necessity) to suspend breathing, and in the final extreme this 'wish' is discontinued by the organism itself, which takes the wheel and resumes respiration. However at times we will have our face in water, and this condition in its turn determines a prevention of respiration that is stronger than the force to resume it. The reasons for this second reflex are obvious: it opposes the possibility of breathing liquid and thus drowning.

One does not always pass straight from consciousness to blackout. There will often be intermediate conditions that go by the name of **pre-blackout states**, in which there is a lack of control, or the subject does not know what he or she is doing even though they have not yet blacked out. There will be movement, although in a disorientated and convulsive manner that is commonly referred to in freediving jargon as **'samba'** (there is an impressive similarity of many pre-blackout states to an uncoordinated dance).

Whether suffering from blackout or pre-blackout ('samba') the subject may exit without any side effects, as long as there is an assistant who can aid the resumption of breathing and stay beside the victim until consciousness is recovered.

It is important to know that there are blackouts from which the subject exits very quickly, and other states in which an expert with resuscitation equipment is required. In fact the jaw can sometimes be violently contracted due to the protraction of the hypoxic condition. This will require an instrument to force the jaw open, artificial respiration, and finally the administration of oxygen.

At times the contractions during the pre-blackout stage are of such force that two people are required to hold the victim and to be able to revive regular breathing.

Even top-level apneists that have experienced and survived blackouts tell of not having clearly acknowledged the threshold of danger, just as many others have achieved important results in this sport without ever experiencing either 'samba' or blackout. Professor Ficini claimed that some people are predisposed, and although there may not be any relevant scientific data, there is probably some truth in the theory.

Another astonishing fact, most of all for the regularity with which it occurs, is that almost all those who have suffered a blackout will categorically deny the fact, and some do not even accept the idea of having been assisted?

To avoid the risk of blackout and 'samba' it is essential to understand your own limits and your apnea capacity, and to avoid pushing past these, but most of all to breath correctly before the dive and thereby prevent hyperventilation.

Nevertheless the most critical and delicate phase after a difficult apnea will always be the exit. The way in which one takes the **first breath after the exit** of a dive determines the

The habit of never exhaling with force at the end of an apnea is a principle of the highest importance. It can be the difference between life and a nasty experience; for the safety of any athlete a controlled breath must become automatic whether following static or dynamic apnea or freediving.

success of the finish and the evasion of a blackout. The first action must always be an expiration to make room in the lungs for new air and therefore oxygen. The most common error is to exhale forcefully and deeply from the mouth immediately upon exiting the water; or worse still to start the expiration whilst surfacing. This will provoke a sudden lowering of the partial pressure of oxygen in the blood, and consequent 'samba' or complete blackout.

Avoid exhaling forcefully after apnea!

Instead we should **calmly exhale through the mouth, without completely emptying the lungs, and then straight away inhale through the mouth to replenish oxygen.** Subsequently we can completely unload our air, returning to normal respiration. This technique will prevent the partial pressure of oxygen from falling below values that would precipitate 'samba' or even blackout.

10.2 PREVENTION

The chemical reactions that make life possible are regulated by neural and hormonal mechanisms that don't take place in the same way or at the same time in everyone. In practice this means that there are different resistances to cold and fatigue, there are different times required for digestion and different tastes for food, different times of apnea and of recovery, and so forth.

Another important aspect to consider is ignorance, or a lack of understanding of the situation, which is the most serious cause of stress. For this reason it is the responsibility of the apneist, as in all other underwater activities, to prearrange a **contingency plan of emergency** and communicate it to companions during the briefing before a dive, together with all other information regarding the activity. The aim is to control every aspect of the dive and thereby lower the risk factor.

Being unprepared is the quickest way to stress, and thus to a potential accident. Therefore the first step is to collect information, and understand the situation on land, on the boat and in the sea.

Be prepared

Marine weather conditions, orography and bathymetries of the dive site all determine how the activity should be planned.

Nautical charts, weather forecasts, sea bulletins, harbourmasters, diving centres, local fishermen and anyone who lives their daily life in this changeable zone will be able to supply the required information.

The following factors must all be established and agreed on: times of entry and exit from the water, general direction of movement and any envisaged stops, depth of descents and the type of training that will be performed. A good dive plan must also predetermine behaviour in case of the unexpected: this is discussed in greater depth in section 10.5.

After having established and discussed the **emergency procedure** with the group, each member revises the signals to be certain that they are speaking the same language as the others and verifies again that they have understood the information regarding the session of apnea.

THE DIVE PLAN

- Do I understand the situation well on land or on the boat?
- Have I briefed everybody?
- In an emergency would I know what to do in the water and on land?
- Have I reviewed the signals with companions?
- Have I established with the group the times of entry and exit, and the operating depth?

The system of pairs

Organisation into a pair system will allow for peace of mind during diving, and most importantly it will allow for each to give more attention to their partner during the dive, supplying the certainty of a 'guardian angel' on the surface. We can confirm that to anticipate the potential risks of apnea in any situation – pool or open water – requires activating an **effective system of pairs.** It remains to identify the qualities of a good dive partner and the rules of behaviour for the apneists that constitute the pair.

Being **good dive partners** means having equal passion, attitudes and ability in apnea. Mutual enthusiasm and dedication in the water allow the sharing of particular emotions and sensations with a companion.

In particular a dive partner should:

- Have a good training; at least equal to that of the partner.
- Have received good instruction and understand all the concerns of freediving.
- Be proficient in techniques of resuscitation (CPR): cardiac massage and artificial respiration.

It is not sufficient just to have a good dive partner; both members must be responsible and follow several simple rules, in particular:

- **Respect the dive plan that has been predetermined and discussed with companions.**
- **Adjust the programme and the expectations to the requirements of the least expert in the group.**
- **Communicate to companions any personal or ambient variations of the situation that require a change of the dive plan.**
- **Adopt the 'one up one down' rule.**
- **Never lose sight of each other.**

Partner support

Every session of apnea starts with the formation of pairs. Once this is established each member must at all times be aware of the location of their partner and what they are doing.

The success of each session is dependant on the conformation of the technical and athletic capacity of the more capable of the two apneists to the capacity of the less expert or less in-form. Here then are some simple safety guidelines for the pair system in static apnea, dynamic apnea and constant weight freediving.

Assistance in static apnea

Static apnea involves staying completely still, floating face-down on the surface for as long as possible. Thus it is very simple, and not the least bit physically engaging for the assistant to guarantee safety. However it will require more commitment of attention, as the assistant will have to announce the times from the chronometer.

The assistant stays close at all times to both the companion and the stopwatch. With a light touch agreed upon in advance the assistant systematically verifies the state of consciousness after a certain amount of time. The apneist must respond to the assistant's safety check with a simple and unequivocal action such as, for example, an OK sign made with the thumb and index finger of one hand. If there is no reply then the assistant immediately repeats the signal, and if this second check is again unanswered then the performance of the companion must be immediately terminated.

When agreeing on the signals with the companion, another important aspect to define is the spacing of safety checks. There are two methods:

A. signals are given at random intervals between 10"-20": this system has the advantage of not conditioning the performance of the companion.
B. signals are given according to predetermined times, for ex-

ample the first after 1' and then every 30". With this method the companion is informed of the passing of time.

Psychologically the second method is more demanding. If it is true that during a static apnea we make 'a voyage outside of time', then this approach will interfere with concentration and relaxation, inciting the apneist to strive to make the time, and thus inducing a forced, not a mental apnea.

The assistant must always remember that his or her task does not finish when the companion moves to terminate the apnea. Experience has shown that blackout can occur even several seconds after surfacing. Remember to carefully observe the companion even after they have exited the water, and continue to check their state of consciousness and respiration for several seconds.

Assistance in dynamic apnea

The aim is to swim as great a distance as possible without surfacing and maintaining a constant depth. The risk will be the greatest in the final few meters of the distance. The assistant follows on the surface, maintaining an almost vertical position to the companion.

Swimming with fins, mask and snorkel, and with a flutterboard in one hand, the assistant is able to breathe whilst watching the companion, ready to intervene if necessary to offer a flotation support (*Fig. A and B page 318*). This technique of assistance is called 'one up one down', and is adopted also for constant weight and all other freediving in open water.

Assistance in constant weight

Constant weight is apnea made at depth in open water, involving a descent as far as possible using the fins and a certain amount of weight on the belt, and returning to the surface with the same weight, still pushing with the fins.

Obviously the supporting companion cannot accompany their partner for the whole of the descent. **Assistance** is given only **in the final meters of the ascent** where the risk of blackout is greatest.

Before the dive begins verify the buoyancy of the companion, remembering that being too positive will make the de-

scent tiring, whilst being too negative will be extremely dangerous during the ascent. Depth of neutral buoyancy must be proportional to the intended maximum depth. The difference between familiarity with deep freediving and being calm and serene, or feeling fear, anxiety, unnecessary muscular contractions and other symptoms of stress will also depend on the amount of trust in the companion and their promptness. If the dives involve demanding depths then it is best to reach the companion between –10 and –15 meters to assist with the final meters of the ascent. This guarantees the greatest safety to the apneist during this, the toughest period of the ascent.

Remember that visual contact will considerably lower the level of stress, aiding control of the situation at the moment of greatest risk. For this reason it is important that the assistant rises beside the companion, maintaining the same velocity. This will make it easier to request the OK, observe the eyes, the expression of the face, and general behaviour to reveal any possible signs of stress.

Upon resurfacing, safety procedure requires the assistant to check that the companion:

- responds to the request for the OK;
- takes the mask off their face;
- breathes properly.

Freediving is unadvisable when you find yourself in any of the following situations:

- Excessive fatigue.
- Excessive eating and/or consumption of alcohol in the preceding 12 hours.
- In the course of digesting food.
- Physical debilitation given to the use of pharmaceuticals.
- Suffering from a pathological condition (bronchitis, otitis etc).
- Adverse weather conditions.
- Lack of dive partner.
- Lack of necessary preparation and/or the adequate technical means for a session of freediving.

KNOWING WHEN TO RENOUNCE DIVING IS AN INDICATION OF RESPONSIBILITY

In some cases pre-blackout symptoms are manifested several seconds after resurfacing, when everything seems to have gone for the best. Therefore make sure that everything is OK even after the companion has surfaced.

10.3 HAND SIGNALS

The auditory apparatus is unable to receive intelligible sounds in immersion; in spite of this it is possible to hear a background noise particular to the marine environment. On land sounds propagate through air with a velocity such that sound waves are perceived first by one ear and then by the other. This means the central nervous system can 'read' the interval of time that passes between the perception of one ear and the other, thus defining the direction of the sound.

Sound travels four times as fast in water due to the greater density of liquid with respect to the gases that compose the atmosphere. Thus our auditory apparatus will hear noise without being able to identify their sources, as the interval of time between perception by one ear and the other is greatly reduced. If you hear a boat's motor when ascending from a dive you will not be able to ascertain the direction it is coming from, so it is a good idea to look around yourself, turning in a complete circle. Only a variation in intensity of the noise will reveal if the craft is approaching or withdrawing, but it will not allow for a judgment of direction.

Breathing and relaxing on the surface in preparation for a freedive constitutes a potentially dangerous situation for the apneist, as it is difficult to hear the noise of an approaching boat's motor. To remain calm and to be able to properly prepare for the dive, a **signal buoy** and a good dive partner are essential. **Being well visible** to boat captains allows them to maintain their distance from the dive site. Here also the system of pairs becomes critical: the assistant must visually check the surrounding area constantly, verifying that there are no threatening boats. This is fundamental to the safety and tranquillity of the apneist who is about to dive.

RECOMMENDATIONS TO THE APNEIST

- Never freedive alone.
- Always use a signal buoy.
- Modify weighting so as have positive buoyancy at –10 m from the surface.
- Always compensate before arriving at the pain.
- Always let water into the hood before diving, eliminating air from between the neoprene and eardrum.
- Always take the snorkel out of the mouth during immersion.
- After the dive never exhale completely or with force.
- Compensate the mask in the descent.
- Avoid apnea if you are not in optimal condition.

Communicating underwater

The impossibility of communicating verbally underwater has forced divers to codify a language of conventional signals, which if appropriately combined can allow the creation of intelligible phrases.

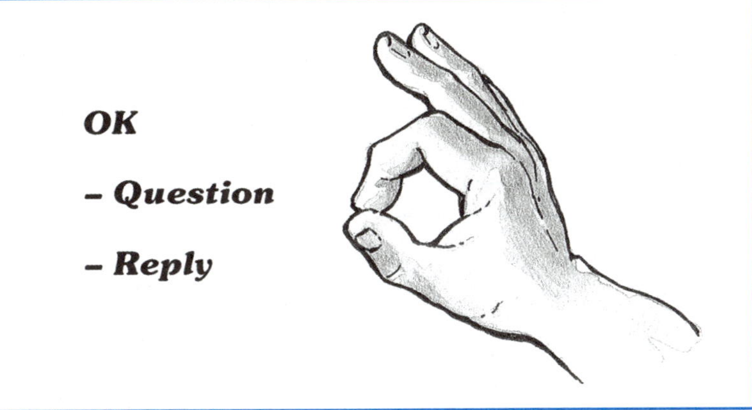

OK

– Question

– Reply

OK? – OK! On the surface at a distance

OK? – OK! With one hand occupied

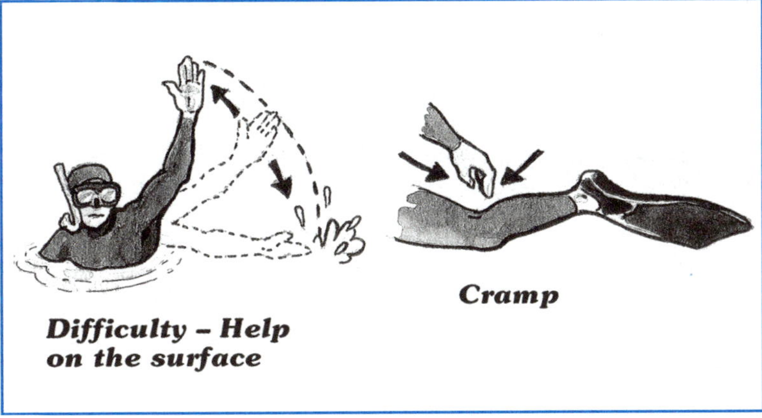

Difficulty – Help on the surface

Cramp

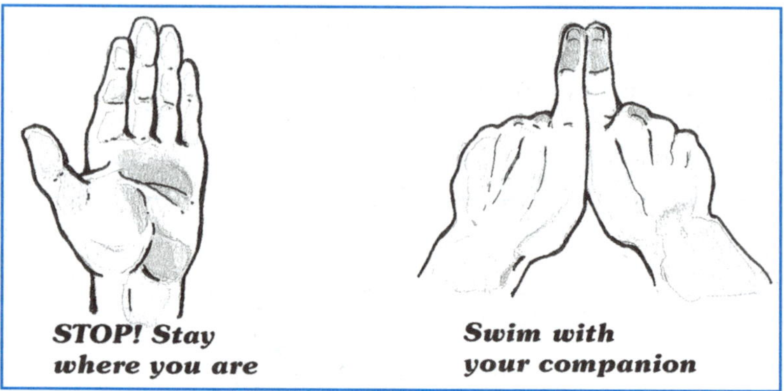

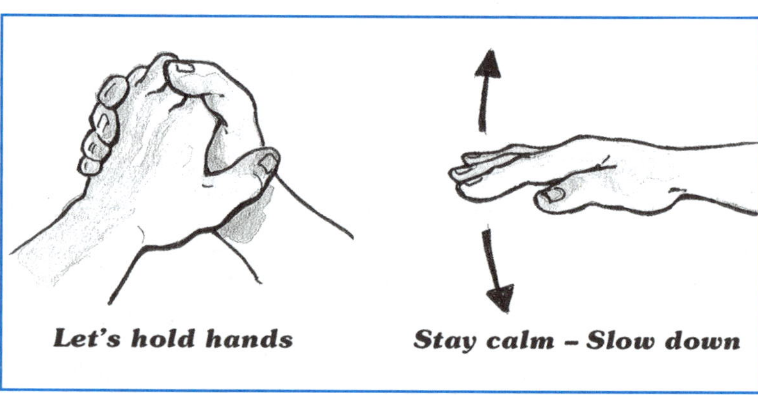

10.4 DIET AND PROTECTION FROM COLD

The relationship between apnea and diet has yet to be defined exactly by research. There is no certain data concerning repeated apnea, but information has been acquired and phenomena recorded that haven't always been supplied with articulate explanations. This is one of the reasons why there is still so much empiricism and improvisation. Some athletes, despite having peculiar dietary habits, obtain excellent results; at times they are clumsily and inaccurately imitated, causing only a worsening in condition of the imitator.

The first indispensable step is the self-examination: it is necessary to know oneself in detail, to trust one's own sensations and to try and respond to them or satisfy them. Fatigue, hunger, thirst, rhythms and cold are factors that will always need to be given attention.

Recognising energy waste is fundamental; although the precise mechanisms are still unknown, there is an elevated energy consumption in apneists that doesn't depend solely on water temperature, marine weather conditions or the 'load' on the individual. Therefore it is important to supply the organism with an adequate nutrition – **never fast before apnea.**

The consumption of glucose accounts for only a part of the energy necessary for physical activity: it was calculated that **in repetitive apnea, a general elevation in energy consumption** ahead of modest muscular activity will result in a fairly consistent consumption of glucose. Thus an apneist, just like any other sweater and grinder, will need energy from all the principal nutrients. We will consider several hypotheses.

Spending an entire day in the sea

The evening before a full day of diving eat a dinner with a main course high in protein (meat, eggs, fish). Legumes (vegetable proteins), though they represent a very dear topic for nutritionists, have several contraindications in our field of activity. The overproduction of gas in the intestine causes abdominal distension (and therefore a slight robbing of lung space), and possible pain due to the variation of pressure of this gas during diving.

Breakfast in the morning must precede entry into the water by at least an hour and a half; a generous liquid content will make the transition through the digestive system more rapid.

Choose which liquid to consume according to your experiences with digestibility, keeping in mind that strong tea or coffee are not recommended as they increase excitability and the use of oxygen. Fruit juices, in particular citrus juices, can sometimes cause 'acidity'; the risk is that in the head-down position gastric acid may enter the oesophagus or even the mouth. Milk requires laborious digestion. Herbal teas and tisane not only have the effects for which they are popular, but other possible side effects also. The conclusion? Know yourself! Consume only that which you have tried and tested.

The 'solid' component should have a high content of complex carbohydrates, which means cereals, bread, biscuits and rusks. Consume these in generous quantities but do not go over the top, otherwise they will limit apnea.

Marmalade and honey are excellent: however allow time for digestion and consume them in moderation. Yoghurt is an excellent substitute for the nutritive qualities of milk, but is less liquid, so for breakfast it should be diluted with other liquids (even water). Bear in mind that yoghurt is acidic and therefore requires the same consideration as for the citric fruit juices.

The 'English breakfast' or the German equivalent are both strongly inadvisable: their high fat content guarantees considerable energy reserves but takes too long to digest. If you stay in the water freediving for many hours then biscuits or a little bread will be helpful, as long as they aren't all consumed at once, but over several occasions.

Upon returning to land after passing several hours freediving in the sea, we will undoubtedly be deficient in water and salts (especially sodium). Fruit and water are excellent reintegrators, equivalent to the specific supplements on the market.

Glucose drinks will go down very well. The most bulky meal (dinner) should then include the principal nutrients that have been lacking during the day (protein), and with the entire night for digestion there are no inadvisable foods. However raw or cooked vegetables are recommended for fibre, which will allow a good intestinal movement and an appropriate elimination of waste.

Spending an afternoon in the sea

A good breakfast in the morning is the best way to start, making sure that none of the principal nutrients are missing. A small sandwich, half a portion of pasta or a couple of pieces of fruit at least two or three hours before diving will guarantee energy through to the evening.

What to eat and what to avoid

- **Gaseous drinks** (*soft drinks, carbonated water, beer*): the addition of CO_2 renders such beverages detrimental before or during the activity of apnea in so much as they distend the stomach and force the diaphragm upwards. It's a different argument for beer, which is forbidden within 4-5 hours before immersion due to its considerable effects on digestion.
- **Alcohol:** the hard liquors are definitely to be avoided, but this applies whatever the case. Small doses of wine (1 glass

per meal) don't have any negative effects; however it is worth being teetotal prior to diving.

- **Sweets:** simple and less elaborate sweets are preferable, for obvious reasons of digestibility. Caramel should be avoided shortly before diving.
- **Chocolate:** contains reasonable amounts of xanthine, which is an excitant similar to caffeine; its effect is greatly reduced in small doses, as in for instance flavouring of breakfast milk. It also contains important mineral salts, and whatsmore... it tastes so good!
- **Chewing-gum:** by chewing we use, even if indirectly, the same muscles used for compensation. Against this sole advantage there is: the stimulation of digestive juices (one of the reflexes of chewing) that can worsen the acidity we have already mentioned, and the increase in saliva secretion that further reduces circulating salts. Best avoided.
- **Garlic, onions, leeks:** it is said that they have positive effects and it was Jacques Mayol who made them famous amongst freedivers. However these effects should be read as unknown pseudo-pharmacological actions, i.e. they are not scientifically proven. It is true that they have a vasodilatory action on the peripherals, which works against the vasoconstriction of apnea that determines the blood-shift described in *Chapter 3*; on this basis they should even be eliminated. However there is no certain data on either the detriments or advantages that derive from these vegetables.
- **Antioxidants:** vitamins C and E in particular have an antagonist action to the free radicals, which have been demonstrated by many studies to be produced in abundance during apnea, when tissues are in a hypoxic condition.

The production of free radicals is the object of careful investigation in both healthy and sick humans since they can contribute to great damage. One of the negative effects of apnea, which for several years was thought to tax the brain cells of anyone who practiced apnea daily, could be directly dependant on the work of free radicals. However it seems that only those who dive very frequently to a great depth are exposed to this risk.

The conditional is again obligatory as research in this field is still very shallow. Science

GOOD DIETARY RULES

- Never fast.
- Drink water constantly.
- Eat one meal a day rich in protein.
- Avoid alcohol.
- Maintain a high consumption of fruit and vegetables.
- Avoid weight gain.
- Listen to yourself and satisfy your needs.

is unfortunately also subjected to the laws of the market, and apnea does not currently have sufficient commercial weight.

We cannot hope to annul the problem of free radicals by eating foods rich in principal antioxidants; however with a suitable intake of food containing vitamins C, E and A and polyunsaturated fatty acids, we will supply countermeasures that reduce damage to a minimum. Therefore fruit and greens, milk and meats (liver), oil, fish and dried fruit should appear frequently on the table.

- **Liquorice:** has two important effects. It reduces the irritation of nasal mucous, which is useful in the winter when the air is particularly cold, or in cases of light coughing. Furthermore it induces the retention of potassium, which is a salt lost in large quantities during apnea. Be careful not to overindulge: one or two sticks is plenty.
- **Dietary supplements:** there are a great many on the market, and products balanced with 55% carbohydrate, 30% fat and 15% protein can be the solution to many problems. They are very easily digestible, have excellent dietary content, afford little waste products, and represent the best way to sustain oneself during a heavy day. Dissolved in water before drinking they can cure the energy deficit that is encountered by those who are unable to eat anything in the morning. They can also be used during weekends spent in foreign places where adequate nutrition is unavailable. Saline supplements can also be helpful for the apneist during psychophysical exhaustion, in particular magnesium, which participates in various biochemical processes connected to respiration.

What and how much to drink

During a session in the sea it is best to sip a little water from time to time, even if you are not thirsty; continuous moistening by seawater of mucous in the mouth sends false signals regarding thirst to our central nervous system. Underwater activity, whatever it may be, provokes a considerable increase in the production of urine. The urine of a freediver during their activity is fundamentally hypotonic – remarkably similar to mineral water. It is produced by the stimulation of a specific hormone that produces a shortage of salt.

This explains why after spending long hours in the water we often have a craving for something salty. If we indulge this craving, and drink plenty of water also, then we will restore our body's correct hydration.

Body temperature

When we immerse ourselves in water we feel a cold shiver. This is due to the fact that body warmth, which is maintained constantly at about 37°C, is dispersed far more rapidly in water, due to its coefficient of thermal conduction being 25 times greater to that of air. Therefore we disperse heat 25 times faster in water than on land.

Generally after a brief period of time in the water there is an adaptation that makes the temperature seem more agreeable. In fact our body adjusts to the cold with a peripheral vasoconstriction, in which the blood vessels tighten and restrict blood flow to the surface. In this way the dispersion of heat is slowed by maintaining it 'in the depths' of the body.

However if we stay at length in the water then the body's mechanisms of adaptation are not sufficient and shivering will commence. Shivers are the physiological response of our body, which tries to warm itself by spasmodically contracting muscles. However this reaction requires energy, and therefore shivers are a message to the apneist that they are 'running on reserve' – a good reason to leave the water.

The cold should never be in control. It can be pre-empted by using a wetsuit of suitable thickness for the conditions, and as we have mentioned for diet, by adopting strategies and targeted nutrition during the period in the water.

During a long session in cold water even the body temperature will start to decrease, shivers will be more intense and prolonged and hands and feet will become numb. When body temperature descends to around 35°C conditions of hypothermia begin to be manifested, representing a serious danger. If the exposure to cold continues and temperature descends to 32°C then the capacity of reason is reduced, and at temperatures below 32°C there is an immediate threat to life.

10.5 MANAGING AN EMERGENCY

The greatest risk to an apneist is without doubt that of drowning. For this reason every apneist should know how to correctly conduct First Aid techniques, in particular cardiopulmonary resuscitation (CPR). This topic cannot be covered adequately within an apnea course, as it requires time, a mannequin, two subjects and most importantly the direction of an expert who is competent in the material – a CPR instructor. There are many organisations that offer courses in First Aid such as PADI, Red Cross and National Health services.

We advise that you complete your training by participating in one of these courses, for peace of mind as well as safety, and ensure also that your companion can capably perform manoeuvres of resuscitation.

PRE-ARRANGING EMERGENCY PROCEDURE

An emergency plan must always be simple and clear. Every member of the group must know what to do in any emergency, quickly carrying out procedures that allow the rescuer to give maximum attention to the victim, as well as calling for medical aid. Whether in the pool or in open water an emergency plan must supply three things in particular:

- **First aid kit.**
- **Oxygen kit.**
- **System of communication with the Emergency Medical Services.**

First aid kit

Should be taken wherever you go. Consists of a box containing a few helpful items that are used to deal with small emergencies in the marine environment. Pay attention to the expiry dates of some items contained in the kit.

Oxygen kit

O_2 is fundamental in the handling of a diving related emergency. There **must** be an O_2 tank available for emergencies at the site of immersion. O_2 is essential to help recover respiration in the case of a blackout.

System of communication with the Emergency Medical Services

Knowing who will call the medical services, as well as how and from where to call them, means that in a serious emergency assistance will come rapidly, saving precious time. Figures from the American Heart Association that plotted the relationship between intervention of ACLS (Advanced Cardiac Life Support) and the time until activation of CPR show that if CPR is activated within 4 minutes of cardiac arrest, and ACLS intervenes within 8 minutes, then the probability of revival is 43%, while if ACLS arrives between 8 and 12 minutes then the probability of revival drops to 10%.

HOW TO HANDLE AN EMERGENCY IN THE SEA

While the managing of an emergency in the pool is the responsibility of the lifeguard, we will see how to deal with an emergency in the sea. Having the local emergency phone number stored in your cell phone's memory is not sufficient – each member of the group must know how to use the phone. This information should be discussed with companions in the briefing.

What to do in the case of an emergency

The moment a freediver is seen to be in trouble a sequence of precise operations must be triggered. Success is dependent on a contingency plan having been pre-arranged that is equal to the situation: we will look at some examples.

Locating the body of a victim

It can happen that the victim is visible from the surface, in which case only dive if you are confident of being able to make a controlled, calm dive. If you have just surfaced, re-immerse only after having recovered completely, and carefully evaluating that emotions have not triggered an **elevated heart rate.**

Abandon all superfluous equipment

Jettison all unessential equipment (speargun, torch, fish holder etc) without being concerned about losing them If you are life-lined try to attach your own line to the victim by passing it under their armpits, free the victim's weights and attempt recovery to the surface. If the lifeline is attached to your belt then the alternative is to free the weights and try to recover the victim holding him or her with your hands. If you are forced to abandon the rescue attempt, or you do not succeed in bringing the victim to the surface you will be able to subsequently recover the victim with the lifeline.

In a case in which **the apneist is not visible** from the surface, make a reconnaissance at a good depth for viewing the bottom.

The search should follow a pattern of concentric semicircles, increasing in width from an easily identified centre that corresponds to the point where the victim was last seen.

Recovery of an unconscious apneist from depth

The aim of this operation is to bring the victim to the surface as quickly as possible. There are different ways of completing this task; whatever the case, as soon as the rescuer has reached the unfortunate he removes their weightbelt as well as his own and abandons both on the bottom.

Now in positive buoyancy, the pair begin the ascent. The rescuer transports the victim by passing an arm underneath the armpits and holding the head with the same hand. If the victim is reached during the ascent, and therefore in midwater, he or she can be transported, after removing the weightbelts, supported by straight arms with the hands placed under the armpits (as described in *Chapter 9.4*). The rescuer can stay in front of or behind the victim, as long as they are able to fin vigorously and hold the victim in such a way as to be hydrodynamic, whilst taking advantage of positive buoyancy.

Surface procedure

Immediately upon reaching the surface, try to establish a positive buoyancy of both victim and rescuer, abandoning any superfluous weight. At this point one must concentrate on preventing asphyxiation and promoting the resumption of respiration, whether spontaneous or artificially stimulated during transport. Therefore position the victim by one shoulder, and support the head by placing the hands under the jaw with the fingers following the line of the bone; keep the chin raised and without removing the mask, take the snorkel out of their mouth.

The rescuer commences the transport, placing the nape of the victim's neck on their sternum and finning dorsally. If respiration does not spontaneously recommence then begin **artificial mouth-to-snorkel respiration** (*see figure on page 365*). This procedure allows the rescuer to effectively raise the chin and maintain the airways open at the same time as swimming easily.

Remove the mask from the victim and replace the snorkel in the mouth, sealing it off with the left hand. The little finger rests under the chin, the ring and middle fingers on the lips around the mouth, exerting a suitable pressure, while the index and thumb close off the nose. **Remember that to maintain open airways it is necessary to keep the head hyperextended.**

Use the right hand to guide the snorkel into your own mouth, and exhale into the snorkel (insufflation) every five seconds, which can be measured by repeating mentally: 'thousand and one, thousand and two, thousand and three, thousand and four, thousand and five'. Before starting the breath make sure that there is no water in the snorkel.

Artificial respiration can be efficiently performed whilst still in the water. Many victims of **pre-drowning** have been saved by the efficient ventilation that they have received in the water. Apneists frequently require artificial respiration in the water due to their distance from the exit point.

Other than that described above, there are other techniques for efficient artificial respiration in water. Between the many methods of the Red Cross and National safety organisations the three following actions are always recommended:

- **Bend the head backwards**
- **Raise the jaw**
- **Open the mouth**

There are very few methods of in-water artificial respiration that provide an adequate support to the jaw so as to keep the victim's airways open. In fact if the airways are incorrectly opened then instead of entering the lungs the air will enter the victim's stomach. The inflated stomach pushes against the diaphragm, further impeding the flow of air exhaled by the rescuer into the lungs. It is highly likely that attacks of vomiting will occur when the air enters the stomach. Therefore, if possible, keep the jaw raised during artificial respiration.

The most efficient method of in-water artificial respiration is the use of a pocket mask (a small mask that covers nose and mouth), with which all three of the required actions can be applied. The two handed hold, raising the jaw, maintains the airways correctly open, helps to keep water out of the victim's mouth, allows ventilation of the subject both through the mouth and nose, eliminates mouth-to-mouth contact with the victim and enables the rescuer to swim efficiently. For this reason every apneist should carry with them a **pocket mask**, perhaps attached to their signal buoy.

Slaps, shaking and other similar procedures should be avoided: they do not have any medical justification.

Removing the victim from the water

Upon reaching the boat or shore, try to remove the victim from the water. Techniques of resuscitation can only be performed effectively on firm ground. The rescuer decides

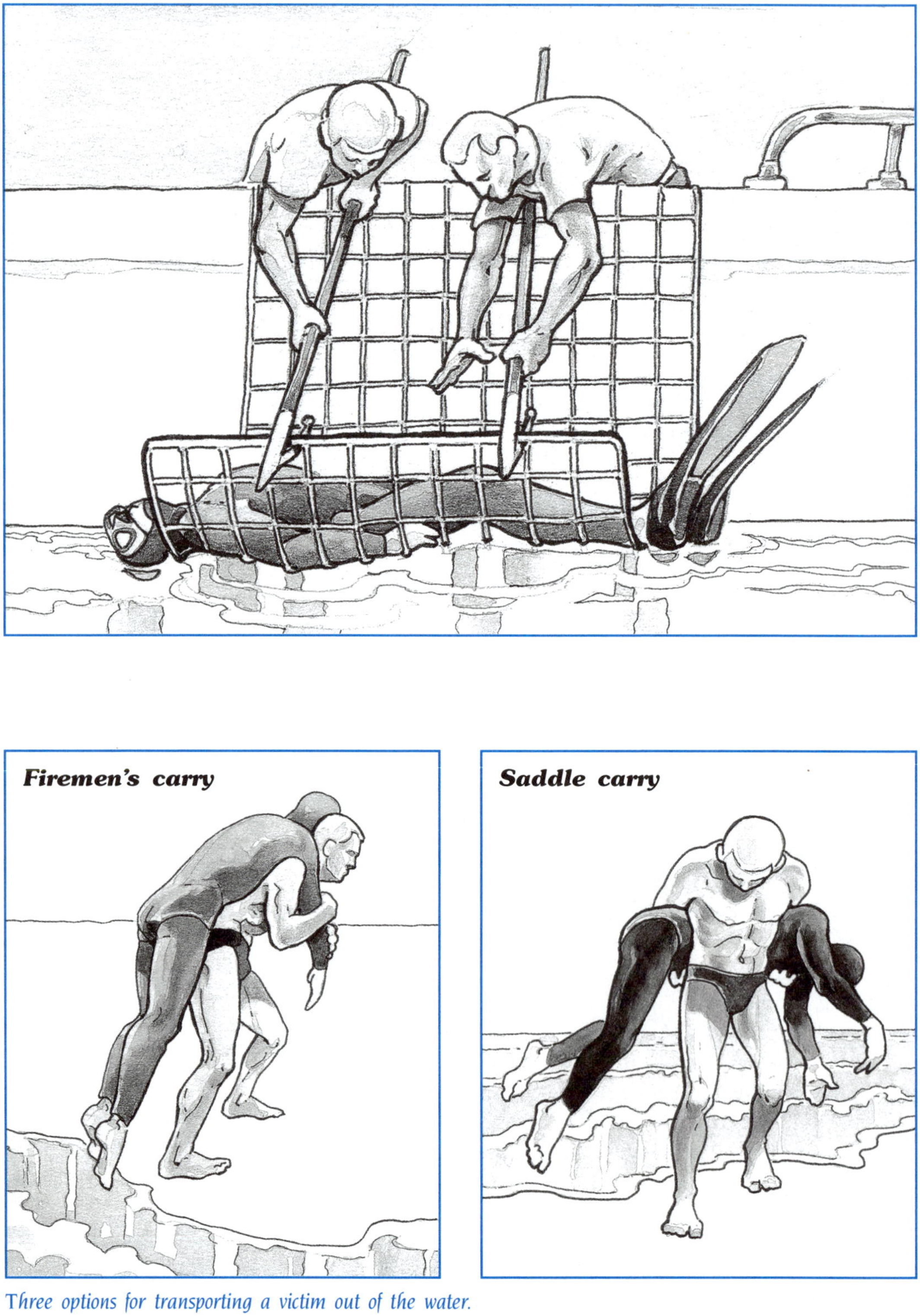

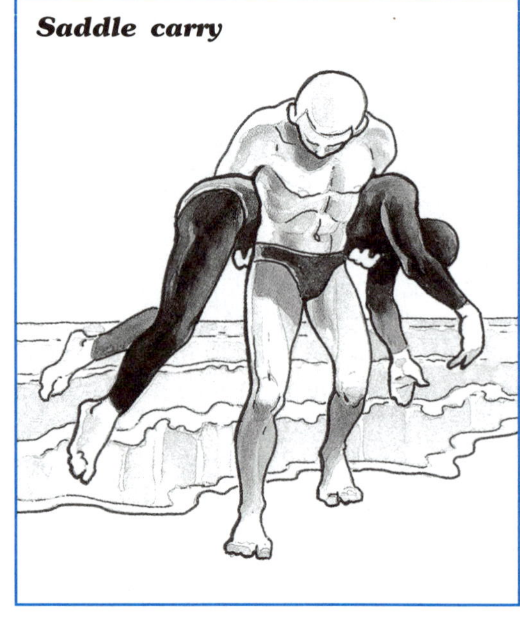

Three options for transporting a victim out of the water.

whether to remove the victim's fins before exiting the water, and evaluates if other people on the surface can help bring the unfortunate apneist onto a dry surface.

There are three possible exit points for a rescue: onto a boat, on a beach, or on rocks. Helping a companion up on to a boat can be very difficult, especially if there is no stepladder or platform. A rope or net can be of help in hoisting an unconscious diver onboard a boat with high gunwales (*see top figure on page 324*).

In this situation the rolling technique works best. By rolling the victim over the edge you will avoid wasting energy. For a boat that is lower in the water such as an inflatable dinghy, the inanimate body can be lifted straight out of the water; it will help to exploit the buoyancy force of the water.

If you come ashore on a beach, use the current to let yourself be taken by the surf as close as possible to the shore. Whilst traversing the area of breaking waves, block the surf with your own body so that the victim does not swallow any water. Upon reaching the shore you can use either the fireman's carry or the saddle carry (*see figures on page 324*) to bring the victim out of the water.

To be able to easily bear the victim in the fireman or saddle position without becoming exhausted or straining your back, you will need to begin in shallow water. Stay bent at the knees so that the shoulders are level with the surface and grasp the victim, arranging them in the chosen mode. Taking the weight on the lower limbs, and not on the back, raise the victim up and walk towards the beach. Upon reaching the water's edge, bend at the legs until you are kneeling. Supporting the head, rotate the unconscious companion until he or she can be placed lying face-up.

Transporting a victim to shore is a difficult task, so use extreme precaution. If the sea is rough then carefully evaluate the most suitable moment, taking advantage of the period of calm between one wave and the next.

If you find yourself on a rocky coastline the rescue will be even more dangerous, and it will be safest to wait for the moment of calm between the waves before swimming towards the rocks. When you reach the shore grasp onto the rocks, and while the water is drawing back try to quickly roll or raise the victim towards the highest place before the next wave arrives. Whatever the method of exit, it will be safer and easier with the help of other people.

Procedure out of the water

Once onshore, and safely out of the water, the victim's head must point back to the water, while the feet point inland; if onboard a boat then the head should be facing aft, with feet pointing to the bow: in this way the head will remain lower than the rest of the body, promoting circulation from the heart to the brain.

It will be easier to perform artificial respiration on a dry surface; and if necessary you should be capable of supplying complete CPR.

Finally, make sure to drain any water that may be in the lungs. This can be accomplished in a boat by simply raising the victim's feet, which should be in a prone position. On the shore you can achieve the same thing by turning the victim's body. On a steep shoreline turn the victim on to their side in the recovery position for several seconds, allowing the water to flow out due to the effect of the slope.

Available time

Up to **8 minutes** may elapse from the moment in which the apneist loses consciousness to the moment in which the heart, if respiration is not restored, stops beating. This is the period used to bring effective aid to the victim.

Once the heart stops beating (clinical death or catalepsy), brain cells will immediately start to die, and the brain sustains irreversible damage due to **anoxia**. After about **3-4 minutes** of cardiac arrest biological death supervenes (flat electroencephalogram).

It is evident that, given the shortage in available time, the rescuer confronted with a subject should be able to quickly diagnose respiratory arrest, check the pulse and upon realising the gravity of the problem, take the decision to intervene in the most suitable way. The elements necessary for a diagnosis can all be verified on the subject's face; this is helpful with apneists, seeing as we usually wear wetsuits that can be particularly difficult to remove.

First of all the **mask must be taken from the victim's face** and the pupils and lips should be examined. If the lips are bluish then it is an indication that the blood which flows under the thin layer of skin covering the lips is poor in oxygen: in this case the state of hypoxia is already advanced.

The situation is even more serious if the **pupils are dilated to the maximum and are not reflexive** (i.e. insensitive to variations of light): this indicates that the part of the central nervous system responsible for the pupil's reflexes has also entered into a state of hypoxia, and more generally, that the brain cells are not receiving oxygen – a sign that the heart has also stopped.

In either case, the first operation to undertake is artificial respiration. It is impossible to execute CPR in the water; therefore the victim must be transported as quickly as possible out of the water.

Do not lose precious time trying to make the victim expel all the water that they may have inhaled: even at the beginning of drowning the primary problem is the lack of oxygen in the tissues; therefore immediately supply air by mouth-to-mouth breathing, or better still with a pocket mask. Delaying intervention in order to empty the lungs, with the aim of making artificial respiration more efficient, can in reality compromise the success of the entire operation.

It is worth mentioning that if blackout occurs in cold water then the reduction in metabolic consumption caused by hypothermia allows for the toleration of a greater reduction in cerebral blood flow: at a temperature of around 30°C the blood supply to the brain can be stopped for 10' without neurological damage. Medical literature reports of cases of reanimation that had a happy ending after some tens of minutes of respiratory arrest. This means that, it being understood that it is necessary to provide resuscitation in as short a time as possible, one can and one should attempt intervention even on subjects who it is assumed have already exceeded the deadline for recovery.

FIRST AID

First aid (the initial phase of emergency treatment required by a patient or casualty) is often, if not forgotten, at least undervalued.

Other than in exceptions that are luckily very rare, the work of the medic begins when the patient arrives at the hospital. There is thus a long and dangerous 'pause in treatment' from the moment of the incident to the start of appropriate care.

This text has deliberately not gone into the techniques of reanimation and first aid, as there are dedicated institutions that organise courses for training of this highly specialised nature.

Clearly it is not just the apnea instructors, but also each and every responsible apneist who should know how to competently handle techniques of reanimation – not for their own security, but for that of their companions.

TRAINING FOR APNEA

CHAPTER

11

If you don't practice you don't deserve to dream.
– Andre Agassi

The world of apnea is undergoing a phase of deep transformation, passing from a pioneering and poetical period to another – which we could define as professional – in which rationalisation of the methods of training and techniques of execution runs closer to scientific research. The programming of physical activity has an increasingly relevant role.

To plan a training program means setting out distinct phases of preparation that are proportioned qualitatively and quantitatively, with respect to the genetics of the athlete and the fundamental principles of training. A top-level apneist is not a Superman, but an athlete that trains seriously, following particular tables and a preparation that separates physical and athletic work from the psychological, technical and strategic.

The idea that an apneist must be someone gifted with particular and mysterious mental capacities or powers that are medically 'unidentifiable' is long dead, disproved by the fact that the number of apneists at the top level has continued to increase. These athletes are training harder, in every direction, and in a serious and coordinated fashion, through identifying and analysing factors that characterise performance, and programming training accordingly.

There are no miracle recipes to become a champion of apnea, only a long labour of patience and determination.

Physical training is the base of all sporting activity, and without an adequate athletic preparation it is impossible to reach satisfactory results. Training of competitive apneists is divided into physical preparation (swimming, running, weights) and specific preparation (stationary apnea, dynamic apnea and freediving).

In the preceding chapters we have seen the principle techniques of freediving. If the passion for apnea has won you over and you decide to improve your performance, then the following pages may well be of use.

11.1 PHYSICAL PREPARATION OF THE APNEIST

The 'dry' training of the apneist must be arranged over the space of a year, during which time the training stimuli, termed the 'work load', can create organic adaptations aimed at the improvement of performance. Consistency and a gradual approach are the two key words in the training (whether physical or specific) of the apneist.

Physical training holds a fundamental role in the winter, away from the competitive season, for a period of about five months. This type of work will then gradually diminish in both intensity and period as it makes way for training in water.

There are still many obscurities concerning man's physiology during apnea, such as the fact that we still do not know at what point during a constant weight dive or dynamic apnea the body transfers from aerobic to anaerobic movement. Another important factor yet to be understood is whether white or red (quick twitch or slow twitch) muscle fibres are preferable for freediving. Once these and other mysteries are solved we will then be able to address the details of physical training for apnea.

In theory, the first two months of training are dedicated entirely to physical preparation; then specific training is gradually inserted up until the period of maximum load (usually in spring) in which the two types of preparation are synchronized. From the beginning of summer onwards the dry physical preparation is reduced until it disappears completely to leave space for only specific training in the water. In this way we approach the most important season – the summer.

While work is predominantly physical we can insert one session per week of apnea training. Clearly we cannot have an elevated performance in the water in the phase of intense physical preparation.

As in all sports, it is not possible to stay in top form for a long period. It is therefore necessary to lay out the training program over the year in order to reach the best conditions in the most important part of the season. Starting well in advance with apnea training tables and then protracting them for too long a period, we run the risk of peaking too soon and finding ourselves in the middle of the season with a form that is already declining (the problem of over-training).

This is one of the problems that the greater part of top-level apneists face: how to train so as to be in form at the right time – neither too soon nor too late. By documenting training and results throughout the year we will better understand how to structure the following year's programme, moving the various phases forwards or backwards depending on whether form in the water was attained too early or too late.

The objective of physical preparation is to train the two fundamental factors: anaerobic capacity and aerobic power (VO_2MAX). Aerobic power is often erroneously neglected when we talk of apnea. On the contrary it is unquestionably an important factor. VO_2MAX measures the quantity of oxygen that the muscles are able to turn into energy in a unit of time. An athlete that possesses a good VO_2MAX has favourable characteristics for apnea: a large red blood cell count, a high value of haemoglobin, low resting heart rate and an elevated vital capacity due to aerobic training.

A well trained anaerobic capacity allows tolerance to a high level of lactic acid, which forms for example after rapid finning in apnea. It is important that all muscles maintain their elasticity (stretching is essential at the end of every session) and that the heart is habituated to working under strain. Every exercise should be started gradually, increasing the rhythm and intensity from one week to the next.

The personalisation of a competitive apneist's training requires the presence of a specialist medical team who can evaluate the starting point of the subject through the methodologies described. Subsequently, with the help of an athletic trainer a schedule can be constructed that allows on one hand the general increase in potential of all systems concerned with athletic performance in apnea; while on the other hand it allows the identification of lacking areas, which can be corrected by weighting the training to their benefit. It is essential to institute intermediary checks to follow the right evolution of training.

The psychological aspect is just as critical, and cannot be neglected: it is important to create a relationship of trust and mutual understanding between the athlete, the trainer, the medical team and the psychologist, with the aim of ensuring that everything is carried out with the maximum scientific thoroughness even if it is invalidated by that which inexorably conditions the duration of apnea in man: the psychosomatic sensations.

The training tables presented in this chapter (relating to running, swimming and weights) have been written up with purely illustrative numbers, to give an exemplification. The values can be modified depending on training and personal level. Out of all the disciplines swimming is the most effective form of training. If you are constricted by time to make a choice then swimming should take priority over running and weights. There are other training activities that are beneficial to apnea (cross country skiing, cycling, rowing etc), which for reasons of space we haven't discussed here.

RUNNING

Running has a fundamental role in the first five months of physical preparation. During the first two months pace should be kept low whilst the duration of the exercise is gradually increased, passing from 30' initially to 60' of running after sixty days.

Upon completing this primary phase of foundation, the remaining three months of running exercises are mostly specific; their purpose is to gradually adapt the organism to tolerate conditions of elevated hypoxia and acidosis.

The main exercises are:

A) **Running whilst controlling breathing:** run at a reduced pace, inhaling and exhaling very slowly, maintaining a constant number of steps in the two phases of the breath. The time of expiration must be twice as long as the inspiration (e.g.: 10 steps in expiration – 5 steps in inspiration)
OBJECTIVE 1: increase the duration of running with the same steps for inspiration and expiration.
OBJECTIVE 2: increase the number of steps per expiration and inspiration, maintaining a constant total time of running.

B) **Running whilst controlling breathing with a brief apnea at the end of each respiratory phase** (e.g. 8 steps in expiration – 2 steps of apnea – 4 steps in inspiration – 2 steps of apnea).
OBJECTIVES: identical to the preceding exercise.

C) **Series of distances in apnea with a brief recovery** (e.g. 10 steps of apnea running – 5 steps of normal breathing ... repeat 20 times)
OBJECTIVE 1: increase the number of apneas.
OBJECTIVE 2: increase the distance covered in apnea.

D) **Maximum distance in apnea at a slow pace with a long recovery** (e.g.: 50 steps of running apnea with a complete recovery, repeated 10 times).
OBJECTIVE: increase the distance run in apnea.

E) **Apnea sprints at maximum speed with a long recovery.** **OBJECTIVE:** increase the duration of the sprint whilst maintaining a constant velocity.

F) **Gradual increase of distance in apnea with a constant recovery** (e.g.: 2 steps of apnea – 10 steps breathing – 4 steps of apnea – 10 steps breathing – 6 steps of apnea – 10 steps breathing... – 20 steps of apnea – 10 steps breathing...)
OBJECTIVE 1: increase the maximum distance of apnea.
OBJECTIVE 2: decrease the amount of steps of recovery for a constant distance of apnea.

HOW TO ORGANISE TRAINING

We propose several training modules to repeat cyclically

Module 1
10' warm-up running, A (20'), C (15'), D (15'); stretching

Module 2
10' warm-up running, B (20'), F (15'), E (15'); stretching

Module 3
10' warm-up running, A (20'), F (15'), D (15'); stretching

Module 4
10' warm-up running, B (20'), C (15'), E (15'); stretching

As you can see, the unit of measure in the various exercises is not minutes or seconds, but footsteps. This makes the training session seem shorter and less monotonous, avoiding having to spend the time with eyes glued to a watch.

Every athlete has their own pace – velocity, stride distance and rhythm – which is like a unit of measure. It can be entirely different to the pace of another athlete, and this is a good reason not to imitate the execution of another apneist.

SWIMMING

Swimming is fundamental for the apneist. A fine swimmer can be easily converted into a good apneist (assuming there are no problems with compensation) since swimming presupposes a high level of aquaticity. Swimming also benefits the respiratory and cardiovascular systems, and trains the musculature in complete absence of gravity, which has considerable advantage to the mobility of joints. A muscle trained through swimming will maintain a long and hydrodynamic form with respect to the same muscle trained during dry activity. Swimming is excellent aerobic exercise.

However there should be distinct sequences of work and successions of different exercises. It is advisable to insert a session of about 20' of fin swimming at the conclusion of each session of pure swimming to maintain the form of the muscles specifically involved in finning. Weightbelts can be used to increase the workload.

In the following pages we present 6 examples of training tables for pure swimming, with purely illustrative times and distances that should reflect an average swimmer.

TABLE A	TYPE OF TRAINING	QUALITIES DEVELOPED IN TERMS OF PERCENTAGE
• 200 m warm-up • 4 × 100 crawl, 10" rest	• interval training	• endurance 80% velocity 20%
• 3 × 200 crawl, arms only, 15" rest	• interval training	• endurance 80% velocity 20%
• swim 1 length slowly, 1 length quickly; 2 L.S., 2 L.Q.; 3 L.S., 3 L.Q.; 4 L.S., 4 L.Q.; 3 L.S., 3 L.Q.; 2 L.S., 2 L.Q.; 1 L.S., 1 L.Q.	• speed play	• endurance 85% velocity 15%

TABLE B	TYPE OF TRAINING	QUALITIES DEVELOPED IN TERMS OF PERCENTAGE
• 200 m warm-up • 4 × 100 crawl, 20" rest • 3 × 100 crawl, 10" rest • 2 × 100 crawl, 5" rest	• interval training	• endurance 80% velocity 20%
• 5 × 50 arms only, 15" rest (hypoxic breathing)	• interval training	• endurance 80% velocity 20%
• 2 × 150, 3' rest	• interval training	• endurance 80% velocity 20%
• 4 × 50 sprints, 1' rest	• sprint training	• endurance 10% velocity 90%

TABLE C	TYPE OF TRAINING	QUALITIES DEVELOPED IN TERMS OF PERCENTAGE
• 200 m warm-up • 2 × 200, 20" rest • 2 × 100, 15" rest • 2 × 50, 10" rest	• interval training	• endurance 80% velocity 20%
• steps: 50, 100, 200, 300, 200, 100, 50 with 1' rest between one exercise and the next, and at a quick pace	• repetition training	• endurance 45% velocity 55%
• 300 m arms only, 2 lengths slowly, 1 length very quickly	• speed play	• endurance 85% velocity 15%

TABLE D	TYPE OF TRAINING	QUALITIES DEVELOPED IN TERMS OF PERCENTAGE
• 200 m warm-up • 3 × 100, 20" rest • 3 × 75, 15" rest • 3 × 50, 10" rest	• interval training	• endurance 80% velocity 20%
• 5 × 50, 10" rest (hypoxic breathing)	• interval training	• endurance 75% velocity 25%
• 6 × 25, departing every minute at maximum velocity	• sprint training	• endurance 10% velocity 90%
• 3 × 50, departing every two minutes at maximum velocity	• sprint training	• endurance 10% velocity 90%

TABLE E	TYPE OF TRAINING	QUALITIES DEVELOPED IN TERMS OF PERCENTAGE	
• 200 m warm-up	• repetition training	• endurance 45%	velocity 55%
• 4 × 50, departing every 1'30"	• over distance	• endurance 85%	velocity 15%
• 400, legs only 400, arms only (hypoxic breathing)			
• 2 × 400, with rest of 30" between one and the next, 1 length slowly, 1 length quickly	• over distance	• endurance 95%	velocity 5%

TABLE F	TYPE OF TRAINING	QUALITIES DEVELOPED IN TERMS OF PERCENTAGE	
• 200 m warm-up	• interval training	• endurance 80%	velocity 20%
• 5 × 75, departing every 1'45" (hypoxic respiration)	• interval training	• endurance 80%	velocity 20%
• 5 × 50, arms only, every 1'45" (hypoxic respiration)	• over distance + repetition training	• endurance 72.5%	velocity 27.5%
• 1000 m, swimming 100 slow, 100 quick, 200 slow, 200 quick, 100 slow, 100 quick, last 200 at maximum velocity			

WEIGHT TRAINING

The period of training with weights is subdivided into three basic phases, which are spread over five months. We shouldn't only train the muscles involved in finning, but also all the other muscle groups of the body.

The apneist must absolutely avoid elevated workloads with slow movements aimed at increasing muscle mass. Muscular hypertrophy causes an increase in oxygen consumption that is unfavourable to apnea.

At the beginning of a training season we complete a period of two months general preparation or **macrocycle**, with 3 or 4 sessions per week.

The objectives are as follows

A) General muscular preparation of the lower parts of the body, torso and upper limbs.

B) Toning of postural muscles (abdominal and lumbar).

C) Maintenance and gradual enhancement of cardiovascular activity (aerobic training).

The two most effective methods for reaching these objectives are PHA (Peripheral Heart Action) training and Circuit training. Alternating between sessions of PHA and Circuit training can help maintain interest in training.

PHA training

PHA consists of 5-10 microcircuits, each composed of 4-6 exercises. Each microcircuit should be repeated 2-3 times before moving to the next. The exercises themselves are repeated rapidly 20-40 times, with a load of about 30% maximum. The recovery between one exercise and the next is 15"-30", and the pause between one circuit and the next consists of 1'30" on an aerobic machine (rowing machine/bike/stepper/treadmill).

Circuit training

Circuit training is a typical mixed aerobic workout, based on a series of exercises that target areas of the body where circulatory problems and accumulation of fat deposits are most frequent. It consists in a circuit of 10-15 exercises that is repeated 2-4 times. Each single exercise is repeated 30 - 40 times, or however many can be executed in a period of 45" to 1'. The recovery between exercises is 15", and the workload should be 25% to 40%.

The heart rate will be greatly raised during the period of work, and oxygen consumption will be high. The muscle groups engaged are predominantly in the lower limbs (quadriceps and femoral biceps, glutei, calves and tibials), abdominals, lower back, pectorals, deltoids, triceps and biceps.

These muscles are targeted with computerised machines that allow more or less faithful reproduction or simulation of exercises typically performed in open spaces: running, climbing, rowing, stair-climbing, etc with the advantage of being able to monitor at any instant the type of effort required (control of heart rate, consumption of oxygen etc).

Upon completing this preliminary phase we start with a period of special preparation, or the **mesocycle**, that continues for 2 months of 2-3 sessions a week in the gym. In this phase we resume the preceding exercises, but they must be executed with a greater velocity, and a load of around 10-15% of maximum that allows for 60 repetitions.

There follows a final very subtle period, the **microcycle**, with a duration of one month of twice weekly sessions. Its worth will depend on the seriousness with which the first two cycles have been completed.

In this phase we repeat the exercises of the second period and with the same load, but this time during apnea. The number of repetitions depends on the level of training and the capacity of maintaining apnea during dry movement.

The objectives are:

- Greater tolerance to elevated concentrations of lactic acid, and improvement of the pain threshold.
- Muscular work in apnea to stimulate muscular acidosis (increase of CO_2 and decrease of O_2).

STRETCHING (Articulation and muscular elasticity)

Flexibility (muscular elasticity and joint mobility) will always guarantee an efficient and harmonious athletic movement; in some sports these two qualities can make the winning difference. Freediving is definitely such a sport, where flexibility greatly influences economy of performance. The apneist must combat the resistance to movement of both the liquid element and their equipment, meaning flexibility becomes indispensable.

Anyone who is confined to a sedentary period will find that flexibility quickly undergoes a considerable regression, together with the physical condition. Although it will always be possible to reacquire muscular elasticity and joint mobility upon resumption of training, it is important not to neglect stretching exercises that should always contribute to a complete training programme.

An inactive muscle quickly weakens and stiffens, losing its elasticity. The main joints are affected in the same way, losing the balance that can only be supplied by a functional and active muscle. As a consequence smoothness and range of movement (articulation) are reduced.

Muscles have incredible qualities, such as the capacity of elongation (although this must occur gradually so as to avoid trauma to tissue and fibre). A muscle that undergoes regular and constant elongation exercises will always respond more quickly and efficiently to any type of movement; the change from a passive to active state will be easier; amplitude of movement is increased, and most importantly risk of injury is reduced. Sprains and 'pulled muscles' are mainly derived from lack of muscular elasticity or tendonitis.

Naturally even a well-trained athlete shouldn't ignore the importance of brief stretching sessions, before and after training. Indeed a well-trained muscle requires even more stretching, both before physical exercise, to avoid damage and to ensure maximum articulation, and after, to re-lengthen the fibres that have shortened and stiffened during muscular contraction.

Many apneists have suffered from tendonitis, especially in the Achilles tendon. Indeed freediving injuries are most often sustained in the lower limbs, which transmit energy to the fins. In particular, apneists that use a monofin should never undervalue stretching, which if combined with proper training guarantees correct articulation of all the involved areas.

The beauty of stretching is that it can be comfortably practiced at home, without the need of any particular equipment. It needn't be coupled with any other form of training and we can stretch whilst watching television or listening to music. A session should be thought of as a period of relaxation, in which we try to restore musculature and joints to their original elasticity and balance. Stretching will greatly benefit skeletal muscle, even in the absence of specific training (which is advisable nonetheless).

Muscular elasticity and the consequent articular mobility will be critical during the start of a dive. The duckdive will be more fluid and natural, without the risk of straining the lower back. The arms, which balance the action of the body and the throw of the legs, will thus be free to extend downwards, maintaining the most hydrodynamic and relaxed position. The lower limbs can develop their propulsive action without constraint, oscillating freely to the maximum amplitude that the hips, knees and ankles allow for.

If we haven't exercised for a long period, and we have lost the flexibility required to (for example) touch the toes without bending at the knees, then the action of the finstroke will also be considerably impeded. The moment we need to increase the amplitude and power of the stroke we will encounter difficulty and even pain. We will not be able to completely extend our limbs in order to gain maximum efficiency from the finstroke, and by persisting with the movement we may easily strain or pull a muscle.

For apneists who use a monofin this discourse on stretching is even more relevant, since to develop a fluid undulating motion a high articular mobility and muscular elasticity are essential. A monofin freediver who is unable to extend their arms past their head in line with the body, or who has limited mobility in the lower back etc will show a significantly impeded propulsion.

When to stretch?

- For a short period in the morning (a great way to start the day).
- During work, to diminish stress.
- After being in a static position for a long time.
- When feeling any rigidity.

Why stretch?

- To reduce muscular tension and assist psychophysical relaxation.
- To develop motor coordination, improving efficiency and freedom of movement.
- To prevent muscular injury due to exercise with cold or untrained muscles.
- To facilitate a demanding physical task by preparing the relevant muscles.
- To develop awareness of the body. The effects of stretching are enhanced when it is coupled with a session of relaxation.
- To allow the mind to detach itself more easily from the body's kinaesthetic perceptions such as disturbances or tension.
- To improve blood circulation.
- To contribute to a feeling of wellbeing.

Flexibility is essential to any underwater movement. During spearfishing, whether hunting in caves or by ambush, a flexible and elastic body will be able to change position, twist, bend and extend without difficulty, making movement in general more efficient. A harmonic and fluid motion will also consume less oxygen.

How to stretch, and for how long

Stretching doesn't require any physical preparation or ability, and exercises can be performed by healthy people of all ages. Furthermore appreciable results can be attained with a practice time of only 10-15 minutes per day.

There are simple rules that need to be followed at the start to ensure that stretching is efficient, without counterproductive consequences. The method of muscular elongation must be gentle and progressive – one shouldn't attempt to stretch the muscle excessively from the very first attempt. It is also a mistake to try and stretch a muscle by 'bouncing' up and down on it. Muscles possess a stretch reflex that intervenes when they are stretched excessively, causing an instantaneous contraction that actually stiffens the muscle. Muscles should instead be stretched progressively, and never to the point of pain. There should be a sensation of receding muscular tension, with a relaxing effect. Working in this way will require more time, but results will come and we will soon realise that we are moving more easily and naturally.

The first session should be characterised by 30-40 second stretches below the pain threshold. The sensation of tension will tend to subside as the muscle decontracts, and the muscle will lengthen more with each repetition. After this mainly static phase we begin to add movement to the stretches. Once the position has been reached and held for several seconds then the stretch can be taken slightly further by moving lightly, within the pain threshold, for a further 30-90 seconds.

The value of a stretching session is greatly enhanced when it is coupled with slow, rhythmic and controlled respiration such as that of Pranayama. We should preferably combine the most intense part of the stretch with the expiration, which must be slow and deep. The position is then maintained during the inspiration, before the stretch is once again extended a little further during the expiration. If there is difficulty in maintaining smooth respiration then this is most likely due to excessive effort, and the stretch should be reduced slightly to allow for more natural breathing. If done correctly this will induce a greater relaxation of both body and mind – a condition fundamental to the conception of modern apnea.

The most important muscle groups to stretch for freediving

As a general rule it is important to stretch the entire body so as to acquire a complete flexibility. We all have different builds and musculatures, meaning we will also need to identify areas that are most in need of specific attention. A session should therefore be divided into targeted as well as generalised stretching.

Once a good base condition has been established we can progress to other specific work aimed at the areas most implicated in freediving. With traditional bi-fins this will be the area between the lumbar muscles of the lower back and the flexors and extensors of the toes. The monofin requires a more complex movement that involves almost all muscles of the body, and so it will be necessary to develop total body flexibility (a condition that wouldn't hurt even those who do not use a monofin).

For the spearfisher it is important to be able to move like an eel on the sea floor; quite often the seabed composition and the sudden advance on prey require elastic movements or changes of direction, and someone who can move in this way will have a definite advantage. In particular the shoulder and hip joints need special attention since the balance of the muscles that regulate them is so delicate.

11.2 TRAINING IN WATER

The best training for apnea is apnea itself. In this section we will discuss the sequence, order and cadence with which one should organise training of static apnea, dynamic apnea and freediving. There are general rules that are best respected, and we have recapitulated these in the table *Recommendations for the apneist on page 354*. One fundamental rule is to never swim prior to an apnea session. Swimming will provoke an increase of heart rate and the intervention of all muscle groups required for the style adopted, thwarting relaxation.

The three types of apnea are very different to each other. However it is possible to find a relationship between them in level of performance: in general **1 minute of static apnea should allow for a dynamic of 20-22 m and a depth of 10 m freediving.** This ratio is not hard and fast, but quite often if it isn't displayed then it is because of limiting emotional or psychological factors, or a lack of technique. A good instructor can help identify and analyse such limitations.

It is critical to possess a logbook, an instrument of checking and comparing to verify progression, in which results and any possible observations from each training session are recorded.

IMPORTANT: In the tables and exercises of this chapter, values of time, distance and depth are given as examples only. Every apneist should work at their own level and capacity.

Training is nothing more than bodily change and adaptation due to work. It is necessary to identify all the parameters of this work in order to be able to program and modulate training. For example in cycling, distance and velocity constitute two variables of the work (that can also be defined as volume and intensity).

In the case of training in apnea, whether in the sea or pool, the work is constituted by time in apnea (or distance or depth) and time in recovery. Returning to the example of the cyclist, we can talk of factors that impact the work: two hours of cycling at 40 km/h when the temperature is 35°C will be a lot harder than an equal period of cycling at the same velocity on a mild day.

In apnea there are many factors that can influence the two variables of interest to us (performance and recovery time). A dive to 30 m in 12°C water is more difficult than the same dive in tropical water. 75 m dynamic apnea in a 25 m pool with rubber fins is harder than 75 m in a 50 m pool with long fins. There are endless examples of this kind. We will see how to identify the factors that can influence a workload in apnea, factors that must be taken into account in order to vary the program and to understand possible improvements or sudden drops in performance. They are:

1) water temperature
2) time already spent in the water
3) intensity of work performed
4) visibility
5) weighting
6) available equipment
7) current
8) concentration
9) physical form
10) stress

We must never dive alone. An apneist must always operate in conditions of safety (*see Chapter 10*).

TRAINING STATIC APNEA

In this section you will find tables for use in organising your training, which will be more effective if you bear in mind the following simple rules.

- Never perform apnea without an adequate assistant.
- Do not warm-up (swimming, dynamic apnea) before static apnea. If the temperature is low then use a wetsuit during the apnea.
- Position depends on personal preference, but should always involve absolute muscular relaxation.
- Before starting a training table it is a good idea to do 3-4 warm-up apneas, allowing a gradual approach to the starting point of the table.
- The tables should be personalised according to ability. **The times indicated correspond to the level of an apneist who has a maximum static apnea of 4'**. Stronger apneists may increase the apnea time or decrease the recovery time. Anyone with a more modest maximum can reduce the times of execution and increase the recoveries.
- **Static apnea in a pool should be performed after filling the lungs to 70-75% of their total capacity.** A full inspiration does not allow for the necessary relaxation and decontraction.
- Partial exhale apnea is another way to increase the workload.
- While following the sequences proposed in these pages, remember never to exceed 8 apneas in a single training table. If 8 apneas is achieved with ease then it is not the number of apneas that should be increased but the intensity of work (extend apnea time or reduce the recovery interval as per the objectives).

Training static apnea does not entail entering the water with the sole intention of trying to last a little longer than the previous training session. These programs will allow the gradual increase of our level of performance. The two tables proposed (A & B) constitute the base for a good session.

The first step is to create a personal training table for static apnea. Therefore the apneist must 'sacrifice' the first training session in order to identify, with the help of their companion or instructor, the times and recoveries that will comprise their starting table.

If during this phase of creating the tables (A & B) you feel out of breath after three or four apneas, then this is a indication that the loads (time of apnea or recovery) must be revised to a lower level. If on the other hand you finish the eighth apnea with great ease then you will be able to increase the times of apnea and reduce recovery times. As a general rule it is best not to exceed 3' in the recovery time. If the base tables do not seem suited to your ability then they will become so through the application of the objectives shown, which increase the difficulty of the tables.

Every apneist will have their own **Table A** and **Table B**: these represent the foundation tables from which we diverge to pursue a precise objective. **In each training session there should be one objective only**.

A training table performed with the achievement of objective 3 will constitute a new base table (that thereafter substitutes the previous table) from whence we depart to attempt the new objectives 1 and 2. A maximum attempt should be performed no more than once every two months.

Table A

CONSTANT TIME OF APNEA, DECREASING RECOVERY TIME			
2' APNEA	>	3'	RECOVERY
2' APNEA	>	2'50"	RECOVERY
2' APNEA	>	2'40"	RECOVERY
2' APNEA	>	2'30"	RECOVERY
2' APNEA	>	2'20	RECOVERY
2' APNEA	>	2'10"	RECOVERY
2' APNEA	>	2'	RECOVERY
2' APNEA			

The time of apnea is 50-60% of personal best.

Objective 1: increase the number of apneas with the minimum recovery interval (in the example start with an initial recovery time of 2'50" instead of 3', and finish with two apneas of 2' recoveries).

Objective 2: decrease the minimum recovery time (in the example start with an initial recovery time of 2'50" and finish with a recovery of 1'50").

Objective 3: Increase the constant time of apnea for the same sequence of recoveries (in the example pass from 8 × 2' apneas to 8 × 2'10" with the same recoveries). **The new table achieved in this fashion will constitute the new base table.**

Table B

INCREASING TIME OF APNEA, CONSTANT RECOVERY TIME				
2'	APNEA	>	2'45"	RECOVERY
2'10"	APNEA	>	2'45"	RECOVERY
2'20"	APNEA	>	2'45"	RECOVERY
2'30"	APNEA	>	2'45"	RECOVERY
2'40"	APNEA	>	2'45"	RECOVERY
2'50"	APNEA	>	2'45"	RECOVERY
3'	APNEA	>	2'45"	RECOVERY
3'10"	APNEA			

The initial time of apnea is 50% of personal best.

Objective 1: increase the number of apneas with the maximum time, for the same amount of recovery (in the example, start with an apnea of 2'10" instead of 2' and finish with two 3'10" apneas).

Objective 2: increase the maximum apnea time for the same recovery (in the example start with an initial apnea of 2'10" and finish with an eighth apnea of 3'20").

Objective 3: shorten the recovery time for the same sequence of apnea times (in the example pass from recoveries of 2'45" to recoveries of 2'30", with the same sequence of apneas). **The new table achieved in this fashion will constitute the new base table.**

The increments of apnea time and decrements of recovery interval will vary depending on the level of the apneist. For someone trying these tables for the first time it will be easy to improve, to reach objective 3 with ease, and to make increments of apnea and decrements of recovery as high as 15". This will become more difficult as the level of the apneist is raised: when working close to the limit the steps can be as small as 2-3 seconds.

There will be days in which we just can't stay concentrated, we don't want to suffer and put up with contractions, and as a result apnea times aren't achieved. We cannot let this be demoralising. Rather than training Tables A and B with their various objectives, we can instead perform different tasks that are less psychologically involving, such as:

- static apnea without required times, during which we train new techniques of relaxation and concentration.
- static apnea with empty lungs.
- series of apneas with a single recovery breath between them.
- series of apneas with very brief recoveries (e.g. 15").

Combining Tables A and B together it is possible to obtain a Table C, in which increasing apnea times are coupled with decreasing recoveries.

Table C

INCREASING TIME OF APNEA, DECREASING RECOVERY TIME				
2'	APNEA	>	3'30"	RECOVERY
2'10"	APNEA	>	3'20"	RECOVERY
2'20"	APNEA	>	3'10"	RECOVERY
2'30"	APNEA	>	3'	RECOVERY
2'40"	APNEA	>	2'50"	RECOVERY
2'50"	APNEA	>	2'40"	RECOVERY
3'	APNEA	>	2'30"	RECOVERY
3'10"	APNEA			

TRAINING DYNAMIC APNEA

Some general advice for dynamic apnea.

- Dynamic apnea generally takes place in a pool where the temperature of the water is pleasant and a swimming costume is sufficient – the wetsuit is unnecessary. Furthermore, direct contact with the water favours sensitivity to the action of the finstroke.
- Before starting a training table it is a good idea to perform 3-4 warm-up dynamic apneas. These apneas serve also to regulate the velocity of finning in cases where the exercise will require a precise time of apnea (*see exercises E and F*).
- It is essential to be able to control and completely slow the velocity of finning, especially at the end of a prolonged dynamic apnea, when we instinctively accelerate the rhythm of the legs.
- Always train dynamic after static in cases where both are organised for the same session.
- In the tables that follow the times displayed are purely illustrative, giving an idea of the type of work to follow. The apneist will adopt distances and times adapted to their own level. The important point is to maintain the trend of each exercise.
- During dynamic apnea the arms must be kept along the sides so as to maintain complete relaxation, while in the sprints at maximum velocity we advise extending the arms forwards, for hydrodynamics and safety at the end of the length.
- It is unadvisable to exceed the number of apneas shown in the tables. To increase the workload it is preferable to raise intensity (increase distance or reduce recovery time).

- The load can also be increased with artificial resistance: dynamic apnea with wetsuits of different thicknesses, weight-belts, wearing articles of clothing, using elastic tied appropriately to the waist and fastened to the edge of the pool, buoyant flutterboards held in a position of resistance to forwards movement.

We recommend working through three different tables per training session.

Table A

SERIES OF DYNAMIC APNEAS
WITH CONSTANT DISTANCE AND TIME

Example: 10 × 50 m with 1' rests

Objective 1: increase distance, with the same recovery time (e.g. 10 × 55 m with 1' rests).

Objective 2: maintain the same distance while decreasing the interval of recovery (e.g. 10 × 50 m with 55" rests).

Table B

SERIES OF DYNAMIC APNEAS
WITH FIXED TIME OF DEPARTURE

Example: 10 × 50 m departing every 2'

In this exercise swimming faster will allow for more recovery time, and vice versa (if 50 m is covered in 50" there will be 1'10" rest, if it takes 1'15" then there will only be 45" rest).

Objective 1: increase distance, with the same times of departure.

Objective 2: decrease times of departure, with the same distance.

Table C

VERY QUICK SPRINTS OVER A SHORT DISTANCE
WITH A BRIEF INTERVAL OF RECOVERY

Example: 6 × 25 m very quickly with 1'30" rests

Objective 1: increase the number of repetitions to a maximum of 10.

Objective 2: increase the distance covered at maximum velocity.

IMPORTANT: to avoid muscular strain this exercise should not be performed cold. The basic idea of this table is to burn as much oxygen as possible over a very short distance. If the exercise is not executed at maximum velocity its purpose will be defeated.

Table D

SERIES OF DYNAMIC APNEAS
WITH AN ACTIVE RECOVERY

(ideal if training in water that isn't very warm)

Example: 10 × 25 m dynamic apnea with 25 m swimming recoveries; 500m total

Objective 1: gradually increase the fraction of the distance performed in apnea.

Objective 2: increase the total distance whilst maintaining an equal ratio of dynamic apnea to swimming recovery.

IMPORTANT: never stop swimming to rest. It is important to be able to manage and economise energy and oxygen consumption over the total distance. If this isn't possible then attempt shorter distances in apnea with longer recoveries.

Table E

PROGRESSIVE SERIES,
PRIMARILY HYPERCAPNIC WORK

(velocity of swimming increases, recovery decreases)

Example:

10 × 50 m	START EVERY	SPEED	REST
2 × 50 m	3'	1'20"	1'40"
2 × 50 m	2'45"	1'10"	1'35"
2 × 50 m	2'30"	1'	1'30"
2 × 50 m	2'15"	50"	1'25"
2 × 50 m	2'	40"	1'20"

Table F

PROGRESSIVE SERIES,
PRIMARILY HYPOXIC WORK

(velocity of swimming decreases, recovery decreases)

Example:

10 × 50 m	START EVERY	SPEED	REST
2 × 50 m	2'30"	50"	1'40"
2 × 50 m	2'30"	1'	1'30"

2 × 50 m	2'30"	1'10"	1'20"
2 × 50 m	2'30"	1'20"	1'10"
2 × 50 m	2'30"	1'30"	1'

If the workloads in tables E and F are too high then we can reduce the distances (10 × 25 m instead of 10 × 50 m) or increase the interval between starts (e.g. begin with 4' instead of 3' in Table E, and 3'30" instead of 2'30" for the recoveries in Table F). The important point is to follow the guidelines of the exercise.

Table G

SERIES OF DYNAMIC APNEAS WITH A SINGLE RECOVERY BREATH

Example: 500 m distance consisting of 10 m dynamic apneas with a single breath of recovery between them.

Objective 1: increase the fraction of the distance performed in apnea.
Objective 2: increase the total distance.

IMPORTANT: never interrupt the sequence of apnea to rest before completing the total distance. If this is not possible then swim shorter dynamic apneas, but always with a single recovery breath.

Table H

SERIES OF DYNAMIC APNEAS COMBINED WITH STATIC APNEA
(Stop and go)

Follow four different 'Stop and go' work patterns

1. STATIC	DYNAMIC	
2. DYNAMIC	STATIC	
3. STATIC	DYNAMIC	STATIC
4. DYNAMIC	STATIC	DYNAMIC

Objective 1: increase the static time, maintaining a constant dynamic distance.
Objective 2: increase the distance of dynamic, maintaining a fixed time in static.
Objective 3: increase both static time and dynamic distance.

When use of equipment (fins, mask, wetsuit, etc.) is impossible, then excellent training for dynamic can still be achieved as follows:

SERIES OF FREESTYLE LENGTHS
(Gradually decreasing the frequency of breathing)

Do not increase indefinitely the number of armstrokes covered in apnea – stop at the maximum number that allows completion of 50 meters.

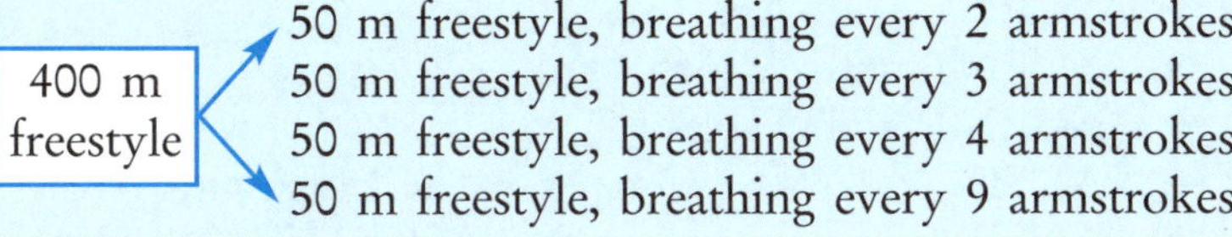

TRAINING FREEDIVING

With many meters of water above our head we must consider actions carefully and take maximum precautions; therefore remember to:

- Always freedive with a guide rope.
- Always dive with adequate assistance.
- Perform two or three warm-up dives before starting the first training table.
- A deep freedive requires a complete and maximum inspiration.
- If freediving to a depth great enough that compensation of the mask and ears starts to become a problem then it may help to start the dive with the mouth also completely full of air.
- Weighting must allow for positive buoyancy from ten meters upwards.
- During the descent the arms will be extended past the head; in the ascent they are relaxed by the sides.
- **VERY IMPORTANT: even in the case of tables with decreasing recovery intervals the minimum recovery time on the surface must always be at least three times as long as the dive time.** For example, if the total dive time is 1 minute then the recovery must be at least 3 minutes.
- The following training tables can also be split and subdivided into several days of training.
- Depths and recovery times are purely illustrative. Every apneist will work at his or her personal level by varying the workload (depth or recovery time).

Tables A and B are not training programs, but rather exercises that allow a gradual approach to a new depth, limiting the amount of doubt and fear that can be provoked by a jump of several meters to a new depth. We reach a new depth through intermediary steps of increasing difficulty. Tables A and B are also very useful to train compensation in conditions of greater security at new depths and at depths in which we have difficulties equalising.

Table A

TRAINING TO REACH A NEW DEPTH WITH A GRADUALLY INCREASING WORKLOAD, USING IDEAL WEIGHT

DESCENT with ARMS	➜	ASCENT with ARMS		
DESCENT with FINS	➜	ASCENT with ARMS		
DESCENT with ARMS	➜	ASCENT with FINS		
DESCENT with ARMS	➜	PAUSE	➜	ASCENT with ARMS
DESCENT with FINS	➜	PAUSE	➜	ASCENT with ARMS
DESCENT with ARMS	➜	PAUSE	➜	ASCENT with FINS
DESCENT with FINS	➜	ASCENT with FINS		

All the descents should be to the maximum (new) depth. Every descent and ascent is made along the guide rope. The last dive prescribed on table A is a constant weight freedive. It is achieved by increasing the difficulty whilst respecting the criteria of gradual progression.

At the end of this training table the operating depth becomes a 'security depth' for the apneist.

All the descents should me to the (new) maximum depth. The difficulty of the dives increases gradually, until the seventh descent is none other than a constant weight freedive. It is necessary to work with two weights, one of which is mobile (and left on the bottom) while the other remains on the waist. The rope that is used to draw the weightbelt back to the surface also functions as the guideline during the ascent.

Table B

TRAINING TO APPROACH A NEW DEPTH WITH A GRADUALLY INCREASING WORKLOAD, USING VARIABLE MOBILE WEIGHT

Example: if the ideal weighting is 4 kg

DESCENT	ABANDON	ASCENT
10 kg	10 kg	0 kg
9 kg	8 kg	1 kg
8 kg	6 kg	2 kg
7 kg	4 kg	3 kg
6 kg	2 kg	4 kg
5 kg	1 kg	4 kg
4 kg	0 kg	4 kg

Tables C and D are proper training programs, in which we always stay above the maximum depth, but with reducing recovery times.

Table C

SERIES OF CONSTANT WEIGHT FREEDIVES (MAX 8), GRADUALLY REDUCING THE INTERVAL OF RECOVERY

Example:	20 m	➜	4'	REST
	20 m	➜	3'45"	REST
	20 m	➜	3'30"	REST
	20 m	➜	3'15"	REST
	20 m	➜	3'	REST
	20 m	➜	2'45"	REST
	20 m	➜	2'30"	REST
	20 m			

This work must be performed to a depth approaching 60% of maximum.

Objective 1: gradually decrease the recovery interval, though maintaining a time at least three times as long as the dive time.

Objective 2: increase the depth for the same sequence of recovery times.

Table D

SERIES OF CONSTANT WEIGHT FREEDIVES (MAX 8), GRADUALLY INCREASING DEPTH WITH CONSTANT RECOVERY

Example:	18 m	➜	3'15"	REST
	20 m	➜	3'15"	REST
	22 m	➜	3'15"	REST
	24 m	➜	3'15"	REST
	26 m	➜	3'15"	REST
	38 m	➜	3'15"	REST
	30 m	➜	3'15"	REST
	32 m			

The starting depth should be about 50% of maximum.

Objective 1: decrease the fixed recovery interval for the same sequence of depths, maintaining a minimum recovery of at least triple dive time.

Objective 2: gradually increase the depths for the same recovery time.

Tables C and D can be performed with a brief pause on the bottom that will further increase the workload. If we do so, we must always remember that the most taxing part of the performance – the ascent – is still ahead of us. Therefore always limit the duration of the stay at maximum depth to a very short interval, which may be increased gradually.

Table E

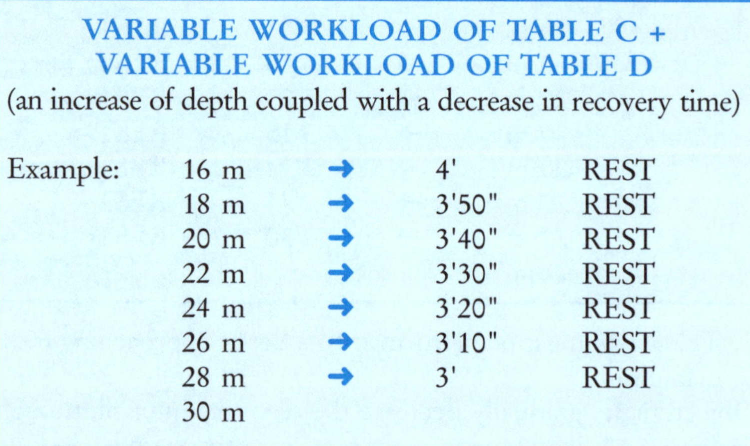

VARIABLE WORKLOAD OF TABLE C +
VARIABLE WORKLOAD OF TABLE D
(an increase of depth coupled with a decrease in recovery time)

Example:				
	16 m	➜	4'	REST
	18 m	➜	3'50"	REST
	20 m	➜	3'40"	REST
	22 m	➜	3'30"	REST
	24 m	➜	3'20"	REST
	26 m	➜	3'10"	REST
	28 m	➜	3'	REST
	30 m			

11.3 THE YEARLY TRAINING PROGRAM

It is important to know how to organise the various training sessions, how to mix the disciplines and with what intensity. Training must be designed so that we enter into form in the most relevant period, neither too late or to early. There is nobody better than ourselves to recognize improvements or deteriorations in our form. In the winter we quickly forget the grand performances, incredible times and abyssal depths. In the winter season and also in spring we must operate at a high workload that diminishes gradually with the onset of summer, the period in which work is predominantly aquatic.

The scheme that follows is an example of how the various activities should be divided during the year with the aim of reaching peak form for deep freediving in the (Northern Hemisphere) summer. If we change objectives then we will necessarily need to change the type of work. It is possible to train more than one discipline in a single day. We recommend spending at least two months a year away from apnea. This gives the organism time to recover from an intense season, re-establishing normal values relating to blood, physiology and functionality. Even the eardrums can do with a bit of rest.

Month	Activity	Plan	Period
DECEMBER	RUNNING:	Base	PERIOD OF PHYSICAL PREPARATION
	WEIGHTS:	1st month macrocycle	
	SWIMMING:	Base	
	APNEA:	—	
JANUARY	RUNNING:	Base	
	WEIGHTS:	2nd month macrocycle	
	SWIMMING:	Base	
	APNEA:	Once per week	
FEBRUARY	RUNNING:	Specific work (*see pages 332-333*)	
	WEIGHTS:	1st month special preparation	
	SWIMMING:	See tables pages 334-336	
	STATIC APNEA:	Once per week	
	DYNAMIC APNEA:	Once per week	
	FREEDIVING:	—	
MARCH	RUNNING:	Specific work (*see pages 332-333*)	PERIOD OF PHYSICAL & SPECIFIC PREPARATION
	WEIGHTS:	2nd month special preparation	
	SWIMMING:	See tables pages 334-336	
	STATIC APNEA:	2 times per week	
	DYNAMIC APNEA:	Once per week	
	FREEDIVING:	—	
APRIL	RUNNING:	Specific work (*see pages 332-333*)	
	WEIGHTS:	Final preparation	
	SWIMMING:	See tables pages 334-336	
	STATIC APNEA:	2 times per week	
	DYNAMIC APNEA:	2 times per week	
	FREEDIVING:	Once per week	
MAY	RUNNING:	Specific work (gradual reduction)	
	WEIGHTS:	—	
	SWIMMING:	See tables pages 334-336	
	STATIC APNEA:	2 times per week	
	DYNAMIC APNEA:	2 times per week	
	FREEDIVING	2 times per week	

COMPETITIVE PERIOD: TRAINING IN WATER ONLY

JUNE

RUNNING:	—
WEIGHTS:	—
SWIMMING:	—
STATIC APNEA:	Once per week
DYNAMIC APNEA:	2 times per week
FREEDIVING:	3 times per week

JULY

RUNNING:	—
WEIGHTS:	—
SWIMMING:	—
STATIC APNEA:	Once per week
DYNAMIC APNEA:	Once per week
FREEDIVING:	As much as possible

AUGUST

RUNNING:	—
WEIGHTS:	—
SWIMMING:	—
STATIC APNEA:	—
DYNAMIC APNEA:	—
FREEDIVING	As much as possible

SEPTEMBER

RUNNING:	—
WEIGHTS:	—
SWIMMING:	—
STATIC APNEA:	—
DYNAMIC APNEA:	—
FREEDIVING	As much as possible

NOVEMBER OCTOBER

REST
SPEARFISHING OR FREEDIVING ONLY

11.4 EVALUATION OF BASE PHYSICAL PARAMETERS

In the athletic preparation of a top apneist several parameters need to be taken into account (and periodically measured), allowing an understanding of the subject's physical condition and of how their body is modifying and regulating itself, whether during physical training or in apnea.

Professor Magno has supplied a list of exams and tests that allow us to detect whether training is proceeding in the right direction. By analysing these results we can personalise training programmes.

Blood cell count

It is necessary to understand in detail the quantity and morphology of the corpuscular part of the blood. Values of haematocrit and haemoglobin and morphology of the erythrocytes are used to calculate the subject's oxygenation capacity.

Radiographic exam of the thorax

Normally we receive a radiogram of the chest in the posterior-anterior projection, which allows us to study the morphology of the ribcage and spinal column, the pulmonary parenchyma and bronchial tree, the main chambers of the heart and the pleural sinuses.

For a complete study it would be optimal to perform two radiograms of the chest – one after expiration and one after maximum inspiration – in order to measure the range of movement of the two halves of the diaphragm, which would then, with specific training, allow to significantly reduce the space of 'dead air'. In reality a study of the diaphragm would require examining the athlete directly with radioscopy, but this methodology is not always well received by subjects due to the obvious increase of exposure to radiation, and the iatrogenic risk of successive exposures.

Electrocardiogram, lying down and under pressure

This test is indispensable to measure the true conditions of cardiac conduction. If the exam is conducted during exertion then it is wisest to use a treadmill instead of the stationary bicycle.

To better understand the body's responses to effort (whether using a treadmill or a stationary cycle) the athlete must be subjected to two trials under exertion, the first with normal respiration and the second during apnea after having performed controlled hyperventilation. The two trials must be well separated and the wattage must be maintained at a constant value of average intensity (80 watts), to measure the modifications of heart rate from rest to the end of the apnea.

Obviously the more the subject has trained, the lower the frequency of heartbeat at the end of the apnea (this data can already indicate the degree of training of an athlete).

Furthermore, during an exam of this nature in apnea the athlete should be prepared for any arhythmias that may be triggered.

Spirometric exam

With this exam the static and dynamic lung volumes can be measured, determining:

- tidal volume (TV)
- vital capacity (VC)
- inspiratory reserve volume (IRV)
- expiratory reserve volume (ERV)
- 1 second forced expiratory volume (1"FEV)
- forced expiratory volume (FEV)

This data is essential for the evaluation of the small and intermediate airways. Before executing the exam it is necessary to hyperventilate to obtain an optimal alveolar ventilation.

There have been very interesting studies made on the reaction of asthmatic patients to apnea: in fact it was noted that if apnea is practiced regularly the symptoms of asthma may actually improve, to the point where they almost disappear completely. In an attempt to explain the reasons for such reactions it was hypothesized that practicing controlled ventilation followed by protracted apnea creates an alveolar distension with a good level of oxygenation, which with time may directly or indirectly 'control' bronchial constriction in response to stimuli induced by an asthma attack.

Measurements of thoracic diameters

Other essential measurements are the dimensions of the intercostal spaces, in particular between the 3rd and 4th ribs and between the 7th and 10th. For an apneist it is not important to improve the pectoral muscles or trapeziums, even if they are indirectly involved in respiration, but rather to improve tone in the intercostal muscles.

Working muscles dedicated solely and directly to the movements of inspiration and expiration can actually result in an increase in the width of movement of the ribcage during breathing, allowing the loading of a greater amount of air before an apnea.

Plicometer

This exam is very useful for measuring density and body mass. Body weight is a very important parameter and must be strictly controlled, as it constitutes a quantitative element of the athlete's energy balance – the relationship between caloric intake and caloric consumption. From trends of body weight it is possible to establish whether the athlete's diet is correct. There are various rules used to determine the subject's ideal weight in relation to height. Of these, Broca's formula is the most popular, and determines body mass index (BMI) as:

BMI = body weight in kilograms / (height in meters)^2, where:

- normal subject 19.5 – 24.0
- overweight subject 24.1 – 29.0
- obese subject > 29.1

Total body weight is constituted by Lean Body Mass (LBM) and Body Fat percentage (BF), which is about 15% in a young sedentary man and 26% in a similar woman. LBM is obtained by subtracting the weight of BF from total body weight; this mass is referred to as muscular mass, even if in reality it is comprised of other tissues and organs (liver, kidneys, bones etc). Muscular mass contributes to about 40-50% of LBM, and this proportion increases with a decrease in body fat.

Using a plicometer we can determine BF by measuring the thickness of the cutaneous folds at the tricep, abdominals and under the scapular.

ORL inspection

The tympanogram and impedance meter exam (*see Chapter 3*) are essential to test the function of the unit responsible for the success of compensation. The apneist needs to dive and surface much faster than a scuba diver and cannot waste precious time waiting for compensation.

Arterial haemogasanalysis

This test is necessary to measure haematic concentration of O_2 that, as we have seen, plays a fundamental role in the carotid and bulbar receptors, which trigger the resumption of respiration. It is best to perform the exam at the moment of finishing a dry static apnea. The measurements of pH, pCO_2, and pO2 are important. Using a saturometer during static apnea is simpler and less invasive, and measures the level of haemoglobin saturation at which the apnea is terminated.

Muscular measurements

Effected on the muscles of the lower limbs before and during training.

Echocardiogram, dry or in water

This exam is useful, whether in conditions of training or repose, for the study of possible modifications to cardiac parameters such as the thickness of sector IV or the posterior walls. As we know, during apnea the heart will undergo bradycardia, with a reduction of the force of contractions and of quantities of expulsion, and therefore considerable savings of O_2.

APNEA ACADEMY

School for the Instruction and Research of Subaquatic Apnea

In recent times Scuba diving has made significant advances in both education and technology. In contrast Freediving, although it is a far older sport, has been left somewhat in its wake.

In 1995 Umberto Pelizzari (multi world record freediver) and Renzo Mazzarri (three times world champion spearfisher) decided to fill this gap with the creation of a school called the Apnea Academy. Together with Angelo Azzinari and Marco Mardollo they would instruct the technical aspects of apnea, while to respond to the necessity of research a scientific group was soon established, with Prof. Ficini studying the physiology of the apneist, Prof Odone, a psychologist with a long history in the field of apnea, Doctor Luigi Magno in charge of hyperbaric medicine and Doctor Nicola Sponsiello for dietology.

In 1996 the first Apnea Academy Instructor course was held on the island of Elba, and after a week of intensive lectures and exercises the first 45 instructors graduated. The school drew on the experience of Pelizzari, who in turn had combined the indefatigable physical training of Enzo Maiorca with Jacques Mayol's techniques of respiration and mental concentration. This new approach to apnea was in complete contraposition to the traditional methods.

In the years since its formation the Apnea Academy has expanded rapidly, with the addition of a printing office, freediving centres, AA trophy competitions, educational literature, videos and specialised courses in such topics as Mental Training and use of the Monofin.

AA Centres are now being established all over the world, and the Apnea Academy is set to become the global standard for the instruction and research of subaquatic apnea.

The emblem of the Apnea Academy is two dolphins, symbols of the bond between man and the sea, and an allusion to Jacques Mayol's concept of Homo delphinus.

The Apnea Academy is a sporting association and a school that has chosen a precise direction (research and instruction) and adopted precise strategies.

The idea is that the students of the Apnea Academy can draw personal health and well being from the practice of apnea. Apnea is therefore a means of improving quality of life.

Vision

A global teaching organisation for underwater apnea.

Mission

To educate the practice of apnea and wellbeing.
or awareness, safety and enjoyment in underwater apnea.

Strategies

- Development and evaluation of individuals that make part of the organisation, by way of:
  - secretary
  - printing office
  - research and development groups
  - mental training and apnea
- Cultural exchanges based on the genuine sharing of values.

Policies

- Maintain total organisational autonomy with respect to any other didactic federation or organisation.
- Collaborate with other entities, associations and federations to develop competitive activity and to preserve the environment.

Objectives

- Promote Apnea Academy courses worldwide – i.e. form new apneists.
- Organise an Instructor Course every year (alternating between Italian and English courses).
- Organise courses of Mental Training and apnea for both instructors and students.
- Promote competitions and gatherings.
- Produce quality teaching supports for students and instructors.

For more information visit the Apnea Academy website at www.apnea-academy.com

BIBLIOGRAPHY

Andersen J.L. - Scherling P. - Saltin B., *Atleti si nasce o si diventa?*, Le Scienze n. 11/2000.
Ballantyne D., *Manuale di tecniche audiologiche*, Masson, Milano.
Barluzzi R., *L'istruttore subacqueo*, Editoriale Olimpia.
Berger G. - Sachs Z. - Sadé J., *Histopathologic changes of the tympanic membrane in acute and secretory otitis media*, Ann. Otol. Rhinol. Laryngol. 1996; 105: 458-461.
Bierman C.W. - Pierson W.E. - Seattle - Wash, *Diseases of the ear*, J. Allergy Clin. Immunol. 1988; 81: 1009 -1014.
Bluestone and Doyle, *Physiology of Eustachian tube and middle ear*, J. Allergy Clin. Immunol. 1988; 81: 1000-1003.
Bruce A. et al, *The Cytoskeleton in molecular biology of the cell*, Garland Edition, 1994.
Buratti M. - Cusaro G., *La rieducazione tubarica*, Masson, Milan, Paris, Barcelona, Bonn, 1991.
Counsilman A., La scienza del nuoto, Zanichelli.
Fireman P., *Otitis media and Eustachian tube dysfunction: connection to allergic rhinitis*, J. Allergy Clin. Immunol. 1997; 99: 787-797.
Herrigel E., *Lo Zen e il tiro con l'arco*, Adelphi.
Lederlé E. - Kremer J.M., *La rieducazione tubarica o rieducazione velo-tubo-timpanica*, Omega edizioni 1991.
Lombardi A., *Apnea: disciplina dell'aria e dell'acqua*, Sperling & Kupfer.
Maiorca E., *A capofitto nel turchino*, Rizzoli.
Maiorca E., *Sotto il segno di Tanit*, Rizzoli.
Martini F., *Fondamenti di anatomia e fisiologia*, EdiSES, 1994.
Mayol J., *Homo Delphinus*, Giunti Martello.
Pelizzari U., *Profondamente*, Mondadori.
Petter G., *Dall'infanzia alla preadolescenza*, Giunti Barbera.
Piaget J., *Lo svillupo mentale del bambino*, Einaudi, Torino.
Piaget J., - Inhelder B., *La psicologia del bambino*, Einaudi, Torino.
Strologo F., *La rieducazione tubarica. Metodologia e risultati a breve e lungo termine*, Tesi di diploma universitario in logopedia, 1999.
Takahashi H. - Hayashi M. - Sato H. - Honjo I. - Dmedsc, *Primary deficits in Eustachian tube function in patients with otitis media with effusion*, Arch. Otolaryngol. Head Neck Surg. 1989; 115: 581-584.
Tedeschi C., *Angela degli abissi*, Edizioni Dare.
Tovaglieri S., *Imparare a sciare giocando*, Tesi di diploma ISEF 1986.
Van Lysbeth A., *Pranayama, la dinamica del respiro*, Astrolabio.
Zanatta D., *Analisi biomeccanica della pinneggiata subacquea e valutazione d'efficienza delle pinne*, Tesi di laurea Facoltà d'Ingegneria, Padova.
Zorpette G., *Muscolosi per sempre in futuro bionico*, Le Scienze dossier n. 4/2000.

DISCLAIMER

Please note that this manual should be used as a supplement to your Apnea Instructor, not a stand-alone learning tool.

It is the precise responsibility of the apneist to understand the associated risks, for two reasons: to cope with the possible emergencies of companions, and to adopt behaviour that guarantees safe activity.

Apnea is a discipline that requires great individual commitment, but this does not mean that it should be practiced alone. The system of pairs constitutes the primary rule of safety for apnea, as with all disciplines that are practiced in contact with the liquid element.

Part of a good apneist's repertoire should be the ability to perform cardiopulmonary resuscitation (CPR), for which we recommend a specific course of theory and practice. Reading a book will not be sufficient. Seek instruction from a specialist and you will be certain to learn how to correctly manage an emergency procedure.

UMBERTO PELIZZARI *was born in 1965 in Busto Arsizio, Italy. 1.89 m tall and 84 kg he boasts a lung volume of 7.9 litres. At 5 years old he could swim perfectly, and at the age of 17 he had already completed eleven seasons of competitive swimming. Umberto graduated from the University of Milan in July of 1990 with a degree in informatics, but his life was to take a very different turn. He would commence on a long sporting career of freediving, establishing seventeen world records in all the disciplines. The only athlete in the world to set records in all three specialities of apnea, Umberto closed his career with – 80 m in constant weight, – 131 m in variable weight and – 150 m in No Limits. You can learn more at his website: www.umbertopelizzari.com*

STEFANO TOVAGLIERI *was born in 1959 in Busto Arsizio, Italy. He graduated in 1986 with an ISEF diploma to teach Physical Education at the Archiepiscopal School of Science in Tradate. As an SSI (Scuba School International) instructor from 1990 and an Apnea Academy instructor from1998, he has taught hundreds of people to dive, whether with a regulator or with a snorkel. From 1999 he was part of 'Club Azzurro' (Italy's national apnea team) of the FIPSAS, the Italian Federation for Underwater Sport Fishing Activities. He dives to over 50m in Constant weight and has a personal best in static apnea of 6'56. In 1999 he was part of the Italian team which won, ahead of France and Germany, the Red Sea Dive Off 99; an international meeting of apnea teams held at El Gouana in the Red Sea. He is responsible for the printing office and is secretary general of the Apnea Academy.*

Also by Idelson Gnocchi Publisher Ltd.

Homo Delphinus
The Dolphin Within Man
by JACQUES MAYOL

ISBN 1928649033 - Hardcover: 398 pages.
The only book written about Man's spiritual connection to the sea. The term Homo Delphinus refers to individuals who are aquatic as dolphin, share a love of the ocean. Mayol believed that some people will be, within a couple of generations, capable of swimming at depths of 200 meters and holding their breath for up to ten minutes. This book is also a limited edition coffee-table size book includes more than 300 pictures. www.thejacquesmayol.com

The Ten Kings of the Sea
Salvage of Santa Isabella's Treasure
by JACQUES and PIERRE MAYOL

ISBN 1928649246 - A novel based on real discoveries and experiences made by Jacques Mayol's around the world during his life who was dedicated to discovering the underwater secrets of the Sea. www.thejacquesmayol.com

The Mediterranean Diet
Origins and Myths
by DARIO GIUGLIANO, M.D.

ISBN: 1928649114 - Hardcover: 266 pages.
This book covers the origins, the history and the myths that have developed regarding the Mediterranean diet. It also applies scientific data and research to reveal the true benefits of the foods of this geographical region and their effects for healthy living. The research has come from ancient literature and contemporary medical studies and by archeological and historical discoveries from countries surrounding the Mediterranean Sea. This book is a limited edition coffee-table size book includes more than 365 pictures. www.boatseafari.com